Brexit, Trump and the Media

EDITED BY
JOHN MAIR, TOR CLARK,
NEIL FOWLER, RAYMOND SNODDY
and
RICHARD TAIT

Published 2017 by Abramis academic publishing

www.abramis.co.uk

ISBN 978 1 84549 709 5

Printed and bound in the United Kingdom

Typeset in Garamond

Abramis is an imprint of arima publishing.

arima publishing
ASK House, Northgate Avenue
Bury St Edmunds, Suffolk IP32 6BB
t: (+44) 01284 700321

www.arimapublishing.com

Contents

Section 5: The 2016 air war
Balance in an unbalanced world
John Mair   205

Acknowledgements

These books are never heroic individual efforts, they depend on the efforts of scores of people, primarily the 50-plus authors who have given their services free of charge with very tight deadlines.

The commissioning editors (services also pro bono) have been steadfast over a period of seven months, from an idle conversation to this tome, and never a cross word in half a year of creative co-operation.

Tor Clark and Neil Fowler have been unflinching in the Herculean task of sub-editing more than 100,000 words.

Finally, as ever, Richard and Pete Franklin at Abramis have done their jobs most professionally.

Now, it is down to you dear reader…

John Mair, Oxford
Tor Clark, Leicester
Neil Fowler, Northumberland
Raymond Snoddy, London
Richard Tait, London

The editors

John Mair has taught journalism at the Universities of Coventry, Kent, Northampton, Brunel, Edinburgh Napier, Guyana and the Communication University of China. He has edited 18 'hackademic' volumes over the last seven years, on subjects ranging from trust in television, the health of investigative journalism, reporting the 'Arab Spring', to three volumes on the Leveson Inquiry. He and Richard Lance Keeble invented the sub-genre. John also created the Coventry Conversations, which attracted 350 media movers and shakers to Coventry University; the podcasts of those have been downloaded six million times worldwide. Since then, he has launched the Northampton

Chronicles, Media Mondays at Napier and most recently the Harrow Conversations at Westminster University. In a previous life, he was an award-winning producer/director for the BBC, ITV and Channel 4, and a secondary school teacher.

Tor Clark is Associate Professor in Journalism at the University of Leicester, UK. After studying Politics and History at Lancaster University, he worked for the Northamptonshire Evening Telegraph, before becoming editor, first of the Harborough Mail in Leicestershire, and then of Britain's oldest newspaper, the Rutland & Stamford Mercury, where he led a successful bid to the Heritage Lottery Fund to preserve its unique 300-year-old newspaper archive. Previously he was Principal Lecturer in Journalism at De Montfort University in Leicester, where he launched two Journalism degrees, one accredited by the NCTJ. He holds an MA in Mass Communications from the University of Leicester and is now researching towards a PhD. He is reviews editor of the academic journal Journalism Education, a regular commentator on politics and media for BBC Leicester and a Senior Fellow of the Higher Education Academy.

Neil Fowler has been in journalism since graduation, starting life as trainee reporter on the Leicester Mercury. He went on to edit four regional dailies, including The Journal in the north east of England and The Western Mail in Wales. He was then publisher of The Toronto Sun in Canada before returning to the UK to edit Which? magazine. In 2010/11 he was the Guardian Research Fellow at Oxford University's Nuffield College where he investigated the decline and future of regional and local newspapers in the UK. From then until 2016 he helped organise the college's prestigious David Butler media and politics seminars. As well as being an occasional contributor to trade magazines he now acts as an adviser to organisations on their management and their external and internal communications and media policies and strategies.

Raymond Snoddy OBE, after studying at Queen's University in Belfast, worked on local and regional newspapers, before joining The Times in 1971. Five years later he moved to the Financial Times and reported on media issues before returning to The Times as media editor in 1995. At present, he is a freelance journalist writing for a range of publications. He presented NewsWatch on the BBC from its inception in 2004 until 2012. His other television work has included presenting Channel 4's award-winning series Hard News. In addition, Snoddy is the author of a biography of the media tycoon Michael Green, The Good, the Bad and the Ugly. He was awarded an OBE for his services to journalism in 2000.

Richard Tait CBE is Professor of Journalism at the School of Journalism, Media and Cultural Studies, at Cardiff University. From 2003 to 2012, he was director of the school's Centre for Journalism. He was editor of Newsnight from 1985 to 1987, editor of Channel 4 News from 1987 to 1995 and editor-in-chief of ITN from 1995 to 2002. Tait was a BBC governor and chair of the governors' programme complaints committee from 2004 to 2006, and a BBC Trustee and chair of the Trust's editorial standards committee from 2006 to 2010. He is a fellow of the Society of Editors and the Royal Television Society, treasurer of the International News Safety Institute and an independent trustee of the Disasters Emergency Committee.

Introduction:

Populism's lessons for Journalism

By Jon Snow, Newscaster, Channel 4 News

The last two years have caught the media, the pundits, and the professional 'know-alls' napping. When Mrs May called the 2017 General Election for June 8, many were talking 'Tory Landslide'. They were even talking of Labour being reduced to 100 MPs in the Commons. We so-called experts, failed to spot that the British people – bitterly divided over Brexit – had no interest in her 'snap election', and determined to punish her for calling it. After the 2015 EU Referendum, the media failed to look at the consequence of such a narrow victory for so controversial and complex an issue as leaving the European Union.

The self-same 'experts' took Mrs May's bid for a bigger mandate than her 17 seat majority in the House of Commons at face value.

Not so the electorate who proved the experts wrong at every turn. No one was predicting a hung Parliament or the nightmare scenario in which the Northern Irish right-wing DUP MPs were summoned to keep the Tories in power. And though many of us understood 'strong and stable' was a PR man's effort to divert us from what proved to be a truer epithet of 'weak and wobbly', few in the media discussed her frailties openly until too late.

But then we, the media/political elite, had already been in trouble in America, failing to spot the populism there that would propel the most unstable and inappropriate presidential candidate into the White House.

In both the UK and America, this is in part because few of us live amongst those suffering most from the actions of those in power. I blame myself for not spotting it when covering the US presidential election in America's frustrated heartlands.

'Bad people – the worst people in the world'

Standing at the back of a sports hall in North Carolina, I realised Donald Trump was now including me in his tirade against the media. I was amongst only 20 or so media present, and perhaps 500 people present in the hall altogether. Suddenly, upon Trump's urging the entire crowd turned around and yelled at us, thrusting their fists at us. In those mad October days in 2016, it was impossible to imagine that this man – whose campaign rallies veered between pantomime and something very dark – was within a couple of months of becoming the so-called 'leader of the free world'.

The same was true as the political elite in the UK chose to ask the British people whether they wanted to leave Europe. The media believed the political leaders who said it would easily be won by those who sought to remain. But it proved an issue of such complexity that few journalists, let alone many members of the general public, had much idea of what it was all about. Hence Europe became a handy receptacle for the resentments over immigration, poverty, and shortcomings of the welfare state, for which the EU was rarely responsible.

Needless to say, the politicians came up with two key themes they thought would work for both Trump and Brexit. Trump wanted to make America 'great again', whilst the Brexiteers wanted to put the 'great' back into Britain; and both campaigns were threaded through with 'fake news'.

The media's failure – and a remedy

In the years before the Referendum, if, as a reporter, one stopped a voter in the streets and asked them to list their top ten issues – Europe rarely figured at all.

In America, the Trump/Clinton battle looked an easy one for the media, but proved illusive. Many regarded Mrs Clinton as a bit of the same-old, same-old, but at least someone who understood America's power structure. Trump simply declared she was 'a criminal'.

None of us had spent time watching years of 'the Apprentice' – unlike many of the voters. They loved this outsider, Donald Trump, firing people noisily on TV. Few of us understood this was exactly what many of them wanted to do with the Clintons, and a lot of other high profile politicians. Many in the media convinced themselves 'sense' would prevail. Few of us realised this blunt, rude, odd-looking man, 'the Donald'– millionaire that he was – had captured the zeitgeist. Ultimately, once again, few in the media sprang from the echelons of those most keenly screaming from Trump.

It would be too simplistic to say – for Trump, read Farage. But UKIP and those who funded it had spotted the deepening alienation which increasing numbers of British voters were feeling for politics. In the case of the UK, it was a 'thing' rather than a 'person' which had become the issue. Europe was the thing. Europe – castigated by the Mail, the Express, the Telegraph and others down the years –

suddenly it had come good as an explosive issue. In a single vote, we were told, leaving Europe would cure all our ills. In a flash we would have

£350m a week to spend on the NHS (fake news, or a straight lie?) Down the 40 years of EU membership, the media had done very little to extol the benefits of Europe, and plenty to attack it.

How much did the Cornish media do to praise the massive EU investment over the decades in the game-changing developments across what is one of the poorest counties in Europe? How much did the national press do to unwind the complex free trade arrangements in Europe which affected not only ourselves but many emergent Commonwealth countries too?

For myself, I feel the media failed, not only over the Referendum, but perhaps over reporting Europe at all down the 40 years of the UK's membership. But once we had failed in reporting EU in the first place, our chance amid the fresh mown lies (or fake news) of the campaign itself, we didn't have a chance. Not that some in the media would have wanted the chance anyway.

For America, the media did not fail. They reported Donald Trump as he was, and is. That is what the people wanted, and as a consequence the people elected him. But on the campaign, they were so far removed from the alienated voters they were reporting, thus missing the potential scale of his success.

Finally, in the June 2017 General Election the media and political classes were hoisted by their own ignorance of the nature of the society they were reporting. Voters thumbed their noses at Mrs May and her hard Brexit. They decisively did not increase her mandate to deliver on leaving Europe. Neither did they vote to have the Northern Ireland's hard-line DUP keeping Mrs May in power for however short a time it may prove.

This book is a timely one, bringing together the two great populist moments affecting the English-speaking world and beyond. It also marks a salutary reminder to we, who report, pontificate, and comment, that we need to render our industry more reflective of the people we serve.

The ground war in 2016: In the trenches

***

Understanding the Brexit result is just the start

Richard Tait

The 'What ifs?' of history can give a valuable sense of perspective in times of dramatic change. They can remind us, for example, that events and personalities matter as well as great social and political movements. If Boris Johnson had sent his draft pro-EU article to the Telegraph on the weekend of 19/21 February 2016, throwing in his lot with David Cameron, rather than the anti-EU article which kick-started his leadership of the official Leave campaign, Remain would probably have won. If Hillary Clinton had not taken winning Michigan, Pennsylvania and Wisconsin for granted, she, not Donald Trump, would probably have won the US electoral college. Both contests were that finely balanced. But he didn't and she didn't and this book is the result.

However, the narrowness of the victories of Leave and Trump should not diminish the significance of what has happened. This is particularly the case with Brexit, for while US voters have an option on whether to continue with President Trump in 2020 (and some of his opponents hope he won't last that long), the British electorate has made a once in a generation decision. The chapters in this section analyse Leave's victory through the eyes of its architects and look at the overall role of the media – social media as well as print and broadcasting – in reporting a unique event which will define the sort of country the UK will be for the foreseeable future.

Nigel Farage MEP can claim with some justification that Brexit would never have happened without his leadership of the UK Independence Party (Ukip) over the last decade. He also thinks it would never have happened without You Tube and social media to compensate for Ukip's initial lack of mainstream coverage. The Referendum won, he found himself a few months later the keynote speaker on the future of journalism at the biggest news media conference in the world – NewsXchange.

His challenge there to journalists was a stark one: "It's not just the political class that is increasingly treated with contempt by the broader public across the West, actually the national broadcasters and the rest of the media are being viewed in the same way". He believes journalism as a profession is out of touch – elitist, metropolitan and far too narrow in its recruitment to understand the people and the ideas, which made Brexit happen. For him, the news media needs to hit the re-set button.

Andy Wigmore and James Montgomery were two of the leading 'Bad Boys of Brexit' – respectively the director of communications and the senior press officer of the Leave.EU team, led by Arron Banks and Nigel Farage, which failed to get designation as the official leave campaign but waged a very effective guerrilla war in parallel to Vote Leave, focusing on social media and immigration. They are not over impressed with the quality of British journalism: 'When it came to print media, inserting ourselves into the debate was surprisingly easy, because most journalists are not the grizzled investigative reporters of yore. For the most part, they are lazy creatures on tight deadlines'.

Television was a tougher nut to crack – but they found being outrageous usually guaranteed coverage. The notorious 'Breaking Point' poster was a classic example – working class voters did not see it as a gaffe. They thought it was showing something that was happening and the outcry proved the elites were out of touch. 'The critical reaction to the poster did more for the Leave campaign than the poster by itself ever could have, but, to this day, most Westminster types still believe it was a misstep'.

While Leave.EU created mayhem, the official campaign, Vote Leave, was a slightly more conventional political and media operation. Matthew Elliott, its chief executive, argues the foundations of its success were laid by Vote Leave's skilful management of expectations around David Cameron's negotiation with the EU – ensuring, with the help of the press, that what the prime minister hoped would launch a successful campaign to remain was denounced as inadequate by the media and by conservative politicians, including six members of his cabinet and Boris Johnson.

The Leave campaign set the bar high enough to be sure the prime minister would not achieve it – but he had helped them by initially promising more than he could deliver. 'By the time Cameron finally presented the results of the deal to the nation, everyone knew it was a dud'. The prime minister, he writes, failed his own exam and Leave's choreography of the coverage over the crucial weekend of 19/21 February meant the campaign started with both sides with an equal chance of winning.

What Vote Leave and Vote.EU had in common was a relentless and successful focus on social media. Alex Connock is one of the UK's leading experts on digital media, currently managing director of Endemol Shine North. He has a simple explanation for why Leave won the digital battle – they used the available tools much more effectively than their opponents. He is sceptical of the worries that heavy investment in targeted advertising tipped the balance in Leave's favour: "Before targeted advertising can work, there does have to be actual people receptive to the message in the first place to build upon."

The harsh reality for Remain, who began the campaign confident that social media would be one of its main weapons, was that users had opinions of their own and many of them were strongly anti-EU. Remain then made life more difficult for itself by refusing to fight fire with fire, rejecting some of the more aggressive and brutal advertising that would have been perfect for social media. "Remain and the Democrats weren't cheated by behavioural data analysis, fake news or armies of bots. They just didn't fight anywhere near smart enough."

This picture of a digital space where most people already know what they think is supported by a fascinating study of Twitter by Max Hanska, senior lecturer in digital journalism at De Montfort University, and independent researcher Stefan Bauchowitz. They analysed 7.5m tweets in the month before the referendum. They found Leave supporters were more numerous and active than remainers by a much larger margin than the eventual result.

While some remainers did engage with leavers, retweeting or quoting people with opposing views, leavers tended to stay in their own echo chamber – interacting only with like minded other leavers. For this group, the Eurosceptic newspapers – particularly the Daily Express – were an important source of information and material and Leave's clear slogans, like 'take control' were better suited to the Twitter format than the more convoluted arguments for Remain. "On Twitter algorithms play only a small role, meaning partisan filtering of news is mostly down to the network of followers users create." Where journalism fits in this new world seems still to be resolved.

Despite the enhanced role of social media, the referendum was still largely fought and probably decided by the campaigns in the traditional press and broadcast media. Loughborough University's Centre for Research in Communication and Culture has been providing expert analysis of election media coverage for 25 years. David Deacon, professor of communication and media analysis, and Dominic Wring, professor of political communication, are not impressed by what they found when analysing the referendum. The national press split 80 per cent for

Leave to 20 per cent for Remain in terms of circulation and, with the exception of The Times and the Daily Star, all the newspapers were highly partisan in terms of editorial balance.

The broadcasters, under their rules of impartiality, were balanced between the two sides, but their coverage was skewed in a number of undesirable ways. It was dominated by David Cameron and Boris Johnson, neither of whom had stated their position on UK membership of the EU until shortly before the campaign started; there were three times as many men on our screens as women, sidelining, among others, Theresa May and Nicola Sturgeon; the campaign agenda itself was very narrowly focused on the economy and immigration, with issues like devolution and the Article 50 process 'neglected concerns'. Given the poll evidence of levels of public ignorance about the EU and the issues in the referendum, they wonder if the media could and should have done more – 'our evidence suggests all national news organisations – publicly-funded broadcasters as much as privately paid newspaper journalists – struggled to present the Referendum as little else than a debate about two issues within one party.'

The next two years of Article 50 negotiations will, ironically, provide a last chance for the UK media to explain some of the key issues as we actually leave the EU. But the EU referendum also shows the enormous challenge facing newspapers and broadcasters to stay relevant as social media becomes ever more influential in political communications. Understanding why Leave won is just the start of the process of meeting that challenge.

The media must be more responsible and more representative

Post-Brexit the media need to be more representative of their audiences, move out of their metropolitan comfort zones and re-think their approach to the big issues facing Europe today, argued former UKIP leader Nigel Farage, in his keynote speech to the 2016 NewsXchange Conference in Copenhagen

2016 has been the year of political revolution. It's been the year of political outsiders. But remember, what made Brexit happen and what got Trump elected were a lot of little people who don't normally vote at all but have simply had enough and want to vote for change. They feel they've been talked down to, they feel they've been sneered at. And I think what this conference needs to face up to is it's not just the political class that is increasingly treated with contempt by the broader public across the West, actually the national broadcasters and the rest of the media are being viewed in the same way.

You are now on a par with the political class – it's not a great place to be is it? And the internet poses you a real challenge. Now let me be clear, from my perspective we would never ever have got UKIP off the ground, we would have been any more than a little fringe party, had it not been for YouTube taking off in 2007 and 2008.

At the time in the European Parliament in Brussels or Strasbourg, I made very helpful, positive interjections and contributions, but the chances of me being covered by a national broadcaster, by a national newspaper in 2008 were just about zero despite the fact I led UKIP into coming second across the entire United Kingdom in 2009. There wasn't a story. People thought what was happening Brussels was boring and didn't really connect with ordinary people's lives. So nobody has made better use of the internet and social media than me. And of course Trump has done exactly the same thing. I think the internet can be very liberating. I think the internet means governments simply can't lie to us any more in the way that they used to. But I think the internet equally can be a very bad thing and a very dangerous thing. If people's trust goes away from you guys and goes completely to the internet there is a genuine and real danger very dangerous or bad ideas will take hold.

Talking to less than half the population

So I think the broadcasters and the media in the wake of 2016 need to press the reset button. I never thought I'd say this but I think you have got to be more responsible, and you have got to be more representative because at the moment you are probably talking to less than half of the population in all your respective countries. I don't want traditional media to disappear, but I do think traditional media needs to move out of your metropolitan comfort zone.

Now my personal experience of this is mostly with the BBC. Some of this is personal, but much of it is backed up by good documentation. Newswatch is an organisation I have helped over the years and since 1999 we have analysed thousands of hours of BBC output on a variety of issues. After getting elected to the European Parliament back in 1999, one of the first things that happened was a joint production between ARTE and the BBC. It was a series to be shown on BBC2 called Desperately Seeking Eutopia. For four months I had a fly on the wall journalist with me, which as you all know is the dream position for your industry to be in.

So I was caught calling Romano Prodi a wanker and one or two other things which does tend to happen when you forget it's there. But it was really interesting. The story was about a 35 year-old politician, who had just been elected from a no-hope party, a party to whom, through 624 hours of election coverage in 1999, the BBC had given 4.5 minutes. And yet we had won three seats and we had won seven per cent of the national vote. So for four months they followed me on my first day and getting the documentation and meeting other MEPs. Anyway the BBC's contribution to this was about £70,000 but it was decided the BBC would not show the programme.

There were questions asked in the House of Lords and elsewhere and no, the BBC said the content would be too damaging. So in the end they relented and they showed the programme at 10am on a channel called BBC Knowledge. I think it's now disappeared, that Channel, and I think the viewership were three old ladies and six cats. But I did tune in to watch it and I kid you not before the transmission it said 'viewers must warned that during the course of the next hour Mr Farage expresses some very extreme opinions'. I mean God help us – all I was saying is we should govern our own country, we should be a democracy, we should control our own borders and maybe think about linking out with a bigger, wider world.

Bias by omission

So I found from the start it was very very difficult and to be honest when it came to coverage of the European issue from 1999 until 2012/3 the BBC's bias on this issue wasn't so much deliberate. It was actually bias by omission. They didn't think issues like open door immigration as a result of EU membership and former communist countries joining was a particularly relevant issue to talk about.

Now I want to be fair to the BBC and to the other UK broadcasters. I will say this, throughout the Referendum campaign itself the BBC did everything it possibly could to make sure there was fair and balanced coverage. And you won't hear a single complaint from any of us on the Leave side about how that was conducted. The trouble is it has all reverted to type. Since June 23, 2016, there have been a whole mass of programmes about Brexit. And I am not just talking about the Today Programme or the Ten O'Clock News. I'm talking about Farming Today. I'm even talking about the Food Programme, in which there was a long Brexit special telling us the disastrous things that could happen to food prices as a result of voting Brexit. I've got a series of letters here with Tony Hall, the BBC director general, in which he has been challenged by Lord Pearson of Rannoch to name a single programme that has been on BBC Television or Radio since June 23 which has discussed the exciting new possibilities of being a free country that can make its own decisions.

Drawing from a much broader spectrum of people
So I have looked at this and thought about this – and particularly what has happened since June 23, 2016. Really the question is not is the BBC biased, is not are all of you biased, the question is do you think you are biased? And I don't think you do. Because when I meet people in the media they assume they are representing a proper reasonable balanced view. When I go into New Broadcasting House and I look at the people who are working there, the vast majority come from at least middle class wealth in many cases; more than that, I bet there is not a single person on the news or research side who hasn't been to a good university. Many live metropolitan lives with lifestyle choices that would not be replicated in those percentage terms once you got outside the M25 and that I think is what I see everywhere.

I think recruitment is absolutely vital, just like politics needed a massive shake up with some outsiders coming in with different backgrounds who were not necessarily career politicians, I think you in the media need to start drawing from a much broader spectrum of people. Now I am not for one moment pretending this is isolated to the United Kingdom. There are countries in which there is even less of debate on some of these issues.

Where the media are out of touch
I picked out the BBC because that is personal experience. But I would say also there are some big issues you need to think very hard about. The European question is one. We have shown with Brexit what is possible and there are now many countries across the European Union seriously questioning their future in this project. On immigration I think still many of you are covering this subject in the way that anyone who dares to raise the issue somehow has malevolent intentions underneath which in the vast majority of cases simply isn't true. I think the coverage of radical

Islam is another area where you are completely losing touch with vast swathes of your own population. It happens in politics too. Dear Hillary couldn't even bring herself to say radical Islam, she couldn't even use the term.

And lastly where I believe you are really getting completely out of touch is on your coverage of the issue of climate change. And I say this with particular reference to the wind industry. I have seen dozens of reports on British media about a new wind farm being built on an upland moor or being built at sea. We are told how wonderful this is how it's going to reduce CO_2 emissions and this new wind farm will power a city the size of Birmingham. What we don't get told is that when the wind doesn't blow it won't even power a single kettle.

What we don't get told is none of this can be done without a vast taxpayer subsidy. What we don't get told is actually wind energy and renewables have led to one of the greatest transfers of wealth from the poor to the rich we have seen in modern times. I haven't heard any of that in the United Kingdom. Increasingly people are wondering why their electricity bills are as high as they are. So I do think this industry needs to press the reset button.

And finally I have to say on Trump, it wasn't just you who were wrong. Everybody was wrong. But I had a very good bet at five-to-one and I've enjoyed 2016 even if you haven't. You have got to change, otherwise you'll come back here in five years time and there'll be fewer of you.

Note on the contributor
Nigel Farage has been a MEP for South East England since 1999. He was leader of the UK Independence Party from 2006 to 2009 and from 2010 to 2016. In the 2014 UK European Elections UKIP won the highest share of the vote – the first time since 1906 that any party other than Labour and Conservative had come first in a national poll. In the 2016 Referendum campaign he appeared with David Cameron in the first of the ITV debate programmes. In January 2017 he joined LBC as the presenter of his own programme, *The Nigel Farage Show*, four nights a week.

How the Bad Boys of Brexit manipulated the media

The Leave.EU campaign team recognised the UK news media had a tired formula and was out of touch with a large swathe of the voting public, so played traditional journalism at its own game – and won, say Andy Wigmore and Jack Montgomery

Leave.EU, which ended up becoming the single largest player on either side of the EU Referendum, was originally designed as a campaign of, by and for the people.

Early on, we decided we didn't want to rely on a load of soundbite-blathering politicians from the mainstream parties who, for the most part, are either unrecognisable to the general public or intensely disliked by them.

We wanted our message to be carried by real people: small business owners who could speak to the strangulating effect of EU legislation first hand; locum GPs who could report on the impact of mass immigration on the health service from the frontline; fishermen who had watched their industry and their communities crumble around them thanks to Brussels mismanagement, and so on.

We realised pretty quickly the old media weren't interested in any of that. Despite all their protestations to the contrary, establishment journalists are encased in the Westminster bubble as firmly as any of the MPs they've invested countless lunches in, and when media requests came through, ordinary people were out of the question – producers wanted politicians.

This is because the old media isn't really all that interested in politics so much as politicking: who's up, who's down, which members of the Cabinet have had a falling out, etc. It is the same sort of Brangelina drama which fills the entertainment pages, basically, but for people who like to think they're above that sort of thing – just substitute Brad Pitt and Angelina Jolie for David Cameron and Boris Johnson. (Shudder).

So, we couldn't be a campaign 'of' the people after all – but we were still determined to be a campaign 'for' the people, and that meant figuring out how to manipulate a media establishment which would have preferred not to deal with a bunch of painfully uncouth, UKIP-tinged interlopers in the first place.

Journalists will give you what you want if you give them what they need

When it came to print media, inserting ourselves into the debate was surprisingly easy, because most journalists are not the grizzled investigative reporters of yore. For the most part, they are lazy creatures on tight deadlines. Almost every Referendum story they churned out followed the same basic formula:

> *Government Department/Think Tank/Global Body X Says Brexit Will Damage Y*

> *A new report/study claims leaving the European Union will result in [insert negative outcome].*

> *"X, y, z," it said.*

> *"This really goes to show that we're Safer, Stronger and Better Off in the EU", said [Remain minister/other spokesman].*

> *But [Leave campaigner] responded, saying [contrary remark]."*

Tailor your press release right, and it can be gummed together with another one and the story is basically already written. This is manna from heaven for journalists, because it means they can file early and have extra time to tweet witticisms at people who are wrong on the internet.

The trouble for Leave campaigners was the initiative was pretty much always given to the Remainers. The Government would have a minister give a speech or wheel out an 'expert' at some factory, promising Brexit would rain fire and brimstone on one sector of the economy or another, more or less every day, and the media would always run with it.

The event itself would be essentially a formality, as a copy of the text would be distributed hours or even a full day in advance. This is why you saw so many 'In his speech, *X* is expected to say *Y*' stories in the press.

Trying to get your own leads this way as a Leave campaigner was a waste of time – if it wasn't a comment from Boris which could be construed as him 'eyeing a potential leadership challenge', the old media wasn't interested.

Responding to the Remainers' prophecies of doom in detail didn't get you anywhere, either. Your argument would just be boiled down to 'but Leave campaigners said this was just scaremongering' – which looks worse than having no comment at all, somehow.

The format did, however, lend itself incredibly well to the kind of unashamedly dirty tactics which became Leave.EU's specialty, because it allowed us to contrive our press releases so they could slot into the churnalism template where we would be guaranteed the last word.

We discarded the Vote Leave method of trying to come up with a minister or 'expert' of our own to balance things out immediately. Remain's strategy depended heavily on burying us under the sheer weight of all the institutional prestige they had on their side – the Bank of England, the International Monetary Fund, the Institute for Half-our-funding-comes-from-Brussels, and on and on.

They had the numbers on their side, no question, and if given a straight choice between two mutually contradictory visions of Brexit according to 'experts', we knew the public would go with the status quo.

Instead, we took the Trump approach and went full anti-establishment: there isn't a banking corporation, economic forecaster or 'respected global body' which doesn't have EU money in its pockets or a recent history of utter failure – or, more usually, both – and we made sure the journos were fed with short, punchy press releases pointing this out before Remain's latest set-piece speech had even been delivered.

"This is the same politician/institution/corporation which said *x* about the euro/ before the recession/etc," a typical comment might read, inserting a reference to the inevitable EU subsidy, pension or similar along the way.

This would often be the last thing readers would see, and quite possibly all they would remember, chipping away at Remain's prestige and appealing to the public's willingness to believe the establishment is, in fact, a useless bunch looking after their own interests.

"If George Osborne, Tony Blair and Goldman Sachs all agree that EU this is good for them, then it's probably not good for the rest of us," was a key and very compelling theme which the insider campaigns couldn't develop like we did, because it implicated them, too.

This supported a wider, largely online campaign of mockery which was based online and bypassed the old media entirely: visually striking picture tiles and satirical videos poking fun at the corporate managers and government ministers puffing themselves up at podiums and trying to persuade the public they knew what was best for the country.

People were more than happy to see them taken down a peg, and our material appealed to the public sense that the political class and their academic and corporate sponsors are all useless, anyway. We didn't have to go over every dot and comma of the economic arguments, we just had to ask people to ask themselves if they really believed the country would crash and burn without Brussels telling it what to do when countries like Australia and Canada seemed to be managing just fine.

The big brand outlets matter less than you think
Another thing we always bore in mind was column inches in the Express, The Guardian and so on aren't as important as people in the bubble think. For the professional politician, the big brand name outlets are a great way of promoting yourself, allowing you to 'cut a figure' among your peers and advance your career. But if you're trying to put a case to the general public, they're surprisingly low-

impact. Most of the national newspapers are silos, with their readerships' minds already made up one way or another, and your 800-word opus isn't going to do much to change minds.

We always made sure we fed a steady stream of comments to the regional and trade-specific outlets, much-neglected by the London-centric establishment. Many rival the declining national papers in circulation, and most have a much more general readership, meaning you're more likely to win people over. They also allow you to deliver targeted messages on issues of particular concern to particular communities, rather than forcing you to rely on the scattergun approach which the nationals require.

Spot the deliberate mistake

That covered the print media, but the big broadcasters were a tougher nut to crack – particularly the BBC. They didn't draw so much on written press releases as the newspapers and news websites, and they played a bigger role in setting the wider tone of the campaign. A video of ours could be shared literally millions of times online, but if they decided it wasn't news, it wouldn't make any impact beyond Facebook.

What they did like to do, though, was feign horror whenever we said something which went beyond the bounds of what they deemed to be respectable debate, particularly with respect to immigration. Milking Arron Banks for outrageous comments became a miniature cottage industry for Remain-leaning journos, in fact.

We learned to manipulate the media by appealing to their eagerness to find 'gotcha!' moments here, too, by making calculated mistakes which drew public attention to us.

I could name numerous examples – a personal favourite was a picture tile featuring comments on immigration by the Dalai Lama, which earned a reaction from the man himself – but the best is obviously the notorious 'Breaking Point' poster.

We knew immigration was our strongest card in the Referendum, but Remainers and Left-liberals more generally had been doing a pretty good job of pretending to believe people had 'legitimate concerns' about it since Ed Miliband produced his daft border control mugs, keeping it low on the agenda.

The 'Breaking Point' poster, which featured a huge column of illegal migrants snaking through Europe with the accompanying text 'The EU has failed us all', pointed a giant foam finger at the very worst of the crisis without any attempt to sugarcoat it, provoking the exact knee-jerk response from the media and political establishment which we wanted.

It appeared like we had blundered to them of course, because the coverage was framed entirely in terms of: 'Haven't you gone too far? Isn't this racist? When are you going to apologise?' – all backed up by quotes from the ranks of the professionally offended, denouncing our supposed racism and xenophobia.

What we understood was most ordinary voters, particularly in working-class areas, didn't see a gaffe. They saw the establishment returning to the old, default position it had been trying so hard to distance itself from: concerns about immigration aren't 'legitimate', they're racist.

The feedback we were getting was: 'Why is it racist? It's happening, isn't it? This reaction just proves they still don't get it'.

The media missed this entirely, of course, since journalists and political anoraks spend all their time talking to each other, not the public. Their outraged reaction to the poster did more for the Leave campaign than the poster by itself ever could have, but, to this day, most Westminster types still believe it was a misstep.

Bring old media an audience, and it will come to you
There are certain things the establishment media – elements of it, at least – do very well, of course. No-one does a better job of shredding a headline-grabbing 'report' or 'study' with no substance to it than BBC interrogator-in-chief Andrew Neil, for example.

The trouble is Neil's one-man seal-clubbing operation on the Daily Politics is only seen by a very select audience, a couple of hundred thousand people, at best, who are at home in the middle of the day on weekdays who probably already have pretty firm political views one way or another already.

Meanwhile, there are amateur political commentators on YouTube the media has never heard of who crush these numbers with little more than a cheap mic and some still images of headlines every day.

Recognising both of these facts, our team would put the good bits of the old media to work for our new media effort: every day we would pore through programmes like Neil's, clipping together the best bits and uploading them to social media so we could bring the spectacle of Remain ministers gasping like recently landed sea trout to the masses.

The old media had no objection to our doubling or tripling their usual public profile; in fact, they seemed rather pleased to be getting a bite of the new media pie. Eventually it got to the point where they'd be doing our work for us, linking us to relevant segments over Twitter and asking if we might had seen them. (We have now – thanks!)

The Remainers and the official Vote Leave campaign, which thought the battle was won so long as they were able to parachute the carbon-copy talking head of the day onto a studio couch to regurgitate a few prepared lines, missed these new avenues of public engagement almost entirely.

Take home lessons

That, in short, is how you manipulate the media as an outsider:

- Recognise how it operates and what it needs to get its work done for the day, and tailor your content appropriately.

- Remember column inches aren't an end in themselves, and don't neglect the little players.

- If the media doesn't want to give you a fair hearing, make calculated mistakes to trick it into giving you an unfair hearing that will make your point for you.

- And, finally, bypass it entirely where you can and demonstrate you can bring them attention they wouldn't otherwise be getting, and they'll come to you.

Not so hard to kick in the doors to the ivory tower after all – in fact, you'll find most of the residents don't even realise you've done it!

By the way, this is exactly what Trump did.

Note on contributors

Andy Wigmore was Director of Communications at Leave.EU. After the Referendum he worked closely with the Donald Trump campaign alongside Nigel Farage, culminating in the now famous meeting three days after the US election and the photo with Trump and Farage in front of a golden door. He still works closely with Arron Banks and Nigel Farage. Jack Montgomery was Leave.EU's senior press officer and Scottish spokesman, and directed social media output during Referendum week. He currently writes for the Breitbart News Network.

Deal or no deal? The weekend Brexit went from outside bet to even chance

Only full-scale treaty change would have kept Britain in the EU, and once the Prime Minister failed to offer that to UK voters, the writing was on the wall, says Matthew Elliott, former Chief Executive of Vote Leave

On Friday, February 19, 2016, David Cameron stepped out of a conference room in Brussels to announce he had successfully concluded his renegotiation with the European Union. The team around him in Downing Street had written the script for what would happen next. The Prime Minister would emerge just after 10pm, in perfect time to commandeer the evening news. The next day, he would hold a Cabinet meeting at which the vast majority of ministers would tell him, and each other, what a wonderful deal he had got. He would then step outside to say the same to the British people. And the Remain camp would get an instant 10-point bump in the polls – a lead which would only build as 'Project Fear' swung into gear.

In fact, that late-night announcement was about the last point things went according to plan for the Remainers. The next day, Cameron shared the headlines with the news Michael Gove had come out for Vote Leave. And on the editorial pages, the renegotiation got a kicking. The Times headlined its editorial 'Thin Gruel' and pronounced: "From the land of chocolate, David Cameron was always destined to bring back fudge." Even the Financial Times admitted the 'fundamental, far-reaching' change Mr Cameron had promised 'was never realistic'.

The Referendum itself was, of course, won on June 23. But it was that weekend in February 2016 that made it possible for us to win it. On the Saturday, the 'Glorious Six' – Cabinet Ministers Iain Duncan Smith, Michael Gove, Chris Grayling, Priti Patel, Theresa Villiers and John Whittingdale – announced they would be campaigning for Leave. On the Sunday, Boris Johnson became number seven, when he announced he was doing the same. And in the days that followed, the bump in the polls Remain had expected – and was relying on – completely failed to materialise. One of the key reasons for this was how we played the expectations game. This was one of the great successes of the Leave movement that has been relatively ignored, yet which was absolutely vital to our eventual victory.

Genesis of Vote Leave

After the Conservative Party's surprise election victory, two things became crystal clear; first, there would be an EU Referendum and second, that it would not be on the vision outlined in David Cameron's famous Bloomberg speech in January 2013. The kind of Europe he'd outlined there was one that even I might have voted for – one which offered a return of powers to the member states and a recognition of national parliaments as 'the true source of real democratic legitimacy and accountability'. Neither of these things was possible once the Prime Minister ruled out treaty change at the June 2015 European Council – which is why the Board of Business for Britain proceeded to set up Vote Leave. Our stance had always been 'Change, or Go'. Once it became clear 'change' was off the table, we had to prepare to fight for 'go'. But even if we were certain in our own minds Cameron's deal wasn't enough, how would we make that clear to the voters?

At the end of 2011, when I was working out what to do after running the NOtoAV referendum campaign, I commissioned Lynton Crosby and Crosby Textor Fullbrook to examine how an EU Referendum campaign could be fought and won. Lynton and his team found in a straight In/Out referendum, Out stood a very decent chance. But if there were a meaningful renegotiation, Remain would walk it: the figures were 43 per cent for Leave come what may, 14 per cent for Remain even with the status quo, and 39 per cent for Remain with reform. CTF's focus groups found the same: the public were overwhelmingly supportive of a renegotiation if one were on the table. Subsequent polls over the following years found the same thing. If you asked people whether they wanted to leave the EU, you got one set of figures. But if you asked a follow-up question about how they would vote if David Cameron were standing there claiming to have secured a great new deal for Britain, In suddenly leapt ahead by 10 to 15 points.

This predicted bounce was the reason why so many of my polling and campaigning friends thought I was crazy for setting up Business for Britain and lining myself up for another referendum campaign. I remember meeting a friend for brunch one Saturday in Brixton Market, who was certain the Leave campaign would lose an EU Referendum. "Matthew," he told me patiently, "you don't understand just how popular the PM is." It wasn't only the public. Many Tory MPs, particularly the 2015 intake, were more Cameron's children than Thatcher's. He'd selected them, campaigned for them, won them their seats. So if we were going to win the Referendum, there were all kinds of things we needed to do.

We needed to make sure the campaign rules in the EU Referendum Bill guaranteed a fair fight. We needed to make sure the Conservative Party stayed neutral, so the other side couldn't get access to its money or its data. We needed to recruit mainstream support from MPs, activists and business figures so people could see that this wasn't a repeat of the 1975 referendum – that there were sensible, normal people who thought leaving the EU was the right thing to do. We also needed to recruit star names who thought the same – so the face people saw on their screens calling for us to Leave was a Boris Johnson or Michael Gove, not a Nigel Farage or George Galloway. And of course we needed to raise money and build a proper campaigning organisation. But we also needed to raise the bar for Cameron's negotiation as high as possible – to take the shine off his deal in the eyes of MPs and the public by making it absolutely clear how far the negotiations had fallen short. And the best way to do that was to hold him to his own standards.

Doing our homework first

At the heart of this game of expectation management was Business for Britain, which I'd founded in 2013. BfB always had three purposes. First, to act as the precursor to a full-on Leave campaign (unless, of course, Cameron delivered on the pledges in his Bloomberg speech). Second, to win support within the business community – it was always very clear if it came out against us, we'd lose. Rodney Leach and Business for Sterling had stopped Britain's entry into the euro by showing the business community was divided on the issue. So we needed to demonstrate business leaders were also split on Britain's future relationship with the European Union. And third, we needed to be able to critique the Prime Minister's renegotiation from a mainstream position. That's why we deliberately pitched our tent to cover all shades of eurosceptic opinion – anyone who thought the status quo wasn't working.

Our mission statement was 'Change, or Go'. If the renegotiation worked, then we'd have helped to make sure it was a proper one. If it didn't (as was always likely), then the only logical course of action was to leave the EU. This was something Arron Banks and his friends at Leave.EU never understood. I lost count of the number of times Richard Tice, a Business for Britain signatory who then became Co-Chairman of Leave.EU, urged me to take a stand. What they couldn't see was if we looked like we rejected Cameron's position out of hand, we'd lose. We had to show we'd actually considered it – we had to make him the guy who was out of tune with the public, not us. At the heart of this was a 1,000-page, five-part report called 'Change, or Go: How Britain would gain influence and prosper outside an unreformed EU', which was published in June 2015 and serialised in the Daily Telegraph. We argued, compared to the status quo, Britain was in a win-win position. We would be better off after a proper renegotiation, but if that didn't happen, we would also be better off out of an unreformed EU. I'm under no illusions about the number of people who actually read Change, or Go all the way through – although one of them was the Foreign Secretary. Anyone who thinks Boris Johnson was being opportunistic by coming on board with Vote Leave, or he didn't care about the issues, should have seen the well-thumbed copy in his office, covered in post-it notes and folded-down corners.

But Change, or Go succeeded in doing exactly what it was meant to, it reassured people that serious, sober, rigorous research had been done into what leaving the EU might look like – that it was not a leap in the dark. It also acted as bait for MPs and ministers. We sent copies to everyone we could think of in Parliament, along with personal letters saying I'd be only too happy to discuss the contents. Above all, it raised the bar for Cameron's renegotiation to the proper height. Not an arbitrary height picked by us, but the height promised in his Bloomberg speech. One of our most popular videos at Business for Britain, subsequently remade and updated by Vote Leave, was a reel of video clips of Cameron saying extremely eurosceptic things, in order to heighten the contrast between promises and delivery. Soon after the election, it became clear the Prime Minister would fail his own exam. At a European Council meeting at the end of June 2015, he had conceded he would not ask for treaty changes to deliver whatever his deal turned out to be. He would instead settle for guarantees that there would be treaty changes at some point in the future. To anyone who knew anything about the EU, this was a white flag.

It was at this point we made our pivot. The board of Business for Britain agreed to come out for Leave; we sent letters to all our supporters telling them so and we began the formal process of setting up Vote Leave. At every stage, we kept Nigel Farage and Arron Banks fully informed of our plans – which is why it was so frustrating journalists swallowed his line that his setting up 'The Know' (as Leave. EU was originally called) had bounced us into launching early. Many people were involved in this game of expectations management, and we can't deny how events like the migrant crisis reinforced our message of Taking Back Control. But by the time Donald Tusk put out a draft of the deal in early February, the scales had fallen from voters' eyes. The draft got an absolute kicking in the press and on social media – one for which the Remainers, unlike us, were oddly unprepared. In polls taken after the Tusk draft appeared, only 21 per cent of the public said they supported its terms. By the time Cameron finally presented the results to the nation, everyone knew the deal was a dud. That's why, during the campaign itself, it was barely even mentioned.

For months, many MPs and public figures had been hemming and hawing about which way to go. Many said they needed to wait until the outlines of Cameron's deal became clear, that they still had faith in him to deliver. But once the deal came out, they couldn't pretend any more. In the end we got 135 Tory MPs on board, far more than Downing Street ever imagined possible. Instead of the PM making the deal look better, the deal made the PM look worse – especially since he suddenly switched from insisting he 'didn't rule anything out' if he didn't get a good deal to campaigning for it 'with all my heart and soul'. From that point, his personal approval ratings dropped sharply. The more he raved about Europe, the less credible he looked.

The moment Cameron lost the Referendum

When I look back on those months before the short campaign, I'm still baffled by how badly David Cameron played his hand. In Europe, he went in talking tough, but what he effectively said to the other countries was: 'Give me something I can sell'. The moment he ruled out treaty change, he effectively ruled out getting anything actually meaningful. Similarly, there was no sustained attempt to speak to his Eurosceptic backbenchers, to find out what the people who had been hammering away on these issues for years actually wanted or thought might be achievable. It wasn't a sham negotiation, clearly, they put a lot of effort into it. And you have to admire Cameron for actually fighting for the EU during the campaign, rather than stepping back as Harold Wilson had in 1975 in order to remain in power whatever happened. But the deal he was defending was never going to come close to what was needed – and both the public and his MPs came to realise it. Ultimately, Cameron and those around him assumed throughout this process that whatever they came back with, they would win. They knew how to win elections. They had the most popular politician in the country. As Iain Duncan Smith has said, it felt at that final Cabinet meeting after the deal was announced as if he and the others were being given a condescending pat on the head, being granted gracious permission to go off and do their usual Eurosceptic nonsense to get it out of their systems.

I write this not to gloat, but because I think it's important people realise the amount of planning that went into the Referendum campaign and that pivotal weekend. We had to do so much groundwork, and take so much time, to get ourselves in shape for those three crucial days – to identify and neutralise Downing Street's advantages. But that weekend, in February 2016, from Cameron coming back with his deal to Boris coming out for Vote Leave, feels in retrospect like the moment we went from underdogs to contenders with an even chance. The foundation had been built from which Vote Leave would win four months later, on June 23.

Note on contributor:
Matthew Elliott has been described by the Financial Times as 'one of the most formidable political strategists in Westminster', having been Chief Executive of Vote Leave, the official Brexit campaign in the 2016 EU referendum. Matthew also led NOtoAV, winning the 2011 referendum on the Alternative Vote. As a policy entrepreneur, he has founded and run numerous award winning campaigns, from the TaxPayers' Alliance (TPA) to Business for Britain (BfB). Matthew is currently a Senior Fellow at the Legatum Institute. He has written four books, appears regularly on TV and radio, and is a frequent speaker both in the UK and overseas.
He tweets @matthew_elliott

Social death: How did millennial liberals lose history's most digital elections?

Since President Obama used social media mastery to win two elections, liberals thought they owned the digital space. But both major elections of 2016 showed things had changed. How did the liberal digital elite go wrong? What did the right get right? And have user profiling and behavioural analysis changed the way elections are fought forever, asks Alex Connock?

Auspiciously or not, it was Friday 13th. That day in May 2016, the bosses of hit websites Facebook, Buzzfeed, The LADbible, and Twitter filed into 10 Downing Street, invited to help get the young to register to vote. There was even someone from casual dating site Tinder[1].

David Cameron was swiping left, hooking up with the millennial, digital generation – and no doubt aware that among his key, targeted Brexit psychographic, the 'Disengaged Middle', 70 per cent sourced their news primarily from Facebook[2].

Once unleashed, the viral dynamics of social media engagement would not behave, but skit like zephyrs over the social timeline. The social media battles of 2016 would then be won at the ballots by the populist right, by the glib agitprop of Brexit and Trump. And tech commentators would hypothesise the roles of paid reach in Facebook, and vote-winning armies of right-wing bots, dispatched by behavioural algorithms in support.

But as coding language entered political science, there were still more likely explanations. Maybe the right won the digital elections just by being better at the punchy output the social news cycle demands – Farage and Trump having perfected the art of saying something outrageous at the vicarage tea party. Or maybe Facebook users are just more alt right than right-on in the first place.

How many Likes have you got?

Nineteen years earlier, Tony Blair gave Noel Gallagher and the Britpop gang a glittering soiree[3] at No. 10 – an Arcadian, pre-internet era where no-one checked Twitter, and everyone cared what tabloids said. The occasion, and Blair's message, was filtered by just a handful of press owners, most of whom a prime minister could have dinner with.

For similar reach in 2016, Cameron would have to feed the Glastonbury Festival. He had to seep out his message through a chaotic tented city of millions of peer-to-peer social feeds. Just 6 per cent of 18-24 year olds now got their news feed from newspapers, versus 28 per cent from social media.[4] Cameron's meeting wasn't so much digital Cool Britannia, as an online bet on 'Europe or bust.'

The best option was to befriend the platforms. The social media elite scrupulously practised Brexit agnosticism, but was still an intravenous line into an audience that newspaper potentates could only fantasise. Buzzfeed was so big it had 168m views for a single video on its food site, Tasty[5] – a very Europe-friendly Greek salad as it happens.

Cameron's push for voter engagement gambled the young would be pro-Europe. If that demographic registered, everyone could get on with Summer and the Euros, a future livelihood secured for 19.5m UK under 25s. And so the 2016 Bite the Ballot campaign launched a 'generation drive' on June 1, presented as Brexit-agnostic. "Politics needs rebranding – and that's where you come in," said its website: "#Turn up for the EU Ref."[6] (Nine months later, no one had had the heart to take the site down.)

Remain weren't only into voter registration – they also plunged into social media campaigning first. In February 2016 they planned a Stronger In Europe 'Twitter war room' and a paid push for Cameron's Facebook page.[7] Meanwhile the Leave camp started badly on social. A key funder emailed a colleague: "The website is awful, the Facebook page worse.... ....If this is your best shot, you should be shot."[8] With the stars aligning like this for Remain, what could go wrong?

Read the comments

What could go wrong was that the users had opinions of their own. Europe stories would generate aggressively 'anti' comments on social sites. The LADbible had not taken a Remain/Leave position but some Facebook users interpreted one anyway: "TheLADbible can you quit with the lefty political views, you're not panafuckingrama, you're here to make me laugh. Now go find me a video of a dog that has a shit catch. Or just like the government, I'll unsubscrbe from you're views (sic)." For that comment: 1350 likes.

The supposed secret army of sock puppets

And then the story took a diversion into tech. Newspapers said[9][10] the Right used arcane data modelling and psychographic profiling. Commentators theorised corporations with armies of automated 'bots'. The inventor of the world-wide web Tim Berners-Lee said (as part of a wider menu of points to improve about the web)[11]: "The increasing sophistication of algorithms drawing upon rich pools of personal data mean that political campaigns are now building individual adverts targeted directly at users."

Targeted advertising bots do exist. Paradoxically, people who run major social sites actually know the fakes in person - because the same faces regularly pop up in Comments section within seconds of a new video upload, even when the video they are liking is a couple of minutes long. But losing to international bots is also way more palatable for a professional political campaigner than losing because you haven't got enough friends on Facebook.

Paid vs earned political advertising

Facebook success comes down to engagement: how many people like and share your stuff, both of which push items up in users' news feed. The Leave side used paid advertising on social – targeting a limited budget towards people most likely to share it. In other words they did what consumer goods advertisers do every day.

The allure of Facebook's advertising model is that if you open a Stroud fishing tackle superstore, you can specifically buy views of Stroud's self-declared anglers – 'paid views.' To the extent the fishermen share the content, anyone taking the bait is an 'earned' view – which is the free stuff you want. Advertisers, and even big social channels, kickstart content with paid views to key demographics and influencers, then watch it go viral as the engagement hopefully kicks in. It's like seeding a cloud to start the rain.

So Leave spent 40 per cent of its budget on a consultancy firm, according to the Daily Telegraph[12], giving £3.5m to AggregateIQ (AIQ), a small tech company in provincial Canada – but unpack that, and it gets less weird. That AIQ is a consultancy in highly-targeted Facebook advertising is a statement of the obvious, because all Facebook advertising is by definition targeted, unless the client is spending their budget like a blind drunk grenadier with a blunderbuss. As Zack Massingham of AIQ told the Telegraph: "The reality is the vast majority of that money was for online advertising to those groups of people the campaign wanted to reach." That was about the 'paid' views, rather than (say) billboard advertising on lorries.

Meanwhile for the 'earned' component, Leave.EU's social media got modern. Campaigner Andy Wigmore reportedly perfected real-time adjustment in posts to maximise effectiveness. "Within an hour, we would change a headline on Facebook or Twitter maybe five or six times just to gauge the reaction. We were monitoring how many people looked and shared it, where it went, and reacted accordingly."[13]

In the focused, cerebral offices of major UK social media channels, doing that is about as exotic as having a Gregg's sausage roll for lunch. It happens every day.

Real news vs fake news

In the US, the context was broadly the same for the alt right as for the Brexiteers; identifying liberal bias in the mainstream media, they aggressively flanked it with social. Breitbart economics editor John Carney said at Columbia Journalism School[14] in February 2017: "Do you think you're predominantly staffed by people who view Trump's point of view as not only wrong, but also evil?" And to right-wing 'populists', that perceived imbalance in the media needed redress.

So the conservative movement grew its own online news outlets. "Breitbart is now bigger than Pornhub", said a headline[15], as it briefly became 29th most trafficked site in the US, and used that traction in the election. The New Yorker said it undermined Hillary Clinton[16] by tracking which stories about her got the most engagement to isolate the most potent weapons against her.

Fake news wasn't what Breitbart did – but it did grow industrially on many other sites. In November 2016 detailed Buzzfeed analysis[17] claimed top fake election stories outranked Facebook engagement on the top stories from 19 major news outlets combined. Of the top false election stories, 85 per cent were pro-Trump.

Fake news aside, was the reach of conservative sites organically driven, or manipulated? Observer journalist Carole Cadwalladr rummaged around in[18] the right's social media toolbox, exploring how analytics companies used data collection and profiling to help Trump target advertising effectively and reach people most likely to share it. The Washington Post agreed it was effective, and said after the election one leading firm in the space won new business from its success.[19] But at a basic level this was still just paid and earned reach, none of which means they circulated fake news or did anything else wrong.

Indeed Mark Zuckerberg, speaking at Techonomy[20] after the US election said: "The idea that fake news on Facebook – of which it's a very small amount of the content – influenced the election in any way is a pretty crazy idea."

For one thing, fake news had massive competition – not always presented in the statistical picture. Facebook made the point[21] that non-text stories like native video, live content and image posts from major news outlets also saw mass engagement, but weren't measured in that Buzzfeed analysis. For instance a Guardian Facebook upload of a Jimmy Kimmel Live video of Barack Obama reading out Trump tweets reached 51m views with 498,423 shares.[22] Those are big numbers.

Meanwhile the story of Breitbart beating Pornhub in site visits wasn't what it seemed either. The Trump-sceptical New York Times was always well ahead. And by March 2017 rankings,[23] the Times was at 27, Washington Post at 42 and Breitbart back at 45; hardly the conservative media upending the news industry, or a black box of battle-winning bots.

Data is not the only information

In fact, the obvious counterpoint to the view that big-data geeks won Trump the election is that one firm who helped him also helped Ted Cruz – who got knocked out of the race.[24] That's probably because before targeted advertising can work, there does have to be actual people receptive to the message in the first place to build upon. A sceptical pre-election piece in AdAge[25] questioned whether behavioural methodology always delivered. The New York Times[26] doubted that any digital 'secret sauce' helped Trump: "Many scoff."

The Columbia Journalism Review of March 3, 2017 had a simpler answer to what happened in the digital elections[27]: people just stick to what they like. If the media blamed externalities for the unanticipated victories – Russian hacking, fake news – Columbia analysis just said the Internet gave people personalised filter bubbles, so they could read 'The Daily Me'. Breitbart developed as 'a distinct and insulated media system, using social media as a backbone to transmit a hyper-partisan perspective to the world'. An earlier book[28] about conservative broadcaster Russ Limbaugh had called that 'the echo chamber.' On social, everyone hears more from people who agreed with them in the first place. Look at your own Twitter or Facebook feed, and see how few of them disagree with what you think.

Strange attractors

So the fact Brexit and Trump won elections does not evidence the 'secret sauce' of behavioural profiling by armies of bots – though their sophistication as paid-view generators of reach is something that will be key in future elections. It could equally be a question of political charisma seeping across peer networks through its sheer outlandishness, in the same way that click-bait, Photoshopped pictures of 'mysterious sea creatures' washed up on beaches go massively viral. Gordon Fletcher of Salford University[29] says: "Politicians like Farage and Trump become beacons for support or critical response, strange attractors. Engaging at all precludes ambivalence." The resulting extreme partisanship can be digitally targeted.

At the London Ad Fest event at in March 2017 a session on classic political advertising pulled out the 'Britain Isn't Working' classics, but also a brilliant Remain advert. It was a picture of IDS, Gove, Farage and Johnson, all looking like plonkers, with the slogan: 'Do you want to be left alone on a small island with these men?'[30]

This was effective, brutal, negative, non-ambivalent, un-nuanced, and perfect material for social sharing. Except, Remain didn't share it.

I wish they had done, because the hard truth is Remain and the Democrats weren't cheated by behavioural data analysis, fake news or armies of bots. They just didn't fight anywhere near smart enough.

Notes

[1] Patrick Christys *Daily Express* (17 May 2016), Cameron 'signs up with TINDER & the LADBIBLE in bid to get youngsters to stick with EU' by http://www.express.co.uk/news/uk/670934/David-Cameron-Prime-Minister-Tinder-LadBible-EU-referendum-Europe

[2] Tim Shipman *All Out War: The Full story of how Brexit sank Britain's Political Class*

[3] Clare Rudebeck *&* Genevieve Atilde *Independent* (27 April 2005), *Eight years later, how the party ended for the Cool Britannia set* http://www.independent.co.uk/news/uk/politics/eight-years-later-how-the-party-ended-for-the-cool-britannia-set-526457.html

[4] Reuters Institute, University of Oxford, *Digital News Report (2016)* http://reutersinstitute.politics.ox.ac.uk/sites/default/files/Digital-News-Report-2016.pdf?utm_source=digitalnewsreport.org&utm_medium=referral

[5] *Tasty* Facebook site (owned by Buzzfeed) (viewed March 2017) https://www.facebook.com/Buzzfeedtasty/videos/1721186814800627/

[6] *Bite the Ballot* website, (viewed March 2017) http://bitetheballot.co.uk

[7] Tim Shipman *All Out War: The Full story of how Brexit sank Britain's Political Class*

[8] Quoted by Tim Shipman in *All Out War: The Full story of how Brexit sank Britain's Political Class*

[9] Carole Cadwalladr, *Observer* (26 February 2017) *The Big Data Billionaire Waging War on Mainstream Media* https://www.theguardian.com/politics/2017/feb/26/robert-mercer-Breitbart-war-on-media-steve-bannon-donald-trump-nigel-farage

[10] Jamie Doward and Alice Gibbs, *Observer* (4 March 2017) *Did Cambridge Analytica influence the Brexit vote and the US election?* https://www.theguardian.com/politics/2017/mar/04/nigel-oakes-cambridge-analytica-what-role-brexit-trump

[11] Tim Berners-Lee *Observer* (March 12 2017) *I Invented the web. Here are three things we need to change to save it* https://www.theguardian.com/technology/2017/mar/11/tim-berners-lee-web-inventor-save-internet

[12] Patrick Foster and Martin Evans *Telegraph* (24 Feb 2017) *How a tiny Canadian IT company helped swing the Brexit vote for Leave* http://www.telegraph.co.uk/news/2017/02/24/exclusive-tiny-canadian-company-helped-swing-brexit-vote-leave/

[13] Quoted by Tim Shipman *All Out War: The Full story of how Brexit sank Britain's Political Class*

[14] David Uberti, *Columbia Journalism Review – Breitbart editor slams mainstream media in Pulitzer Hall* http://www.cjr.org/covering_trump/Breitbart-editor-columbia-stelter.php?facebook&utm_content=buffer54e8e&utm_medium=social&utm_source=facebook.com&utm_campaign=buffer

[15] Ben Kew, *Breitbart*, 19 February 2017. *Breitbart News 29th most trafficked site in America, overtakes Pornhub and ESPN* http://www.Breitbart.com/big-journalism/2017/02/19/Breitbart-news-traffic-surpasses-Pornhub-espn/

[16] Jane Mayer, *The New Yorker, The Reclusive Hedge-fund Tycoon Behind the Trump Presidency* 27 March 2017 http://www.newyorker.com/magazine/2017/03/27/the-reclusive-hedge-fund-tycoon-behind-the-trump-presidency

[17] Buzzfeed News – *This Analysis Shows How Viral Fake Election News Stories Outperformed Real News on Facebook* https://www.Buzzfeed.com/craigsilverman/viral-fake-election-news-outperformed-real-news-on-facebook?utm_term=.xbnW5QBOW#.ajPJOvbDJ

[18] Carole Cadwalladr *The Observer* () *Robert Mercer: the big data billionaire waging war on mainstream media* https://www.theguardian.com/politics/2017/feb/26/robert-mercer-Breitbart-war-on-media-steve-bannon-donald-trump-nigel-farage

[19] Matea Gold and Frances Stead Sellers *Washington Post*, After Working for Trump's campaign, British data firm eyes new US government contracts. https://www.washingtonpost.com/politics/after-working-for-trumps-campaign-british-data-firm-eyes-new-us-government-contracts/2017/02/17/a6dee3c6-f40c-11e6-8d72-263470bf0401_story.html?utm_term=.a0da7e9583e5

[20] Kim Kolaticheva, *Fortune* (November 11, 2016) Mark Zuckerberg says Fake News Affecting the Election is a 'Crazy Idea.' http://fortune.com/2016/11/11/facebook-election-fake-news-mark-zuckerberg/

[21] Craig Silverman, *Buzzfeed* (November 16, 2016.) *This analysis shows how viral fake news stories outperformed real news on Facebook* https://www.Buzzfeed.com/craigsilverman/viral-fake-election-news-outperformed-real-news-on-facebook?utm_term=.mpreJM6Ye#.wsGgZ5Ykg

[22] *Guardian* Facebook video *When Donald J. Trump tweeted that Barack Obama is the worst president in the history of the United States – he probably didn't expect Obama to read it out on live television.* https://www.facebook.com/theguardian/videos/1507085585985170/

[23] Alexa rankings US March 2017 http://www.alexa.com/topsites/countries/US

[24] Kate Kaye, *AdAge* (August 16, 2016) *In DC, Cambridge Analytica not exactly Toast of the Town* http://adage.com/article/campaign-trail/cambridge-analytica-toast/305439/

[25] Kate Kaye, *AdAge* (August 16, 2016) *In DC, Cambridge Analytica not exactly Toast of the Town* http://adage.com/article/campaign-trail/cambridge-analytica-toast/305439/

[26] Nicholas Confessore and Danny Hakim New York Times (March 6 2017) *Data Firm Says 'Secret Sauce' Aided Trump: Many Scoff* https://www.nytimes.com/2017/03/06/us/politics/cambridge-analytica.html?smprod=nytcore-iphone&smid=nytcore-iphone-share&_r=2

[27] Yochai Benkler, Robert Faris, Hal Roberts and Ethan Zuckerman *Columbia Journalism Review* (March 3 2017) *Study: Breitbart-led right-wing media ecosystem altered broader media agenda* by http://www.cjr.org/analysis/Breitbart-media-trump-harvard-study.php?link

[28] Jamieson, K. and Cappella J. (2010) *Echo Chamber: Rush Limbaugh and the Conservative Media Establishment*, Oxford University Press: Oxford.

[29] Interviewed March 2017

[30] John Plunkett *Guardian* (1 July 2016) *Rejected Remain Campaign Posters Revealed by Ad Agencies* https://www.theguardian.com/media/2016/jul/01/rejected-remain-campaign-posters-revealed-by-ad-agencies

Note on contributor:

Alex Connock is Managing Director at TV production company Endemol Shine North, and has worked across viral advertising video production for many clients, including hit social platform LADbible, where for a period in 2016 he was head of video. He is also visiting professor at Salford, Sunderland and Manchester Metropolitan universities and Entrepreneur in Residence at Insead. He has recently completed a study with IpsosMori into the effectiveness of different styles of video in e-commerce.

Tweeting for Brexit: How social media shaped the Referendum campaign

Eurosceptic Twitter users outnumbered and out-tweeted pro-Europeans in the EU Referendum campaign, but were more confined into their own echo-chambers than Remainers. Max Hänska and Stefan Bauchowitz analysed 7.5m tweets and found the predominance of Euroscepticism on social media mirrored its dominance in the press.

Since the EU Referendum in June 2016, and even more so since Trump's election victory in November, pundits have not tired of asserting the supposedly wide-reaching influence of social media on our politics. It has been commonplace to speculate social media was a key conduit for misinformation, or 'fake news' more generally, that it confined citizens to echo chambers, that it may have been decisive in shaping the outcomes of the Referendum, and, indeed, the election of Donald Trump in the United States. There is no doubt social media have transformed our communication, how we access, and engage with information. It is also clear that the mediated relationship between politicians, citizens, and journalists, how these groups communicate, engage with and relate to each other, has changed.

Consider the evidence on the increasing importance of social media as an information source. The Reuters Institute's Digital News Report found that in 2016 social media's rise as a news source pulled even with print's decline, both serving as a source of information for around 35 per cent of the UK's public. After dedicated news sites, social media is the second most important place people discover news online (Newman et al 2016). A 2015 Ofcom report found 43 per cent of those who get news online, receive it through social media. The figure rises to 61 per cent among 16-24 year olds, 16 per cent of whom rely exclusively on social media for news (Ofcom 2017). Across the Reuters report's 26 country sample, social media served as a news source for 51 per cent of its respondents, and as a main news source for 28 per cent of 18-24 year olds. But of course social media is not merely a channel for delivering news to audiences. Users share, post and comment on news, and can engage directly with politicians and journalists.

It is hardly surprising news organisations increasingly use social media to reach audiences, and engage them. Journalists are fond of Twitter for sharing updates, particularly on ongoing stories. General research is also a staple Twitter use, allowing journalists to follow sources, and sometimes to crowd-source information. Those who are very active users also tend to be more audience-oriented than their less social media-active peers. And just as audiences can engage with journalists, given the multi-directional interactivity Twitter affords, journalists have also begun to seize social media as an opportunity to engage with audiences, to offer behind-the-scenes views, gauge reactions, and build relationships. Some journalists also use Twitter to build a strong personal news brand, by displaying their professional values and practices, their ability to network and cultivate a community of followers (Hedman 2015). In doing so journalists are building direct relationships with their readers.

Twitter is also particularly popular among politicians. 87 per cent of British MPs have Twitter accounts. Of course Donald Trump's use of Twitter as a primary means of reaching his followers is now notorious. But this is hardly surprising. As ever more citizens use social media, and as it becomes a more important source of information, it also becomes an obvious channel through which to reach them. To some extent politicians, like journalists, are cutting out intermediaries and reaching their audience directly.

Why does social media matter?
Evidently Twitter is an important part of the changing news ecosystem, through which politicians, journalists and citizens communicate and compete for eyeballs. Users are able to customise their informational environment by selecting who they follow or engage with, a tendency amplified by social media algorithms which optimise users' social feeds with content they may find congenial. However, on Twitter algorithms play only a small role, meaning partisan filtering of news is mostly down to the network of followers users create. Consequently, the social feed of an avid Eurosceptic would likely have been filled with stories about how inimical the EU was to British democracy, with confident assertions that millions of pounds would be saved by leaving the EU, that the NHS would benefit, and Remainers were scaremongering.

Perhaps most important, as noted above, social media disintermediates the diffusion of news and information, so traditional information intermediaries have seen their gate-keeping capacity diluted. In the past politicians and commentators needed to rely on news media to relay their messages to the general public. Now Farage's or Trump's tweets can reach millions directly, unadulterated by pesky journalists fact-checking and contextualising their message on the evening news. The increasing importance of social media as a source of news and information, its popularity with journalists and politicians, and the ways in which it changes the ecosystem through which news is shared and accessed, make it crucial for us to understand its role in the UK's EU Referendum.

How leave won Twitter

To map Twitter's info-sphere, and examine how Eurosceptic (Leave) and pro-European (Remain) activity compare on Twitter in the run-up to the Referendum, we collected more than 7.5 million Brexit-related tweets in the month preceding the Referendum. We ask whether there was a relationship between Twitter activity and the actual vote, what kind of information was shared on Twitter, and whether Leavers and Remainers were confined to echo chambers which kept feeding them information congenial to their views, or whether the two sides engaged openly with one another.

It is clear from our analysis that Twitter users who supported leaving the EU were more numerous, and Eurosceptic users in general were more active (they tweeted more frequently) than Remain users. We estimate Leave users were more numerous and more active on Twitter by a factor of 1.75-2.3. Other researchers examining Google search trends, Instagram posts and Facebook found similar patterns of Eurosceptic views being communicated with greater intensity by a greater number of users on those platforms (Herrman 2016, Polonski 2016).

We also found local authority districts with a greater share of Twitter users supporting Leave tended to vote for leaving the EU, so Twitter activity correlated with voting in the Referendum. This is not to say an analysis of Twitter activity could have predicted the Referendum. It is not clear how the Leave margin on Twitter should have been interpreted prior to the Referendum, even with such a robust observation of more pronounced Eurosceptic activity. After all, the factor by which Leavers outnumbered and out-tweeted Remainers on Twitter was much larger than the margin with which Leave won the vote.

We also analysed the nature of openness and homophily on Twitter, which crucially affords users the ability to interact and engage with each other. To do so we examined the extent to which users who supported Leave and Remain interacted with each other, that is, for instance, whether a user who supported leaving the EU replied, quoted or retweeted a user who supported remaining in the EU. We found Leave users tended to be less open, and mostly engage with other Leave supporters, indicating important hallmarks of an echo-chamber. In contrast Remain supporters were much more open. Specifically, 83 per cent of interactions initiated by Leave supporters were with other Leave supporters. For Remain supporters this figure drops to 46 per cent. Remainers replied to, retweeted or quoted Leavers 49, 39 and 50 per cent of the time, respectively. Contrast this with Leavers who replied to, retweeted or quoted Remainers only 19, 8 and 11 per cent of the time, respectively.

This tendency to interact only with the like-minded is also reflected in the URLs shared. Leave users tended to share Eurosceptic domains, including The Express, the Daily Mail, and Breitbart. But Leave users also linked more frequently to Bloomberg and Reuters than Remainers. Remain users tended to share links to The Guardian, BBC, The Independent, and less frequently The Mirror, The Financial Times, and The Economist. Overall, the most frequently linked domains were The Guardian, YouTube, BBC, and The Express. The prominence of The Express over the Daily Mail was somewhat surprising, given the latter is well known for running a hugely successful website which attracts around 29m monthly readers from the UK alone.

YouTube was the second most prominent domain linked, indicating the importance of video as a way of distributing information about the campaign. The single most shared video was to a clip of John Oliver's comedy-news show Last Week Tonight which was supportive of remaining in the EU. Eurosceptic videos were numerous, but no single one rivalled the reach of John Oliver's clip. Prominent Eurosceptic videos included 'Brexit the Movie' and other clips featuring, among others Toby Young, and Joseph Watson, who attempted to debunk 'Project Fear' and characterised the EU as a dictatorship by the bureaucratic gravy train.

Overall, Twitter users who supported leaving the EU were much more active and motivated in advancing their cause, than Remainers were in advocating continued EU membership. One possible explanation of the dominance Leavers achieved on Twitter may be that slogans such as 'vote Leave', 'take control', or even 'Brexit' were more suited to simple, soundbite messaging than the Remain campaign's slogans and arguments (which is particularly useful given the character constraints of a tweet). Press coverage of the Referendum also favoured leaving the EU. Weighted for circulation, 82 per cent of newspaper articles in the lead-up to the Referendum supported leaving the EU, as other contributors to this book have noted (Deacon 2016). The balance of Eurosceptic information, views and opinion on Twitter thus appear to be leaning in the same direction as the balance of information in the press, meaning both online and offline citizens were more likely to encounter Eurosceptic voices.

As social media changes the ways news and information is distributed, accessed and engaged with, we are forced to consider its implications for both journalism's role in shaping public discourse, but also for the way media conveys information back-and-forth between citizens and the political system. How can people's desire to engage and participate in the creation and distribution of information be reconciled with journalism's role in making judgements about the importance and veracity of competing pieces of information? As the linear and hierarchical gate-keeping structures which define the broadcast age have ever-less purchase on our evolving news and information ecosystems, the messy, multi-directional, bottom-up practices of diffusing and absorbing information will play an ever-greater role in processes of public opinion formation.

References

Deacon, David (2016). 82% circulation advantage in favour of Brexit as The Sun declares, Centre for Research in Communication and Culture, Loughborough University, June 14, Available online at https://blog.lboro.ac.uk/crcc/eu-referendum/sun-no-longer-hedging-bets-brexit/, accessed on December 5, 2016.

Hedman, Ulrika (2015) J-Tweeters, *Digital Journalism*, Vol. 3, No. 2 pp 279–297

Herrman, John (2016) 'Brexit' Talk on Social Media Favored the 'Leave' Side, New York Times, July 16, Available online at http://www.nytimes.com/2016/06/25/business/brexit-talk-on-social-media-heavily-favored-the-leave-side.html?nytmobile=0, accessed on August 5, 2016.

Newman, Nic; Fletcher, Richard; Levy, David A.; & Nielsen, Rasmus Kleis (2016) Reuters Institute digital news report 2016, Oxford: Reuters Institute for the Study of Journalism, University of Oxford.

Ofcom (reissued in 2017) News consumption in the UK: Research Report, London: Ofcom.

Polonski, Vyacheslav (2016) Social Media Voices in the UK's EU Referendum, Medium, May 15, Available online at https://medium.com/@slavacm/social-media-voices-in-the-uks-eu-referendum-brexit-or-bremain-what-does-the-internet-say-about-ebbd7b27cf0f#.wtk0mbjfq, accessed on December 6, 2016.

Note on contributors

Max Hänska is a Senior Lecturer in Digital Journalism and Media Discourse at De Montfort University in Leicester. His research explores the impact of digital technologies on political communication and citizen journalism, and the impact of communication on political decision-making.

Stefan Bauchowitz is an independent researcher. He holds a PhD in Development Studies from the London School of Economics.

One party, two issues: UK news media reporting of the EU Referendum campaign

It was meant to be a fundamental debate over the future direction of the UK for generations to come, but too much of the media coverage focused on a narrow range of arguments inside the Conservative party, say Professor David Deacon and Professor Dominic Wring

Controversy surrounds mainstream news media reporting of the United Kingdom's exit from the European Union and it is unlikely to go away. Since the Referendum vote on June 23, 2016, there have been repeated allegations about the broadcasters' perceived lack of impartiality in coverage of the Brexit process. The BBC, in particular, has been attacked for adopting what is claimed to be an unduly negative and pessimistic approach when discussing the implications of the UK's withdrawal[1].

Elsewhere, the right wing press have been criticized for their aggressive endorsement of 'hard' Brexit, most notably following their splenetic response to the British High Court's judgement that the UK Parliament had to be consulted before Article 50 could be triggered. On this occasion, Theresa May pointedly defended the need to respect press freedom, ignoring wider concerns about the constitutional implications of untrammeled press attacks on the judiciary. Her stance contrasted starkly with that of her predecessor. Prior to the Referendum, David Cameron had approached the owner of the Daily Mail in an ultimately unsuccessful attempt to try and influence the newspaper's editorial position that involved the removal of its editor[2].

The controversies over the BBC and Mail are some of the preliminary skirmishes in what is going to be a protracted debate over a contested process. Television and newspaper coverage matter in the Brexit negotiations because research consistently demonstrates how important they continue to be in informing public knowledge about, and attitudes towards, the European Union. This significance still far exceeds that of social media and internet sources[3]. At the time of writing the invocation of Article 50 has just happened and therefore media discussion about the form and effects of Brexit to this point has been essentially conjectural. It will be intriguing to see how the material effects of Brexit influence future journalistic interpretations and evaluations. But news media don't simply reflect reality, they contribute to its construction – highlighting particular issues, ignoring others; privileging certain viewpoints and deprecating others. This chapter focuses on what was arguably the most crucial period in the reporting of the issues: in the white heat of the Referendum campaign itself.

Referendum coverage

The results presented are derived from a content analysis conducted by Loughborough University's Centre for Research in Communication and Culture. The content analysis examined EU Referendum related coverage in the weekday coverage of the following mainstream, national news outlets between May 6 and June 22, 2016.

- Television: Channel 4 News (7pm), Channel 5 News Tonight (6.30pm), BBC1 News at 10, ITV1 News at 10, Sky News 8-8.30pm.

- Press: The Guardian, The Times, Daily Telegraph, Financial Times, Daily Mail, Daily Express, Daily Mirror, The Sun, Daily Star and The i[4]. The total analysis covered 2294 news reports, articles and editorials.

The 'continuum of opinion' in Figure 1 illustrates how both Leave and Remain enjoyed the support of five titles with the size of the individual columns representing the extent of the said newspaper's partisanship. The larger the column, the more the title's reporting privileged its favoured camp over its rivals. This measure accurately forecast the intensity and direction of every newspaper's eventual formal editorial declaration. Consequently The Guardian and the Express were adjudged to be the most committed and, perhaps more intriguingly, the Star and The Times the least partisan and therefore placed next to one another on the continuum despite being very different kinds of newspaper. Whereas the Star's position reflects its preference for 'soft news', The Times' stance was markedly at odds with its notoriously Eurosceptic proprietor Rupert Murdoch and that of its sister paper, the Sunday Times.

Although five newspapers supported Leave and the same number Remain, collectively evaluative reporting of the campaign favoured Brexit by a margin of roughly 60:40. But even this does not fully reflect the huge quantitative advantage Leave enjoyed over its rivals in terms of editorial reach. When circulation is taking into account, the pro-Brexit camp benefited because newspaper items supporting their cause out-sold those favouring Remain by a ratio of 80:20.

The newspapers' propensity to privilege one side over the other during the Referendum was further reflected by the space afforded to quotes from representatives of the rival campaigns (see figure 2). Pro-Leave titles were more likely to feature the words of Brexit supporters and pro-Remain papers advocates for the status quo. The broadcast media differed from their print counterparts on this important measure. Across seven different television news programmes sampled, the near parity in airtime devoted to Leave and Remain spokespeople is remarkable and reflects the various channels' adherence to long established rules and practices governing their impartiality, at least concerning airtime.

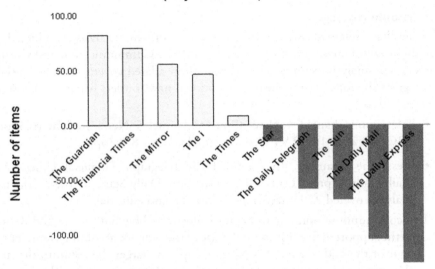

Figure 1: Volume of Pro-Remain to Pro-Leave Items
(May 6 - June 22)

Note: these figures are calculated by subtracting the number of items favouring Remain from the number of items favouring Leave. A positive value indicates an overall pro-Remain stance for a newspaper, a negative value, a pro-Leave stance. The larger either value is, the greater the support for that position

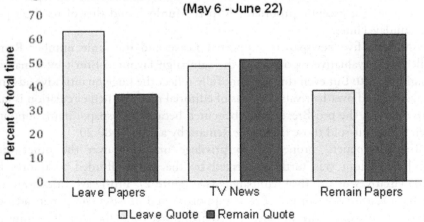

Figure 2: Quotation time for Remain/ Leave supporters
(May 6 - June 22)

However, referenda present broadcasters with challenges which differ from those arising from more conventional election campaigns. Consequently although impartiality ensured Leave and Remain spokespeople received similar television exposure, the party political nature of this representation was markedly skewed in favour of the ruling Conservatives across all news sectors (see Table 1). Prime Minister David Cameron and his potential successor Boris Johnson became the primary figures and de facto leaders of the rival camps judged by the media covered they received in what was a highly personalised even presidential contest (see Table 2). This was particularly remarkable given as recently as a few months before polling day neither Cameron nor Johnson had publicly declared how they would vote in a by then inevitable referendum their party had promised. Now they were attempting to influence the millions of votes of others.

Table 1: Comparison of the frequency of appearance of all news sources by media sector

	Pro Remain papers	Pro Leave papers	TV
Conservative	35.7%	50.3%	29.3%
Labour	11.9%	10.0%	10.0%
UKIP	3.7%	4.5%	4.2%
SNP	1.0%	0.7%	0.7%
Liberal Democrats	1.1%	0.2%	0.7%
Other party (incl Green)	0.7%	0.5%	0.5%
Celebrities/ media	2.9%	2.6%	4.6%
Experts	4.9%	3.5%	4.7%
Business	8.2%	3.6%	4.1%
Trade union	.9%	.5%	.5%
Citizens	5.8%	4.5%	26.0%
Other ref. pressure group	9.0%	6.2%	3.5%
Government depts/ agencies	4.9%	5.3%	2.7%
Other UK	3.3%	3.0%	0.9%
EU organisations	2.2%	1.6%	0.7%
Other non-UK	3.9%	2.9%	6.9%

Note: up to 5 sources could be coded per news item/ article.

Table 2: Top twenty media appearances (May 6 – June 22)

Position	Name	Number of appearances	Percentage of Referendum items in which they appeared
1	David Cameron (Conservative REMAIN)	499	24.9%
2	Boris Johnson (Conservative LEAVE)	379	18.9%
3	George Osborne (Conservative REMAIN)	230	11.5%
4	Nigel Farage (UKIP LEAVE)	182	9.1%
5	Michael Gove (Conservative LEAVE)	161	8.0%
6	Iain Duncan Smith (Conservative LEAVE)	124	6.2%
7	Jeremy Corbyn (Labour REMAIN)	123	6.1%
8	Priti Patel (Conservative LEAVE)	65	3.2%
9	Gordon Brown (Labour REMAIN)	52	2.6%
10	John Major (Conservative REMAIN)	47	2.3%
11	Jacob Rees-Mogg (Conservative LEAVE)	35	1.7%
12=	Chris Grayling (Conservative LEAVE)	33	1.6%
12=	Gisela Stuart (Labour LEAVE)	33	1.6%
14=	Theresa May (Conservative REMAIN)	29	1.4%
14=	Donald Tusk (President European Council REMAIN)	29	1.4%
16	Nicola Sturgeon (SNP REMAIN)	28	1.4%
17=	Bernard Jenkin (Conservative LEAVE)	24	1.2%
17=	Sadiq Khan (Labour REMAIN)	24	1.2%
19	Liam Fox (Conservative LEAVE)	23	1.1%
20	Jean-Claude Juncker (President of the EC REMAIN)	21	1.0%

The disproportionate focus on the Conservatives reflected divisions over the EU within the Government as well as intrigues over what might happen to the various leading ministerial figures including Cameron after the vote. The Conservative dominance in TV news was partly mitigated by the prominence given to 'citizens', but television and press coverage similarly marginalised Labour and UKIP although each had at least some profile compared with politicians from the other mainly pro-Remain parties who collectively received negligible coverage. If the range of partisan voices was limited then so was the gendered nature of the reporting. This was largely a 'he said-he said' campaign. Women were conspicuously sidelined in media terms and this led to complaints from various protagonists in the debate, notably former Cabinet minister Harriet Harman, who expressed dismay over the imbalance in broadcast coverage. Two female politicians were particularly sidelined: the Scottish First Minister Nicola Sturgeon, who had made such a striking impression on the news reporting of the 2015 UK General Election campaign, and Theresa May, Prime Minister-in-waiting, who would subsequently abandon her pro-Remain position and commit the nation to withdrawal from the EU.

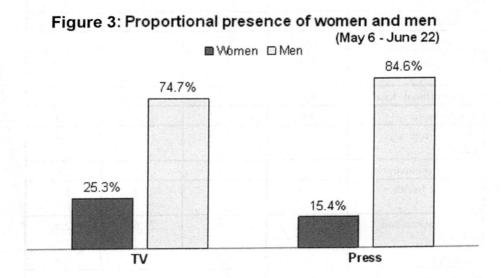

Figure 3: Proportional presence of women and men
(May 6 - June 22)

■ Women □ Men

As the range of politicians featured in media reporting of the Referendum was limited, so were the topics covered (see Table 4). The economy was the major substantive issue across all media. The prominence of the topic reflected the sustained attempts by both Remain and Leave to make their respective financial-based cases for wanting to stay in or exit from the EU. Immigration was the next most high profile substantive topic. Its prominence increased significantly four weeks before the vote, following sustained attempts by pro-Brexit campaigners to make it a salient issue and thereby frame perceptions of the Referendum among a large part of the electorate. Figure 4 shows the growing attention given to the immigration issue in the last stages of the campaign was not restricted to the Leave supporting press, indeed the patterning of attention was temporally consistent across all media and in relative terms, immigration received most prominence in TV news coverage in the latter stages of the Referendum campaign.

The dominance of these two substantial issues contributed to making the campaign a very narrow one, especially in terms of the topics that would subsequently come to dominate the post-mortem. Devolution and Article 50 were, by contrast, neglected concerns.

Table 4: Most prominent issues by all media and media sector (6 May – 22 June)

	All Media	Pro Remain papers	Pro Leave papers	TV News
	%	%	%	%
Referendum conduct	30.9	33.5	29.6	28.9
Economy/ Business	18.9	18.9	18.9	18.8
Immigration	13.2	9.9	14.8	15.6
Public opinion and citizens	8.0	8.8	5.0	11.3
Constitutional/ legal	6.1	5.8	6.7	5.5
Employment	3.6	3.9	3.4	3.4
Defence/ military/ security	3.4	2.9	4.4	2.7
Standards/ corruption	2.4	2.1	4.2	.3
Health & health services	2.3	2.7	2.2	1.7
EU operations and activities	1.7	1.4	1.6	2.4
Housing	0.9	0.7	1.1	0.8
Crime/ law and order	0.9	1.1	1.2	0.0
Social security	0.8	0.6	1.2	.7
Devolution in UK	0.8	0.8	0.3	1.5
Other foreign policy	0.7	0.8	0.7	0.5
Taxation	0.6	0.6	0.7	0.5
Public services	0.6	0.1	1.0	0.6
Agriculture	0.6	0.6	0.3	0.9
Environment	0.5	0.7	0.6	0.0
Education	0.5	0.4	0.7	0.2
All other issues	2.7	3.5	1.5	3.4

Figure 4: Weekly prominence of 'Immigration' coverage in TV and Press

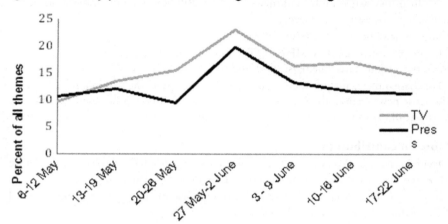

The failure of news media

'You can almost hear the sound of people across the country grappling with the issues in this campaign. For what it's worth, I suspect that despite all the confusion …most people have grasped the basics: migration – we're more likely to limit European migration if we leave; the economy – the vast bulk of financial and business opinion thinks it would be best to stay; sovereignty – Brussels will have less power over us if we leave, but we'll have less power over Brussels if we do that. Frankly, the rest is just detail anyway.' Evan Davis, BBC 2 Newsnight, 22/6/2016

The question mark that hovers behind all of these figures is the extent to which these trends in Referendum coverage, particularly the partisan press, affected the eventual outcome. Such a search for media causality is likely to be fruitless. In a media-saturated environment it is almost impossible to isolate the influence of particular news organisations. Moreover, commercial self-interests as much as doctrinaire agendas often shape chosen editorial positions.

In our view, it is more appropriate to consider the extent to which national news organisations succeeded in presenting a diverse, informed and pluralistic debate about a decision of such momentous consequences. This need for public orientation could not have been greater, as poll after poll has highlighted how under-informed UK citizens are about the EU and its role. Our evidence suggests all national news organisations – publicly-funded broadcasters as much as privately paid newspaper journalists – struggled to present the Referendum as little else than a debate about two issues within one party.

Notes

[1] e.g. http://www.telegraph.co.uk/news/2017/03/20/bbc-risks-undermining-brexit-damaging-uk-pessimistic-skewed/.

[2] http://www.bbc.co.uk/news/uk-38816692

[3] http://ec.europa.eu/COMMFrontOffice/publicopinion/index.cfm/Survey/getSurveyDetail/search/media/surveyKy/2098

[4] For these outlets, analysis was restricted to the front page, the first two pages of the domestic news section, the first two pages of any specialist section assigned to the coverage of the campaign and the pages containing and facing papers' leader editorials.

Note on contributors

David Deacon is Professor of Communication and Media Analysis at the Centre for Research in Communication and Culture, Loughborough University

Dominic Wring, Professor of Political Communication at the Centre for Research in Communication and Culture, Loughborough University.

Why Leave won in 2016

***

The uncertainty of a binary vote

Raymond Snoddy

The explanations for Brexit in the UK and Trump in the US are many and various, and range effortlessly from the psychological, philosophical and political to the sociological, geographical and economic. Then there are the polls and the economic forecasters – they got it all wrong again. Didn't they?

Eric Kaufman, professor of politics at Birkbeck, University of London, believes the mainspring of the votes for Brexit and Trump lie in values and the demographic change represented by immigration rather than inequality and anti-elitism. He accepts that education and the difference between degree and no degree is important but it is the different world views represented that is key.

Invisible psychological values are more important than group differences and an individual's place on the authoritarian – libertarian axis is more relevant in predicting a Leave vote than views on economic questions. Leave voters are poorer than Remain supporters but the difference is small.

Two issues markedly divide people on Brexit and support for Trump – attitudes to child-rearing and to the death penalty. Ask whether you want a child who is considerate or one which is well-mannered – those who answered considerate were more likely to vote Remain while Leave supporters opted for well-mannered – i.e. those obeying rules.

Those who oppose capital punishment had only a 20 per cent chance of voting Leave.

Another important predictive value is conservatism – those who wish to minimise change – especially when allied with authoritarianism.

"Authoritarian and conservative values, not deprivation or anti-elitism drove Brexit and Trump," Kaufman argues. But why now? The answer from Professor

Kaufman is that rapid ethnic change led to an increase in anti-immigration sentiment and populism.

Author and journalist David Goodhart has identified a different divider and one that has increasingly overlain the old distinctions of class and economic interest. It is the difference between those who see the world from 'Anywhere' and people who see it from 'Somewhere.'

For Goodhart the worldviews of Anywhere and Somewhere – those who remain where they were born and brought up – are equally valid. But the balance of power between them has shifted in recent decades, encouraged by the spread of higher education and liberal ideas.

"The helter-skelter of expansion of higher education in the past 25 years and the elevation of educational success into the gold standard of social esteem has been one of the most important, and least understood, developments in British society. It has been a liberation for many and for others a symptom of their declining status," says Goodhart.

Things are not as mobile as many believe with only 3 per cent of the world's 7.3bn population living outside the country of their birth. Globalisation may be a powerful force but the particular forms that globalisation takes is not inevitable and is a matter of politics that can be adjusted, Goodhart argues.

As an economist it is hardly surprising that Professor David Blanchflower takes an economic view of Trump and Brexit and points to the 'tide of technology' that has destroyed manufacturing jobs as one of the key underlying factors.

Former coal mining towns in the UK voted overwhelming for Brexit while counterparts in the US transferred their allegiance from the Democrats to Trump. In most English seaside resorts hit severely by British tourists leaving for warmer climes on cheap flights, it was the same story-high percentages of Brexit votes.

Blanchflower also emphasises how slow the recovery has been from what he calls The Great Recession of 2008 and the associated rise in underemployment – the part-timers who would like fulltime jobs.

"Votes for Brexit and for Trump were cries for something better. Relative things matter and 'the left-behinds' see others doing well. The concern is nothing can be delivered and the voters have been sold snake oil," Professor Blanchflower fears.

Former Conservative Treasury Minister Lord Jim O'Neill spent much of his earlier career forecasting currency movements at Goldman Sachs and wonders whether the vilified expert forecasters might not be proved right after all.

After all the forecasters got one post-Brexit prediction very right – the fall in the value of Sterling.

"It is not entirely impossible sustained Sterling weakness might end up delivering strong negative consequences for the real economy (such as inflation), albeit somewhat more delayed than forecasters initially suggested," Lord O'Neill argues.

Consumers will probably see their real incomes erode and this could be followed by a sharp rise in interest rates by the Bank of England. Then the consumer weakness could be dramatic, not least as house prices could suffer significantly. "Sounds familiar? It could still happen," insists the former forecaster.

Professor John Curtice, professor of politics at Strathclyde University is sympathetic to the plight of the opinion pollsters in trying to call the Referendum result. It was far more complicated than a General Election. People's inclination to vote for Remain or Leave cut across party preferences, and while education background was important in predicting the outcome, this is information that is time-consuming to obtain and is not normally collected by pollers.

According to Curtice, one of the polling industry's main problems was that it tried too hard, repeatedly adjusting how they were conducting, analysing and reporting their raw data.

The raw unweighted data of the final polls on average put Remain on 50 per cent with Leave on 50 per cent. While this still over-estimated the Remain vote this was partly to do with judgements on don't knows and how to estimate who would actually vote.

Professor Curtice also wonders whether pollsters were themselves caught up in the expectations that referendum polls were in danger of overestimating the willingness of voters to embrace radical change.

Matt Singh, polling analyst and founder of Number Cruncher Politics, accepts that opinion polls did not cover themselves with glory on Trump, Brexit and the 2015 UK general election.

In their defence he cites the increasing difficulty of getting a sample of people that is representative of the target population and then predicting which of them will go on to vote. The opinions of easier-to-contact people, and those more willing to share their views, may be systemically different from the views of the harder-to-find. To some extent pollsters were caught out with both Trump and Brexit when 'unlikely voters' – some who had abstained for decades - came out to vote.

White people who didn't go to university, but who voted for Brexit and Trump, were also a problem for the pollsters. Many have little interest in politics and may be less likely to take part in opinion polls.

Singh fears that polling organisations in attempts to make their findings interesting have also failed to communicate uncertainty and highlight the appropriate caveats, or even the fact that public opinion research is not a perfect science.

"Polls have got it wrong in the past and will again at some point in the future. But as a science, polling has adapted before and can once again. There may come a time when genuine alternatives to polling exist. But that time has not yet come," he argues.

Brexit and the polls: Too big a challenge?

The polls are widely thought to have anticipated a victory for Remain in the EU Referendum, but a closer look at the evidence casts doubt on the validity of this judgement, says Professor John Curtice

The EU referendum posed a particular challenge for the polling industry. Pollsters do at least try to learn from their past mistakes. But the Referendum was a one-off event where the accumulated wisdom of previous general elections was not necessarily of much use in knowing how best to estimate the balance of opinion in the forthcoming ballot.

Indeed, it was clear from the outset, UKIP apart, people's inclinations to vote for Remain or Leave cut across their party preference. All parties had many Remain and Leave voters amongst their current supporters. Consequently, even if the polls were accurately representing the current balance of support for the parties – and thus had overcome the difficulties that had beset their efforts to produce an accurate estimate of Conservative and Labour support in the 2015 general election (Sturgis, 2016) – they could still be inaccurate in their estimate of support for Remain and Leave.

One key reason why party preference did not align with Referendum vote intention is the EU ballot was about a very different set of concerns from those which usually predominate at a general election. The choice offered by Conservative and Labour is typically between whether there should be a bit more state spending and an attempt made to secure a little more equality, and a little less spending and an effort made to create rather more incentives for people to pursue economic success. This choice is, indeed, what we usually mean by 'left and right'. But the merits of state spending and equality were not the focus of the debate during the Referendum campaign. Rather it was primarily about the merits or otherwise of sharing sovereignty and allowing people as well as goods and services to move freely between one country and another. This meant it was a choice between a socially liberal outlook that is relatively comfortable living in a diverse society and tolerates the presence of a variety of social mores and cultural practices, and a more socially conservative point of view which places a greater premium on social order and cultural homogeneity.

The distinctive character of the ideological division which lay the heart of the Referendum is evident in Table 1, which, using data from the British Social Attitudes survey, compares the relationship between (a) being on the left or on the right, and (b) being inclined to a liberal or an authoritarian (that is, socially conservative) outlook and how people voted in (a) the 2015 general election, and (b) the EU Referendum. People are classified as 'left' or 'right' according to whether they agree or disagree with a set of propositions about economic inequality and whether the Government should try to reduce it, and as 'liberal' or 'authoritarian' depending on how they answer a set of propositions about respect for the law and punishing criminals (for further details see Curtice, Phillips and Clery, 2016: 12-13).

Table 1. The Ideological Patterns of Electoral Choice in the 2015 General Election and in the 2016 EU referendum

	Left	Right	Liberal	Authoritarian
2015 general election	%	%	%	%
Conservative	23	58	34	48
Labour	45	20	37	28
EU Referendum	%	%	%	%
Remain	50	50	66	34
Leave	49	51	34	66

Sources: British Social Attitudes survey 2015; NatCen mixed mode panel survey, Sept/Oct 2016. Left = the one-third of respondents with the most left-wing views. Right = the one-third of respondents with the most right-wing views. *Et simile* for Liberal and Authoritarian

In the 2015 General Election those on the right were much more likely to vote Conservative rather than Labour, while those on the left were more inclined to vote Labour than Conservative. Although it was also the case that the Conservatives were ahead amongst authoritarians while Labour enjoyed a narrow advantage amongst liberals, the differences between liberals and authoritarians were less marked than those between left and right. In contrast, whether someone was on the left or the right made absolutely no difference at all to the likelihood they would vote Remain or Leave. Both those on the left and those on the right divided their support equally between the two camps. In contrast, liberals were twice as likely to vote Remain rather than Leave, while authoritarians were twice as likely to vote Leave rather than Remain.

The different character of the choice being made by voters in the EU Referendum made a difference to the demographic features of the electorate that it was most important for pollsters to reflect accurately in their samples. The division between social liberals and social conservatives is rooted primarily in educational background; graduates tend to be socially liberal while those with few, if any, educational qualifications are more likely to be social conservatives (Surridge, 2010; Park and Rhead, 2013). Indeed, around three-quarters of graduates voted in the Referendum to Remain, while three-quarters of those with no educational qualifications backed Leave (Swales, 2016). Yet educational background is not only time-consuming to collect accurately but also, because it does not make a great deal of difference to whether someone votes Conservative or Labour, is not routinely collected by the polls. As a result, pollsters found they had to adapt their methods for the Referendum. Either they collected information about respondents' educational background and ensured the educational profile of their sample matched that of the general population or else they asked some questions which tap people's social liberalism versus social conservatism and weighted the attitudinal profile of their sample so it matched the profile obtained by a previously conducted high quality academic survey.

The performance of the polls
So measuring the balance of support for Leave and Remain in the EU Referendum presented the pollsters with a distinct and difficult challenge. Still, how well did the polls do in meeting it? There is a widespread impression they did not do very well at all (Duncan, 2016; Moore, 2016). Certainly, it seems not only did most commentators expect Remain to win, but so also did most voters (Ashcroft, 2016). Consequently, Leave's success came as a 'shock' to many (BBC, 2016). Yet it is far from clear the polls did give good grounds for believing Remain was clearly set to win.

Table 2 Estimated support for Remain during the long campaign by type of poll

	Average % vote for Remain in Polls conducted by:	
	Internet	Phone
1.12.15-18.2.16	50	60
19.2.16-31.3.16	50	56
1.4.16-30.4.16	50	55
1.5.16-26.5.16	50	56
27.5.16-22.6.16	49	51.5

Note: Don't Knows excluded from the figures upon which these averages are calculated

Consider, first of all, Table 2, which shows separately for those polls conducted over the internet and those conducted by phone the average level of support for Remain across all polls conducted in the six months leading up to polling day. For most of this period the two kinds of poll produced distinctly different pictures of the state of the referendum race. Until the last four weeks of the campaign, polls conducted over the phone did tend to put Remain well ahead. However, those conducted via the internet did not. Rather, these persistently suggested support was evenly divided between Remain and Leave and it was a toss-up as to which side would win. Given that nobody could be sure which set of estimates was right (Curtice, 2016a), the polls did not provide a sound basis on which to form the judgement that Remain was clearly in front.

Meanwhile, it is apparent from Table 2 that during the final four weeks of the Referendum campaign, that is, the official 'pre-Referendum period' when campaigning was at its height, both internet and phone polls pointed to a narrow outcome. Indeed, of the 35 polls of voting intention conducted during this period by companies which belong to the British Polling Council, slightly more (17) put Leave ahead than did Remain (15), while three polls put the two sides neck and neck. This makes it rather surprising there should have been such a widespread expectation the polls pointed to victory for Remain.

We can, perhaps, gain some understanding as to why this impression was formed by looking at the trajectory of the polls during the course of the Referendum campaign. In the first two weeks the polls on average put Remain and Leave neck and neck on 50 per cent each. But in the third week, a week book-ended by the murder of the Labour MP, Jo Cox, the polls began to tilt in favour of a Leave victory; on average they put Leave on 51 per cent and Remain on 49 per cent. But thereafter it looked as though a swing in favour of Remain was taking place. During the last seven days of the campaign it was Remain that was put narrowly ahead, by 51 per cent to 49 per cent.

Expectations of a swing-back
This apparent swing back then fed into a prior expectation many commentators appeared to have – that there would be a swing in favour of Remain in the final days of the campaign as risk-averse voters decided departure from the status quo represented too much of a gamble (Kellner, 2016). Was this not, after all, what had happened in the Scottish independence referendum? Indeed, international comparative study of referendums suggested there was often a swing-back towards the status quo in the final phase of referendums on major constitutional change (Le Duc, 2003). It seemed those expectations were being fulfilled and Remain would be home and dry. Relatively little attention was paid to warnings that this swing back did not always occur, and especially so in close referendums, and that even if it did happen it was not particularly likely to be a very large movement (Fisher and Renwick, 2016).

In the event, the expectation of a swing-back was not fulfilled. A better interpretation of the final polls was while Remain might have a slight edge, the outcome was likely to be very close and the prospect a majority might vote for Leave should not be discounted. Two of the final six polls actually put Leave narrowly ahead, while two others reported a lead for Remain so small it could simply be a consequence of the chance variation in results to which all polls are subject. The polls certainly did not simply 'get it wrong'.

Table 3 Estimated Outcome of the EU Referendum in the Final Polls

	Remain	Leave
	%	%
Result	48	52
Opinium	49	51
TNS-BMRB	49	51
YouGov	51	49
Ipsos MORI	52	48
ComRes	54	46
Populus	55	45

That said, they clearly did not 'get it right' either. If the errors in the polls could simply be accounted for by the chance variation to which they are all subject, while some would have underestimated support for Leave, others would have overestimated it. But, as Table 3 makes clear, none managed to overestimate Leave support. That suggests the distinctive challenge of estimating the balance of support for Remain and Leave was one the pollsters did not fully crack – though there is probably the thought in many a pollster's mind that if the Referendum had taken place a week earlier when most polls had Leave ahead, the industry's efforts would have been regarded as a success.

Ironically, however, one of the industry's problems was perhaps it tried too hard. Aware of the distinctive challenge posed by the Referendum, the pollsters were repeatedly adjusting how they were conducting, analysing and reporting their raw data (Curtice, 2016b). The net effect of these decisions on the estimates of the final polls was to increase the estimated level of support for Remain. On average the published estimates of the final polls in Table 3 pointed to a 52 per cent vote for Remain, 48 per cent for Leave. But if we look at the raw unweighted data collected by the final polls, on average these put Remain on 50 per cent, Leave on 50 per cent. While these unweighted figures also somewhat overestimate support for Remain, they suggest the error in the final polls was not simply a consequence of an inability to reach Leave voters or of any reluctance on their part to declare their support for Leave. Rather it was also because of the decisions made by the pollsters as to what to do about the don't-knows and how to estimate who would make it to the polls. Most of those decisions, made on the basis of imperfect information about a unique contest, in practice increased estimated support for Remain. Perhaps the pollsters themselves were also caught up in the expectation the Referendum polls were at risk of overestimating voters' willingness to embrace radical change?

References

Ashcroft, Lord (2016), How the United Kingdom voted on Thursday....and why', Available online at http://lordashcroftpolls.com/2016/06/how-the-united-kingdom-voted-and-why/, accessed April 6 2016.

BBC (2016), Brexit: Europe stunned by UK Leave vote. Available online at http://www.bbc.co.uk/news/uk-politics-eu-referendum-36616018

Curtice, John (2016a), The divergence between phone and internet polls: Which should we believe? London: NatCen Social Research. Available online at http://whatukthinks.org/eu/analysis/the-divergence-between-phone-and-internet-polls-which-should-we-believe/, accessed April 6 2016

Curtice, John (2016b), How Leave won the battle but Remain may yet still win the war, Available online at http://whatukthinks.org/eu/how-leave-won-the-battle-but-remain-may-still-win-the-war/, accessed April 6 2016

Curtice, John., Phillips, Miranda. and Clery, Elizabeth, (2016), Technical Details, Curtice, John, Phillips, Miranda and Clery, Elizabeth (eds), British Social Attitudes 33, London: NatCen Social Research. Available online at http://www.bsa.natcen.ac.uk/media/39042/bsa33_technicaldetails.pdf, accessed April 6 2016.

Duncan, Pamela (2016), How the pollsters got it wrong on the EU referendum, The Guardian, June 24. Available online at https://www.theguardian.com/politics/2016/jun/24/how-eu-referendum-pollsters-wrong-opinion-predict-close, accessed April 6 2016

Fisher, Stephen, and Renwick, Alan (2016), Do people tend to vote against change in referendums?, Available online at https://electionsetc.com/2016/06/22/do-people-tend-to-vote-against-change-in-referendums/, accessed April 6 2016

Kellner, Peter (2016), Don't celebrate too soon Brexiters: history favours Remain, New Statesman, June 6, Available online at http://www.newstatesman.com/politics/elections/2016/06/dont-celebrate-too-soon-brexiters-history-favours-remain, accessed April 6 2016

Le Duc, Lawrence (2003), The Politics of Direct Democracy: Referendums in Global Perspective, Peterborough, On.: Broadview Press.

Moore, Fraser (2016), Brexit: How did the pollsters get it so wrong", Daily Express, 24 June, Available online at http://www.express.co.uk/news/uk/682990/Brexit-EU-referendum-polls-wrong-predictions-2015-election, accessed April 6 2016

Park, Alison, and Rhead, Rebecca (2013), Personal relationships: Changing attitudes towards sex, marriage and parenthood, Park, Alison, Bryson, Caroline, Clery, Elizabeth, Curtice, John and Phillips, Miranda (eds), British Social Attitudes 30, London: NatCen Social Research. Available online at http://www.bsa.natcen.ac.uk/latest-report/british-social-attitudes-30/personal-relationships/introduction.aspx, accessed April 6 2016.

Sturgis, Patrick. (chmn.) (2016), Report of the Inquiry into the 2015 British General Election Opinion Polls, Southampton and London: National Centre for Research Methods and British Polling Council. Available online at http://eprints.ncrm. ac.uk/3789/1/Report_final_revised.pdf, accessed April 6 2016.

Surridge, Paula (2010), The making of social values, Stillwell, John., Norman, Paul, Thomas, Claudia, and Surridge, Paula. (eds), Spatial and Social Disparities, Dordrecht: Springer, pp. 179-98.

Swales, Kirby (2016), Understanding the Leave Vote, London: NatCen Social Research. Available at http://whatukthinks.org/eu/wp-content/uploads/2016/12/NatCen_Brexplanations-report-FINAL-WEB2.pdf, accessed April 6 2016.

Note on contributor

John Curtice is Professor of Politics at Strathclyde University, Senior Fellow, NatCen Social Research and the ESRC's 'The UK in a Changing Europe' initiative, and President of the British Polling Council

Polling – battered and bruised but still alive

A combination of President Trump, Brexit and the 2015 UK General Election gave a massive hit to the polling industry. Nevertheless, the lack of a suitable alternative within the time and cost constraints means that polling is unlikely to disappear in the near future, says Matt Singh

Recent years haven't been happy for pollsters, with a number of high-profile mishaps. Though some of these incidents have involved relatively small errors in contests that – by chance – both had high stakes and narrow margins, the industry has faced criticism and encountered increasing distrust.

Let's not downplay the challenges

To be sure, there are often genuine mitigating factors, in particular the fact that any survey will have a degree of inaccuracy – the margin of error – solely due to statistical chance. But errors across multiple polls should not all be in the same direction. And although there has been some unfair criticism, there is little upside in trying to downplay the difficulties that the industry has had.

The 2015 UK general election didn't see large average errors, but the gap between the two largest parties was substantially underestimated. This was particularly significant because in Westminster elections, the gap between the two main parties is by far the most important single determinant of seat numbers.

The EU Referendum campaign saw a number of polls with Leave leads, but as anyone that has studied referendums will know, averaging polls over the entire campaign period is misleading (Fisher, 2016a). History tells us to expect voters to shift towards the status quo in the final stages, and the evidence presented in Fisher (2016b) is that this is exactly what happened. Polls of respondents recontacted on the day of the vote showed Remain between four and eight points ahead. A better defence would be to highlight that the UK's EU Referendum was a one-off event without a remotely recent precedent, which was always likely to make it difficult to poll (Singh, 2016a). So while it is correct to say that the EU referendum polls were inaccurate, it is far more understandable than a similarly-sized miss in a general election would have been.

And while national polls in the US presidential election were broadly accurate, the errors in state polls – which are still being investigated at the time of writing – were not (Kanagasooriam, 2016). Moreover, the pattern of errors raises at least the possibility that the national polls had benefited from offsetting errors that by chance cancelled each other out, not unlike the 2010 UK general election. To some extent, polling relies on probabilities balancing out, but incidents like this should still be taken as seriously as those that actually pick the wrong winner.

Why things have been going wrong
There have been two particular problems recently; firstly getting a sample of people that is representative of the target population, and secondly predicting who of them will actually vote.

At the UK general election in 2015, polls on average measured accurately the collapse of the Liberal Democrats and the surge of UKIP, but mismeasured which of the two main parties was benefiting and which was losing out. The ex Lib Dems were meant to be going disproportionately to Labour and the Ukip surge was supposed to be hurting the Conservatives more. In reality, the impacts of both realignments were far more evenly distributed between the two main parties.

What went wrong was rooted in the unrepresentativeness of pollsters' samples, but happened in 2015 because the statistical techniques that pollsters had been using in response to earlier difficulties couldn't cope with the fluid nature of politics of the preceding term; there were too many people that had ditched the Coalition parties, too few that stayed loyal to the Conservatives, and too few former Labour voters that switched to UKIP (Singh, 2016c).

The sampling problems had been building for some time. Getting 1,000 or so people that are genuinely representative of the population has become harder and harder over time, for the simple reason that easier-to-contact people, and those that are more willing to share their views, often have systematically different views to the harder-to-contact.

A genuine random probability sample is achievable, but normally at extremely low speed and high cost, by choosing people from randomly selected addresses which are then contacted as many times as necessary to make contact. It can in some cases be replicated through ever more advanced statistical techniques. But what appears to have happened at the EU referendum (and is at least a possibility with the state polls in the US) is a trend of 'unlikely voters' turning out in increasing numbers, sometimes after decades of abstention (Singh, 2016b). A survey could provide the most perfectly representative sample that money can buy, and still get it wrong, if turnout patterns are not as expected. And although the problem of differential turnout can be exaggerated, it can still tip the balance in a close election or referendum.

One key demographic group are white people who didn't attend university (Silver, 2016). They are thought to have voted heavily for Donald Trump and to leave the EU. Many of them have little interest in politics and as such may be less likely to participate in opinion polls (Curtice, 2016). The problem can be particularly acute in countries like Britain and United States where turnouts are normally low (and in British case, much lower than a generation ago), meaning a large pool of potential 'unlikely voters'.

At the same time, they have increased in significance, due to changes in the political landscape. Various studies have shown that education is a very strong predictor of attitudes toward social progressivism. Those attitudes, in turn, have become an important divide, alongside and interacting with, the traditional fiscal axis concerning the size of the state. Or to use the characterisation of Blair (2007), 'left versus right' has been joined by 'open versus closed'.

That is an interesting development purely from a political science perspective. But combined with the issues around sampling and turnout, it also becomes a significant challenge for pollsters and forecasters.

The role of the media
It has often been suggested in response to the events of 2016 that the media (and the 'establishment' more broadly) ought to make more of an effort to get out of their cosmopolitan urban bases more and meet a wider range of people.

It is potentially problematic that the media is, in polling parlance, an unrepresentative subset of the wider population. Young, university-educated people in urban areas – a disproportionately well-represented demographic – usually move in very different circles and have very different perspectives to the voting public as a whole; and, crucially, their perspectives tend to differ in ways that have become politically relevant. That is certainly not to suggest that anyone with a duty of impartiality is failing in it. However there is at least a risk of unrepresentative demographics holding unrepresentative views.

But there is another, longer-standing problem, namely the need to communicate uncertainty, given that public opinion research is not a perfect science. There can be a conflict between making a poll result seem interesting and giving due regard to the appropriate caveats. In 2015, for example, the media gave very little credence to the possibility of the polls being wrong, despite their historical record being mixed. The 'inevitable hung parliament' narrative went almost unquestioned. When Singh (2015) presented analysis suggesting that this was very unlikely to be the case, it was met by disbelief by many until the broadcasters' exit poll was published.

This can be made worse by the problem of pollsters (individually or collectively) 'marking their own homework'. Independent experts are much freer than pollsters to highlight the limitations and quirks of polling in general (and of individual polls in particular), but there is room for their expertise to be called upon more often.

Another problem concerns probabilities in roughly the 10 to 40 per cent range being misunderstood. It is intuitive to most that a binary outcome with a probability of between 40 and 50 per cent is only narrowly the outsider and that there is a high chance of either outcome materialising. Conversely, something with a 0 to 10 per cent probability is extremely unlikely. But scenarios in which a probability lies in the awkward range between the two – unlikely, but nowhere near impossible – seems frequently to be misunderstood. If the chances of Leave or Donald Trump winning had been likened to the probability of a spot kick being missed in a penalty shootout, the uncertainty might have been clearer.

It is possible that these two factors could even have interacted. Could it have been that some in the media did not believe that the voters would 'really do that'? Such a hypothesis may be difficult to evaluate objectively, but some journalists have suggested that such thinking may have been present in 2016 .

What's the alternative?

Before polling can plausibly be declared dead, first something needs to replace it. The alternatives available at the time of writing remain as yet unproven at best and potentially thoroughly misleading at worst.

The suggestion that journalists 'get out and about' is a good idea in and of itself. But it cannot be a substitute for the scientific measurement of public opinion. Case in point, before the EU referendum, one journalist that visited Stoke-on-Trent estimated that 'nine out of ten' there were voting for Brexit (Harris and Domokos, 2016). The result in the city was actually 69.4 per cent Leave, the difference between the two being far larger than any conceivable polling error.

Predictions of elections using the results of other elections – such as using local authority elections to predict general elections or using local by-elections to predict local elections – is an alternative method in some cases. However it isn't usable in most countries and is best employed in combination with other tools, as Singh (2015: 8) did before the 2015 UK general election.

There is, unsurprisingly, a great deal of excitement around social media sentiment analysis, though its problems, even if they eventually prove surmountable, are considerable at present. People choosing to express their opinions in public may not be representative of the country, whether in terms of their geography, demographics, or politics. Even ensuring something as simple as 'one person, one vote' is not straightforward. But above all is the lack of history. The social media era has seen an unfathomable number of tweets, but the relative infrequency of elections means there are at best a handful of data points on which to test any analysis.

Nor is it likely – as is sometimes claimed – that polls distort the democratic process by influencing voting behaviour. While it is arguable that voters may be influenced, it is by expectations of the outcome based on opinion polls, not by the polls themselves. If there were no polls, those expectations would be based on guesswork, rumours, cherry-picked leaks of party data and personal prejudices, and would very likely to be even more distorted, not less. Opinion polls may be imperfect, but they are scientific and impartial. It is worth considering how many of the commentators that later criticised opinion polls for failing to call Donald Trump's victory would even have expected the 2016 US presidential race to be close without the benefit of polling to show that it was.

The way forward – evolution

The way probability is communicated needs to be improved. Most audiences would find it more intuitive to think of forecasts as point estimates, rather than as probability distributions. This may lead them to treat some events as near-certainties, when the data suggests a more balanced picture.

Pollsters will always have a role to play in communicating their work, but journalists need to be ready to ask them difficult questions. There needs to be a greater role for experts with an in-depth understanding of polling but independent of the polling industry.

As for the representativeness of the media, given that journalists will inevitably be young, well qualified and situated in the major conurbations, there are no easy solutions. But as with so many things, in order that a problem be solved, first it must be understood.

And on a technical level, the recent problems in polling – particularly sample quality – need further to be analysed and understood, and solutions developed. Polls have got it wrong in the past and will again at some point in the future. But as a science, polling has adapted before and can once again. There may come a time when genuine alternatives to polling exist. But that time has not yet come.

Note
[1] However some journalists have argued that was a bias. See, for example, Rahn (2016).

References

Blair, Tony (2007) speech at Blenheim Palace, October 1. Available online at http://www.tonyblairoffice.org/speeches/entry/tony-blair-speech-at-blenheim-palace, accessed on April 3, 2017.

(Curtice, 2016) The Benefits of Random Sampling: Lessons from the 2015 UK General Election, NatCen, January 14. Available online at http://bsa.natcen.ac.uk/media/39018/random-sampling.pdf, accessed on April 3, 2017.

Fisher, Stephen (2016a) How good are referendum polls in the UK?, Elections Etc, May 31. Available online at https://electionsetc.com/2016/05/31/how-good-are-referendum-polls-in-the-uk

Fisher, Stephen (2016b) Treatment of don't knows and turnout weighting, presentation at the Royal Statistical Society, December 7.

Harris, John and Domokos, John (2016) The Labour supporters backing Brexit in Stoke-on-Trent heartland, The Guardian, June 14. Available online at https://www.theguardian.com/commentisfree/video/2016/jun/14/labour-supporters-brexit-stoke-on-trent-eu-referendum-video, accessed on April 3, 2017.

Kanagasooriam, James (2016) How did the polls get it so wrong – again?, The Times Red Box, November 10. Available online at http://www.thetimes.co.uk/article/how-did-the-polls-get-it-so-wrong-again-xdwgvrtp7, accessed on April 3, 2017.

Rahn, Will (2016) The unbearable smugness of the press, CBS. Available online at http://www.cbsnews.com/news/commentary-the-unbearable-smugness-of-the-press-presidential-election-2016, accessed on April 3, 2017.

Silver, Nate (2016) Pollsters Probably Didn't Talk To Enough White Voters Without College Degrees, FiverThirtyEight. Available at https://fivethirtyeight.com/features/pollsters-probably-didnt-talk-to-enough-white-voters-without-college-degrees, accessed on April 3 2017.

Singh, Matt (2015) Is there a shy Tory factor in 2015?, Number Cruncher Politics, 6 May. Available online at http://www.ncpolitics.uk/2015/05/shy-tory-factor-2015.html, accessed on April 3, 2017.

Singh, Matt (2016a) Brexit probability increases sharply, Number Cruncher Politics, June 13. Available online at https://www.ncpolitics.uk/2016/06/forecast-update-brexit-probability-increases-sharply.html, accessed on April 3, 2017.

Singh, Matt (2016b) The 2.8 Million Non-Voters Who Delivered Brexit, Bloomberg View, July 4. Available online at https://www.bloomberg.com/view/articles/2016-07-04/the-2-8-million-non-voters-who-delivered-brexit, accessed on April 3, 2017.

Singh, Matt (2016c) The failure of a generation: the polling debacle of 2015, Cowley, Philip and Ford, Robert (eds) More Sex, Lies and the Ballot Box, London: Biteback pp 1-5

Note on contributor

Matt Singh is a polling analyst and the founder of Number Cruncher Politics. Among his most noted works are an analysis (Singh, 2015) published before the 2015 general election with the rare distinction of correctly predicting an opinion polling failure (and the Conservative victory) before the event, together with Singh (2016c) detailing why it happened. He acts as an advisor to governments, financial markets, corporations, think tanks and polling companies and has been cited by academic research and fact checking websites. He can be reached via https://www.ncpolitics.uk and tweets at @MattSingh_.

Values and immigration – the real reasons behind Brexit and Trump

The general perception is the group known as the 'Left Behinds' exerted a dreadful retribution on the power elite by voting for Brexit and for Donald Trump. Not so, says Eric Kaufmann, there were other reasons

The shockwaves from Brexit and Trump had barely finished rippling through leading media outlets before pundits were pronouncing this a protest by the 'Left Behind'. It was a comforting thesis. Rather than a crisis of cosmopolitan values, this was really an old-fashioned problem of economic inequality coupled with a remote power elite. The post-2007 economic crisis and bailouts of rich bankers by political elites turned the people against their masters. The path to defanging the new right-wing populism was simple: use traditional policy levers to move money to deprived communities. At the same time, improve responsiveness to the concerns of everyday citizens by devolving power away from Westminster and Washington.

Unfortunately, these narratives are built upon the sands of anecdote and ideology, rounded off with a crude eyeballing of geographic results. The closer one gets to fine-grained data, and the more forensically one analyses it, the faster the mirage disappears. As I'll argue, economics has little to do with Brexit and nothing to do with Trump.

What matters? Two things – values and demographic change

Before addressing these drivers, let's first note what is common knowledge to most observers of the populist right. That education level, not income, is most closely correlated with its support. In both the Brexit and Trump cases, average education level is far more closely aligned with the vote than average income. This is especially so for whites.[1] Income is correlated with education, but there are many successful people – think successful building contractor – without qualifications. Similarly, there are many poor people, such as struggling artists, who have degrees but little money. When you control for education, income has no effect on whether a white person voted for, or supports, Trump. With Brexit, income has a small effect.

Why is education – especially the line between degree and no degree - so important? Because it reflects not just material circumstances but worldview. A number of studies show that those with more open and exploratory psychological orientations and worldviews in their early teens are more likely to self-select into university.[2] This, much more than the content of the education people receive, makes them more liberal. In effect, education level offers a window onto the cultural values of a voting district, which is why it's the best predictor of populist support. The main effect works through individuals: those with a degree were much less likely to back Brexit/Trump than those without. For instance, in Ashcroft exit polls, 57 per cent of those with a degree supported Remain. In the British Election Study (BES), 59 per cent did so, while 39 per cent of those lacking degrees did.[3] In American exit polls, Trump won whites without college degrees 67-28, compared to 49-45 for whites with degrees.[4]

In addition, educated people tend to cluster, usually in nodes such as Silicon Valley where the knowledge economy is most intense. When they do, they set the tone and can affect the views of those without a degree, and vice-versa. For instance, those with low qualifications were 16 points less likely to vote to leave the EU if they lived in an area with the highest as opposed to lowest education levels. Those with A levels or a degree living in these high-skill areas were 30 points less likely to have voted Leave than their similarly qualified compatriots living in the lowest-educated areas.[5]

The combination of educated individuals voting their worldview, and educated contexts shaping the worldview of those less educated, results in the sharp geographic divisions observed in both countries. Add in the effects of ethnic diversity and age (young and minority voters were less likely to back right-wing populism) and you arrive in the polarised political geography of 2016. Successful cities such as London or San Francisco appear to be surrounded by a sea of populist revolt.

This has little to do with rustics' envy of the big smoke but has everything to do with the educational, age and ethnic composition of liberal cities. Strip these characteristics out, and there is no difference between city and country. A white working-class Londoner, for instance, is just as likely to have voted Leave as a white working-class Cumbrian. And every Leave community has at least a quarter, and often 40-45 per cent, of the population who voted Remain. The myth that provincial Britain and urban Britain are different worlds is a gross exaggeration. The big divide is between individuals in communities. Nonetheless, as Daniel Kahneman and Amos Tversky – subjects of Michael Lewis recent book *The Undoing Project* - remind us, our minds are attuned to vivid images such as rustbelt factories or London café-sipping elites. This is why the geographic and class stories work so well. Yet, as another of Lewis' classics, *Moneyball*, revealed, we would do better to place our trust in the data rather than gut instinct.

The data tell us invisible psychological differences based on core values are more important than group differences, including ethnicity and education level. Value divides cut through community, group and family. A good friend of mine works for Microsoft and is a classic 'Anywhere', to use David Goodhart's phrase for those who are attached to their mobile credentials and lifestyle.[6] He was stunned to find that while his teenage son was a Remainer, his twin teenage daughters were fervent Brexiteers. Countless versions of this story unfolded across the country on voting day.

Values

Values are the social psychological orientations we hold across a wide range of questions that confront us in everyday life. At the lowest, most general, level come the so-called Big 5 orientations – extraversion, openness, agreeableness, conscientiousness and neuroticism. On top of these are more domain-specific orientations of which authoritarianism is one of the most important. These are typically measured with a suite of questions asking about our views on childrearing, sentencing for criminals and censorship. Among the Big 5, low openness predicts support for populist right parties and Brexit. Conscientiousness – being fastidious about one's obligations – tends to correlate with populist right support. The authoritarian-libertarian axis is even more consequential. It crosscuts the economic left-right dimension, which has structured voting and ideology through much of the post-war period.

Are these not simply a reflection of the group or community one happens to inhabit? Yes and no. Young people, the educated and those in liberal spots or countries are more likely to be libertarian than authoritarian in their values. But most of the variation in authoritarianism is within-district and within-group, not between-group. In the BES, it is the authoritarian-libertarian axis that tells us most about a person's likelihood of having voted Leave, not their views on economic questions. This four-item scale predicts 12.5 per cent of the variation in Brexit vote, compared to just 4.9 per cent of the variation in Brexit accounted for by age, education, income, gender, ethnicity and region combined.

As Jonathan Haidt remarks, twin studies suggest that somewhere between a third and a half of political behaviour is inherited.[7] Karen Stenner argues that authoritarianism is very deep-rooted, linked to both heredity and personal biography. Thus it cannot be educated out of people – indeed, campaigns that flag the importance of diversity and dissent are likely to stoke rather than soothe authoritarians.[8] Authoritarianism is a bit of a misnomer: these are not scary people but the scared – seeking protection from what they perceive as a dangerous world. They are more likely to say people cannot be trusted, and that they fear walking alone at night. Their preference is for order, security and stability, not diversity and change. The open-closed schema mentioned by Tony Blair, or Goodhart's

Anywhere-Somewhere distinction, come closer than 'authoritarian' in capturing the essence of this mindset.[9]

In late August 2016, thanks to funding from Policy Exchange, I fielded two YouGov surveys, one in the US and one in Britain, each based on a sample of around 1400.[10] The British survey asked people how they had voted in the Referendum, the American one asked them to rate Trump on a thermometer scale, from 0 to 10. Surveys included two measures of authoritarianism. The first is based on a classic, longstanding childrearing question, 'Is it more important for a child to be considerate or well-behaved?' The questions sound identical, but they differ in the deep associations they trigger. A well-behaved child obeys the rules of society, hierarchy and tradition, a considerate child is other-directed and empathetic within a horizontal world of equal individuals.

I also asked about people's income, so we are able to evaluate what is more important, people's economic circumstances, or their authoritarian values score. The results are presented in figures 1 and 2, one for each of Brexit and Trump. Let's begin with the Brexit vote. The sample is skewed 54-46 toward Remain, but what we are interested in are the differences between Remainers and Brexiteers, not the absolute levels. Samples are restricted to White British in Britain, and non-Hispanic whites in America. On the horizontal axis at bottom is income. On the vertical is the probability that a person reported voting Leave. The slope of the line indicates the extent to which poor and rich differ in their reported Brexit vote. The lines also control for age, education, gender and region, so we are looking only at differences associated with income and this childrearing measure of authoritarianism.

Note two things. First, the difference between the endpoints of both lines between the poorest (at left) and richest (at right) is only five points and this is not statistically different from chance. So white Leavers are poorer than white Remainers, but this is only a small difference. By contrast, the gap between lines is substantial and significantly different from what could have occurred by accident. This means those who answered 'considerate' to the authoritarianism question (lower line) have only a 35-40 per cent likelihood (depending on income) to have voted out compared to those who said 'well-mannered', represented by the higher line at 55-65 per cent likelihood. In fact, the difference between the lines is 20-25 points, five times that for income.

When we move to a more domain-specific question such as support for the death penalty, the relationship becomes even stronger. In work I did on the EU referendum voting intentions using the British Election Study, those most opposed to capital punishment on a five-point scale, once demographics were taken into consideration, had only a 20 per cent chance of voting Leave, compared to 75 per cent for those most in favour.[11] Values, not income, tell us how people voted.

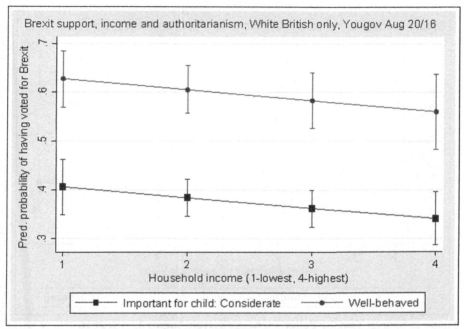

Figure 1: Source: YouGov-Policy Exchange survey, August 17-18, 2016

It's much the same story in the US in figure 2, where this time, wealthier whites rate Trump half a point higher on a 0-10 thermometer scale than poor whites. So much for all those images of rustbelt towns, tales of opioid addiction and the mournful strains of J. D. Vance's Hillbilly Elegy. Those are poignant stories that make good copy and sell books, but they overstate the importance of group membership and class compared to the inner psychology of Trump supporters. What matters is, once again, authoritarianism, which is only partly linked to group and region. In figure 2, white Americans who answered that it was more important for children to be considerate scored Trump an average of two points lower than those who said it was more important for them to be well-mannered. Income makes no significant difference.

The second major value set which Stenner mentions is conservatism. This describes those who wish to minimise change, an orientation that overlaps with authoritarianism. But whereas authoritarians are opposed to diversity and dissent, even if present for generations, conservatives are only opposed to diversity if it represents a change from a past they once knew. The question, 'Things in America/ Britain were better in the past,' nicely measures this orientation. In both the US and Britain, this has a similar power to the four-item authoritarianism scale in predicting support for Trump and Brexit.

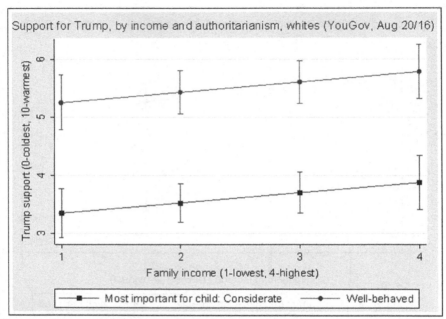

Figure 2: Source: YouGov-Policy Exchange survey, August 17-18, 2016

Anti-elitism matters less than income for the Brexit vote. Which is to say it doesn't count for much. The BES asked a series of questions of its 25,000 sample, including whether people trust MPs and whether they would rather put their trust in ordinary people than politicians. Neither significantly predicts a Brexit vote when other factors are considered. A set of populism questions were also asked on a smaller sub-sample, including whether people agreed that 'the politicians in the UK parliament need to follow the will of the people.' This had only a borderline impact on Brexit voting intention, which was not significant after authoritarianism and conservatism were added to the model.

Finally, just in case you think resentment of elites lies behind all this, consider the following question, 'What annoys you most about the American elite?' Respondents to a small survey of 361 Americans I ran on March 19, 2017 could answer 'they are politically correct,' 'they are rich and powerful,' or 'they don't annoy me.' While this is far from a large sample, it turns out Trump voters were actually less anti-elite than Clinton voters, with just 60 per cent saying elites annoyed them, compared to 64 per cent of Clinton voters. This is not significant given the sample size. But the real difference lay in *which kind* of elite rankled each voter. While there is a baseline resentment of elites in the US population for being rich and powerful, this was cited by 55 per cent of Clinton supporters but just 27 per cent of Trump voters. By contrast, 34 per cent of Trump voters but only 9 per cent of Clinton voters cited 'political correctness' as their main anti-elite gripe. Thus Trump voters are better characterised as anti-liberal elite than anti-elite.

Ethnic demography

We have established that authoritarian and conservative values, not deprivation or anti-elitism, drove Brexit and Trump. But this cannot answer the 'why now?' question. In order to do so, we need to bring in demography, specifically ethnic change and immigration. In my YouGov-Policy Exchange data, I ask people what the most important issue facing the country is. Nearly 40 per cent of those who gave Trump 0 out of 10 said inequality was the top issue facing America. Among those rating the Donald 10 out of 10, just 4 per cent agreed.

By contrast, immigration is the top concern for 25 per cent of white Trump backers but hardly registers among Trump detractors. An Ipsos-Mori study during the primaries came to the same conclusion: opposition to immigration, and a cluster of orientations dubbed 'nativism,' not economic worries, best explain support for Trump.[12] For Brexiteers, it's a similar story, with 43 per cent of those who voted Leave citing immigration as the most important issue facing Britain compared to only 5 per cent of Remainers. The picture for inequality is the reverse: 20 per cent of Remainers, but barely 5 per cent of Leavers, call it their top concern. So much for the 'Left Behind' thesis.

The US was about 90 per cent white in 1960; it is 63 per cent white today and more than half of American babies are now from ethnic minorities. Most white Americans already think they are in the minority, and more high-identifying whites are beginning to vote in an ethnopolitical way. The last time the share of foreign born in America reached current levels was the 1900-1920 period when immigration restrictionist sentiment was at fever pitch. We should not be surprised to see this issue rising to the fore.

Ethnic change can happen nationally or locally, and it matters in both Britain and America. Figure 3, which includes a series of demographic and area controls, looks at the rate of Latino increase in a white American survey respondent's zip code (average population around 30,000 in this data). The share of white Americans rating Trump 10 out of 10 rises from just over 25 per cent in locales with no ethnic change to almost 70 per cent in places with a 30-point increase in Latino population.

The town of Arcadia in Wisconsin – fittingly a state that has flipped to Trump – profiled in a recent Wall Street Journal article, shows what can happen. Thomas Vicino has chronicled the phenomenon in other towns, such as Farmer's Branch, Texas or Carpentersville, Illinois.[13] There are very few zip codes that have seen change on this scale, hence the small sample and wide error bars toward the right. Still, this confirms what virtually all the academic research shows: rapid ethnic change leads to an increase in anti-immigration sentiment and populism, even if this subsequently fades. The news also spreads and can shape the wider climate of public opinion, even in places untouched by immigration.

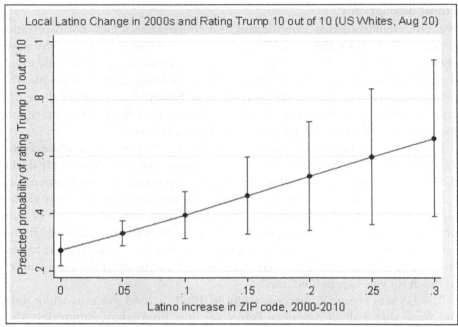

Figure 3: Source: YouGov-Policy Exchange survey, August 17-18, 2016

In Britain, it's a similar story: when we control for the level of minorities in a ward, local ethnic change is linked with a significantly higher rate of Brexit voting. From under 40 per cent voting Brexit in places with no ethnic change to over 60 per cent voting Leave in the fastest changing districts such as Barking in London or Boston in Lincolnshire.

Values and demography

Put values and demography together and you get political polarisation: authoritarians and conservatives respond negatively to diversity and change, while libertarians and liberals embrace it. Consider the relationship between authoritarianism and immigration attitudes in Europe in figure 4, based on data for 16,000 native-born white respondents to the 2014 European Social Survey. Authoritarians, who place a high value on safe and secure surroundings, are more likely to perceive immigrants as making their countries a worse place to live. But in countries with low Muslim populations (e.g. Ireland or Finland, where Muslims are less than 1 per cent), authoritarians and others don't diverge much in their anti-immigration views: 3 per cent of those who say safety and security are important 'strongly agree' that immigrants make their country worse compared to 2 per cent for others.

Now look at the right side of the chart, where data is drawn from countries where Muslims exceed 4 per cent of the population. The gap between the red and blue lines is now over twice as large, with more than 6 per cent of safety-conscious individuals now strongly anti-immigrant. If you are white and less concerned about safe and secure surroundings, the share of Muslims in your country has only a small impact on your view of immigrants. If you care about safety and security, Muslim share makes a big difference to those views.[14] This shows how demographic shifts interact with values to create political polarisation.

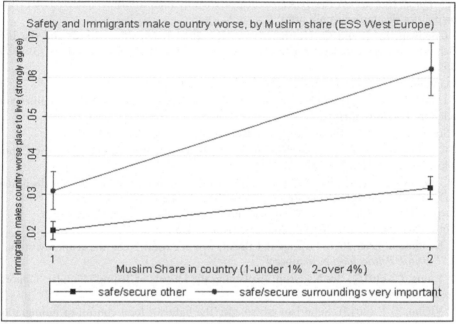

Figure 4: Source: Data from European Social Survey 2014. N=16,029. Pseudo R2= .084. Controls for country income; also individual income, education and age. Countries: Austria, Belgium, Switzerland, Denmark, Germany, Finland, France, Ireland, Netherlands, Norway and Sweden.

Conclusion

Value differences and immigration, not inequality and anti-elitism, fuelled the Trump and Brexit votes. In this era, the values divide – especially the question of whether western societies should become increasingly diverse – is emerging as the primary axis of politics. Economic questions are losing their centrality even as mainstream politicians stubbornly insist on viewing the new nationalism through old spectacles.

Notes

[1] Silver, N. (2016). Education, Not Income, Predicted Who Would Vote for Trump. Five Thirty-Eight. November 22; "Brexit: voter turnout by age," Financial Times, June 24, 2016

[2] Surridge, P. (2016). "Education and liberalism: pursuing the link." Oxford Review of Education 42(2): 146-164; Lancee, B. and O. Sarrasin (2015). "Educated Preferences or Selection Effects? A Longitudinal Analysis of the Impact of Educational Attainment on Attitudes Towards Immigrants." European Sociological Review 31(4): 490-501.

[3] Fieldhouse, E., et al. (2016). British Election Study, 2016: General Election Results Dataset [computer file], July.

[4] *Election 2016: Exit Polls, New York Times* https://www.nytimes.com/interactive/2016/11/08/us/politics/election-exit-polls.html

[5] Goodwin, M. J. and O. Heath (2016). "The 2016 Referendum, Brexit and the Left Behind: An Aggregate-level Analysis of the Result." The Political Quarterly 87(3): 323-332.

[6] Goodhart, D. 2017. The Road to Somewhere (London: Hurst)

[7] Haidt, J. (2012). The righteous mind : why good people are divided by politics and religion. London, Allen Lane.

[8] Stenner, K. (2005). The authoritarian dynamic, Cambridge University Press.

[9] Goodhart, <i>Road to Somewhere</i>; Blair, T. (2017). 'Against Populism, the Centre Must Hold.' <i>New York Times</i>, March 3.

[10] For data, see: https://d25d2506sfb94s.cloudfront.net/cumulus_uploads/document /u12mloq9ox/PolicyExchangeResults_160907_Authoritarianism_UK.pdf; https://d25d2506sfb94s.cloudfront.net/cumulus_uploads/document/aage6nsrqj/ PolicyExchangeResults_160907_Authoritarianism_US.pdf

[11] Kaufmann, Eric. 2016. 'Trump and Brexit: why it's again NOT the economy, stupid,' *LSE British Politics blog*, November 9

[12] Young, C. (2016). 'It's Nativism: Explaining the Drivers of Trump's Popular Support.' Ipsos, September.

[13] Vicino, T. J. (2012). Suburban crossroads: The fight for local control of immigration policy, Lexington Books.

[14] ESS Round 7: European Social Survey Round 7 Data (2014). Data file edition 2.1. NSD - Norwegian Centre for Research Data, Norway – Data Archive and distributor of ESS data for ESS ERIC.

Note on contributor

Eric Kaufmann is Professor of Politics at Birkbeck, University of London. He is writing a new book entitled Whiteshift: immigration, populism and the myth of majority decline. Penguin will publish it in 2018.

The Somewheres vs the Anywheres: Britain's new dividing line

David Goodhart is, or was, an intellectual iconoclast. His prescient book, The British Dream, foretold in 2013 the tsunami of populism that came to fruition in 2016. In his newly-published book The Road to Somewhere he looks into the social typology of modern Britain and finds a new great divide

Much of the British commentariat see an 'open v closed' divide as the new political fault-line. Tony Blair dedicated a speech to the distinction in 2007 just before he left office: "Modern politics has less to do with traditional positions of right versus left, more to do today, with what I would call the modern choice, which is open versus closed."

He was partly right, but he failed to grasp why so many people find his version of open so unappealing. To understand that we have to consider the great value divide in British society, echoed to varying extents in other developed societies. The old distinctions of class and economic interest have not disappeared but are increasingly over-laid by a larger and looser one, between the people who see the world from **Anywhere** and the people who see it from **Somewhere**.

Anywheres dominate our culture and society. They tend to do well at school – Vernon Bogdanor calls them the 'exam-passing classes' – then usually move from home to a residential university in their late teens and on to a career in the professions that might take them to London or even abroad for a year or two. Such people have portable 'achieved' identities, based on educational and career success which makes them generally comfortable and confident with new places and people.

Somewheres are more rooted and usually have 'ascribed' identities – Scottish farmer, working class Geordie, Cornish housewife – based on group belonging and particular places, which is why they often find rapid change more unsettling. One core group of Somewheres have been called the 'left behind' – mainly older white working class men with little education.

They have lost economically with the decline of well-paid jobs for people without qualifications and culturally, too, with the disappearance of a distinct working-class culture and the marginalization of their views in the public conversation. However,

Somewhere ambivalence about recent social trends spreads far beyond this group and is shared by many in all social classes, especially the least mobile. Despite recent increases in geographical mobility, about 60 per cent of British people still live within 20 miles of where they lived when they were 14.

Of course, few of us belong completely to either group – we all have a mix of achieved and ascribed identities – and there is a large minority of Inbetweeners. Even the most cosmopolitan and mobile members of the Anywhere group retain some connection with their roots and even the most small town Somewhere might go on holiday abroad with EasyJet or talk on Skype to a relative in Australia.

The South East (of England) rules

A large section of Britain's traditional elite remains rooted in south east England and London, in a few old public schools and universities. Indeed they are more southern-based than in the past as the dominant families of the great northern and midland towns have gravitated south. But even if this part of the elite has not moved very far physically they are much less likely than in earlier generations to remain connected to Somewheres through land ownership, the church, the armed forces or as an employer. They are, however, connected to the new elites.

As has happened before in British history, the old elite has absorbed the new one, the rising 'cognitive' elite of meritocrats, from lower social class and sometimes immigrant backgrounds. In doing so it has often exchanged traditional conservatism for a more liberal Anywhere ideology. Consider George Osborne in whom the economic liberalism of the right and social liberalism of the left is said to combine.

In any case Anywheres and Somewheres do not overlap precisely with more conventional social categories. Rather, they are looser alignments of sentiment and worldview. Both groups include a huge variety of people and social types. Somewheres range from northern working class pensioners to Home Counties market town Daily Mail readers; Anywheres from polished business executives to radical academics.

Although I have invented the labels, I have not invented the two value clusters clearly visible in a host of opinion and value surveys, with Anywheres making up 20 to 25 per cent of the population, compared to around half for Somewheres, and the rest Inbetweeners.

The Anywhere/Somewhere categorisation is both a frame for understanding what is going on in contemporary politics and a plea for a less headstrong Anywhere liberalism. The Anywheres have counted for too much in the past generation – their sense of political entitlement startlingly revealed after the Brexit and Trump votes

– and populism, in its many shapes and sizes, has arisen as a counter-balance to their dominance throughout the developed world. It can be a destructive counter-balance, but if we are to be tough on populism we must be tough on the causes of populism too, and one of those causes has been Anywhere over-reach.

Who are the Anywheres?

Extrapolating from opinion surveys, and adding my own judgments and observations, I have assembled a loose Anywhere ideology I call 'progressive individualism'. This is a worldview for more or less successful individuals who also care about society. It places a high value on autonomy, mobility and novelty and a much lower value on group identity, tradition and national social contracts (faith, flag and family). Most Anywheres are comfortable with immigration, European integration and the spread of human rights legislation, all of which tend to dilute the claims of national citizenship. They are not in the main anti-national, indeed they can be quite patriotic, but they also see themselves as citizens of the world. Work, and in fact life itself, is about individual self-realisation. Anywheres are comfortable with the achievement society; meritocracy and most forms of equality (though not necessarily economic) are second nature to them. Where the interests of Anywheres are at stake, in everything from reform of higher education to gay marriage, things happen. Where they are not, the wheels grind more slowly, if at all.

..and who are the Somewheres?

By contrast, the Somewheres are more socially conservative and communitarian by instinct. They are not on the whole highly religious, unlike their equivalents in the US, and only a small number on the far-right fringes are hard authoritarians or consistent xenophobes. They are moderately nationalistic and, if English, quite likely to identify as such. They feel uncomfortable about many aspects of cultural and economic change, such as mass immigration, an achievement society in which they struggle to achieve, the reduced status of non-graduate employment and more fluid gender roles.

They do not choose 'closed' over 'open' but want a form of openness that does not disadvantage them. They are also, in the main, modern people for whom women's equality and minority rights, distrust of power, free expression, consumerism and individual choice, are part of the air they breathe. They want some of the same things Anywheres want, but they want them more slowly and in moderation. Their worldview – as with Anywheres I have assembled it from opinion surveys and my own observations – is best described by a phrase many would regard as a contradiction in terms: 'decent populism'.

The relative powerlessness of British Somewheres in recent times is shown by, among other things: the miserable state of vocational education and apprenticeship provision in a graduate-dominated society, the double infrastructure failure in housing (in the south east) and transport links (in the north), and the bias against domesticity in family policy.

From Somewhere to Anywhere and back again?

Both Anywhere and Somewhere worldviews are valid and legitimate and their divergence from each other is neither new nor surprising. What has changed is the balance of power, and numbers, between them. Until 30 or 40 years ago the Somewhere worldview remained completely dominant. It was British common sense. Then in the space of two generations another Anywhere common sense has risen to challenge and partly replace it. This is thanks, above all, to two things; the legacy of baby boomer '1960s' liberalism and the expansion of higher education, which has played a key role in disseminating that legacy. We are now entering a third phase – Brexit might be said to mark its beginning – in which neither worldview is so clearly dominant.

The helter-skelter expansion of higher education in the past 25 years and the elevation of educational success into the gold standard of social esteem has been one of the most important, and least understood, developments in British society. It has been a liberation for many and for others a symptom of their declining status. The Anywhere world of geographical, and often social, mobility, of higher education and professional careers was once the preserve of a small elite.It has now become general, though not universal. For Somewheres, meanwhile, post-industrialism has largely abolished manual labour, reduced the status of lower income males and weakened the national social contract. Neither the affluent nor employers feel the same obligation towards 'their' working class they once did.

In a democracy the Somewheres cannot be ignored. And in recent years in Britain and Europe, and in the US through Donald Trump, they have begun to speak through new and established parties and outside party structures altogether. In Britain they helped to win the Brexit Referendum and then the vote itself, and by constantly telling pollsters how worried they are about immigration they have kept that issue at the centre of British politics.

The Anywhere ideology is invariably a cheerleader for restless change. Consider this from Tony Blair, again, at the 2005 Labour conference:

> "I hear people say we have to stop and debate globalisation. You might as well debate whether autumn should follow summer... The character of this changing world is indifferent to tradition. Unforgiving of frailty. No respecter of past reputations. It has no custom and practice. It is replete with opportunities, but they only go to those swift to adapt, slow to complain, open, willing and able to change."

This from the leader of the party which historically represented the people who benefited least from capitalist modernisation.

Change makers and change resisters?

When change seems to benefit everyone, such as broad-based economic growth or improved healthcare, the conflict between the two worldviews recedes. But when change does not seem to benefit everyone, as with the arrival of the two 'masses', a mass immigration society and a mass higher education system for almost half of school leavers, the restrained populism of Somewheres can find a voice.

One of the implicit promises of modern democratic citizenship is some degree of control over one's life. This translates most easily into a right to stop things happening, the right, at its most basic, to some stability and continuity in the place and the way one lives. Given the nature of the modern world even this is not a promise democratic politicians can easily deliver, especially when committed to an economic liberalism which has exported factories and imported workers. Consider the extraordinary ethnic and physical changes in London and Birmingham in the past 30 years.

Somewheres are often said to be myopic, unable to see that accepting change brings longer-term advantage. Yet it is also the case the people from Anywhere with more fluid identities and an educational passport to thrive are well equipped to benefit from change, while the people from Somewhere are often not, even in the long run.

Anywheres tend to see Somewhere conservatism as irrational or as a backlash against the advance of liberal social values. It can be, but it is also to be expected people who feel buffeted by external events with little political agency, social confidence or control over their destinies will cling all the harder to those spaces where they can exercise some control, in the familiar routines of their daily lives and beliefs. Somewhere conservatism may have shed many of the historical trappings of mid-twentieth century classic working-class conservatism – the protestant faith, jingoism, white supremacy – but the instinct to stick with the familiar and to those small zones of control and esteem means Somewheres are often hostile both to market change and to top-down state paternalism.

Are the somewheres nowhere?

Most Somewheres are not bigots and xenophobes. Indeed much of what I call the 'great liberalisation' of the past 40 years in attitudes to race, gender and sexuality has been absorbed and accepted by the majority of Somewheres. But compared with Anywheres the acceptance has been more selective and tentative and has not extended to enthusiasm for mass immigration or European integration. Somewheres are seldom anti-immigrant but invariably anti-mass immigration. They still believe there is such a thing as Society.

The 1960s were not just about challenging traditional ideas and hierarchies. The decade also marked a further dismantling of the stable, ordered society in which roles were clearly ordained. Individuals became freer to win or lose. That was disorientating to many. Most Somewheres did not share the optimism of baby boomer Anywhere liberalism and instead found the emerging post-industrial, post-nationalist, post-modern Britain was in many non-material ways a less hospitable place for them.

Somewhere in the USA?

This chimes with the view that at least part of Trump's success came through appealing to a hitherto latent white identity politics. In any case, populist politics is certainly here to stay and, though many of the parties themselves are unstable and often dominated by furious personality clashes, the demand for their product shows no sign of fading.

Their appeal is primarily motivated by cultural anxiety and hard to measure psychological loss. Economic loss is a factor too – a significant majority of the 56 per cent of British people who describe themselves as 'have-nots' voted Brexit – but if it was primarily about economic loss the populists of the left would surely be stronger.

There is another important aspect to this argument. Anywheres often claim the trends they support are historically inevitable, whether it is mass immigration, the current form of globalisation or the decline of settled communities. But in reality, rich societies are much less mobile than Anywheres assume and the same is true for humanity as a whole: a little over three per cent of the world's 7.3 billion people live outside their country of birth and this percentage has only increased slightly in recent decades. Only 25 years ago, net immigration to Britain was zero. It is true inflows into rich countries have risen quite sharply since then but that has been partly the result of policy choices. Large scale immigration is not a force of nature. Also economic globalisation, at least in a technical sense, is less developed than is often assumed. If globalisation is defined as the emergence of a single global economy, with transnational corporations with worldwide production networks and few barriers to the free flow of goods, labour and capital, then it has barely started.

The Global picture

The globalisation story tends to focus on its impact on trade, finance, transport and communications technologies and immigrant diasporas, all of which are either inherently international or easy to internationalise. Even here the impact is much less than usually assumed and all these activities are governed by national laws or international agreements drawn up between national governments. According to the trans-nationality index of the United Nations Conference on Trade and Development, even the 100 most global corporations still have nearly half of their sales, assets and employment in their home country (where they may still benefit from formal and informal protections).

The vast majority of workers in advanced countries work in the service sector serving the domestic market, not in the global economy. And while states have to take account of global market forces, they continue to have a large amount of potential discretion over fiscal, tax and welfare policy. Recent globalisation has in part represented a welcome rebalancing of power and wealth away from rich Western states like Britain towards developing countries like China and India. But there is no reason why it should actively disadvantage the poorer people in rich countries.

Is Globalisation good for all?

The global openness of the past 25 years has been on balance a blessing for most British people, but the blessing becomes more mixed the further down the income and education spectrum you move. The particular forms globalisation takes are not, however, set in stone. It is a matter of politics and can be adjusted. If the Anywhere technocrats who dominate the World Trade Organisation, the EU, the international human rights courts, and so on, are forced to concede their version of globalisation is, in part, a choice, not an irresistible force like the seasons, as Tony Blair claimed, then by extension they must persuade us it is a desirable destination. And that is very much harder. A better globalisation is possible and a world order based on many Somewhere nation states co-operating together is far preferable to one big supranational Anywhere.

Note on contributor

David Goodhart was founding editor of Prospect, the current affairs magazine. He is the author of British Dreams (2013), which has been hailed as predicting many of the issues made apparent during and after the 2016 EU Referendum. This chapter is an edited version of the first chapter of his new book The Road to Somewhere: The Populist Revolt and the Future of Politics, published by Hurst.

How the 'left-behinds' gave us Brexit and Trump

All the evidence says people who have been 'left behind' since the onset of the Great Recession voted for Brexit and Trump and – despite populist promises – their decision is unlikely to improve their lives, with potentially frightening consequences, predicts Professor David Blanchflower

*"For it is a possibility that the duration of the slump may be much more prolonged than most people are expecting and much will be changed both in our ideas and in our methods before we emerge. Not, of course the duration of the acute phase of the slump, but that of the **long, dragging conditions of semi-slump**, or at least sub-normal prosperity, which may be expected to succeed the acute phase."*   John Maynard Keynes (1931)[1]

Since 2008 Western countries have been experiencing the long dragging conditions of semi-slump. Their people are hurting. Trump and Brexit offered hope. The promise was the good times would start to roll again. It seems unlikely any of this will be delivered. The hope was false.

There is no spare £350m a week to spend on the NHS. Obama didn't wiretap. The inauguration crowds were smaller than previous ones. The size of Trump's electoral college win was not record setting and he lost the popular vote by 2.9m votes. There were not millions of illegal votes in the presidential election and thousands were not bussed in to vote in New Hampshire. There is evidence that not a single fraudulent vote was cast in the Granite state where I live and voted. There was no Bowling Green Massacre or a terrorist attack in Sweden.

Trumpcare, according to the Congressional Budget office would have removed health insurance by around 26m, many of whom voted for Trump. The plan was the poor would pay for tax cuts to the rich. Under the Republican plan, the premium for a typical low-income 64-year-old, many of whom supported Trump, after subsidies, would jump to $14,600 a year, from $1,700 a year.[2] There is no sign of an infrastructure or tax-cut plans to create jobs. Trump will not be able to turn back the tide of technology that is primarily responsible for the destruction of manufacturing jobs. Even Mitch McConnell, Republican majority leader thinks the wall isn't going to be built and there is no chance Mexico is going to pay. A border adjustment tax would be paid for by American consumers through higher prices. This isn't what voters were told would happen in Kentucky, West Virginia, Ohio, Wisconsin, Michigan and Pennsylvania. Somebody will have to be blamed.

In 1914, 181,000 miners were employed in the anthracite mines of Northeastern Pennsylvania. On January 22, 1959, the Knox Coal Company's mine in Luzerne County, under the Susquehanna River, in the vicinity, of Port Griffith, a small town, midway between Wilkes-Barre and Scranton, collapsed and the mighty Susquehanna River poured into the mines, flooding them throughout the interconnected underground system. Shortly after the flooding of the Knox Mine, two of the area's largest coal companies announced a full withdrawal from the anthracite business. Other companies whose mines lay some distance from the Knox disaster continued to operate on a much smaller scale into the early 1970s. The only anthracite production that still occurs in the area is large-scale surface mining of shallow old works.

Luzerne county's website[3] suggests even though the anthracite resource remaining in the ground is substantial, the complex geologic structure, steep terrain, and the inefficient early mining of the thicker and more accessible blocks of coal 'now preclude the use of modern mechanized equipment underground'. The website says: "Billions of tons of anthracite are still in the ground but remain inaccessible because of underground flooding."

Donald Trump held a rally in Luzerne County to raise the locals hopes things might change. He told a crowd at Wilkes-Barre, the seat of Luzerne County on October 10, 2016: "Oh, we're going to make Pennsylvania so rich again, your jobs are coming back. We're going to be ending illegal immigration. We're going to stop the jobs from pouring out of our country." In 2016, 5,644 Democrats in Luzerne County changed their registration to Republican. Luzerne County flipped from voting for Obama by five points in 2012 to voting for Trump by 20 points.

Coal production in the UK in the 1960s was around 177m tonnes and the industry employed half a million miners. Output fell to 114m tonnes by the mid-1970s and 300,000 workers. By the time of the year-long national strike in 1984-5 output was down to 133m tonnes and 180,000 workers. Pit closures continued through the 1990s and only 21m tonnes mined with 1,300 workers. From 2000-2010 the coal industry contracted further with output falling to 10m tonnes. Kellingly, the UK's last deep mine was closed in 2015. In 1982, the NUM had 170,000 members. By 2015 the number of members had fallen to 100. In 1984 Yorkshire had 56 collieries. Today there are none. The coal mines were concentrated in a few towns. For example, Barnsley, had 11 pits in 1984, Doncaster had nine, Rotherham had ten and Wakefield had 15. Each of these towns voted Brexit by large majorities; Barnsley 68 per cent, Doncaster 69 per cent, Rotherham 68 per cent and Wakefield 66 per cent, against 52 per cent nationally. There is nothing governments can do to raise the world coal price. Tariffs would just mean consumers would switch to cheaper oil, gas or solar.

On March 23, 2011, the UK Chancellor of the Exchequer George Osborne, claimed in his Budget speech he wanted: "The words 'Made in Britain', 'Created in Britain', 'Designed in Britain', and 'Invented in Britain' to drive our nation forward – a Britain carried aloft by the march of the makers."

Six years later UK manufacturing output is still 9 per cent below its pre-recession peak and 1 per cent below its level in March 2011. Manufacturing as a share of total employment in the UK as measured by the number of workforce jobs has fallen from 9.2 per cent in June 2007 to 7.6 per cent in September 2016. The total number of manufacturing jobs has fallen from three million at the peak to 2.6 million now. There has been no march of the makers just a march of the unemployed ex-makers. In the United States, according to the BLS, manufacturing employment in January 2-17 was 12.3 million down from 14 million in January 2007, down 12 per cent. Coal mining employment is down from 77,500 in March 2007 to 49,900 in March 2007, or by a third.

English seaside towns also mostly voted for Brexit with one major exception, Brighton and Hove – where I was born – which voted Remain. Examples are Blackpool 68 per cent, Great Yarmouth 72 per cent, Southend-on-Sea 58 per cent, and Torbay 63 per cent. The main reason for their decline is British tourists left for warmer climes when cheap flights became available. We don't have details for every town but here are the ones we have. Of the 20 neighbourhoods across the UK with the highest levels of working-age people on out-of-work benefits, seven are in coastal towns. Even with global warming the weather in the UK is still worse than it is in Spain.

The lack of recovery from the Great Recession is what did it. It took an unusually long time to restore the output lost in the Great Recession especially if we adjust for the growth of the population. According to the OECD, output per head in 2015 was 4.7 per cent higher in the US than it was in 2008, compared with 3.3 per cent in the UK, 5.7 per cent in Germany and 0.3 per cent in France. Output per head in Italy was still 8.2 per cent lower. We do know in the case of the UK the recovery took longer to restore output than the five other documented recessions of the last century. It took 72 months to restore lost output compared with 48 months or less in the other five documented recessions. The only documented recessions that were slower were after the South Sea Bubble, and the Black Death which was the slowest recovery for 600 years. Data on this is now available from the Bank of England on their Three Centuries of Macroeconomic Data, webpage.[4] The data shows the recession of 1720 took 16 years to recover from, the 2007 one took six years, 1815 and 1839 took five. 1973; 1979 and 1920 took four, 1907 took three and 1891 took two. The Great Recession took over six years to restore lost output.

One of the features of the Great Recession, especially in the UK and the US was there has been a recovery in jobs, with the unemployment rates returning to approximately their pre-recession levels. At the time of writing in March 2017 the unemployment rate in the US is 4.7 per cent and in the UK 4.8 per cent. But in both countries, there has been a marked rise in underemployment, especially in the number of part-timers who want full-time jobs. For example, in the US the broader measure of labour market slack which includes the underemployed stands at 9.2 per cent, up from a low of 8.2 per cent in 2007. In the U.K., the number of workers saying they are part-time but want a full-time job at the time of writing is at 1,118,000 up from a low of 610,000 in April 2006. Of note, in Chart 1 is, despite the unemployment rate having returned to pre-recession levels the employment to population rate has not, noting it has done so in the UK.[5] There is an issue whether this decline is structural or cyclical. Janet Yellen in a speech at Stanford University on January 19th, 2017 claimed

> "Of course, both the labour force participation rate and the employment-to-population ratio are still much lower than they were a decade ago. But the cyclical element in these declines looks to have largely disappeared, and what is left seems to mostly reflect the ageing of the population and other secular trends."

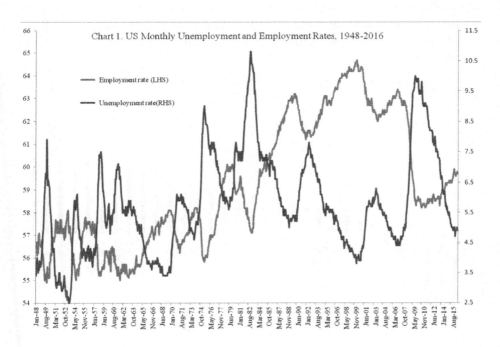

Chart 1. US Monthly Unemployment and Employment Rates, 1948-2016

This looks wrong given the UK and Canada, for example have had access to the same technology and other secular trends and have more generous benefits. As can be seen below they have similar ageing patterns.

	Canada	USA	UK
15-24	14.0%	16.3%	14.4%
25-34	15.9%	17.1%	16.6%
35-44	15.1%	15.4%	15.1%
45-54	16.3%	16.0%	17.4%
55-64	16.7%	15.9%	14.5%
65 and over	22.0%	19.2%	21.9%

If the UK or US economies were anywhere close to full-employment we should expect to see rapidly rising wage growth and we don't. Nominal wage growth in both countries is just above 2 per cent. Chart 2 illustrates for OECD countries and shows how poor real wage growth has been in the UK, behind only Greece and Mexico. The US is in the middle of the pack, but the long run lack of real wage growth looks scary. Real weekly earnings of US production and non-supervisory, blue-collar workers, who make up 82 per cent of the private sector workforce are 11 per cent lower than they were in 1973. Real weekly earnings for these blue-collar workers are the same as they were FIFTY years ago in 1964. The American Dream is over.

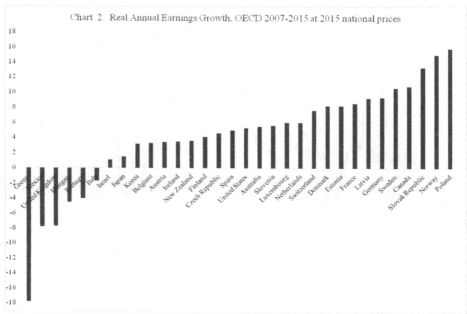

Chart 2. Real Annual Earnings Growth, OECD 2007-2015 at 2015 national prices

Wage growth matters. Chart 3 by county shows the vote to Leave the EU was higher in UK counties which had lower wage levels, based on data from the Annual Survey of Hours and Earnings (ASHE). Chart 4 for the US by state, using wage data from the Quarterly Census of Employment and Wages (QCEW) shows a similar result.

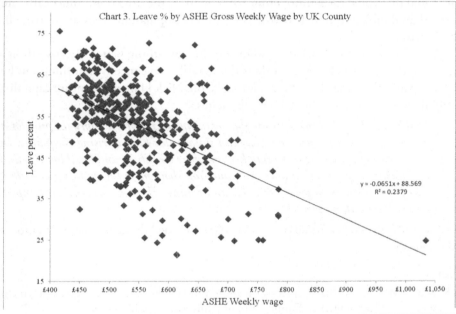

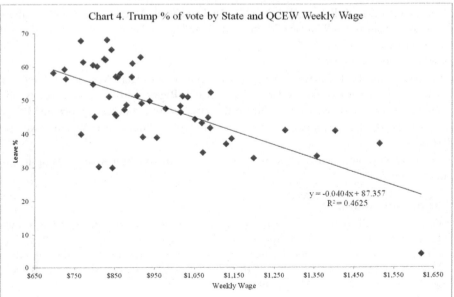

There is evidence votes for Brexit and Trump were higher in areas which had higher obesity rates, heavy drinking, smoking and suicide rates along with lower life expectancy. Deaths in the US from drug poisoning doubled between 2010 and 2015 and at 52,000 now exceed those caused by homicide and road accidents. Poisoning death rates were especially high in states like West Virginia, Kentucky and Ohio that voted for Trump. From 1999 to 2015, the drug poisoning death rate more than doubled from 6.1 to 16.3 per 100,000 population. They are hurting in the heartland.

Votes for Brexit and for Trump were cries for something better. Relative things matter and 'the left-behinds' see others doing well. The concern is nothing can be delivered and the voters have been sold snake oil. Nick Hanauer, venture capitalist and billionaire, wrote to 'My fellow zillionaires':

> "*If we don't do something to fix the glaring inequities in this economy, the pitchforks are going to come for us. No society can sustain this kind of rising inequality. In fact, there is no example in human history where wealth accumulated like this and the pitchforks didn't eventually come out. You show me a highly unequal society, and I will show you a police state. Or an uprising. There are no counterexamples. None. It's not if, it's when.*'[6]

The problem is sub-normal prosperity that succeeded the acute phase. Pitchforks to the ready.

Notes

1 Keynes, J.M. (1931), 'The originating causes of world unemployment', in Unemployment as a World Problem, edited by Quincy Wright, University of Chicago Press.

2 Haeyoun Park, K. K. Rebecca Lai, Jugal K. Patel and Sarah Almukhtar, 'C.B.O. Analysis: Republican Health Plan Will Save Money but Drive Up the Number of Uninsured', New York Times, March 13th, 2017.

3 www.Luzernecounty.org

4 Thomas, R and N. Dimsdale (2016) "Three Centuries of Data - Version 2.3", Bank of England, http://www.bankofengland.co.uk/research/Pages/onebank/threecenturies.aspx. The data are also available on FRED here https://fred.stlouisfed.org/categories/33839.

5 In the U.K., the 16+ employment rate was 60.4 in January 2008 versus 60.5 in November 2016.

6 http://www.politico.com/magazine/story/2014/06/the-pitchforks-,are-coming-for-us-plutocrats-108014

Note on contributor

Professor David Blanchflower is Bruce V Rauner Professor of Economics at Dartmouth College, New Hampshire, Professor of Economics at the University of Stirling, UK, Research Associate at the National Bureau of Economic Research and Contributing Editor at Bloomberg TV. He was member of the Monetary Policy Committee of the Bank of England from June 2006 to May 2009.

Why did the forecasters get it so wrong?

Hang on… says longterm economic forecaster and former Conservative Treasury Minister Jim O'Neill, it is not clear yet that forecasters have got it wrong. Yes, the near term collapse of the economy never happened on the back of the Referendum, but they did get the pound's decline bang on. And if it continues to be weak, then the other parts, about decline in British people's real incomes, related significant weakness in consumption, and all the rest of it, could still turn out to be right. The economy has held up much better than anticipated so far, probably a combination of an improving world economy, an easier monetary and fiscal policy, and because of an initial buoyant consumer, but he explains how it isn't something to declare victory on, yet

The specific nature of this question is somewhat presumptive, given it will be a year since the EU Referendum in the UK when this book is published. Maybe the forecasters will end up being right, to which I shall return. Let me start at a more basic level. In my considerable years as both an economic forecaster, and as a manager of a large team of economic forecasters, I have some awareness of the pitfalls.

In my earlier professional life as a forecaster, I spent much of my time forecasting foreign exchange rates, and indeed, this was the primary purpose, for which I was initially hired by Goldman Sachs. Even at that stage of my career, already having experienced more than a decade forecasting financial markets, particularly exchange rates, I learnt plenty, especially how easy it was to get things spectacularly wrong in the forex markets.

I think the Andy Warhol '15 minutes of fame' is a concept that sits well at home in that business. I have often previously said publicly, as far as foreign exchange market forecasts are concerned, I reckon somebody who gets it 'right' 60 per cent of the time was fantastically good, and this was my neverending goal. I knew at least 40 per cent of the time I would be wrong, sometimes more than 50 per cent. I believe the fact I acknowledged I could get such things wrong at least 40 per cent of the time actually helped me be a better forecaster and at times I learnt to have the honesty and self-belief to say 'I don't know' when someone would ask me what I thought about the dollar.

So in this spirit, one aspect of the answer to the question is: why the surprise? Forecasters are frequently wrong especially about financial markets. By nature, these things are really hard to do, and only a few, very few, are truly good at it.

An irony of the question and how I start responding, actually is, when it comes to the foreign exchange market, this is one of the areas where, especially initially, the consensus was right. Leaving the EU was seen by many, me included, as a potential negative productivity shock, which would reduce the permanent equilibrium value of the Pound, and so it would decline. It was quite likely many business investors, both long-term and more speculative, would be less eager on investing in the UK, which would also point the way towards Sterling weakness. For a country with a persistent balance of payments current account deficit, one that had widened in the couple of years running up to the referendum, it was not one of the more difficult predictions foreign exchange forecasters had to make.

So, contrary to what is generally perceived, the consensus forecasters have got it right on one key area, namely the anticipated weakness of the pound, which from my experience is not often the case. A strong consensus about a currency's future is often more likely to turn out to be wrong than other forecasters. But here, they have been right.

And linked to my opening response, it is not entirely impossible sustained Sterling weakness might end up delivering strong negative consequences for the real economy, albeit somewhat more delayed than forecasters initially suggested. If the pound's decline either directly causes inflation to rise, or has occurred simultaneously to a period where inflation is on the rise, then potentially difficult real economic consequences lie ahead still. In particular, if inflation were to rise more than expected, and show signs of being persistent, and also contributed to a significant pickup in domestic inflation, two related negative effects will still emerge.

Firstly, consumers will probably see their real incomes erode, making it harder and harder for them to sustain the surprisingly buoyant consumption at the heart of the post-Brexit economic strength to date. More disturbingly, and what turn weakness into a rout still, would be if this caused the Bank of England to raise interest rates sharply, then the consumer weakness could be dramatic, not least as house prices could suffer significantly. Sound familiar? It could still happen.

Now, what has meant, at least so far, this widely projected risk didn't come to pass? My honest answer is, I don't know. I am merely an economist, which as I always try to emphasise is a social science. There are no definites in economics, and maybe that is where the problem lies. Too many people, economists themselves, pretend it is a science. It is not.

Here's the possible reasons why forecasters got it wrong, so far. Firstly, when a country is facing such an apparent major structural change, the truth is perhaps it is a time when alternative forecasts, ones with reasonable equal probability, should be considered. I was asked by a senior economist working for a UK concern, what I thought their forecast for the UK should look like for 2016, 2017 and 2018, soon after I had left government. At first, I said I was pleased it was many years since I had formal forecasting responsibilities, and I didn't envy them. But I also quickly added that, in reality from my experience of forecasting and especially from managing economists, what they typically do is use the more reasonably useful short and slightly longer leading indicators they prefer (as well as their in-built bias) to forecast the year ahead, and then for the subsequent years if they had to, they simply would forecast the trend, or historic rate of growth for that country. This is usually greatly driven by a country's productivity rate and its workforce dynamics, of which the population and its age make-up are the main driver. Most evidence going back for most countries for a long time shows a country's underlying growth rate is quite stable. So for somewhere like the UK pre-Brexit analysis of historical growth trends, population dynamics and the productivity performance, leads most to believe the growth trend is around 2.0 per cent, perhaps a tiny bit above if you were generous.

The challenge my friend has is leaving the EU could be seen in a classic economic textbook sense as a negative productivity shock, primarily through reduced access to as many external trade markets, so it is entirely reasonable the majority of economists would adopt a negative long term bias to a post-Brexit UK economic outlook.

But as I suggested to this person, it might just be the case the UK could either handle Brexit better than conventional analysis might suggest, or the rest of the world might perform better than expected, or even the shock and horror of the possible consequences would cause policymakers to work harder than before and introduce smarter economic policies, in terms of both cyclical monetary and fiscal terms, but also structurally, and have better success than seemingly otherwise, in raising productivity.

Of course, my friend didn't buy any of this, but to me, here was a reasonably strong time when I would sympathise with the cautious types, and have two forecasts, as both are reasonably plausible. So here was the first 'error' as such.

A second reason is that the UK is a reasonably open economy in so far as it engages a lot in trade and investment with the rest of the world. This means the UK often gets economic influence from the rest of the world, for good, and bad. Remember the mess of 2008? That happened because of the interplay between our financial system and the rest of the world. Even though our domestic economy suffered badly, the initial cause was events overseas, especially in the US housing market.

What has, perhaps fortunately, happened since mid-2016, especially towards the end, is the rest of the world economy has improved. For a long time I have followed a number of indicators, which collectively give me reasonable confidence about exactly what is going on at any moment in time. Of the six I find really helpful – US weekly job claims; the US monthly ISM purchasing managers' survey; its subcomponent for new orders and inventories; the German monthly IFO survey; the Korean monthly export numbers; and the ratio of retail sales spending relative to industrial production in China – nearly all of them are looking more robust, and supportive of the idea the world economy experienced its strongest growth for a number of years in the final quarter of 2016. I suspect the world economy picked up to around 4 per cent in terms of world GDP growth, probably a full 1 per cent more than consensus expectations. This is pleasant news for somewhere as open as the UK, which the flipside of the inflationary risk of the lower pound, is we might be getting some business lift up from increased competitiveness. We might.

So, just at a time when we appear to have opted to disengage from the world, or at least, in the same manner as the previous 40-plus years, the rest of the world is helping lift our growth. If you look at the sources of stronger than expected UK growth, it doesn't appear to come from overseas, but it cannot have harmed our improved outlook. Additional explanations are less clear, but all plausible. Not least due to the graveness of their own pre-referendum forecasts, both the Bank of England and the Treasury responded quickly to the shock result, with positive policy responses.

So thirdly, as the textbook would argue, easing monetary policy and easing fiscal policy, are supposed to help the economy. So, again, is that such a surprise? In its own after-the-fact explanation for its upward revision to 2 per cent real GDP growth for 2017, the Bank of England cited its own actions, and those of the Government as to significant reasons why. Perhaps the shift in the tone of fiscal policy in particular has played an important role, and more subtle than forecasters themselves may think. Not only did the Treasury become more friendly through its own spending, but by being so public about abandoning its previous plan for a fiscal surplus by 2020, this might have persuaded many consumers to feel more relaxed. It is hard to know, but quite plausible.

This is especially the case, as when you look within the overall economic data as to why the economy has performed better than forecasters expected, virtually all of the evidence comes from a stronger consumer and a weaker savings rate.

So no one should get carried away, as it might not last. If the most hostile critics of the forecasters were to be justified in feeling so self-satisfied, they should await evidence of strengthening investment spending, improving exports, and of course, all of this withstanding our actual end of being in the EU, which is still some way off, even if Article 50 was finally triggered in March.

On the other hand, it is also equally plausible, especially if the Pound were to stabilise, the inflationary impetus starts to fade, productivity also starts to pick up, allowing and supporting more real wage growth, then the consumer could carry on with its post-Brexit strength, but importantly, probably allow for more investment spending to accompany it too.

So, at the time of writing (February 2017), the possible paths for the UK are still quite diverse.

One of the features of the EU Referendum campaign, courtesy of Michael Gove to some degree, became the idea people didn't want to listen to experts, which was a clever opportunistic line which seemed indeed to resonate. It tended to bracket all experts into one, especially the economists and their forecasts. But this is silly in reality, for a country addicted to weather forecasts and many forecasts depend on it. You wouldn't dispense with weather forecasters for getting an important moment badly wrong, as Michael Fish knew very well from the autumn of 1987.

It is the same with economic forecasting, although it is a social science so it is intrinsically more difficult, and this is a takeaway from the Referendum (and the 2007-8 crash) of which many forecasters need to be more conscious.

Note on contributor:
Jim O'Neill, Baron O'Neill of Gatley, was appointed Commercial Secretary to the Treasury by former Prime Minister David Cameron in May 2015, a position he held until his resignation in September 2016. Previously he had a distinguished career in banking and economics, including as chairman of Goldman Sachs Asset Management, and is well known for originally coining the acronym BRIC to describe the then developing economies of Brazil, Russia, India and China. He is Honorary Professor of Economics at the University of Manchester.

Section three
Brexit in the press

***

Just how much influence did the press have over the Brexit vote?

Tor Clark

The debate over the influence of the press over voters' democratic choices is as old as the hills and the subject of constant enquiry and debate, by politicians, journalists, academics and their students. It's the key issue which, for many, legitimises the study of the media and, for others, fills them with fear.

The knee-jerk notion that if The Sun says 'vote Conservative', the Tories win an election because newspaper readers are so easily influenced by a paper still with millions of readers is interesting, but largely overtaken by the argument that longer-term factors are more influential.

But the debate has progressed in interesting ways since that paper claimed to have delivered the Tories a narrow victory in 1992, with much opinion believing a long-term stance by a newspaper or newspapers can in fact influence voter behavior.

Roy Greenslade covers the debate over the 1992 General Election's narrow Conservative victory in Press Gang (2003: 607-608) in which both Neil Kinnock, the defeated Labour leader and Alastair Campbell, then Daily Mirror political editor, both agree the long-term character assassination of Kinnock over the nine years of his leadership of the Labour Party before the 92 election, was what ultimately did for him, rather than specifically the vitriolic campaigns of the Tory tabloids during the immediate election campaign. That election was the ultimate debating example of the influence of the press on democracy... until 2016, when once again attention turned to the influence of a (much smaller) press in the EU Referendum because of the narrowness of the Leave victory.

The right-leaning press, with about 4.8m sales, came out for Leave, while more liberal and left-of-centre papers, with about 1.8m sales, backed Remain, but the tone had been set years before as the Eurosceptic papers had taken a broadly anti-

EU line right back to Margaret Thatcher's 'No. No. No' Commons speech and The Sun's 'Up yours, Delors' headline of 1990.

The belief that this kind of long-term right wing prejudice influences voters, possibly against their best interests, has been the concern of liberal and left analysts since the study of the media first developed and can only have been intensified by press coverage before, during and after the EU Referendum result.

Proudly lauding the Daily Express role as an early champion of Britain leaving the EU, its editor, Hugh Whittow, believes his paper deserves credit for taking up the Brexit cause directly in 2010, supporting Ukip, the political party campaigning for it, and ultimately delivering a Leave victory in 2016.

He says unequivocally: "Our five-year record demonstrated beyond dispute it was the Daily Express which had been, all along, the architect of an editorial campaign which brought about a dramatic political victory."

He believes the result was a vote of confidence in the positive role of the press, across the board, adding: "Our campaign, with its daily agenda of thought-provoking critical analysis and commentary, was designed to boost the confidence of Leave supporters that victory was possible, thereby ensuring a high turnout for the Referendum vote. In fact, the turnout for the Referendum was 72.2 per cent, eclipsing the turnout for the previous year's general election of 66.1 per cent. So it's fair to say the press on both sides of the argument did an effective job of stimulating public interest and action."

Many other leading national newspapers had developed strong Eurosceptic tendencies, over many years, and it was no surprise that Leave was enthusiastically backed by The Sun, the Daily Mail and the Daily Telegraph. But long-term national journalist Liz Gerard has detected a worrying triumphalism in the tone of some of these papers, which has continued long after the victory of the cause they championed.

She says: "Having secured their dream result in the vote to leave the EU, the Daily Mail and Daily Express were not happy to sit back and celebrate. Rather, both seemed determined to continue the fight until any resistance movement had been pulverised."

She describes the tactics of the Daily Mail and Daily Express during the campaign but also sees an unwillingness to celebrate the victory and then just move on in the aftermath. She adds: "The zero-tolerance approach to dissent had been established within days of the Referendum, and while both papers have loudly defended the press's right to free speech, they seem reluctant to respect that right for others."

Hugo Dixon is chairman and editor-in-chief of InFacts, a journalistic enterprise he helped set up before the Referendum to make the fact-based case for staying in the EU. He criticises the pro-Brexit press for running misleading articles – starting with The Sun's 'Queen Backs Brexit' – and failing to correct them with due prominence. He believes his experience of complaining frequently to the Independent Press Standards Organisation (Ipso) offers evidence to make the regulator more responsive. And while he acknowledges the BBC's duty to 'balance' Referendum coverage, he also criticises what he sees as some of its main programmes' failure to challenge infamous claims – specifically the '£350m sent to Brussels' slogan.

Discussing the most inaccurate of newspaper claims he says: "Inadequate prominence is not the only problem with press corrections. They also take incredibly long to appear.

"InFacts secured 10 corrections to inaccurate pre-Referendum stories after complaining to the Ipso. But it took between one and seven months for the newspapers to set the record straight after we first alerted them to their errors. The average delay was 89 days."

We can all have our opinions on what the press did and didn't do in their coverage of this vital national decision, but what does academic analysis of the coverage tell us?

A major study by Billur Aslan Ozgul, David Levy and Diego Bironzo is instructive in suggesting there is a good case to be made that voters were influenced by the press in the Brexit vote. They say: "Although it is hard to ascribe any causal link between press readership and voting patterns, a large number of studies have revealed what appears in newspapers has an influence on how readers think and what they think about."

They add: "Our results revealed the majority of articles... discussing the EU Referendum campaign reinforced the longstanding Eurosceptic narrative of the British press during the campaign period."

And damningly, their research says the way the press skewed their coverage towards their own editorial agenda, was damaging to informed choice. "The relatively narrow range of information sources, when combined with a strong partisan approach, did little to respond to the need of those seeking high quality information to make up their minds."

Martin Moore and Gordon N Ramsay have made a thorough survey of the UK press coverage of immigration and ask whether that coverage was discriminatory.

They write: "In news, features and opinion pieces, migrants were blamed for many of Britain's economic, social and political ills. Migrants were, for example, blamed for taking primary school places, overwhelming the NHS, putting strains on maternity services, creating a housing crisis, stealing jobs, taking benefits, reducing wages, undermining Britain's security and increasing criminality.

"The language used to describe migrants was frequently analogous to language used to describe the movement of water, insects, or epidemics. Migrants were swarming, swamping, storming, invading, stampeding, flocking, over-running, and besieging the UK."

The British press, much of British humour and, indeed, some might say a large part of British culture has always been at best wary at worst insulting about people from overseas. Britain is an island and you don't have to go far anywhere to find the island mentality well established in thought and deed. Whilst the outcome of the 2016 EU Referendum was profoundly shocking to the UK's liberal governing elite, and its educated middle class generally, what was the reaction overseas?

'The Germans' have taken much abuse over the years from the UK's culture and tabloid journalism. Leading London-based German journalist Dianna Zimmermann followed the campaign and its aftermath with a mixture of fascination and horror, but has major fears for the future. She says "Of all people, the Brits, who the Germans admire and envy for so many things, have fired the starting pistol on an era of post-truth. Four million people voted for Nigel Farage in the last election, 17m were seduced by Boris Johnson and convinced by Michael Gove that we have all had enough of experts. They will now be drawn into a Brexit à la Theresa May which, in my view, is likely to be most damaging to anyone who does not belong to the ultra-rich elite."

And over in the world's most dynamic economy, how was the UK's most significant constitutional and historic democratic decision perceived? China-based media researcher Xiaochen Guo analysed coverage from papers based in mainland China, Hong Kong and Taiwan. She says: "With the popularity of globalisation, people are becoming closer to each other. Britain is no longer an isolated island. The world has been affected by Brexit and China is no exception.

"In the case of Brexit news reporting, Taiwan, Hong Kong and mainland China had their own different agendas. News styles of the mainland media are greatly affected by the antecedence of the media. However, on the whole objective journalism was maintained."

It is clear the UK press was once hugely influential; from the Shells Scandal to the Zinoview Letter, from the three-day-week to Neil Kinnock's head being put in a light bulb, the press has sought to get its views over, to bully and cajole its readers into seeing the world its way and voters to achieve that view. The short-term influence of the press is there but its extent is debatable. What is largely agreed is the long-term press focus on a particularly issue or position, in many cases a distortion, based around achieving that view, can indeed be influential.

In a landslide result press influence will play a part in racking-up votes for the victors, but probably will not be the deciding factor. Deciding factors will be many and based on voters' own backgrounds, prejudices and personal experiences.

But in a binary vote, where socio-economic background is not the main criterion on which people vote, where truthful and useful information is hard to come by, where politicians trade in tit-for-tat exchanges over dubious and spurious facts and where the whole vote is based on what might happen in a future we don't yet know, it becomes much easier to make a case for the press being influential on the outcome.

When the margin of victory is 52 per cent against 48 per cent, the argument that the pro-Leave press may have tipped the balance on the most significant postwar decision the British people had to make becomes compelling.

The Daily Express and Brexit

The Daily Express fought for five years to get a Referendum on EU membership. Editor Hugh Whittow says its coverage reflected the positive message of a Leave campaign which captured the popular mood

Can a newspaper set the national mood or does it merely follow it? That is a question which editors have wrestled with since mass circulation papers came into being a century or more ago. I firmly believe the Referendum result has provided us with a definitive answer; the press (as opposed to the media, which includes supposedly impartial broadcasters) reflects then reinforces the views of its readers. A newspaper which believes it can dictate what readers think or how they should vote is doomed to failure – as we saw in the Referendum campaign, part of the reason people voted Leave was because they were tired of being preached to by people who thought they knew better, but didn't.

A newspaper that is doing its job properly is a living, breathing organism that has fresh oxygen pumped into it each day by the people who buy it. The answer to my opening question can be found in the reason most people buy a paper each day – because it is in tune with their beliefs and values, because it speaks with their voice and because it listens to what they have to say. The Referendum campaign demonstrated that perfectly; I cannot remember an issue on which the press was more polarised and, as the result showed, public opinion was so divided. There were few grey areas in the press and not many don't-knows in the electorate.

A five-year crusade
For 123 days in 2016, the Daily Express campaigned vigorously for Britain to vote to leave the EU. It was the culmination of a five-year crusade to have our membership put to the popular vote which began on November 25 2010. That day we ran a front page cartoon of the Crusader – symbol of the Daily Express – standing on the White Cliffs of Dover with a message that said: We Want Our

Country Back. More than 373,000 readers filled in a coupon published in the newspaper and that is when I knew there was a groundswell of opinion on which we could ride. I'd go further – on which we *must* ride.

The Daily Express became the first national newspaper to declare outright support for the UK Independence Party (UKIP) and in January 2011 we published a unique 24-page supplement carefully setting out the case for a UK withdrawal. Despite the implacable opposition of the three main political parties, support for our campaign grew daily and in October 2011, 81 Tory backbenchers defied a three-line whip to support a parliamentary motion calling for a referendum. By reflecting the views of our readers, we were able to influence the actions of MPs who recognised a powerful common thread between what appeared in our editorial columns and what their constituents were telling them in letters and emails.

As our campaign captured more and more the popular mood, UKIP began securing remarkable results in by-elections – so much so that on January 23, 2013, Prime Minister David Cameron had no option but to announce a referendum would be held if his party won the 2015 General Election.

Our unfaltering campaign saw UKIP secure 3,881,000 votes at that election – more than the Lib Dems and the SNP put together – and on February 20, 2016, Mr Cameron signalled a victory for the Daily Express by announcing the Referendum would be held on June 23. Thus started the 123 days of the most significant and successful Daily Express editorial campaign in living memory.

Capturing the mood

In the newspaper and online, front page editorials, news analysis and political commentaries totally captured the mood of the 17m-plus people who eventually voted for Brexit. Some other newspapers, belatedly sensing the rising tide of support for our campaign which had unleashed people power, tried to emulate us. While we were happy and flattered to indirectly receive their support, our five-year record demonstrated beyond dispute it was the Daily Express which had been, all along, the architect of an editorial campaign which brought about a dramatic political victory. There was no gloating triumphalism; no silly claims it was 'The Express wot won it', just a sense of relief we had delivered to the people who matter the most – our readers – the result they wanted, a result which went totally against the expectations of the Prime Minister, the City, the Bank of England, the CBI and much of the media, such as the BBC.

How did this David and Goliath victory come about? Despite what critics of the Leave campaign might claim, it was not built on anti-EU stories about straight bananas or 27,000-word laws on the sale of cabbages. Its foundations were constructed out of what readers knew to be the truth – that the EU was the political dream of people they had not and could not vote for, that open borders meant the country had surrendered control and that laws for Britain should be made in the British parliament and administered by the British courts.

Project Hope vs Project Fear

I must be honest and admit some surprise the Leave campaign was, in fact, so positive and on the whole straightforward. While there is no doubt it reflected the fears of many people about immigration and loss of sovereignty, it was not as doomladen as the Remain campaign with its warnings of economic, social and political catastrophe if readers were crazy enough to vote Leave.

It was Project Hope versus Project Fear and as we have seen in the months following the Referendum, the fear factor was grossly exaggerated. I hesitate to say we were lied to but many of my readers have written, phoned and emailed to complain bitterly about the misleading and mendacious half-truths they were bombarded with by the Remain campaign. If there's one thing an editor who is doing his job should know, it's that the people who buy the paper aren't stupid. They aren't easily conned, they don't believe everything the Establishment tells them and they don't cower in the face of bullying.

Where those newspapers backing the Leave campaign scored well in the effectiveness of their campaigning was in the variety of issues they covered in such a positive way. By doing this they were able to reach out and hold the attention of a wide-ranging audience. Those who backed the Remain campaign seemed unable to find any message that was upbeat. It became a constant daily diet of doom and gloom about the economy and one which resonated with fewer people. President Clinton may have pontificated about the big American election issue being 'the economy, stupid' but at my daily editorial conferences the agenda was much bigger. And we never doubted the intelligence of the people who were going to make the big decision about their futures.

Stimulating public interest

Equally, the Daily Express never once believed those who wished to leave the EU were in the minority in the UK. Our campaign, with its daily agenda of thought-provoking critical analysis and commentary, was designed to boost the confidence of Leave supporters that victory was possible, thereby ensuring a high turnout for the referendum vote. In fact, the turnout for the referendum was 72.2 per cent, eclipsing the turnout for the previous year's general election of 66.1 per cent. So it's fair to say the press on both sides of the argument did an effective job of stimulating public interest and action.

The longer-term challenge was more acute. It was vital during our five-year campaign on traditional and digital platforms that our brand identity should be rigorously protected and enhanced. The multitude of messages about politics, economics and social issues had to be carefully co-ordinated so what the Daily Express proudly states is The Voice of Britain was always on-message.

Taking on the Establishment

Almost all of the Establishment, and big business such as the CBI, was against the aims of our campaign, so we constantly faced powerful opposition on TV, in other newspapers and in hugely-expensive advertising campaigns. The Conservatives, Labour, Lib-Dems, SNP and Plaid Cymru were committed to securing a No vote in the Referendum. The Daily Express and its unswerving support for UKIP was constantly being denigrated by accusations of racism, xenophobia and a 'Little Englander' mentality.

To maintain credibility, confidence and public support in the face of such overwhelming and unfair criticism was a massive challenge which our editorial team took on every day. While the Daily Express could rely only on its own editorial resources, the Government spent £9.3m of taxpayers' money on printing and distributing a glossy booklet to every home in the UK.

Another challenge we had to overcome was the stream of opinion polls which were being produced throughout the campaign, all of which were given wide publicity throughout the media. To counter this, the Daily Express held frequent polls in the newspaper and online which although not as allegedly scientific as face-to-face and telephone polls (nearly all of which failed to predict the correct result), gave a reliable indicator of the public mood overall and how individual issues were viewed by the electorate. The findings of our own polls directly influenced the content and tone of our campaign day to day.

Campaigning on the web

Does the press still have the same power it was able to wield a generation ago? Here are some facts which suggest it does: Traffic to the Express website (express.co.uk) exploded in the build-up to (and aftermath of) the Referendum. Unique users in the ten days before the June 23 vote were up 40 per cent and page impressions up 97 per cent compared with the same period the year before as our campaign reached its peak. In the ten days after the result, unique users were up by 102 per cent and page impressions up 155 per cent as people bookmarked us as the go-to Brexit news destination, a trend that has continued since.

More than one million people took part in our online polls in the final four weeks before the referendum. And 220,000 people watched our live debate – held in front of a politically-balanced studio audience and chaired by LBC presenter Nick Ferrari – two weeks before the vote. This event was streamed on Facebook Live and on the Express website.

In a high-speed modern world of instant communication via the internet, the Referendum showed the tried and trusted traditional method of putting words on paper is still devastatingly effective and, by working hand in hand with online partners, rather than seeing them as rivals for our readership, we can perform an even more powerful role in galvanising public opinion.

Journalists can draw great heart from the way the Referendum demonstrated that powerful and consistent advocacy is the key to the success of any crusade. The public appetite for intelligent analysis is as strong as ever and that can only be good for the continued well-being of newspapers. John F Kennedy summed it up perfectly: "And so it is to the printing press – to the recorder of man's deeds, the keeper of his conscience, the courier of his news – that we look for strength and assistance, confident that with your help, man will be what he was born to be: free and independent." Those who voted on June 23 to be free and independent were surely delivering a similar vote of confidence in the newspaper industry.

Note on the contributor
Hugh Whittow began his newspaper career on the Western Telegraph and the South Wales Echo before moving to the London Evening News, the Daily Star and The Sun. He became deputy editor of the Star, editor of the Daily Star Sunday and in 2003 deputy editor of the Daily Express. Since 2011 he has been the Editor of the Daily Express.

The match is over, but the winners won't leave the pitch

After decades of grumbling about Europe, the Daily Express and Daily Mail threw everything they had at the referendum campaign to ensure Britain would break free of Brussels. Liz Gerard looks at their tactics before and after the vote

'Thwart' is not a headline word. It is ugly. It is quite hard to say. It isn't a word people tend to use in general conversation. But in the months after the EU referendum it became a white-top tabloid favourite, invariably paired with the phrase 'the will of the people'.

Having secured their dream result in the vote to leave the EU, the Daily Mail and Daily Express were not happy to sit back and celebrate. Rather, both seemed determined to continue the fight until any resistance movement had been pulverised.

If anything, the language became more aggressive once the 'enemy' was no longer the 'undemocratic' Eurocrats across the Channel, but people on these islands. To suggest that leaving the EU, the single market or the customs union might not be in the country's best interests was to be denounced as 'unpatriotic' and labelled a 'Remoaner' (in the Express) or 'Bremoaner' (in the Mail). Such terms were not confined to opinion pieces, but spattered through news reports as though they were as valid a description as 'carpenter' or 'estate agent'.

And the biggest sin anyone could commit was to seek to thwart the will of the people.

A sovereign Parliament and an independent judiciary?
Both papers had supposedly been fighting for the primacy of British institutions – but not, it seemed, when it came to Brexit: the people had spoken and no member of either House of Parliament (whose sovereignty was the central issue of the June 23 vote) had any business asking awkward questions. So when a Guyana-born woman with a 'gilded lifestyle' went to court to argue that it was their duty to do just that, the white-tops were apoplectic.

Character assassins were set to work on Gina Miller, the financial adviser who led the legal challenge to Theresa May's belief that she could start the process to leave the EU without consulting Parliament. But the real fury was aimed at the 'out of touch' judges who decided in her favour.

The court had been asked to rule on a constitutional issue rather than on the merits or otherwise of Brexit, but the papers saw the verdict as an impertinent interference. 'Enemies of the people' shouted the Mail from a wanted-poster style front page with photographs of the three guilty men. 'We must get out of the EU' screamed the Express against a Union Flag backdrop – a device it had used on polling day and again when the result was announced. The story began: "Today this country faces a crisis as grave as anything since the dark days when Churchill vowed we would fight them on the beaches," and ended "Fight, fight, fight". Inside a telephone poll asked: "Is blocking Brexit a scandalous betrayal of the will of the people?"

The assault on the judiciary brought gasps from people on both sides of the Brexit argument, as did Lord Chancellor Elizabeth Truss's failure to stand up for the judges. Asked her view, the Prime Minister – who had already announced that the Government would appeal – said: "I believe in the value of the independence of our judiciary. I also value the freedom of our press." Her response might be seen as an expected defence of two pillars of democracy, but the Mail took it as vindication and proclaimed: "May backs press in judges row".

The report was accompanied by a pre-emptive strike on the Supreme Court judges who would hear the final appeal, headlined: "And now here's the next lot lining up to have a go…"

It noted that the panel included a judge who was 'a Brussels man to his fingertips', an 'unashamed champion of the Human Rights Act', and a third who was fluent in several languages.

There was more in similar vein the day before the hearing, which the Mail heralded with six pages of judge-bashing. This time Guy Adams was charged with digging into the judges' backgrounds, discovering that one was a progressive feminist, two liked classical music, and one had a string of racehorses. Another worked with English National Opera, whose chief executive had said she feared Brexit, while a guest conductor had called the Leave lobby 'upsetting'.

The Attorney General's argument made the lead for the paper, under the headline 'Why judges were wrong', but when Miller's side came to put their case, reporting was restricted to a Quentin Letts sketch.

When MPs did finally get their chance to speak – and agreed Theresa May should invoke Article 50 – the Mail was still on the alert for 'dirty tricks from the 114 who, to their shame, voted against implementing the people's will'.

When one insurer equals 300 scientists

The papers' battle (or 'crusade' in the Express) to leave the EU began long before the last general election and David Cameron's manifesto promise to give the public an in/out vote. It stepped up a gear once he was safely back in Downing Street, up again when he went off to Europe to try to persuade fellow leaders to toss him bargaining chips, and again when Boris Johnson and Michael Gove rewarded his efforts with the announcement they were joining the other side. Both papers were in full flow by the time the official campaign started in April – and neither was in the mood to make any pretence of impartiality or even balance.

It is customary in covering elections for newspapers to set out the big issues and the rival arguments, to visit key constituencies to test the water and see what most concerned voters there. This campaign, however, was unique in that there were no manifestos, no policies to be argued, just predictions and speculation. It would still have been possible to visit areas which had benefited from EU investment as well as to consider the plight of communities which felt too many asylum-seekers had been 'dumped' on them. But that didn't happen. Only statistics and opinions were reported. Nigel Farage was given free rein to roam across the Express, his face looking out at readers almost daily.

If someone put forward an argument to leave the EU, the story would be given prominence and the person making the statement made to sound as authoritative as possible, as in 'the head of one of Britain's biggest...' Any right of reply for the Remain side would be tagged at the bottom.

Arguments in favour of staying in the EU would be played down if possible, or if making them a page lead was unavoidable, they would be discredited at the outset with an intro such as: "Downing Street was accused of fearmongering when it said..." A Vote Leave quote would be included in the first few paragraphs and a 'fact box' published alongside showing how whoever was speaking had been proved wrong in the past. The Governor of the Bank of England, the Treasury, the IMF, the CBI and assorted 'experts' were all given this treatment.

At the end of May, more than 300 Cambridge academics wrote a letter expressing concerns about the impact leaving the EU might have on universities and Stephen Hawking said Britain needed to stay in to protect its economy, security and scientific research programmes. The Mail reported its view in a double-column story at the foot of a spread, with Hawking a blob paragraph at the end. A matching story to the left was entirely devoted to the opinion of one man, retired insurer Robert Hiscox, who accused No 10 of disseminating propaganda.

Project fear: the scare stories about immigration

In the early days of the campaign the focus was on the economy, including George Osborne's 'Project Fear' predictions and the red bus promise of £350m a week for the NHS. But Mediterranean boat tragedies and the sight of refugees trudging through southern Europe put migration centre stage and the pro-Brexit papers never looked back.

In a poll based on crystal ball gazing, there was only one certainty; for as long as Britain remained in the EU, it would have no power to deny admission to people from fellow member countries. But that wasn't scary enough. Economic migrants from Albania buying dinghies on eBay to paddle to the UK, Syrians trying to escape their war-riven homeland, Somali rapists and murderers, Romanian chambermaids, Polish plumbers, asylum-seekers camped in the Calais Jungle while their applications were processed – plus the entire 79m population of Turkey – all apparently wanted to settle in Britain. All were lumped together to form one amorphous mass as a symbol of why Britain should vote Leave.

No mention was made of the contribution made to society of the immigrant workforce already here, nor was there acknowledgement that an illegal immigrant would still be illegal, in or out of the EU. Stories about the vast numbers of people born abroad now living in the UK failed to note that such statistics include sporting champions like Bradley Wiggins, Mo Farah and Chris Frome – and Brexit superstar Boris Johnson (born in the US).

An audit of immigration coverage by the SubScribe website found during 2016, the two papers carried a total of 1,768 pages containing stories about 'foreigners', an average of three a day for the Mail and two for the Express (which has far fewer pages). The coverage, which was overwhelmingly negative, increased through the spring to a peak just before the referendum. The Mail gave over six pages to migration on the day before polling, the Express managed five.

Once the votes had been counted, interest in migration fell away sharply – until the autumn, when the Jungle was dismantled and the child migrants started arriving.

The Mail had shown its compassionate side in April when it had supported the Dubs scheme to offer 3,000 children a new start in Britain, with a spread on their plight and a full-page leader. But it changed its tune when the first arrivals were not the smudge-faced it had hoped for, but hulking youths whose ages were immediately questioned. When the Dubs scheme was halted in February, the Mail did not protest.

Dissent will not be tolerated

Over the year, the Express splashed on migration 72 times, compared with 56 for the Mail, with almost every story being presented as a reason to quit the EU. But this was only part of the picture, for there were a further 120 lead stories about the perils of remaining and the profits of leaving. An interesting aspect of this coverage was the fact there were actually more anti-EU splashes in the six months after the referendum than there had been before.

These included reports of shameless attempts to block Brexit and frequent updates on how wonderful everything was going to be once the decree absolute had been issued. One, headlined 'EU exit boosts house prices', was a report of the state of the housing market in the three months from March to June. Clearly, an EU exit could not have influenced anything before voting had even taken place, and the press regulator ordered the Express to run a front-page correction – the second such humiliation in a week.

The Mail has a more diverse news agenda than its rival, so its front-page Brexit coverage was modest compared with the Express: 82 lead stories, with two-thirds of them about immigration. Of the rest (17 before the referendum, 10 after), most were personal attacks on David Cameron – the man whose 2015 election victory was hailed as 'a vote for sanity' and the Prime Minister who gave it the referendum it wanted'.

If the Mail has kept its front-page powder relatively dry, it has been firing at will on the inside pages, complementing news stories with a barrage of opinion pieces. In the two weeks after May's party conference announcement of her planned Article 50 timetable, the paper ran 11 leaders and six comment columns on Brexit, all but three of them attacking 'Bremoaners'.

Free speech for the Press, but not for luvvies

The zero-tolerance approach to dissent had been established within days of the referendum, and while both papers have loudly defended the press's right to free speech, they seem reluctant to respect that right for others.

'Bleeding heart luvvies' who have been advised to shut up after speaking out for refugees include Amal and George Clooney, Gary Lineker, Lily Allen, Emma Thompson, Benedict Cumberbatch, Carey Mulligan and Juliet Stevenson – or, as Christopher Hart described them in the Mail, 'the whole ghastly smug cosseted self-adoring crew'.

Remain MPs should also keep their heads down. When Parliament returned after May had spelt out her thoughts on Article 50 and the single market, there was a move for MPs to have a say on Britain's strategy. At the same time, the CBI repeated its concerns about the economy and a Treasury briefing paper on the cost of Brexit was leaked. It was like lighting the blue touch paper.

'Time to silence the EU whingers', declared the lead story in the Express, while on the op-ed page, Chris Roycroft-Davis found the 'rabble of MPs demanding a Commons vote' guilty of 'snake-like treachery that cannot go unpunished'. The sentence? 'Clap them in the Tower of London. They want to imprison us against our will in the EU, so we should give them 28 days against their will to reflect on the true meaning of democracy'.

The Mail was sufficiently annoyed to run a full-page editorial, signposted on the front page in a double-depth puff above the masthead, and headlined: "Whingeing. Contemptuous. Unpatriotic. Damn the Bremoaners and their plot to subvert the will of the British people."

The leader began: "Waking up yesterday, it was as if Britain had been transported back to those febrile, fractious days in May and June, when the EU referendum campaign was being so ferociously contested."

Indeed. The white-tops have been fighting for so long, they don't seem able to stop.

Note on contributor:
Liz Gerard worked in Fleet Street for more than 30 years, latterly as night editor of The Times. She now writes SubScribe, a blog about newspaper journalism, at www.sub-scribe. co.uk. In particular, she has been monitoring and analysing media coverage of migration since 2013. She was named Editorial Intelligence's media commentator of the year in 2014 and 2016

Facts as newspapers saw them, IPSO's role – and a weak BBC

The media let the public down badly during the Referendum says Hugo Dixon. The pro-Brexit press – led by the Daily Mail, Telegraph, Sun and Express – were not only hugely partisan, they often ran inaccurate or misleading stories, which they were reluctant to correct

InFacts, a journalistic enterprise I helped set up before the Referendum to make the fact-based case for staying in the EU, had a ringside view of what happened. Day in, day out we rebutted inaccurate stories that appeared in the press – or the misleading statements politicians were able to get away with on the BBC. We also made multiple complaints to the Independent Press Standards Organisation (Ipso). Here's what we learnt.

Front page corrections needed to stop press errors
The pro-Brexit press produced many false front-page splashes during the EU Referendum. Even when papers acknowledged their errors, the corrections were never as prominent as the original stories. They were normally small articles tucked away on the inside pages.

When the sanction for a huge misleading story is a minor slap on the wrist, it's hardly surprising we are living in a world of 'fake news' and post-truth politics. If we want to stop the pollution of our democracy, we need to do better.

As far as the press is concerned, the single most important reform would be to force papers to print corrections that are as prominent as the original story. If the article appeared as a front-page splash, the correction should also be on the front page – and appropriately large.

If papers had to make big front-page corrections every time they printed misleading front-page splashes, the psychology around getting the facts right would change dramatically. Such corrections would involve a loss of credibility with readers. They would embarrass proprietors and editors. The journalists who made the mistakes would probably receive dressings down from their bosses. There would be a much bigger incentive to take care to get things right in the first place.

All the large offending papers – the Express, Mail, Sun and Telegraph – abide by the industry's main code of practice. It merely calls for corrections to be given 'due prominence', a phrase that in practice normally means they are rarely prominent at all. It should be modified to 'equal prominence'.

The evidence from the Referendum debate is compelling. Here are six inaccurate front-page splashes and the accompanying corrections.

1. Queen Backs Brexit – The Sun, March 9

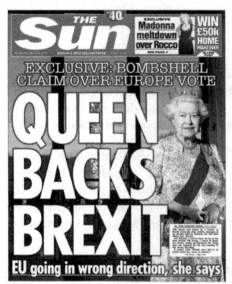 

This was a huge story. Stating the monarch backed Brexit may have influenced how patriotic royalists voted. The Sun was <u>required</u> to correct the story by Ipso, which enforces the code, after Buckingham Palace complained. There was a reference to the correction on the bottom of the front page, with the full ruling published on page 2. But the correction was in no way as prominent as the original error.

Ipso has required papers to mention corrections on their front pages following two other inaccurate Brexit stories, both in the Daily Express. These splashes appeared after the Referendum – one incorrectly stating Brexit had boosted house prices, the other that 98 per cent were opposed to an EU deal and wanted to quit without talks. In each case, the references to the corrections were small and at the bottom of the front page, and so much less prominent than the offending stories.

2. We're from Europe, let us in – Daily Mail, June 16

The Daily Mail front-page splash, just days before the Referendum, detailed a Metropolitan Police operation. which found a family of migrants stowing away in the back of a lorry. Saying these migrants were from Europe added to the toxic brew over migration the pro-Brexit press had been stirring throughout the Referendum campaign. The only problem was the migrants told police they were from Iraq and Kuwait, not Europe. The Mail did acknowledge its error the following day, but the correction was tiny and on page 2.

3. Abu Hamza and latest blow to UK sovereignty – Daily Telegraph, February 6

The sub-head of the story said: "The daughter-in-law of Abu Hamza cannot be deported from Britain despite a criminal past because of human rights laws, an EU law chief has ruled." The story fitted neatly into the Leave campaign's message that we needed to quit the EU to 'take back control'. The snag is there was no court ruling, just an opinion by one of the European Court of Justice's advocates general, who added that under 'exceptional circumstances' Abu Hamza's daughter-in-law could still be deported. Ipso agreed a small correction on page 2 was 'sufficient'.

4. EU seeks control of our coasts – Sunday Express, March 6

"Britannia will no longer rule the waves as Brussels threatens our island sovereignty," said the sub-head. The story would have inflamed the passions of anybody concerned about loss of control to the EU. The only problem is it was not true. The EU's plans for a coast guard only covered the Schengen Area – of which the UK is not a member. After InFacts complained to Ipso, the Sunday Express published a small correction on the bottom of page 30.

5. Brits Not Fair! – The Sun, May 19

'4 in 5 jobs' go to foreigners, said the sub-head. This article would have angered voters who thought foreigners were taking our jobs – another recurrent theme of the pro-Brexit press. It was based on a misreading of data from the Office of National Statistics. The Sun was forced to publish a correction after InFacts complained to Ipso. However, the watchdog concluded a small correction on page 2 was 'sufficiently prominent'.

6. Soaring cost of teaching migrant children – Daily Express, May 16

"The cost of educating 700,000 children from the EU in British schools has hit £3.2bn a year", said the story's first paragraph. This was another inflammatory story about migrants, targeting a key issue of concern for voters. It was false because it wrongly described anybody with at least one parent from the European Economic Area as migrant children. Such a definition would include Nigel Farage's children with his German wife. After InFacts complained to Ipso, the Express published a small correction at the bottom of page 27.

Small corrections tucked on inside pages – and even small mentions at the bottom of the front page – are not remotely adequate to deal with serious errors splashed on the front pages.

Justice delayed is justice denied

Inadequate prominence is not the only problem with press corrections. They also take incredibly long to appear.

InFacts secured 10 corrections to inaccurate pre-referendum stories after complaining to the Ipso. But it took between one and seven months for the newspapers to set the record straight after we first alerted them to their errors. The average delay was 89 days.

The length of time it takes to get justice is at odds with the Editors' Code, which says inaccuracies must be corrected 'promptly' and 'editors must maintain in-house procedures to resolve complaints swiftly'.

One reason it takes so long to get corrections is Ipso has a long drawn-out complaints process with no fewer than five stages:

- Its staff assess whether the complaint raises a possible breach of the code.

- If so, they refer the complaint to the paper, which normally has 28 days to resolve the matter directly with the complainant.

- If no resolution is found, Ipso staff investigate the matter themselves and seek to mediate, trying to conclude their probes within 90 days.

- If the two sides still don't agree, Ipso's complaints committee gives its judgment.

- After this, both sides can ask the watchdog to review its decision, but only on the basis that the original process was 'substantially flawed'.

This quasi-judicial process is designed to ensure that complaints are handled thoroughly and both sides get a chance to put their points of view. But it also gives newspapers an opportunity to drag their heels, hoping that complainants will be worn down. Even if the paper is eventually forced to make a correction, the later it is published, the less its readers will remember what all the fuss was about.

Another reason for delay is that a complainant may not appeal immediately to Ipso. Given the exhausting process, this makes sense. On the other hand, papers often don't take complaints seriously unless the watchdog is involved.

InFacts always first sought to persuade newspapers to correct their stories without bringing in Ipso. We were able to secure five corrections to pre-Referendum stories in this way. But in 20 other cases, we complained to the watchdog – in two batches, on May 19 and June 1. In half of these, we got corrections or clarifications. Here's what happened.

1. "EU migrants convicted of 700 crimes each WEEK – but only thousands of them are deported"
Express, February 17

2. "More than 700 offences are being committed by EU migrants every week, official figures suggest"
Telegraph, February 17

The official data the papers referred to was for criminal 'notifications', not convictions or offences committed. InFacts pointed out the error to both papers on the day the stories were published. The Telegraph corrected the story on June 9 as did the Express – nearly four months later.

3. "EU seeks control of our coasts"
Sunday Express, March 6

We pointed out the error on the day of publication. After a marathon email exchange, mediated by Ipso, the Sunday Express corrected the article on October 9 – seven months later.

4. "Britain could stop ten times more terror suspects from entering the country if it leaves the EU, justice minister says as he blasts EU rules for allowing terrorists to 'waltz into Britain'"
Mail Online, March 30

Dominic Raab, then Justice Minister, didn't say this. InFacts contacted the Mail Online journalist on April 11. The story was corrected on June 11 – two months later.

5. "Report shows the NHS is nearly at breaking point as massive influx of EU migrants forces doctors to take on 1.5m extra patients in just three years"
Mail Online, April 3

The newspaper website provided no evidence EU migrants were responsible for the NHS being at breaking point. The data it relied on didn't even record the nationality of the patients. InFacts contacted the Mail Online six times starting on April 4 before complaining to Ipso. The website corrected its story on June 8 – more than two months later.

6. "Isis has taken advantage of Europe's open borders to plant sleeper cells in the UK, Germany and Italy, head of American intelligence warns"
Mail Online, April 27

7. "EU free movement has allowed Isis sleeper cells into the UK, warns security chief"
Express, April 27

The US director of intelligence did not say open borders had let terrorists into Britain. InFacts pointed this out to the Mail Online and the Express on the day the stores were published.

The Mail Online story was corrected on June 11 – six weeks later. The Express story was clarified on August 17 nearly four months after publication. Ipso rejected InFacts' request that the Express make a formal correction.

8. "Soaring cost of teaching migrant children – £3bn bill 'another reason to quit EU'"

Express, May 16

The story wrongly described anybody with at least one parent from the European Economic Area as migrant children. We informed the Express of the error on May 27. The story was corrected on Referendum day – nearly one month later.

9. "Brits not fair! 4 in 5 jobs go to foreigners"

The Sun, May 19

We pointed this out to The Sun on the day of publication. Ipso <u>ruled</u> the record must be set straight on October 14. The correction was finally <u>published</u> on November 5 – nearly half a year after the original story appeared.

10. "NHS will be £10bn in the red in three years' time – creaking under weight of migrants"

Express, May 23

The report on which this story was based didn't even mention migration. InFacts informed the Express of the error on the day the story was published. The story was corrected on June 22, one day before the Referendum and almost a month after publication.

Such delays in publishing corrections – which are not confined to stories about Brexit – are not good enough. Ipso needs to vet newspapers' complaints procedures to ensure they react more rapidly – especially before it is involved.

The watchdog should also review its own process with a view to speeding it up. Sadly, an external review of the body last year didn't delve into this issue deeply. If Ipso requires more resources to move faster, it should ask the papers – which fund it – to pay up.

After all, justice delayed is justice denied.

Press code honoured in letter, not spirit

One reason the pro-Brexit press hasn't been forced to correct stories is because they weren't technically false, even when they were misleading.

That's not good enough. The Editors' Code is supposed be 'honoured not only to the letter, but in the full spirit'. The experience InFacts gained through complaints to Ipso suggests the opposite is often the case.

Clause 1 of the code says: "The Press must take care not to publish inaccurate, misleading or distorted information or images, including headlines not supported by the text." It goes on to say: "A significant inaccuracy, misleading statement or distortion must be corrected."

In half of the cases, which we took to Ipso, the press watchdog sided with the newspaper. Here are four of the cases we lost – and why.

1. Daily Telegraph, Grand Canyon story, May 13

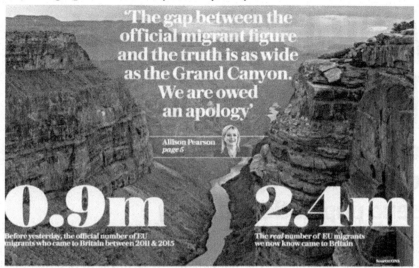

'The gap between the official migrant figure and the truth is as wide as the Grand Canyon. We are owed an apology'

Allison Pearson
page 6

0.9m
Before yesterday, the official number of EU migrants who came to Britain between 2011 & 2015

2.4m
The *real* number of EU migrants we now know came to Britain

Source: ONS

The Daily Telegraph

The headline on page 5 read: "The extra EU migrants the ONS has found down the back of a sofa are six Newcastles".

The Telegraph columnist Allison Pearson used her 2.4m figure to claim EU migrants are responsible for kids not getting into secondary schools of their choice, for people not getting on the housing ladder and for pregnant women being turned away by maternity units.

To get to the 2.4m figure, Pearson added five years' worth of short-term EU visitors to the Office of National Statistics' (ONS) estimate of long-term migrants. We argued that adding the two numbers together in this way was misleading since short-term visitors leave within a year. The claims Pearson used her 2.4m figure to support were spurious because it was implausible that many migrants who hop over for a few months' work would put their kids into secondary schools, get on the housing ladder or attend maternity units.

Ipso rejected our argument on the basis: "It was not inaccurate to state that 2.4m EU migrants had 'come to' the UK, and did not accept the suggestion that doing so implied that this was also the number of EU migrants who had stayed in the UK."

While it is true the Telegraph didn't state these short-term migrants had stayed, the headline on the inside page about the ONS finding 'six Newcastles' of extra EU migrants down the back of the sofa and the tenor of the whole article implied that many if not most were still in the UK.

2. Daily Mail, housing crisis, May 20

MIGRANTS SPARK HOUSING CRISIS

Now EU tells Britain to build more homes as open borders send population soaring

The first sentence read: "Britain has been ordered by Brussels to build more houses – to cope with all the EU immigrants." It went on to describe the EU's recommendations as a 'demand'.

We argued the words 'ordered', 'demand' and 'tells' were inaccurate. Not only does the EU not have any powers to order the UK to adopt any housing policy, the Daily Mail was referring to 'country specific recommendations' which, as the term implies, are recommendations, not orders.

Ipso sided with the Daily Mail, saying the EU's recommendation: "Was presumably done on the basis that some attention would be paid to the recommendation. In these circumstances, it was not significantly inaccurate to characterise the recommendation as an 'order', or the EU 'telling' the UK to build more houses, or 'demand' that it does so."

3. The Times, EU army, May 27

EU army plans kept secret from voters

Details of Brussels power grab buried until day after referendum

The Times quoted plans drawn up by the EU's foreign policy chief for 'new European military and operational structures, including a headquarters'. We argued these could not reasonably be described as plans to create an 'EU army' – a term that would imply military forces under a single command structure. The headline was therefore misleading.

Ipso disagreed, saying: "It was not misleading to characterise the proposed new European military structures as an "EU Army", particularly in circumstances where the precise nature of the plans were explained in the article; the headline of the article was supported by the text."

4, Daily Express, Asylum power grab, March 8

NOW EU WANTS ASYLUM CONTROL

Madness as Brussels plots to tell us who can come and stay in our country

By **Macer Hall** Political Editor

BRUSSELS chiefs last night unveiled plans to end Britain's control over asylum seekers.

They want a centralised EU asylum force with power to meddle in the immigration policies of member states.

It is the European Commission's response to a crippling migration crisis and would give responsibility for overseeing asylum claims to a quango, the European Asylum Support Office. It could impose quotas of asylum seekers on countries – another huge extension of EU supremacy over national laws.

Ukip leader Nigel Farage warned Britain would be left with no control over who can and cannot stay. David Cameron vowed that TURN TO PAGE 5

This was a story about European Commission plans to require member states to take quotas of asylum-seekers. InFacts argued there was never any chance the UK would be part of this system since we had an 'opt-out' on matters of justice and home affairs and David Cameron had made clear he would exercise that opt-out. As such, we argued the story was misleading.

Ipso rejected our argument on the grounds that: "As a member of the EU, there was a possibility that the UK could be subject to these new proposals." It added at the time of publication: "The UK had not exercised its opt-out."

In each of these cases, newspaper published screaming front-page headlines. The Editors' Code says the press must take care not to publish misleading headlines. It also says the code must be honoured in the 'full spirit'.

The papers' actions – and Ipso's support of them – have at best honoured the code's letter. If we are to stamp out the fake news that has blighted the Brexit debate – and could continue to do so over the Article 50 process – the press watchdog will have to do better.

Learning the lessons

We need to learn the lessons from the Referendum campaign. After all, fake news is rampaging around the world like a genie let out of the bottle – and there are many other political battles to come where facts will be twisted and where the public needs to be informed by good journalism.

We also need to do better in future because the Brexit process is not yet over. It will probably drag on until early 2019. The decisions taken in the intervening period will significantly affect our lives for years, perhaps generations to come. It is vital they are subjected to proper scrutiny by the media

Meanwhile, over at the BBC….where the public was failed

At the same time, the BBC failed in its duty to educate and inform. It didn't do nearly enough to challenge those who appeared on its programmes. Instead, it allowed itself to be turned into a forum for endless Punch-and-Judy shows.

It has rightly been criticised for its weak Referendum coverage. If the broadcaster had done a better job of challenging interviewees, informing the public and making room for a variety of viewpoints, voters would have had a better chance of sifting fact from fiction. The BBC, after all, dominates our news coverage: 77 per cent of the public use it as a news source, according to Ofcom.

The most common criticism aired against the BBC is one of phoney balance – namely that it gave equal airtime to experts and their opponents' unsubstantiated bluster. But this is probably not the most serious charge. After all, it would not have been fair to deny the two sides of the Referendum equal airtime or to keep off the air campaigners who were telling fibs or spinning fantasy.

However, what the BBC could and should have done was grill its guests more vigorously – and make more space for coverage that didn't fit into the tired Punch-and-Judy style battle between spokespeople put up by the two official campaigns.

James Harding, the BBC's director of news, gave a defence of its Referendum coverage in The Observer, writing: "We have to deliver 'due impartiality' and 'broad balance', terms designed to ensure that we are free to make judgments on the validity of stories, that we challenge facts and figures, that we acknowledge that different people speak with different levels of authority on a subject."

Harding backed up this argument with four examples of how the BBC had challenged the 'squeakier claims' made by politicians. There were, indeed, some cases in its thousands of hours of coverage when journalists grilled their interviewees effectively. And there were some broadcasters who really made their guests squirm. Andrew Neil stands out, in my mind, as the most effective interviewer.

Not enough grilling

But there were many times when the BBC didn't challenge its guests adequately. I paid special attention to its agenda-setting Today programme in the early period of the campaign – when the terms of the debate were largely set – and noted many such cases.

For example, it let Andrea Leadsom say we send £350m a week to the European Union on March 8 and Gisela Stuart say the same on April 15. During that interview, the Vote Leave chair also promised to use the money for the NHS – a disgracefully false promise. As late as May 11, the Today programme allowed Boris Johnson to say we are sending the EU £20bn a year.

Other failures included letting interviewees spread the myth the EU needs us more than we need them. Chris Grayling said this on March 10, without being adequately challenged, as did John Redwood on March 22 – though, to be fair, he was quizzed on this when he returned to the airwaves on April 18.

David Davis was allowed on March 24 to get away with saying we can't stop killers with EU passports coming to the UK. We can. And Leadsom wasn't challenged sufficiently, in her interview on March 8, when she said 60 per cent of our laws are made in Brussels.

I wish I could play these interviews again and share them with readers. But they are no longer available on the BBC's website. When I asked for clips, a spokesperson wrote back: "Unfortunately the website is the only public source."

I am not sure why the Today programme didn't rise to the occasion. Maybe its presenters and researchers were not on top of the subject matter in those early weeks. They certainly sometimes appeared ill-prepared for so important and complicated a subject, although to be fair they did seem to challenge some of the arguments such as the lie about sending 'Brussels' £350m a week as the campaign wore on.

Maybe they were taken aback by the sheer ballsiness of some of the Leave camp's claims. When Johnson came on air, he flattened John Humphrys like a Challenger tank, telling the presenter at the end he could 'take back control of the interview'.

Maybe the BBC's Referendum guidelines are also to blame. The word 'challenge' doesn't appear anywhere in the long document.

Punch and Judy shows

This wasn't the BBC's only failing. It also allowed too much of its coverage to become a Punch-and-Judy style battle between the official campaigns. The broadcaster, of course, had to give a lot of airtime to Vote Leave and Stronger In. But it allowed its coverage to be virtually dictated by their agendas.

I know the Remain side of the story better. Stronger In had a 'grid', on which it set out what stories it wanted to push on particular days and which people it wanted to push those messages. It coordinated this grid closely with Craig Oliver, David Cameron's director of communications. Indeed, Stronger In was effectively in Number 10's pocket. It rarely put forward people who weren't on message with its Project Fear strategy.

The BBC should not have allowed itself to be manipulated in this way, particularly since it was aware of the potential problem. Its guidelines said: "Where there is a range of views or perspectives, that should be reflected appropriately during the campaign." They went on to say: "The designated Campaign Groups – whilst offering spokespeople to programme-makers and other content producers – cannot dictate who should or who should not appear on BBC output."

But the broadcaster didn't do enough to resist the pressure. As a result, Downing Street and its puppets dominated the Remain camp's share of airtime, and people who wanted to make a positive case for Britain's involvement were edged out. Even Gordon Brown – who was trying to argue we should lead Europe, not leave Europe – found it hard to be heard.

Another consequence was the BBC didn't do enough to advance its mission, 'to enrich people's lives with programmes and services that inform, educate and entertain'. One way to inform would have been to rely less on shrill, highly scripted voices from the campaigns and encourage contributions from more nuanced voices. This would have done more justice to the complexity of the issues. But experts such as Charles Grant, founder of the Centre for European Reform, arguably Britain's preeminent European think-tank, and Lionel Barber, the Financial Times editor, struggled to get on the airwaves.

For every such example, the BBC could presumably come up with a counter-example. But when its senior figures search their souls, do they really think they fulfilled their mission of informing and educating the public well during the Referendum? And, if not, what are they going to do about it? How about an independent, public audit of how the BBC fared during the Referendum backed up by recommendations on how to do better in future?

The world is not getting any simpler. Hard, honest thinking about how to cover often very complicated questions could stand the BBC in good stead. Audiences and licence fee payers definitely deserve it.

Note on the contributor
Hugo Dixon is chairman and editor-in-chief of InFacts. This chapter is based on a series of articles which appeared on InFacts.org

The EU Referendum campaign – UK press and game framing

This study by Billur Aslan Ozgul, David Levy and Diego Bironzo shows the UK press was highly partisan during the EU Referendum campaign period. It also engaged in game-oriented reporting by sidelining the voices of experts and academics and heavily focusing on the contest and strategies and on politicians

Blumler defines the EU Referendum campaigns of 1975 and 2016 as being 'as different as proverbial chalk and cheese' (Blumler 2016). The press reporting can be identified as one of the primary points of difference between the two campaigns. During the first referendum on continued membership in 1975, Eurosceptic journalists comprised a minority. In line with the press, 67 per cent of voters approved of the UK's European Community membership. The positive tendency of the UK press towards European Community membership changed after the passing of the Single European Act in the 1980s (Wring 2016). In the run up to the 1997 elections, the Eurosceptic discourse was to be found in titles such as the Daily Mail, The Sun, the Express, The Times and the Daily Telegraph (Anderson and Weymouth 2014: 63).

In 2013, lobbying from Eurosceptic MPs and the rise of UKIP once more fuelled discussion of Brexit. Having won the election in 2015, David Cameron kept his promise to hold an EU membership referendum and started renegotiating the terms of Britain's membership with European leaders. He achieved some of his goals, but failed to deliver on his original promise to control immigration from the EU. As a result of this, Conservative politicians such as Michael Gove, Boris Johnson and Chris Grayling started campaigning in favour of 'Leave', with David Cameron leading the 'Remain' camp. The newspapers were generally slow to explicitly endorse one side. While the Daily Mail, the Sun, Daily Express, Daily Telegraph and The Sunday Times urged their readers to vote for Leave; The Times, The Guardian, Daily Mirror, Financial Times and Daily Mail's sister paper the Mail on Sunday urged their readers to vote Remain.

How the UK press covered the entire EU Referendum campaign in 2016 is the central research question in this chapter. Although it is hard to ascribe any causal link between press readership and voting patterns, a large number of studies have revealed what appears in newspapers has an influence on how readers think and what they think about (Page 1996: 23).

People can in particular make different decisions when the same problem is framed in different ways (Tversky and Kahneman 1981). For instance, how British policy towards European integration has been represented to the people by the media had an influence on how public opinion formed (Anderson and Weymouth 2014: 2). Moreover, despite the effect of the internet on press readership and revenues, newspapers remain influential and the stories they select and opinions they express often appear in the main TV and radio current affairs programmes. Hence, the continuing agenda-setting role of the press merits detailed analysis.

Our aim is not to assess the quality of the coverage of the European Referendum, but rather to conduct an in-depth analysis of the positions adopted by the UK newspapers both in their editorial and news items. We also analyse the volume/visibility and tone of the articles published throughout the campaign. To capture voices and arguments which were dominant in the press, we also explore the main stories and issues deployed on each side of the argument.

Our results demonstrate press coverage was highly partisan. It portrayed the campaign as a game or contest with a heavy focus on UK politicians and particularly on those in the Leave campaign. Game coverage is defined by scholars Capella and Jamieson as a 'strategy frame' that emphasises 'who is ahead and behind and the strategies and tactics of campaigning necessary to position a candidate to get ahead or stay ahead' (Capella and Jamieson 1997: 33). Game framing of the UK press marginalised the voice of academics and experts. Consequently, the press was generally better at reinforcing the views of decided voters than in providing broad facts and high quality information to undecided voters.

Methodology

Our data were provided by a team of media analysts from PRIME Research, a communications research consultancy. The analysis focused on the London editions of the five largest tabloids and mid-market papers, namely the Daily Mail, The Sun, Daily Star, Daily Express and Daily Mirror as well as the four broadsheets, The Guardian, Daily Telegraph, the Financial Times and The Times. PRIME's proprietary content analysis system was used to analyse all EU Referendum news published in the above mentioned newspapers on Tuesdays and Saturdays between February 20 and June 23. The reason we focused on two days in each week was to have a manageable number of articles, because of the resource-intensive nature of human content analysis of newspaper content. To capture all EU Referendum related stories, the analysts used various keywords such as EU Referendum, EU membership, Brexit, Vote Leave, Vote Remain, Leave campaign, Remain campaign, Project fear, Project fact, Euro, Euro scepticism, Euro sceptic/s, Cameron's deal, Cameron's negotiation, Exit terms.

In total, 3,403 articles discussing the EU Referendum were collected. Of this only 2,378 articles directly focusing on the EU Referendum were used for the analysis in our study. Most of the content analysis is based on article level analysis, but when it came to detailed examination of the topics covered and the sentiment attributed to those, the researchers found message-level analysis to be more robust. For message level analysis, researchers subdivided the articles into content units, ie a single thematic unit, ranging in size between a single sentence or image and a paragraph. This allowed us to capture the full range of issues tackled within each article, rather than just the main issue covered (see Levy et al 2016 for further information).

Findings
Volume:
We first assessed the amount of attention devoted to the Referendum by the UK press. Across the nine newspapers analysed there were 66 articles focused on the Referendum on an average day. The volume of EU Referendum news was greatest in the Daily Mail, with 403 articles focused on the EU Referendum. This was followed by the Daily Telegraph (360), Times (336), Financial Times (318), Daily Express (275) and Guardian (271). On the other hand, The Sun had slightly fewer articles (249) on the EU Referendum than The Guardian. Despite being the same size as The Sun, the Daily Mirror published around half as many EU Referendum articles (119), while the Daily Star (47) had the lowest number of articles focused on the Referendum.

Figure 1.1: Total number of articles by newspaper

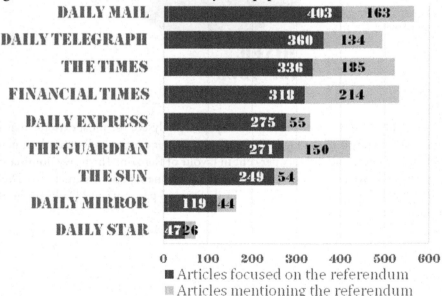

Degree of Partisanship:

To define the Referendum stance of the nine UK newspapers, we summarised and compared the number of pro-Leave and Remain messages in the 2,378 EU Referendum articles across nine newspapers. The articles containing 60 per cent or more messages in favour of Leave or Remain were marked as biased. Our analysis suggests the majority of EU Referendum news (41 per cent) was skewed in favour of Leave, while only 27 per cent supported Remain. The percentage of articles which took no position was only eight per cent. The articles with mixed or undecided messages comprised 24 per cent of all EU Referendum-focused articles in our sample.

Figure 2.1: Overall degree of partisanship classified at article level

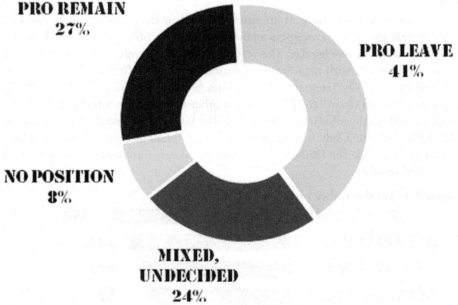

PRO REMAIN
27%

PRO LEAVE
41%

NO POSITION
8%

MIXED,
UNDECIDED
24%

The results also show, of the nine newspapers analysed, the most extreme bias in favour of Brexit was in the Daily Express, with 74 per cent of its Referendum news in favour of Leave and only six per cent in favour of Remain. The heavy dominance of pro-Brexit articles was also present in five other newspapers, namely the Daily Mail (58 per cent), Sun (44 per cent), Daily Star (43 per cent) and Daily Telegraph (47 per cent).

Figure 2.2: Article position by newspaper

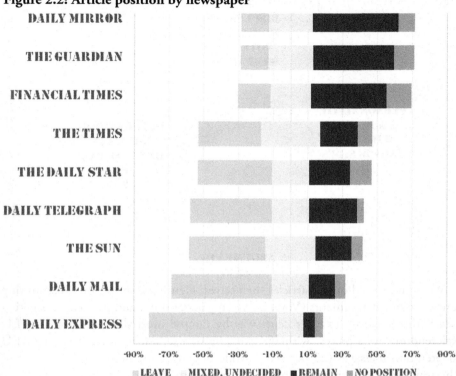

On the other side, the Daily Mirror had the highest share of Remain articles (50 per cent) with a plurality also in The Guardian (46 per cent) and Financial Times (43 per cent).

Popular topics/arguments discussed by the UK press

We categorised issues and sub-issues discussed as part of EU Referendum news into eight broad topics: 1) news about political personalities and other public figures taking a side; 2) discussions around the vote and campaigns; 3) other, broader topics (such as the concept of Brexit, Euroscepticism or the Referendum in general). The remaining five categories consisted of the arguments discussed on each side of the campaign, namely: 1) the economy; 2) issues discussing migration and mobility; 3) regulations; 4) security; and 5) the idea of sovereignty.

When we analysed the headlines of the EU Referendum news, we found almost half concerned discussions of the vote and campaign. Seven per cent of headlines focused on the personalities and public figures taking sides in the campaign and two per cent discussed the Referendum and Brexit in general. Only 42 per cent of the headlines focused on the arguments cited by each camp.

Figure 3.1: Headline topics in EU referendum-focused articles

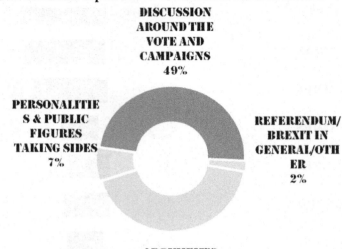

DISCUSSION AROUND THE VOTE AND CAMPAIGNS 49%

PERSONALITIE S & PUBLIC FIGURES TAKING SIDES 7%

REFERENDUM/ BREXIT IN GENERAL/OTH ER 2%

ARGUMENTS 42%

We then focused on the articles themselves. Figure 3.2 shows after discounting non issue-based arguments (Vote, Brexit in general/other and personalities taking sides), the economy (45 per cent) was by far the most discussed topic in EU Referendum news pieces, with UK sovereignty accounting for a quarter of EU Referendum messages (25 per cent), while migration accounted for 16 per cent. The topics of regulations (10 per cent) and terrorism/security (4 per cent) were side-lined in our sample.

Figure 3.2: Topic analysis classified at message level where arguments were used

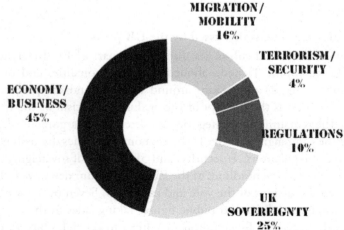

MIGRATION/ MOBILITY 16%

TERRORISM/ SECURITY 4%

ECONOMY/ BUSINESS 45%

REGULATIONS 10%

UK SOVEREIGNTY 25%

Base: 9,189 argument-based messages after excluding 9,969 messages about the Vote, Brexit in general, other and personalities taking sides

Tone:

We scrutinised each message unit within the EU Referendum articles to see whether articles had a positive, negative or neutral tone, finding the EU Referendum news was dominated by negative messages; 46 per cent of all messages discussing the EU Referendum were negative and only 12 per cent were positive.

Figure 4.1: Overall tone of messages

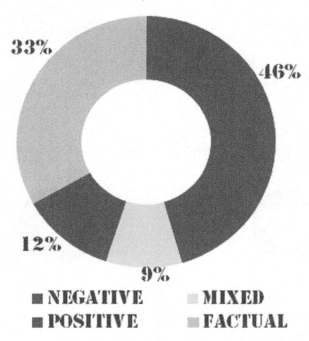

33%
46%
12%
9%
■ NEGATIVE   ■ MIXED
■ POSITIVE   ■ FACTUAL

What was particularly striking was the high percentage of pro-Remain messages adopting a negative tone. It was surprising only 27 per cent of pro-Remain messages were positive about the present, compared to 36 per cent which were negative. The Leave camp, by contrast, was much more negative about the status quo with 76 per cent of pro-Leave messages adopting a negative tone. Yet, our findings show they managed to balance their positive and negative messages by criticising the present but offering hope for the UK's future outside the Union. 34 per cent of Leave messages about the future thereby advanced a positive tone.

Figure 4.2: Tone of messages by position and time perspective

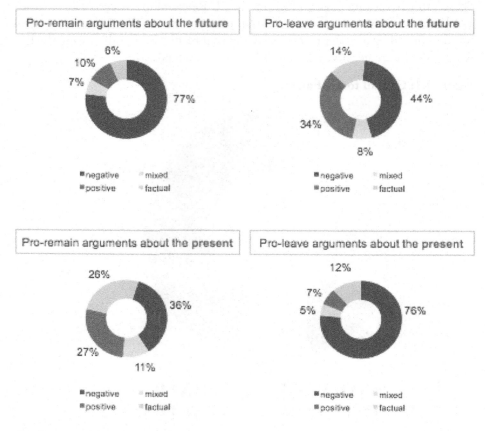

Spokespeople in the UK press:

Finally, our study focused on people quoted in the UK press during the campaign period. We categorised the name and affiliation of each spokesperson according to eleven categories (listed in figure 5.1). The analysis reveals UK politicians received a high level of press attention (34 per cent), followed by campaign representatives quoted in 14 per cent of EU Referendum news. On the other hand, analysts, economists and experts were only quoted in 11 per cent of EU Referendum news. Similarly, the press rarely cited members of the public (10 per cent), businesses (six per cent), foreign politicians (five per cent), government and public bodies (four per cent), lobbies and organisations (three per cent) and celebrities (two per cent). What was particularly striking was the low level of attention granted to academics – only two per cent of EU Referendum news pieces quoted an academic.

Figure 5.1: Spokesperson groups quoted in articles

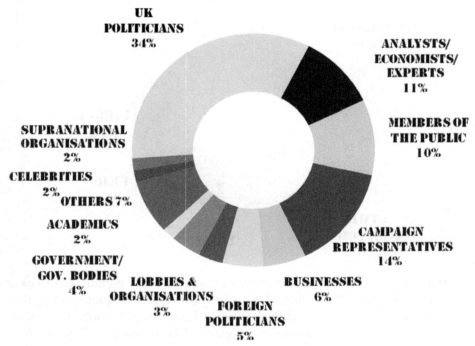

Where academics were quoted, 12 articles – more than 20 per cent of the total – cited the prominent pro-Leave academic, Patrick Minford, Professor of Applied Economics at Cardiff Business School, making him the most cited academic in our sample.

When we analysed which political party was the most cited, our results (Figure 5.2) showed Conservative Party members (64 per cent) dominated the press coverage. As the leading figures of both the Leave and Remain camps were from the Conservative Party, these results were not surprising.

Figure 5.2: UK politicians quoted in articles

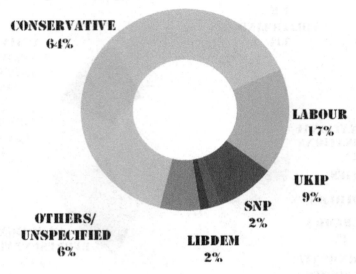

However, what was particularly interesting was the heavy dominance of Leave camp representatives in the press. Of 14 per cent of articles quoting campaign representatives, 74 per cent cited those from the Leave camp. According to a study by Keaveney (2016), the effective campaigning of Leave and its CEO, Matthew Elliott, were the two factors behind this success.

Figure 6.4: Campaign representatives quoted in articles

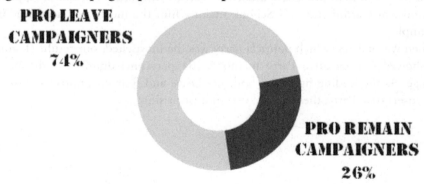

Game-oriented framing of the EU Referendum campaign

Our results revealed the majority of articles (41 per cent) discussing the EU Referendum campaign reinforced the longstanding Eurosceptic narrative of the British press during the campaign period. This was partly because the majority (six out of nine) of the newspapers analysed were skewed towards Brexit, but also the volume of the Referendum news was greatest in the pro-Leave newspapers.

When the tone of news is analysed, we found the negative tone prevailed in the majority of Referendum news, but in particular the future-focused messages of the Remain camp tended to be negative. In contrast, the percentage of positive and negative messages of the Leave camp appeared to be more balanced, as Leave campaigners offered more positive messages on issues such as sovereignty and migration in a post-Brexit future.

In addition to its partisan stand, the press also engaged in game-oriented reporting. More than a half of the Referendum-focused articles (55 per cent) either concentrated on personalities, public figures or on the vote, campaign and Brexit in general. Only 45 per cent of the Referendum articles focused on arguments pertaining to the economy, sovereignty, migration, terrorism and regulation. Press framing is particularly important, as it confers legitimacy upon particular aspects of reality while marginalising other aspects (Lawrence, 2000). Our results show the game framing marginalised the academic and expert voices while putting forward the statements of politicians. Thirty four per cent of coverage focused on UK politicians and of these, the Conservatives (64 per cent) dominated the news. The results also show amongst the campaign spokespeople, the Leave camp succeeded in receiving most of the coverage (74 per cent) in the press. This politicised coverage may have worked well for those who had already established strong views on the Referendum. Yet, the relatively narrow range of information sources, when combined with a strong partisan approach, did little to respond to the need of those seeking high quality information to make up their minds.

References

Anderson, Peter and Weymouth, Anthony (2014) Insulting the Public? The British Press and the European Union, Routledge: Taylor and Francis Group

Blumler, Jay (2016) EEC/EU Campaigning in long term perspective, Jackson, Daniel; Thorsen, Einar and Wring, Dominic (eds) EU referendum analysis 2016: Media, voters and the campaign, Bournemouth: Centre for the Study of Journalism, pp:12. Available online at: http://eprints.bournemouth.ac.uk/24337/1/EU Referendum Analysis 2016 - Jackson Thorsen and Wring v1.pdf

Capella, N. Joseph and Jamieson, Kathleen Hall (1997) Spiral of Cynicism: the press and the public, Oxford University Press

Lawrence, G. Regina (2000) Game framing the issues: Tracking the strategy frame in public policy news, Political Communication, Vol. 17, No. 2 pp 93-114

Levy, A.L. D. Aslan, B. and Bironzo D. (2016) UK press coverage of the EU Referendum. Reuters Institute for the Study of Journalism at the University of Oxford. Available online at: http://reutersinstitute.politics.ox.ac.uk/sites/default/files/UK Press Coverage of the EU Referendum_0.pdf

Page, Benjamin (1996) The mass media as political actors PS: Political Science& Politics, Vol.29, No.1 pp 20-24

Wring, Dominic (2016) From super-market to Orwellian super-state: the origins and growth of newspaper scepticism, Jackson Daniel; Thorsen, Einar and Wring, Dominic (eds) EU referendum analysis 2016: Media, voters and the campaign, Bournemouth: Centre for the Study of Journalism, pp:11. Available online at: http://eprints. bournemouth.ac.uk/24337/1/EU Referendum Analysis 2016 - Jackson Thorsen and Wring v1.pdf

Tversky Amors and Kahneman Daniel (1981). The framing of decisions and the psychology of choice, Science New Series Vol. 211, No. 4481 pp 435-43e8

Note on contributors

Dr Billur Aslan Ozgul received her PhD from Royal Holloway, University of London. Her research interests lie in the fields of media and politics.

Dr David AL Levy is Director of the Reuters Institute for the Study of Journalism at the University of Oxford. He is an expert in media policy and regulation.

Diego Bironzo is Account Director at PRIME Research UK, where he runs international media analysis and communications measurement programmes on behalf of corporate clients and institutions.

Brexit and discrimination in the UK press

Did British newspapers discriminate against migrants during the EU referendum campaign, ask Martin Moore and Gordon N Ramsay

Discriminate: v. 2 (usu. **Discriminate against**) make an unjust distinction in the treatment of different categories of people, especially on the grounds of race, sex or age

Discrimination: n. 1 the action of discriminating against people

Oxford English Dictionary

12. Discrimination (i) The press must avoid prejudicial or pejorative reference to an individual's race, colour, religion, sex, gender identity or to any physical or mental illness or disability

IPSO Editors' Code of Practice

Did parts of the British press discriminate against migrants, or against specific nationalities, during the UK 2016 EU Referendum campaign? If so, then why was there no investigation or sanction on the basis of the code of practice to which most of the press subscribe? These questions have particular relevance given that, following the Referendum, there was an increase in hate crime towards migrants, and East Europeans in particular, which some ascribed to the way the campaign had been conducted, and to media coverage in particular (Weaver, 2016).

The European Commission against Racism and Intolerance (ECRI) Report on the United Kingdom, published a few months after the Brexit campaign in October 2016, made special note of the role of some newspapers in contributing to a heightened environment of racism, xenophobia and intolerance centred in the debate around immigration and Islam in the UK: "Hate speech in some traditional media, particularly tabloid newspapers, continues to be a problem, with biased or ill-founded information disseminated about vulnerable groups, which may contribute to perpetuating stereotypes" (ECRI, 2016).

"It is no coincidence," the Chair of the ECRI continued, "that racist violence is on the rise in the UK at the same time as we see worrying examples of intolerance and hate speech in the newspapers, online and even among politicians" (*Independent*, 2016).

These accusations ought to be treated seriously, particularly since they appear difficult to reconcile with the large quantity of creditable, serious and valuable journalism published in the UK each day by a wide range of news outlets.

This chapter examines these claims on the basis of the articles themselves. It is based on analysis of every article about the Referendum published across 20 leading national news outlets online during the ten-week official EU referendum campaign (14,779 in total) to assess whether the articles, and the way they were presented, can – either individually or collectively – be shown to have moved beyond hostility to being discriminatory. The analysis focuses on news and opinions about migrants, and about specific nationalities, rather than on migration generally or on migration policy. It has been conducted using software called Steno developed specifically for the purpose of digital news content analysis (see Moore and Ramsay, 2015). Following the analysis of the articles themselves, this chapter assesses whether certain coverage can be considered discriminatory. It does this using three separate definitions of discrimination taken from: the Oxford English Dictionary, the UK Equality Act (2010) and the IPSO Editors' Code of Practice.

The research for this chapter is separate to, and methodologically different from, quantitative and qualitative research about media and the EU Referendum done elsewhere. Liz Gerard has done important and exhaustive content research on coverage of immigration in the printed press in 2016 (Gerard, 2017). The RISJ published a report in September 2016 which looked at the main stories deployed by each side in the campaign, based on a sample of national print press coverage (Levy, Aslan and Bironzo, 2016).

Our research found coverage of immigration was both prominent and voluminous in the national press during the EU Referendum campaign. Over the ten-week campaign there were a total of 99 front-page leads about immigration across 15 national print newspapers. Over half these front pages were published by three papers: the Daily Express; the Daily Mail; and The Sun. As well as being prominent, there was also a high volume of coverage overall. The 20 national news outlets studied published a total of 4,383 articles online about the EU Referendum mentioning migrants or immigration. Three in every ten articles about the Referendum, therefore, referred to immigration.

Of the 99 front-page leads about immigration and migrants, 88 (89 per cent) presented a negative picture and 11 presented a neutral perspective. No front-page lead about migration presented a positive picture. Many of the negative front pages focused on the migrants themselves. These included, for example: 'Soaring cost of teaching migrant children' (Daily Express, 16/5/16); 'Migrants cost Britain £17bn a year' (Daily Express, 17/5/16); Brits not fair! 4 in 5 jobs go to foreigners' (The Sun, 19/05/16); 'Migrants Spark Housing Crisis' (Daily Mail, 20/5/16); 'Record number of jobless EU migrants in Britain' (Daily Mail, 27/05/16).

In news, features and opinion pieces, migrants were blamed for many of Britain's economic, social and political ills. Migrants were, for example, blamed for taking primary school places, overwhelming the NHS, putting strains on maternity services, creating a housing crisis, stealing jobs, taking benefits, reducing wages, undermining Britain's security and increasing criminality.

The language used to describe migrants was frequently analogous to language used to describe the movement of water, insects, or epidemics. Migrants were swarming, swamping, storming, invading, stampeding, flocking, over-running, and besieging the UK. Descriptive words were those one usually associates with natural disasters or catastrophes: bombshell, blow, crisis, chaos, soaring, surge, mayday, floodgates, terror, and meltdown.

Migrants were frequently associated with criminality. In some instances this association was explicit. The Daily Express, for example, claimed 'HALF of all rape and murder suspects in some parts of Britain are foreigners' (23/05/16). The Daily Mail led one of its front pages with 'EU killers and rapists we've failed to deport', and The Telegraph with 'European criminals free to live in Britain'. In other instances the association was implicit. The Daily Mail reported on 'A rapist protected by police and the neglected mining town in the East Midlands that has turned into Little Poland'. The man they were referring to was Polish.

News articles about individual migrant stories were used as a platform for columnists to generalise about the criminal tendencies of migrants and the damage caused by migration. A news story about an Albanian migrant, Saloman Barci, for example, was used as an illustration of how migrant criminals are given more money and support than British citizens. The Barci case was, Leo McKinstry wrote in the Express, 'all too typical of our society where the Government neglects the rights of Britons but bends over backwards to support foreigners'(McKinstry, 2016). Richard Littlejohn in the Daily Mail claimed the case 'highlights the madness of Britain's lax border controls, insane interpretation of the Yuman Rites [sic] Act and cavalier disregard for taxpayers' money' (Littlejohn, 2016).

Though the majority of articles mentioning nationalities did so in passing, where evaluative statements were included these tended overwhelmingly to be negative. Certain nationalities were singled out for particularly negative coverage – most notably Albanians and Turks. During the ten weeks, 90 articles were published in which evaluative statements were made about Albanians. All of these articles presented only negative statements. 111 articles were published in which evaluative statements were made about Turks. 98 per cent of these articles presented only negative statements. Were the UK to remain in the EU, these articles asserted, then millions of Turks and Albanians would flood to Britain, bringing with them organised crime, gang violence and general criminality. It was extremely rare in these articles to find someone from either nationality speaking in their own voice.

Coverage of other nationalities, such as Romanians, Poles and Bulgarians, was also substantially negative, though occasional articles referred to benefits associated with migrants from these countries. Often these nationalities were stereotyped – Poles as plumbers or builders, Bulgarians as low-skilled or 'goatherds'. As with Albanians and Turks, other Eastern European nationals were strongly associated with criminality, being called crooks, offenders, lawbreakers, gangsters, murderers, drug dealers, rapists, terrorists, and spongers.

Coverage across all publications was not equal. A small number of publications published a disproportionately high amount of negative coverage of immigration from most of the countries identified, with the Express, Daily Mail and Sun, for example, accounting for 65 per cent of negative statements about Albanians and 73 per cent of those about Turks.

Reflecting public concern and campaign rhetoric?

The news outlets responsible for publishing many of the articles which were highly negative about migrants argued that significant coverage of immigration was necessary, given demonstrably high levels of public concern. This claim is borne out by the monthly Ipsos MORI Issues Index, which shows immigration was one of the top concerns of the public for many months leading up to the Referendum. The amount of coverage, based on public concern, can therefore be justified. This does not, however, explain the overwhelmingly negative tone or the extent to which migrants were blamed for many of Britain's social and economic problems.

The negative reporting can partly be rationalised as a reflection of claims made by campaigners themselves. Leading Leave campaigners including Michael Gove, Priti Patel, Penny Mordaunt and Iain Duncan Smith all made numerous negative statements about the effects of migration on the UK. These included pejorative claims about Albanians by Michael Gove, and about Turks by Penny Mordaunt.

Yet, these outlets also sought out information on their own initiative, particularly with respect to migrants and crime. 'Free to walk our streets,' the Daily Mail reported, '1,000 European criminals including rapists and drugs dealers we should have deported when they were released from prison' (Drury, 2016). 'Shock revelations British port staff face migrants on a DAILY basis many armed with KNIVES' the Express reported on 14 June (Daily Express, 2016). These stories and others were sourced, quite legitimately, by the newspapers themselves, not from campaign leaders. These same newspapers, however, did not seek out countervailing stories which presented a different or more positive picture of migrants.

Was coverage discriminatory?

Coverage of migrants, particularly of Poles, Albanians, Turks, Bulgarians and Romanians was, as illustrated above, consistently and generally unfavourable in certain news outlets. Whether this coverage was discriminatory, however, depends on the definition used.

Using the definition in the Oxford English Dictionary (quoted at the start of this chapter), their coverage was discriminatory. It was consistently unfavourable and made imbalanced and in many cases demonstrably unjust generalisations about categories of people. The OED definition is, however, broad. The Equality Act (2010) has a more detailed definition of discrimination. It defines direct discrimination as 'treating someone with a protected characteristic less favourably than others'. Protected characteristics include; religion, nationality, ethnic or national origin. Again, however, based on this definition it would be difficult not to conclude the coverage by the Daily Express, the Daily Mail, and the Sun was discriminatory.

Yet, it is harder to make such a conclusion based on the Editors' Code of Practice to which these publications subscribe. Clause 12 of the Code of Practice states: 'The press must avoid prejudicial or pejorative reference to an individual's, race, colour, religion, sex, gender identity, sexual orientation or to any physical or mental illness or disability.' The reference to an 'individual' means an article is not discriminatory unless it identifies a specific person. Articles which denigrate nationalities, whether they be Turkish, Polish or Albanian, do not count as discriminatory. Moreover, unlike the Equality Act, the Code of Practice does not include nationality, ethnic or national origin.

This may be why, since it was set up in September 2014 until February 2017, the self-regulatory body which oversees these publications – IPSO – had upheld only one complaint on the grounds of discrimination. This was an individual complaint from Emily Brothers made about transgender discrimination by the Sun (IPSO, 2015). In a general complaint brought against a paper for discrimination against migrants in July 2016, IPSO recorded 'the newspaper [the Daily Express] noted that the complainant had not alleged discrimination towards any individual on the basis of any of the characteristics protected by Clause 12. As such Clause 12 was not engaged' (IPSO, 2016).

It is hard to see when the Code could identify discrimination of nationalities or minority groups. Indeed, arguably the Code gives license to general discrimination by explicitly excluding it from its definition. News outlets know if they do not refer to an individual then they cannot be accused of discrimination under the Code. There is therefore nothing to stop news outlets publishing articles that – by most definitions – are discriminatory against migrants, nationalities, ethnic groups and religious minorities, knowing they will not breach their own code.

References

Daily Express (2016) 'Shock revelations British port staff face migrants on a daily basis many armed with knives,' *Express*, June 14, 2016, http://www.express.co.uk/news/uk/679753/British-port-staff-face-knife-wielding-migrants, accessed April 11, 2017

Drury, Ian (2016) 'Free to walk our streets, 1,000 European criminals including rapists and drug dealers we should have deported when they were released from prison,' *Daily Mail*, April 26, 2016, http://www.dailymail.co.uk/news/article-3558603/Freed-walk-streets-1-000-European-criminals-including-rapists-drugs-dealers-deported-released-prison.html, accessed April 11, 2017

European Commission against Racism and Intolerance (ECRI) (2016) *ECRI Report on the United Kingdom (fifth monitoring cycle)*, Strasbourg: Council of Europe, http://www.coe.int/t/dghl/monitoring/ecri/Country-by-country/United_Kingdom/GBR-CbC-V-2016-038-ENG.pdf (p9), accessed on March 12, 2017

Gerard, Liz (2017) A year of immigration at the white-tops. Available online at http://www.sub-scribe2015.co.uk/whitetops-immigration.html#.WL6DbxKLQdU, accessed on March 14, 2017

Independent (2016) 'Brexit vote has led to noticeable rise in UK xenophobia, watchdog warns,' October 4, 2016, http://www.independent.co.uk/news/uk/home-news/brexit-vote-has-led-to-noticeable-rise-in-uk-xenophobia-watchdog-warns-a7343646.html, accessed on March 14, 2017

IPSO (2015) 00572-15 Trans Media Watch v The Sun. Available online at https://www.ipso.co.uk/rulings-and-resolution-statements/ruling/?id=00572-15, accessed on March 14 2017

IPSO (2016) 04864-16 Young v Daily Express. Available online at https://www.ipso.co.uk/rulings-and-resolution-statements/ruling/?id=04864-16, accessed on March 14 2017

Levy, David, Billur Aslan and Diego Bironzo (2016) 'UK Press Coverage of the EU Referendum', Reuters Institute for the Study of Journalism, Oxford University

Littlejohn, Richard (2016) 'One-legged Albanian killer on benefits,' *Daily Mail*, May 24, 2016, https://www.pressreader.com/uk/daily-mail/20160524/281848642840660, accessed on April 11, 2017

McKinstry, Leo (2016) 'This man is proof we are a nation in moral decline,' *Express*, May 23, 2016, http://www.express.co.uk/comment/columnists/leo-mckinstry/672814/Leo-McKinstry-comment-Immigrant-Saliman-Barci-national-decline, accessed on April 11, 2017

Moore, Martin and Gordon N. Ramsay (2015) 'Data Journalism and the 2015 UK General Election: Media Content Analysis for a Digital Age', Mair, John et al (ed.), *Data Journalism*, Bury St Edmunds: Abramis

Weaver, Matthew (2016) 'Hate crimes soared after EU referendum, Home Office figures confirm' *The Guardian*, October 13, 2016, https://www.theguardian.com/politics/2016/oct/13/hate-crimes-eu-referendum-home-office-figures-confirm, accessed on March 14, 2017

Note on contributors:

Martin Moore is director of the Centre for the Study of Media, Communication and Power at King's College London, and Senior Research Fellow at the Policy Institute, King's College London.

Gordon N Ramsay is deputy director at the Centre for the Study of Media, Communication and Power at King's College London, and Research Fellow at the Policy Institute, King's College London.

A German reaction to Brexit

As well as the challenges Brexit poses to normal journalistic reporting, it also urges us to consider the role of the media in politics and the ever recurring theme of journalistic objectivity. In this context it forced Diana Zimmermann to think about whether the way she perceived it was partly due to her own nationality

I reacted to Brexit in the same way that any other liberal continental European would, or did. I was confused, upset, angry, disappointed. As a journalist I also felt frustrated. When you suddenly have the feeling that a country, which exercises freedom of the press, makes a decision that potentially jeopardises its own well-being, then journalism has somehow failed.

Confessed subjectivity and best-possible objectivity

During the Referendum campaign I tried to gain a deeper understanding of what it was about being German that made me respond to it the way I did.

I am very sceptical of journalists who claim their reports are objective. I do believe in facts, just to be clear on that. But I think an approximation of objectivity can only be achieved if the subjective narrator – in this case the journalist – understands, acknowledges and reveals their own subjective viewpoint.

The majority of my colleagues in the UK make their opinion on certain issues very clear, whereas in Germany, many journalists still believe that they can tell a story 'as it really was' (Leopold von Ranke)[1], even though modern media studies usually reject this. But my delight in reading the wonderfully straightforward and very entertaining views of the British press gradually began to fade away when my attention was diverted to mass provocation in right-wing publications. Stirring up hatred can never be the function of journalism.

In how far what you write about something or someone is as revealing about you as about what you are describing is something I dealt with while working on numerous different topics as a correspondent in Germany, France and East Asia.[2] When I arrived in the UK I had to learn that large sections of the Conservative Party talk similarly to Nigel Farage. And though it contradicted everything I had ever heard about trade negotiations – especially with China – this is a country in which leading politicians appeared to seriously believe they would be better off making a deal with China than to be represented alongside 27 other markets. That baffled me.

It was easy to understand the position of those anti-Europeans left economically deprived by globalisation and, I would claim, by their own government. Many really believe things can't get any worse for them, and travelling throughout the Midlands and Wales it is quite easy to see why.

The biggest challenge for me was to try and understand those Brexiteers who enjoy all of the advantages that come with belonging to the EU but still decided to demonise it for being either a socialist conspiracy or a particularly grotesque embodiment of capitalism.

In a more or less desperate attempt to view the situation more objectively, I visualised to what extent the EU is an institution particularly profitable to Germany, politically and economically, and the way it has been glorified by the Germans throughout recent history. I came to realise how distorted the German view of the EU is – distorted by affection, as opposed to the hostility I was observing in the UK.

For the vast majority of Germans, being European is seen as a perfect way of being a good German. Europe to us has always meant a widening of horizons; a shining future in exchange for a dark past. Its political benefit is obvious, but what is discussed less often is the economic advantage the EU offers Germany, sometimes at the expense of others. The issue of how far this economic benefit is behind our supposed non-material admiration for the EU is discussed even less.

When it became clear the UK, on reviewing its cost-benefit calculation, considered the EU to be unprofitable, it was perceived by the Germans as a narcissistic insult. As a German you are used to people not wanting to have anything to do with Germany, but rejecting the European Union, specifically the idea of European solidarity, is so difficult to understand it is almost unforgiveable, mainly, of course, because Europe saved us. Germany was a nation rescued from fascism by the Brits (among others) and, despite the fact, quite rightly, Germany found itself at the very bottom of every national ranking it was once again allowed to have a say – make decisions even. Europe helped Germany gradually make its way back into the circle of civilised nations and that is why renouncing the EU is considered particularly unsettling.

That is one reason. The other is that the EU was an institutionalisation of a painful recognition in the wake of the Second World War nationalism was the origin of fascism. It was to embody the fact conflict is best avoided through co-operation and by considering everyone as equal. It is difficult to see Brexit as anything other than an expression of a feeling of superiority; we're better off without you. Because we are better.

Disbelief

Despite how surprising the result of the EU Referendum was for almost everyone including Boris Johnson (reassuringly, most of my British colleagues were as stunned as I was) it was still possible to make sense of it and after months of reading, interviewing and reporting I felt well prepared.

We had made visits to every corner of the country for our documentary "Das gespaltene Königreich" (The Disunited Kingdom, ZDF). We travelled through Northern Ireland, Scotland, the south of England and the Midlands, where very often not a single person had anything positive to say about the EU and believed it was responsible for all problems facing the UK – unemployment, lack of integration, low wages, overcrowded schools and hospitals, traffic and the downfall of British industry.

I was genuinely shocked by the state of some of the towns, and by the many people I met who felt neglected and who were now driven by resentment. It made me feel very German because I longingly thought of the Bundesfinanzausgleich (Equalization Payment Mechanism), a system that aims at balancing the wealth of the Bundesländer and leads to a fairer distribution of funds throughout the country.

Whenever I returned to London from these trips I gave a truthful report of how it seemed increasingly unlikely that the UK would remain in the EU. But always, after a few days back in London and some time to soak up the predominantly pro-European sentiment, and the analyses by political economists that 'people will always vote for economic security' I found myself back in the safe familiarity of the bubble. I even put down 52 per cent for Remain in our office bet. Since we are predominantly German, we didn't put any money in. Luckily.

My reluctance to believe in what I had seen and heard, rather than what seemed sensible to me, may also explain why certain aspects of our reporting to Germany from the UK didn't really sink in. Denial. Not because of the echo-chamber phenomenon, and not because we manipulated what was happening in any way, but because the average German views Brexit with even more disbelief than a German correspondent in the UK.

I don't know how often I and my colleagues told audiences of millions that, yes, the Brits have voted for Brexit and it will happen. Yet in Germany there is still the unfaltering belief that the Brits deeply regret what has happened. The days succeeding the referendum result only reinforced this belief.

The German audience watched the mass desertion by those who would have been responsible for seeing it through – Cameron, Farage, Johnson, Gove. This, and the soundbites from one or two taxi drivers grumbling that probably nothing would change for them anyway, consolidated the opinion that someone would somehow realise what a fatal error it all was and would straighten things out again. Even in February this year a news presenter asked me: Is there really no going back?

No. Even on June 24 there was no going back. But the way it seems to be developing is not only starting to gnaw away at the well-meaning belief of the German europhile. They are also refusing to believe it in Scotland, which leads German news anchors to ask foreign correspondents like me: Would the Scots rather stay with *us* (in the EU)?

Nationalism

Us against them. This was the message the Leave campaign sent out. The most serious piece of collateral damage in the fallout of the Referendum is nationalism in Great Britain has fuelled that of other countries. Tit for tat. Bizarrely those promoting this ideology don't seem to understand it. How else is it possible to explain why Theresa May would announce during her speech at Lancaster House that she was ready to wave goodbye to the Single Market, at the same time convinced the EU would offer the UK a good deal. Her reasoning: "I do not believe that the EU's leaders will seriously tell German exporters, French farmers, Spanish fishermen, the young unemployed of the Eurozone, and millions of others, that they want to make them poorer, just to punish Britain and make a political point."[3] This coming from Britain, a safe refuge for pragmatism, the understatement, and ironic distance.

Of all people the Brits, who the Germans admire and envy for so many things, have fired the starting pistol on an era of post-truth. Four million people voted for Nigel Farage in the last election, 17m were seduced by Boris Johnson and convinced by Michael Gove that we have all had enough of experts. They will now be drawn into a Brexit à la Theresa May which, in my view, is likely to be most damaging to anyone who does not belong to the ultra-rich elite.[4]

Balance in the face of lies

The role of the UK media in the Referendum was very educational. As mentioned, I very much admire British journalism in general, but as soon as things started to become serious, it wasn't as much fun anymore. Its very partisan nature eventually came to dominate both sides of the campaign making it seem as though it was okay to leave out factual arguments.

That was one extreme. But the post-referendum discussion surrounding the BBC was even more revealing. In an attempt to occupy the middle ground throughout the debate the BBC was then accused its reporting had been 'too balanced'.[5] This was a lesson I hope will be learned in Germany, especially now we are preparing for general elections in September. Breitbart News hasn't made its debut in Germany yet, and there is much doubt as to whether the concept will catch on there, simply because of the media's very different perception of itself and its role.[6]

The lesson I have learned from the UK media and from Brexit also leaves me thinking it would be much more beneficial for German mass media to take on clear positions. Now, more than in a long time, a journalist who is, as a result of

professional research and investigation of their own subjectivity, convinced of the fatal consequences of a certain political path has a responsibility to make it known.[7]
Translated by Elizabeth Moseley

Notes

[1] "To history has been assigned the office of judging the past, of instructing the present for the benefit of future ages. To such high offices this work does not aspire: It wants only to show what actually happened (*wie es eigentlich gewesen*)". Leopold von Ranke, Sämtliche Werke Bd. 33/34, Leipzig 1885, S. 7

[2] When you are in Germany, you naturally don't spend much time thinking about what makes your reporting German. In France you certainly do. But in terms of the significance of the EU, France and Germany are, by way of exception, *d'accord*. Of course in France there is the Front National, and in Germany the AfD, and in both countries there is increasing skepticism with regard to the EU, but there is no traditional party where a large majority of its members or MPs seriously believe in leaving an institution famou sly known to be powered by a Franco-German engine. However China, a centralised state which (albeit falsely) claims to have made barely any adjustments to its governmental form for 3000 years, doesn't really understand the concept of the EU. At the peak of the Euro Crisis, it was always a question of why Angela Merkel couldn't just get on and solve the problem. But the Chinese have come to accept the idea that the EU is a rational concept. The *Global Times*, mouthpiece of the Chinese Government, reacted surprisingly bluntly to the referendum result: "The UK is just over 300 years old. In its heyday it was known as an empire on which the sun never set, with colonies all over the world. Now it is stepping back to where it was. Britons are already showing a losing mind-set. They may become citizens of a nation that prefers to shut itself from the outside world." http://www.globaltimes.cn/content/990440.shtml

[3] Theresa May, Lancaster House, 17.1.2017

[4] On March 22 *The Guardian* reported both on rising inflation that would most affect the poorest households and also on the fact that the majority of British millionaires would welcome a Brexit.

[5] https://www.dropbox.com/s/8rp7fbc1zbv8qd2/EU%20Referendum%20Analysis%202016%20-%20Jackson%20Thorsen%20and%20Wring%20v1.pdf?dl=0
The fact that there are currently a number of reports about the potentially fatal consequences of Brexit has not only prompted 70 MPs to come forward and complain about the BBC presenting a negative picture of it, but it also raises the question of why such reports did not materialise before the referendum. http://www.telegraph.co.uk/news/2017/03/22/stop-bias-against-brexit-face-fine-bbc-warned/

[6] It is no coincidence that in Germany there is a current attempt to ban hate speech on the Internet, despite concerns regarding European and constitutional legislative concerns about the right to freedom of speech.

[7] Anyone who grew up in Germany during the 70s and 80s, and who considered journalism as a continuation of "Education to Maturity" will be familiar with Theodor W. Adornos definition:
"The foremost requirement from all education is that Auschwitz cannot happen again."

(„Die Forderung, daß <u>Auschwitz</u> nicht noch einmal sei, ist die allererste an Erziehung."
Erziehung zur Mündigkeit, Frankfurt a.M.:Suhrkamp, 1. Auflage 1971, S. 88.)

Note on contributor

Diana Zimmermann was born in 1971 in Frankfurt/Main and is the ZDF correspondent in London, responsible for the UK and Ireland. She studied comparative literature, sinology and history in Berlin, Paris and Kunming. She was a reporter for ARTE in Strasbourg and Berlin and a correspondent for German public broadcaster ARD in Beijing (2003). She has worked for ZDF in China and East Asia from 2007-2011 and from 2011-2015 was the head of auslandsjournal, ZDF's foreign affairs magazine.

The Chinese media on Brexit: a matter of perspective

What impact did Brexit have in China and across its vast population, if anything? Was it reported? Did anyone care? Xiaochen Guo has collected reports on Brexit from more than six journalistic institutions across the mainland, Hong Kong and Taiwan and offers a comprehensive description of Brexit in the eyes of Chinese media from various perspectives

China's mainland, Hong Kong and Taiwan are very different, not least in policy and tradition. This chapter considers content and structural issues around the reporting of Brexit in these three distinct areas.

Mainland media: Different, but respectful

The state-owned media, in the guise of People's Daily and the business media represented by Nanfang Metropolis Daily, are two groups well-matched in strength. As the national party newspaper, People's Daily has a very high impact on the public, while Nanfang Metropolis Daily, one of Chinese most respected newspapers, has the largest circulation among domestic metropolitan newspapers. These two newspaper brands are quite representative when chosen to be sources to research significant international events and public opinion.

All the news on Brexit in the two newspapers starting from Referendum day June 23 to December 23 was researched. During the six months, People's Daily published 25 articles related to the theme of Brexit, whereas Nanfang Metropolis Daily put up 42 related articles. Figure 1 shows the number of reports in 30-day time frames.

The quantity of reports in Nanfang Metropolis Daily is nearly twice that of People's Daily. Both media maintained a high degree of attention to the event within the first 30-days after the Referendum. However, the reports in both media in the following five 30-day time frames were almost none, resulting in difficulty for the public to follow events.

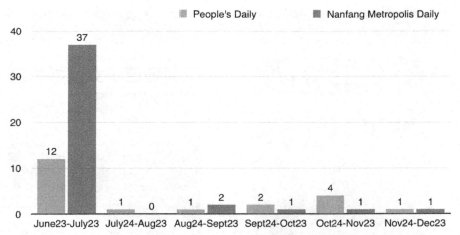

Figure 1. Quantity of reports on People's Daily and Nanfang Metropolis Daily of each 30-day time frames

The reason was largely due to the rapid ending of the Brexit debate itself, from the finish of the Referendum to the change of Prime Minister from David Cameron to Theresa May.

In terms of the form of news reports, the difference between the state-owned media and business media was quite pronounced. In the 25 reports of the People's Daily, more than a quarter of the news was reported in the form of news briefs in thumbnail size, including the results of the Referendum, Mrs May becoming prime minister, the verdict of the Supreme Court etc. It was interesting that Brexit and related news never appeared on the front page of the newspaper in six months.

In contrast, Brexit news occupied the front page of Nanfang Metropolis Daily twice (see Figure 2) – once on June 25 about the results of the Referendum, and the other on July 12 about the new Prime Minister Theresa May. In addition, in June, there were four special reports, explaining in depth the whole process of the Referendum and analysing varying points of view from different social communities. Much space was used to argue impacts of Brexit for the United Kingdom, the European Union and even the rest of the world. At most there were 17 reports about the event in one day, including two editorials.

Besides news of Brexit itself, Nanfang Metropolis Daily used other forms of support coverage, such as profile and historical commentaries. After the departure of David Cameron, the entertainment section published a major article titled 'Cameron's Story', tracing his childhood and political experience in a sympathetic tone. Two months later, its historical comment section published 'Iron Lady's Road to Prime Minister', which compared the political experience of Theresa May with that of Margaret Thatcher. Different from the seriousness of a national party newspaper, the Nanfang Metropolis Daily was able to put a human focus on details that made the articles more accessible.

Figure 2. British news on the front page of Nanfang Metropolis Daily

As a crucial function of mass communication, agenda-setting plays an important role in news selection. Different media have different standards of agenda-setting. From the aspects of content, People's Daily and Nanfang Metropolis Daily obviously have different emphases.

The main issues People's Daily discussed can be summarised into the following three aspects:

Consequences of Brexit especially in economic terms

Economic issues were reported from both domestic and international aspects. Fluctuations in the property market and the panic of British business executives were mentioned many times. Prospective inflation and changes in the pattern of imports and exports caused by Sterling devaluation were also the focuses of discussion.

Diplomatic relations between the United Kingdom, the United States and the European Union

'The United States is Facing its Closest Ally's Departure from the European Union' concluded although the United States will have more difficulty in interfering in European affairs after Brexit, Britain is still its most reliable partner. 'Britain Hopes for Stable Relationships with Germany and France' showed although the British chose to leave the European Union, still, they cannot leave Europe.

Alternative Brexit models

More than a quarter of the reports explored the two Brexit models – hard and soft. 'Hard' Brexit implies the UK can refuse to compromise on any issues just like any other country outside Europe, and 'soft' Brexit suggests UK can enjoy the benefits of European Union while holding its own sovereignty. People's Daily never gave a preference of solution, but it did conclude it was a tough choice to make for Britain.

In content terms , Nanfang Metropolis Daily is less serious. There were more Brexit reports, ranging from the economy, politics, entertainment and even sports news. Nanfang Metropolis Daily usually pays more attention to individuals rather than events.

For example, new Prime Minister Theresa May, her predecessor David Cameron, or even murdered Labour Party MP Jo Cox came to be core characters in Brexit stories.

Secondly, reports about Theresa May were not confined to her political activities, but her gender became a highlight. There were seven features with the title containing words like 'female' or 'Iron Lady', accounting for one-sixth of the total reports. An article tilted 'Two Women's War' described the competition between the two female Conservative Party leadership candidates Andrea Leadsom and Theresa May.

Thirdly, a wide range of other Brexit-related ramifications were reported. '300 Non-resident Players May Leave Due to Brexit' stated the possibility the English Premiership would be hit by both losses of footballers and reduction of sponsorship.

However, there was a report describing the benefits for Chinese customers of shopping in the UK because of Sterling's devaluation, and a big picture took more than half of the page listing luxury brands and products, showing price differences before and after Brexit, which made news reporting attractive to the consumer audience.

In general, reporting on Brexit in mainland China is quite neutral. State-owned media were more serious and restrained with accurate sources of information; business media had diverse forms and perspectives to make articles more readable. All media paid a great deal of attention to Brexit and reported the process factually. Most importantly, all media showed respect for the choice made by majority of British people through the civil and democratic process.

Taiwan media: This is not about Britain; this is about us

Although Taiwan is an integral part of China, its political system differs from the mainland.

It is necessary to study the reports from Taiwan media to better understand the overall Greater China reaction to the Brexit. Reports on Brexit from United Daily News Net (https://udn.com) and Liberty Times Net (http://www.ltn.com.tw) were used for data collection. These are Taiwan's two most viewed news websites. Not surprisingly, Brexit was reported in time and with a high accuracy, but editorial sections were not that harmonious.

Affected by the opposing parties, Taiwanese media is mainly divided into two camps – one is pro-mainland (United Daily News Net) whose reports are almost the same as the mainland's, and the other is Liberal (Liberty Times Net), advocating independence, accustomed to stigmatising the Beijing government, trying to separate Taiwan from the mainland. The object of its reports on Brexit was quite explicit to use the process of referendum as an example to be independent from the People's Republic of China. Editorials stated the system of a referendum was flawless to express the people's will. In general, Taiwan media reported Brexit more or less to have their own political purpose instead of pure journalistic duty.

Hong Kong media: Finance, still finance.

As one of the world's financial centres, economic development is the top issue as far as Hong Kong is concerned. Reports from the Ming Pao and Hong Kong Economic Journal, which are the two most widely circulated serious newspapers and have good credibility across the public, were researched.

To both publications the main concern was the impact of Brexit on the worldwide economic situation. The dominant view was the British had created a precedent, causing the suspicion other European countries to question the value of the European Union, and thus provide potential ripple effects of leaving the EU, which would become one of the factors of future financial market fluctuation (Chuangcheng Ye 2016).

For this reason, some editorials appealed for the Hong Kong Government to be cautious about the Brexit effect, to stay vigilant against radical politics, and to protect the relationship between Hong Kong and the mainland, so they could mutually benefit and remain a win-win situation.

Conclusion

With the popularity of globalisation, people are becoming closer to each other. Britain is no longer an isolated island. The world has been affected by Brexit and China is no exception. As an important part of mass communication, media should disseminate accurate information, and to help guide public opinion positively.

In the case of Brexit news reporting, Taiwan, Hong Kong and mainland China had their own different agendas. News styles of the mainland media are greatly affected by the antecedence of the media. However, on the whole objective journalism was maintained.

Taiwanese media, controlled by parties with extremely different points of view, can be a good way to reflect the current political ecology of Taiwan. Although the history of Hong Kong and the United Kingdom are inextricably linked, now the two are more like just economic cooperative partners. That is why the Hong Kong media focused on the economic aspect. However, no matter what style reporting is undertaken, most media in Greater China largely exist based on the principle of recording and respecting what has happened. The wheel of history rolls along: people go, but stories remain.

References

BBC (2017) Brexit: What are the options? January 15. Available online at http://www.bbc.co.uk/news/uk-politics-37507129, accessed on March 9, 2017.
Chuangcheng Ye (2016) Hanjie He: There are certainly challenges. October 11. Available online at http://news.mingpao.com/pns/dailynews/web_tc/article/20161011/s00004/1476121683231
LTN (2016) Liming Yao talked about referendum in Taiwan, June 23. Available online at http://news.ltn.com.tw/news/politics/breakingnews/1739871, accessed on March 9, 2017.

Note on the contributor

Xiaochen Guo is a postgraduate student at the School of Journalism, Communication University of China, majoring in New Media Journalism. Her interest lies in the study of media ecology. She most recent research looked at sports communication and promoting sports brands using new media. Her email is melody_0509@126.com.

The ground war across the UK's nations, regions and communities

***

What script? Whose script? Our script!

Neil Fowler

The clear message that emerged from the 2016 Referendum was that many voters, and especially substantial numbers from outside London and those not living in the lee of the more elite universities, didn't necessarily follow the script that had been written for them.

That script, which broadly meant they should subscribe to the lead of their elders and betters and vote to remain, had been drafted for them by senior politicians of all the traditional political parties, rubber stamped by many leading journalists and academics, and endorsed by the right-thinking class amongst us.

The only trouble, of course, was that they rebelled. Not everywhere, evidently, but in sufficiently large numbers to bring about the result to leave the European Union.

Why did no-one see it coming? Nigel Farage, Boris Johnson and Michael Gove had all apparently gone off to their beds early on Referendum night, convinced they had lost – so they didn't spot it either.

Well it cannot be said all these groups and individuals hadn't been warned. A small perusal of Matthew Goodwin's and Robert Ford's detailed research in their book Revolt on the Right, which exposed in plain sight the depth and breadth of anti-EU feeling across the political spectrum, should have struck a few warning bells. But Goodwin and Ford talked about those members of society away from the mainstream of London and Oxbridge life – and many failed to see that not everyone would do what they were expected to do.

In this section our authors take a wander around the UK, looking at how voters and the media interacted, and try to ascertain why it all actually happened.

Michael Gilson has edited daily newspapers in three of the UK's four nations (and held senior responsibility on a paper in the fourth), so he is supremely qualified to cast an overview and look at why local publications didn't predict the outcome.

In talking to editors on the ground he believes the result, along with the limited role regional and local papers were able to play in it, had dealt a mortal blow to the sector.

"We simply did not have the troops on the ground nor the support of enough of the citizens to fight the battle against what we now know to be the 'post truth' society we were entering," he says.

"For years we had known we were at risk of irrelevancy as our business model was eroded by digital technology, the flight of advertising and failure to build subscription on the back of decent, revelatory journalism."

Sunderland is renowned for its ability to produce speedy election results – so its early announcement that the city had overwhelmingly voted Leave produced the night's first shock wave.

Lee Hall is a media academic at the city's university and he has talked to three close observers of how Sunderland was castigated for voting the way it did and how it is fighting back.

"Now Sunderland, like the rest of the UK, awaits the outcome of Brexit negotiations," he says. "Nissan has been handed undisclosed Government assurances that the Sunderland plant will be cushioned from any trade tariffs. The predicted Eurogeddon has not transpired. And only time will tell whether Sunderland and Britain hurt its own interests by voting for Brexit. For now the city is working on a new image to project to a post-Brexit world."

Martin Shipton has covered Welsh politics for some 20 years, working on The Western Mail and Wales on Sunday. Like many he was surprised at the way the principality voted as the nation has benefited greatly from European funds over the years

"In Wales it wasn't a case of biting the hand that feeds you, but of biting off the hand that feeds you," he says. He believes the weakness of the Welsh indigenous media, along with London's disregard of Wales may have been a factor.

"In the main, the more than 90 per cent of newspaper buyers living in Wales who choose to buy a title published in England, will find out little about decisions affecting their lives made by the Welsh Government and the Welsh Assembly."

If Wales was being seen to turn on a generous benefactor, what was happening in Northern Ireland? Here the vote to remain was at odds with the overall result and put in to play, again, the whole future of the island of Ireland.

Steve McGookin, a long-time staffer at the Financial Times, has recently returned to his native Belfast. He asks whether the challenge of Brexit proves to be the issue that finally helps break Northern Ireland's traditional political and sectarian impasse? Or will it simply represent one more area of continuing division? Many commentators have differing views.

Broadcaster and former BBC Scotland Business Editor Maurice Smith believes Brexit almost passed the Scottish political and media scene by. So few people in Scotland – and certainly none of the commentariat, right or left, nationalist or unionist – expected a Brexit victory that it scarcely registered on the media Richter scale.

And no-one saw a President Trump, scion of a Scottish emigrant, arriving, too, he says. Now the focus is on a renewed independence campaign – but neither side will be looking to recruit the nation's latest export to make it big overseas.

Tor Clark, co-editor of this book, and with a detailed knowledge of the Leicestershire media marketplace, spoke to journalists closely involved in reporting how the Referendum debate evolved across the county at the same time as the local football club was creating its own earthquake. And they found the debate lacking.

"Regional journalists, in this fairly representative area, approached the Referendum like a normal political campaign and found it was different," he says. "They justify their balanced and impartial approach to trying to serve their readers but are honest enough to admit some of the most spurious arguments perhaps ought to have had greater interrogation."

And staying in Leicester – well initially anyway – Barnie Choudhury looks at how another trick the media missed was not focusing enough on the 'Eastern Exiters', voters whose background in the UK may not have been as long established as others.

"Over the decades," he says, "the media has failed to report on a self-evident truth: after a period, many immigrants, no matter their colour, begin to share the same values, assumptions and thoughts as the native population, on most issues."

And can his conclusion be extrapolated to cover all aspects of how the media and politicians in the nations and the regions of the UK looked at the Referendum debate in the run up to June 23, 2016?

To paraphrase Choudhury, could it be that: "Over the decades (local) media and politicians have failed to realise a self-evident truth: after a period, many journalists, MPs and councilors, no matter their political colour, begin to share the same values, assumptions and thoughts as themselves on most issues. The native population doesn't."

One for much further discussion.

Despatches from the frontline.
Did Brexit finally plunge the regionals into irrelevance?

Losing the war to a tsunami of prejudice and opinion, swept away by social media, bypassed by voters or a finest hour, standing by facts and a real voice for readers? Michael Gilson canvasses opinion and adds his own

You could tell which one was the sole Leave-supporting journalist in the newsroom. After a long night out in the counting halls most sat around in stunned silence or muttered in shocked tones. The Brexiteer, vocal in calling out his liberal colleagues before the vote, now decided discretion was the better part of valour, only a semi-embarrassed smile betraying him. He was on the victorious side.

Every single other journalist now in the newsroom in the early hours of June 24, 2016, including this editor, had simply not seen it coming. Had, if you like, underestimated the groundswell moving under our feet. Sure enough we were covering a patch, Brighton, which voted almost 70 per cent to Remain, but around us in the estates that border the city a bloody nose had been dealt.

We might have guessed Eastbourne would go. But more than 57 per cent to Leave? Worthing and Adur similar votes that outstripped national support for Brexit, fuelled, we now surmised, by those left behind by the sunny South Coast's surface sense of well-being. And liberal Lewes, a narrow verdict for stay, those living outside the picture-postcard centre, the spiritual home of Thomas Paine, almost delivering one of the shocks of the night.

Beneath the tiredness another feeling stirred. How had we, those whose job it is to have our ear to the ground, guessed it so wrong?

There were two thoughts that followed. Had we enough troops these days to accurately reflect the sense of disillusion and disenfranchisement that was arising in the run up to the vote outside of 'right-on' Brighton city where our main business was done, our contacts largely made? And secondly had we simply been swamped by social media?

Our attempts to explain and spell out, report all sides, hold live debates, finally to gently ask our readers to err on the side of caution, refrain from a leap into the unknown been a pointless waste of time compared to the avalanche of self-affirming digital communications that we saw happening out there?

We still believed it would be trusted journalism, not rabid opinion, that people would in the end turn to help them decide. We doubt this now. On June 24 no-one had heard of 'fake news' and 'post-truth society' was only something written about in academic journals.

And perhaps other thoughts emerged only later. Had the absence of journalists in numbers in the crumbling towns and estates of England helped create a democratic deficit that, over the years, led to voices of anguish from those places going unheard? Was the vote to leave the EU an almost cathartic two fingers to the liberal establishment, which included journalism, staffed overwhelmingly as it is by those with the financial support needed nowadays to get into the trade and then survive on its meagre wages?

The sign of the monkey

Peter Barron is what many would call a proper editor. For 17 years he was, and in truth still is, the face of the Northern Echo. He didn't just decide the splash every day, drive the news agenda and write leaders. He was a PR man, a revenue generator, a glad handler, a marketer and an evangelical for his title too. This job description is fast disappearing.

It was H'Angus the Monkey who first alerted Barron to the rise of an anti-establishment feeling in 'left-behind' Britain. In 2002 in Hartlepool Stuart Drummond standing as a joke candidate dressed as the local football team's mascot and promising free bananas for all voters beat the establishment Labour candidate to become Mayor.

"Why on earth would they vote for a man in a monkey suit unless there was a deep dissatisfaction with mainstream politics?" says Barron.

So his newspaper learnt that lesson and factored it in to its reporting. But there's a difference between an election for the Mayor of Hartlepool and leaving the country's biggest trading partner for the unknown.

For the EU Referendum the lessons of Hartlepool would be acknowledged. The views of politicians would be respected but not given undue weight. For Barron it was North East business leaders, a large constituency for his newspaper, who he would turn his ear towards. And they were virtually unanimous. Flagship companies like Nissan and Hitachi were all expressing concern to him. He had absolutely no qualms about pinning his newspaper's colours to the mast in a regional industry whose leaders are generally loathe to express any political opinion at all.

"After the referendum was announced I decided the paper should come out in favour of Remain based on a business leaders over politicians philosophy," he says,

"Jobs and the economy were the biggest issues in the North East and we asked readers to listen more closely to the job creators than the politicians."

In the end 57.3 per cent of voters in Darlington, core Northern Echo territory, voted to Leave but Barron is unrepentant, based on his understanding of his readership. There has been no backlash against the paper and recently, while filming a Brexit documentary for the BBC, he detected signs that opinion in the North East was swinging.

"The main theme that came out of talking to voters for the documentary was that they didn't really understand the full implications of what they were voting for," he says.

Barron would have been only too happy to stand by his decision at the Northern Echo and continue the debate as Britain moves towards divorce. He was shuffled towards the exit door a few months before the vote as the financial cuts sweeping the regional press became a torrent.

What steel in Sheffield?

Jarvis Cocker, lead singer of Pulp and probably one of Sheffield's greatest imports after steel was shocked that his home city voted narrowly to Leave. "That wasn't the outcome I expected," he told The Observer recently. Nancy Fielder, editor of The Sheffield Star for a little more than a year, was not.

"It's funny the BBC came on to us the following morning and were asking us to talk about the shock in Sheffield, but we didn't feel that. Perhaps nationally but we definitely picked up the Leave mood in our city. There was real fear out there, people were scared about jobs and the future, whether those fears were justified around the EU is another matter," she says.

Unlike Barron, Fielder is determinedly opposed to having the Star take a political stance on issues like Brexit and neither on the front page nor in its leader columns did the newspaper ever take a view.

"I don't think that was our job," she says." Our job is simply to inform and educate. We did know though that to come down for Remain would have flown in the face of what a lot of our readers were thinking."

She puts this understanding down to the structure of the Johnston Press-owned newspaper. While she also edits the Doncaster Star, the weekly Sheffield Telegraph and two other weeklies, it is the seven communities journalists (another team fills the back of the newspapers) working across all those titles, she insists, who were out of the ground picking up the aforementioned fears of voters.

While Fielder maintains that her titles do have enough resources to cover what is a large multi-title patch, she does worry about diversity in the newsroom. Few reporters now can afford to enter journalism from what we used to call working-class estates when most newspaper groups now insist on a degree and a post-graduate qualification.

"I come from a working class area of Sheffield so I do bring in stories myself from those places but you do have to worry about that connection," she says. "There's a real danger we will lose it if we don't have people from those areas coming into newsrooms. Even older women who know the struggles of life are thin on the ground."

She adds that in 17 years working across the region she's only ever worked with two non-white journalists.

Dark messages from the Black Country

The messages being received from his readers were clear to editor of the Express and Star, Wolverhampton, Keith Harrison.

The Black Country was becoming disillusioned with high levels of EU immigration into its communities. That, and border control, were the issues picked up in the newsroom and through the title's digital platforms.

For Harrison the support for these feelings led the newspaper into a subtle, rather than overt, support for Leave. Wolverhampton eventually voted 62.6 per cent Leave. Critics argued he was decidedly less subtle nor that balanced ahead of this year's General Election when he told his readers that Theresa May would make a "far superior" Prime Minister than Jeremy Corbyn.

Despite that controversy, on Brexit, he was, he says, surprised to see some regional titles boldly declaring for one side or the other believing the risk of alienating some readers was too great.

"People trust their local newspaper, far more than a politicised national title," he says, "But to win that trust, newspapers have to maintain high editorial standards without being drawn into political partisanship or tabloid name-calling.

"It has to be interesting. It has to be credible. But most importantly, it has to be right."

Harrison bristles at suggestions the media should challenge readers' views on immigration seeing a danger that the implication is they are 'inherently wrong, at best, or racist, at worst'.

"I don't think it is right for a newspaper to respond to people who are unhappy with their lot on a Wolverhampton council estate by telling them they are wrong," he says. "There is a risk that this merely feeds into the disconnect felt between the populace and the 'establishment' that undoubtedly played a role in the Brexit result."

Harrison does see dangers presented by lack of journalistic resources on the ground but believes social media must be harnessed by newspapers, to supplement reporting, rather than letting it fill the void left behind.

"Sometimes the best way to 'speak truth unto power' is to provide a platform and let people speak for themselves – no matter how unpalatable that may be to social norms elsewhere," he says.

A lack of local and regional resources?

Sarah Kavanagh, campaigns officer for the National Union of Journalists, finds it hard to accept that regional titles now have the resources to properly represent the news and views of the communities they represent.

But she agrees journalism, particularly on a regional and local level, is struggling to represent huge swathes of the country because of a lack of diversity in newsrooms. While she says it is too big a leap to blame this for any democratic deficit that might have led to Brexit she does have concerns that voices are now missing from mainstream media.

"If the media is seen as homogenous and not representative of anything other than the middle class then people will turn away from it," she says, "If they can't see themselves and their concerns and lives reflected in it they will conclude it is not for them and what fills the gap will often be fake news.

"I think the identity of the journalist must affect the questions they ask, the angles they report, the experience they bring to what they think is a story. Lack of diversity in the news room must have an impact on the breadth of coverage"

But even if this wasn't so the wider concern for the NUJ is boots on the ground.

"The main players Johnston Press, Trinity, Archant, Newsquest are still making profits but cutting back further and further. Journalists have no time to cover patches or even get out of the office. There are less publications and those still lucky enough to live in an area where there are still titles find smaller numbers of journalists trying to hit click targets and turn around press releases," she says. "How can journalists get close to communities? If you look at the Newsquest titles in south London 12 journalists are producing news for 11 titles and eight websites. It's unsustainable."

A disconnect between the trade and its role

Today few give journalism an importance that its dwindling band of practitioners do. There is a disconnect between the trade itself and an understanding of the role it performs in democracies around the world. Digital technologies having opened up a closed shop for all to become involved, goes the theory.

To compound this sense of self-importance I choose an overblown historical metaphor to illustrate my own view of Brexit and journalism's role in the debate.

For rather like Rome when the Visigoths and Vandals came calling in the 5th Century we were just too worn down by internal strife, indecision, shrinking resources and lack of leadership to do much about the seismic eruption the EU Referendum visited upon us. We simply did not have the troops on the ground nor the support of enough of the citizens to fight the battle against what we now know to be the 'post truth' society we were entering.

For years we had known we were at risk of irrelevancy as our business model was eroded by digital technology, the flight of advertising and failure to build subscription on the back of decent, revelatory journalism.

Brexit delivered a heavy blow, certainly to print journalism and its digital bolt-on. The rise of nationalism and the crumbling of post-war liberal consensus embodied by the European Union was fuelled by global capitalism and given impetus by the 2008 economic meltdown for which few responsible paid any penalty at all. The lack of control over our lives and the ineffectual nature of governments in the face of these global forces inevitably brought a backlash, a protectionism, which traded on our forgetfulness about our history.

Genuine concerns about a deskilled society gave rise to fear and from fear it was an easy leap to hate. Foreigners, Muslims, Mexicans, the list is long and getting longer. Those who saw their chance to hark back to simpler days of British supremacy were quick to realise objective journalism would have to be bypassed if they were to reach their high-walled rose garden. That was the easy part. So powerful and woven into our lives was the white noise of social media and so denuded were parts of the media that it was a no contest.

But there is a simple question we must ask ourselves. Where do we get our information about the world, whether that be Syria or in the neighbourhood where we all live? Journalists would deserve all the opprobrium they would get to claim the answer lies solely with them. But if we do not stake a genuine claim for a role in this process we will forfeit our right to relevancy.

For it is true the role of journalism, where not simply chasing clicks and car chase video, is to continue to speak truth unto power, to lift the rocks and find out what is underneath, to do all this for its citizens. For what is obvious is that when journalism is removed a void fills its place. For what else is fake news but the filling of that void with rumour, red herring, spin and mischief making?

Despite the noble efforts of Barron, Fielder and Harrison we saw this only too clearly in the run up to the Referendum. When they weren't working around the clock to put objective questions to all sides of the debate journalists watched in awe as social media piled up Everests of clicks on the flimsiest of self-affirming half-truths. And when they did bother to engage with us it was often a hundred of so Facebookers simply writing 'Leave' under our free-to-air stories.

In the days that followed the vote Brighton MP Caroline Lucas told The Argus how distraught she was by what had happened. It was a heartfelt lament. 'Get over it you bitch' was the first comment on our Facebook page, its poster, place of work and likes proudly identified, pictures of his family festooning his own page. The next ten comments congratulated him on this perspicacity.

Of course the blurring of fact and opinion is nothing new. Newspapers pioneered it. Hearst's titles turned into a high art form. Some will say we are reaping what we sowed. But there is another side.

A decade ago newspapers, radio stations and local TV were the glue of social cohesion. Hardly a council decision was made nor a crime committed without citizens knowing about it from us. Leaders were held to account, views aired. In truth trainee journalists got bored doing stories about crumbling council house stock and jobless figures, about waiting lists and pelican crossing campaigns, but they were giving voice to the community and more often than not they got results or at the very least there was debate.

Of course this is still happening but in nowhere near the quantity and quality of a decade ago. Journalists often joke they got into the trade because they were poor at mathematics but even we can work out that the loss of 8,000 jobs since 2008 and the need to feed multi-platforms at the same time has seriously damaged the ability to properly rather than superficially cover the patch. The democratic deficit caused by journalism's crisis is not just a neat phrase. It is real and, for me, it played a part in the degradation of debate, whatever side you were on, that we saw in the run up to June 23 last year.

Note on the contributor
Michael Gilson was a long-serving newspaper editor. He was editor of The Argus, Brighton and before that the Belfast Telegraph, The Scotsman, The News, Portsmouth and the Peterborough Evening Telegraph. In 2013 he was the Northern Ireland Journalist of the Year. He was one of only four regional newspaper editors to give evidence to the Leveson Inquiry in 2011-12.

Sunderland: Brexit city to culture club

How a city became a media symbol for divided Britain and fought back. Lee Hall gathers new perspectives from the Daily Mirror's Kevin Maguire, the Sunderland Echo's Gavin Foster and Sunderland 2021 UK City of Culture bid director Rebecca Ball

On the face of it, Sunderland's Brexit vote was an act of monumental and wilful self-harm. This city, apparently so reliant on Nissan and the Japanese car company's supply chain for jobs and a major recipient of EU infrastructure funding, appeared to reject ties to the European marketplace and risk plunging its economy into uncertainty. But, why?

Daily Mirror associate editor Kevin Maguire, a visiting professor in journalism at the city's university and devoted Sunderland football fan, believes the vote was a clear rejection of the status quo. "Brexit split Britain every way it could," he said. "In Sunderland it felt like a protest vote by people with little to lose when wages are stagnating, living standards falling, job insecurity spreading and public services deteriorating."[1]

Just days before the Referendum, Maguire and his Sky News punditry foil Andrew Pierce were in Sunderland. In a university lecture hall they addressed the topic of Brexit before an audience of 200 people, many of them students and most of them young voters. After their Punch and Judy political sparring ended in a unanimous points win for Maguire in front of a home crowd, the pair surveyed the audience. 'Who will vote Remain?' A sea of hands went up. 'Who will vote Leave?' Fewer than half a dozen hands. That's certainly not how it went on the night.

First to Leave

By the end of June 23, Sunderland was on the verge of becoming a poster city for Brexit Britain – in part because it was the first to declare for Leave – 61.3 per cent to 38.7 per cent. As ever on polling night, the eyes of the media were fixed on the city, thanks to a track record for producing results in record time. The electoral production line here has drawn inevitable comparisons with the car plant that has been such a boon to the city's economy. Sunderland is usually first to declare, but this time was pipped to the post[2] by near neighbours Newcastle.

In fact, it was Newcastle's results that sounded the alarm bell for the Remain campaign and therefore could be seen as a more profound moment in the story of Brexit night. Just ten miles up the road from Sunderland, the margin of victory was slender – much narrower than had been expected. Newcastle voted remain by 50.7 per cent to 49.3 per cent. The currency markets wobbled. The pundits sat up. More eyes gazed at Sunderland.

Most commentators were expecting Wearsiders to back the Leave campaign, but not by such a convincing margin. When Sunderland's returning officer declared the result, the winning tally surpassed the 60 per cent benchmark viewed as a strong showing for Brexit. Commentators veered into 'too close to call' territory, though a wafer thin margin in favour of remain was still widely touted as the most likely outcome. As those blinking at screens into the night and many people waking up the next morning discovered, the polls were wrong – again.

Iconic image

In reality, Sunderland's result was not the decisive moment of an extraordinary night. Nor was the margin of victory especially high – 80 areas of the country voted more strongly to exit the EU. But its status as a Brexit city – and a perceived decision to fire a bazooka into its foot at point blank range – was making headlines.

"It was the early hours of the morning and newsdesks across the country were looking for snapshots," said Sunderland Echo managing editor Gavin Foster. "Unfortunately with Sunderland being the focus and the first to declare, the snapshot was an image of a handful of people being held aloft. That image of Sunderland went around the world."[3]

The Sunderland story was picked up by the New York Times, which ran a feature based on in-the-field reporting with quotes from punters drinking in The Speculation pub. Journalist Kimiko De Freytas-Tamura (2016) characterised the Leave majority as a poke in the eye for the Establishment. The Referendum had: "Exposed deep regional divisions and a rift between classes – a working class that feels it has lost out from globalization, and a more mobile, educated class of people who have prospered from free trade and movement."

According to The Times' analysis, Sunderland's Brexit vote reflected a schism between those who worked in factories and those who felt the benefit of EU investment in the region. They quoted locals who don't own shares and weren't fazed by macroeconomic doom-mongering.

It's a description of a disenfranchised electorate recognised by Kevin Maguire, who said: "The European Union billed as delivering greater prosperity and security is another world for many. Class and education played its part when working class people with the fewest qualifications are suffering most from changes in the economy."

Pledges to invest billions in the NHS written on buses would doubtless hit home with those accessing health services more regularly than they check the stockmarket ticker. And the £350m banner seemed more tangible than the vagaries of models for trade with Europe in or out of the EU.

In fact, the quality of the debate itself as well as the messages, frustrated Maguire. He said: "The campaign to stay in the EU was useless, a Tory dominated nightmare. Few had made a positive political case for EU membership in decades while the demonising of migrants, relatively few of whom live in Sunderland, was undoubtedly a factor."

Hung out to dry

The New York Times article did not play well in the local press. Gavin Foster – in operational charge of the venerable Sunderland Echo – was not amused. "Disaffected people voted with their feet," he said. "But equally, you can't take a city and hang it out to dry – which is effectively what the New York Times did."

The Echo splashed on a defence of the city, declaring one of the world's most forward-thinking media operations 'Behind the Times', at least in terms of its portrayal of Sunderland – if not its pioneering approach to digital storytelling. The Echo demanded an apology from the New York Times, urging it to revisit the city for a second look at a place that had been unfairly damned as past its best.

The Guardian's media columnist Roy Greenslade (2016) adjudicated on the side of the Times, rejecting the response from the Echo as an overreaction and calls for an apology as ridiculous. "It was not, in any sense, an attack on the city or its citizens," he wrote. "Nor was there any question of inaccuracy. It was simply one reporter's thoughtful take on the situation. If it was partial in any way, then surely it was reflecting the fact that the Brexit vote was itself overwhelming partial."

Passionate Foster stands by his call for an apology. He believes the paper fulfilled a duty to fight the corner of his community against comments from a London-based journalist who was just as eloquent in her explanation of her right to publish (Clark: 2016). Foster said: "We weren't arguing there aren't challenges. We weren't arguing that people aren't disaffected. The argument was you can't come here, paint the city with the old-fashioned cloth cap and whippet that people in the South love to use to portray the Northeast. It simply isn't that. And so we came out fighting with the front page."

Building bridges

Post-Brexit Sunderland is looking to boost its industry, address perceptions of the city and turn around its fortunes. And the question for those charged with selling a message of hope is how a city, which seems to feel its best days are behind it, comes to believe the future is bright.

Beyond the headlines and the noble defence rallied by the Echo, there is a significant investment in infrastructure – the city is literally building bridges with a new Wear crossing to improve access and ease congestion for those linking to the rest of the region. Traffic is two-way – with plenty of investment heading inwards, around £1.5bn over the next seven years.

Sunderland is bidding to follow in Hull's footsteps by becoming UK City of Culture in 2021. Director of the Sunderland 2021 campaign, Rebecca Ball, acknowledges the challenge of stepping out from the perceived shadow of a great industrial past. She said: "In Sunderland there is a real sense of pride about the city, about what it was, what it achieved and its role in industry. There is a sense of a city that was a national driver as the greatest shipbuilding town, or fuelling the nation. There is a large number of people in the city that feel it doesn't have that role today."[4]

Media portrayals, and even the pen portraits generated through the kind of public consultation undertaken by the Sunderland 2021 team, can't capture the complexities of a diverse city with differing views on a range of issues. "Actually," said Ball, "there are people in the city who are excited about the future and their role in that future. I think there are too many people who see the best days as being behind them."

The Sunderland 2021 bid was launched before the Referendum. So what, then, was the impact of the Brexit vote and subsequent media coverage on the campaign? "There were clear themes coming through the consultation long before the Referendum," Ball said.

"In some ways the Referendum cast the spotlight on some of those themes. It suddenly meant Sunderland was in headlines and people were interested in what was going on – and that puts a different angle on the bid. It went from a sense these were almost invisible issues, to a sense these are issues where Sunderland became something of a barometer for cities where things had been better before."

Kevin Maguire welcomed the bid 'as a golden opportunity to unite Sunderland behind a common goal and bind wounds'.

There is, however, an inherent risk with large-scale cultural regeneration. And there are echoes of the EU referendum attached to that narrative. Investment in cultural assets, infrastructure and experiences can only change opinions about the city if it reaches the same constituency who felt moved to vote Leave, those seemingly disenfranchised under the status quo.

"If you look at the facts of £1.5bn being invested it is a huge amount of opportunity coming into the city, but that opportunity is not necessarily being felt by everybody. That sense of 'who is that opportunity for, who will benefit, who owned it?'" said Ball. That's the sentiment that links back to the Referendum, she believes. "That sense of 'who is benefiting from globalisation, from the digital future, from investment in the city of London?' All of those questions we were aware of bubbling in the city obviously had an impact on the way the referendum went."

EU-turn

Six months after the Referendum, the Echo was again splashing on the Brexit vote, this time to report a poll that suggested the city had changed its mind about leaving the EU. Under the splash 'EU-Turn' they highlighted an almost exact reversal of June's figures, with 61 per cent now backing Remain.

Kevin Maguire is not convinced by a poll he takes with a 'Siberian mine of salt'. "As a guide to popular opinion it is as legitimate as some of the lies we heard from the Leave and Remain camps before the Referendum. Self-selecting clickbait polls are at best a bit of fun and encourage engagement but they are not a reliable barometer," he said.

Gavin Foster warns pundits to ignore such polls at their peril. "All the polls and exit polls said the Referendum would be for Remain. They all stood there and made their commentaries and were as shocked as everybody else. But our original online vote predicted the result after 5,000 people voted. We listen to our readers and see them on our social channels. We could feel what was happening in the city and we have felt it since."

Now Sunderland, like the rest of the UK, awaits the outcome of Brexit negotiations. Nissan has been handed undisclosed Government assurances the Sunderland plant will be cushioned from any trade tariffs. The predicted Eurogeddon has not transpired (Maguire 2017). And only time will tell whether Sunderland and Britain hurt its own interests by voting for Brexit. For now the city is working on a new image to project to a post-Brexit world.

Notes

[1] All quotes from Maguire taken from an interview with author, March 20, 2017.

[2] Gibraltar was first to declare, with Newcastle the first, large, mainland area to return results.

[3] All quotes from Foster taken from an interview with the author, March 21, 2017.

[4] All quotes from Ball taken from an interview with the author, March 20, 2017.

References

Allison, David (2016) Sunderland Echo poll shows U-turn on Brexit, Sunderland Echo, December 2016. Available online at http://www.sunderlandecho.com/news/politics/sunderland-echo-poll-shows-u-turn-on-brexit-1-8282851, accessed on March 16, 2017.

Clark, Kevin (2016) New York Times reporter says it was not her intention 'to upset residents of Sunderland', Sunderland Echo, June 27. Available online at http://www.sunderlandecho.com/our-region/sunderland/new-york-times-reporter-says-it-was-not-her-intention-to-upset-residents-of-sunderland-1-7991032, accessed on March 18, 2017.

De Freytas-Tamura, Kimiko (2016) Pro-'Brexit' City of Sunderland Glad to Poke Establishment in the Eye, New York Times, June 27. Available online at https://www.nytimes.com/2016/06/28/world/europe/european-union-brexit-sunderland-britain-cameron.html?_r=2, accessed on March 14, 2017.

Foster, Gavin (2016) Give us an apology, New York Times – Sunderland Echo's message after 'irresponsible' article, June 30, 2016. Available online at http://www.sunderlandecho.com/our-region/sunderland/give-us-an-apology-new-york-times-sunderland-echo-s-message-after-irresponsible-article-1-7989825, accessed on March 16, 2017.

Greenslade, Roy (2016) Sunderland Echo wrong to demand an apology from the New York Times, The Guardian, July 6. Available online at https://www.theguardian.com/media/greenslade/2016/jul/06/sunderland-echo-wrong-to-demand-an-apology-from-the-new-york-times, accessed on March 16, 2017.

Maguire, Kevin (2017) in interview with the author, March 20.

Note on the contributor

Lee Hall is principal lecturer, head of journalism media and cultural studies at the University of Sunderland. He has published on hyperlocal journalism, social media and discrimination. He's also contributing editor of the Professional Footballers' Association magazine. Email: lee.hall@sunderland.ac.uk

Brexit Wales: Biting off the hand that feeds you

One of the most startling elements of the Referendum result was Wales voting Leave. Martin Shipton asks why the UK nation which has benefited most from European aid decides to reject the body which has poured billions of pounds into it

In Wales it wasn't a case of biting the hand that feeds you, but of biting off the hand that feeds you. The vote for Brexit in the UK country which has profited more than others from the EU in financial terms, is a shocking tale of how an alienated and ill-informed electorate made a decision based on misconceptions that is almost certainly against its own best interests.

It also illustrates the worrying cultural and communication gap that exists between large sections of the population and their elected representatives, as well as what can happen when a weak indigenous media is swamped by opinion formers based in London.

Many Remain voters in Wales, as well as in the rest of the UK, were astonished that despite billions of pounds from EU aid budgets having been ploughed into the Welsh economy since the turn of the century, the country voted Leave by 52.5 per cent to 47.5 per cent, with 17 of the 22 local authority areas wanting out.

Brexit warning signs

Yet for several years there had been warning signs that the perception of Wales as a country with a predominantly left-of-centre and outward-looking political culture was an inaccurate caricature.

Wales came a little late to the Ukip table. In 2007 Nigel Farage spent a disappointing evening chain-smoking at Cardiff's Welsh Assembly election count, convinced 'one or two of our guys' would win seats. When they didn't, the established parties asserted complacently, and certainly prematurely, that Wales wasn't Ukip territory.

Conventional wisdom insisted with all the EU aid money Wales had received, the country was impervious to the Europhobia that by then had become endemic in much of England.

171

Two years later, however, Ukip saw its first MEP elected in Wales, comfortably winning the fourth and final seat thanks to the D'Hondt system of proportional representation.

Five years later, Ukip stunned everyone in the political class by coming within less than 5,000 votes in an all-Wales constituency of topping the poll at the 2014 European Parliament election, pushing the Conservatives into third place and Plaid Cymru into a humiliating fourth.

With this result the penny finally dropped that Ukip posed a real threat to the settled order, even though plenty of politicians and commentators were prepared to console themselves by arguing that many of the party's voters backed it not out of hostility to the EU as such, but because of some general sense of disaffection with aspects of modern life.

At the Welsh Assembly election in May 2016, Ukip won seven PR seats across all five electoral regions. With a seamless transition in political campaigning to the following month's referendum, politicians on the Remain side quickly encountered hostility on the doorsteps of a kind they had never experienced before.

Huge concern, but tiny number of immigrants
Plaid Cymru AM Simon Thomas later told how he had met huge concern in Pembroke Dock, a town with a tiny number of immigrants, EU or otherwise, about foreigners who were supposedly a serious drain on public services. Only a few days after hearing such comments did he come to the conclusion that by reading the Daily Mail's website first thing in the morning, he would be able to guess what would be quoted back to him as he canvassed housing estates a few hours later.

So far as the local situation in his Mid & West Wales region was concerned, the perception was miles away from the reality.

Official statistics tell us Wales receives around £680m in EU funding annually. The bulk of the money comprises receipts under the Common Agricultural Policy and Structural Funds (regional aid distributed to poorer regions of the EU), with the balance made up from Horizon 2020 (a research and innovation programme) and other smaller, but economically significant, pots of funding such as Creative Europe (a cultural support initiative). This means the funding received in Wales is greater than the amount contributed by Welsh taxpayers via the UK's payments into the EU budget.[1]

According to the Welsh Government, EU funded projects have, since 2007, helped support nearly 73,000 people into work and 234,000 people to gain qualifications. They have helped to create nearly 12,000 businesses and some 37,000 jobs.[2]

Figures of this kind were, of course, quoted frequently during the Referendum campaign by First Minister Carwyn Jones and other Remain-supporting politicians. But as with the large amounts of EU money spent on infrastructure and community projects in Wales, if you didn't see yourself as having benefited directly from such spending, messages of this kind had little resonance for those living in deprived communities.

And in comparison with the extensive coverage given to assertions from the Leave campaign that billions of pounds of UK taxpayers' money sent to the EU would be far better spent on the health service, together with negative perceptions of EU migration, Carwyn Jones' advice to the people of Wales was barely noticed.

Equally, if like many people in the poorer parts of Wales - most of the country - you were on low pay or working on a zero hours contract, you'd be unlikely to be impressed.

Figures relating to voters' attitudes towards EU migration in Wales further demonstrate the gap between what was real and what was imagined:

- Recent survey data suggest people in Wales are less sympathetic to EU migrants than people in other parts of the UK. One survey found 71 per cent of respondents from Wales thought EU migrant workers brought more costs than benefits, a larger proportion than in any other part of Britain.[3]

- As many as 86 per cent of people in Wales believe immigration should be reduced, again, a higher proportion than any other part of Britain.[4]

- Yet in fact a lower proportion of people living in Wales are migrants than is the case in the UK as a whole. In Wales 2.6 per cent of the population are EU migrants and 3.2 per cent are non-EU migrants compared to the UK average of 5.2 per cent EU migrants and 8.5 per cent non-EU migrants.[5]

- In the last decade the proportion of EU migrants has increased in Wales, but more slowly than the EU average.[6]

- Most long-term EU migrants come to Wales to work, with more than half reporting they already had a job to go to on arrival.[7]

- Working age EU migrants in Wales are more likely to be in work (79 per cent) than the rest of the population (71.3 per cent).[8]

- Wales is home to 4.8 per cent of the total UK population but just 2.3 per cent of the UK migrant population. This means it has a smaller share than every other part of the UK except the North East of England.[9]

Why so unappreciative?

The contrast between what many people in Wales were prepared to believe about the economic impact of migration on their communities and the objective reality is clear. But how can this be explained? And why weren't they more appreciative of the EU aid money that had helped to rejuvenate their communities?

What cannot be avoided is the fact that a disconnect exists between those who see themselves as part of a reborn nation that has acquired the trappings of a quasi–state, and those for whom the Welsh Assembly is a dimly understood entity whose relevance to their lives is barely, if at all, apparent. The disconnect is a fruitful ground for misunderstanding.

In May 2014 an ICM poll for the BBC revealed that less than half the population of Wales realised the NHS in Wales was run by the Welsh Government: just 48 per cent correctly answered that was the case against 43 per cent who thought it was run by Westminster.

In March 2016 a YouGov poll for Cardiff University's Wales Governance Centre showed Nathan Gill of UKIP was Wales' most recognised MEP: just 16 per cent could name him. Runner-up was the fictitious Elwyn Davies, 'recognised' by 12 per cent.

Journalists often like to scoff at politicians, blaming them if voters don't recognise who they are, or cannot distinguish between their election promises. But in Wales the weakness of the indigenous media is a bigger factor. In 2016 the average daily sale of the Trinity Mirror-owned and Cardiff-based Western Mail fell to just 15,259 copies. In June 2016 the North Wales Daily Post, also owned by Trinity Mirror, decided to make its Assembly reporter redundant.

The Daily Mail has a captive Welsh audience

While London-based papers do not publish separate sales figures for Wales, industry sources are unanimous in saying the biggest seller is the Daily Mail, well–known for its hostility to the EU.

None of the London 'nationals' employ reporters based in Wales, although a Guardian reporter who lives in the west of England does cover significant Welsh political stories. In the main, however, the more than 90 per cent of newspaper buyers living in Wales who choose to buy a title published in England, will find out little about decisions affecting their lives made by the Welsh Government and the Welsh Assembly.

When Carwyn Jones, therefore, set out the economic case for continued membership of the EU and warned about the negative economic consequences of Brexit, many of the voters he would have wanted to reach did not hear him. Instead they were reading anti–EU stories in the Mail, The Sun and the Express.

Days before the Referendum Jones visited the Cardiff City football stadium with Plaid Cymru leader Leanne Wood for a joint media appearance, in which they both said how important a Remain vote was for Wales' economic prosperity. But Wood appeared to lack confidence in the prospect of victory. She had been shocked by the number of people who, weeks before, had helped her secure a famous victory in the Assembly election over a Labour Minister in Rhondda, but were now saying they were intending to vote for Brexit.

Backing a pro-EU politician, and then voting for Brexit

Voting for the fervent EU supporter and Welsh nationalist Leanne Wood in May and for British nationalist Brexit in June may seem to defy logic, but Wood wasn't prepared to criticise those who did so. In a speech delivered nearly two weeks after the Referendum, she said: "Most of the Leave voters I have spoken to during the campaign and since the result did so chiefly because they wanted change, felt voiceless, and are fed up with being taken for granted by an out-of-touch political establishment. I get that and I respect that."

She was also careful when referring to a spike in hate crimes against immigrants to make the point that most Leave voters were not racists.[10]

Welsh Labour didn't get the message that the majority of voters in Wales would vote Leave until the ballot boxes were opened. On the evening of Referendum day, former Cabinet Minister Peter Hain rang me in the Western Mail newsroom to say feedback was good for a Remain victory.

Since the Referendum, Carwyn Jones has maintained a more coherent stance than Labour in Westminster, consistently arguing Wales' future prosperity depends on retaining 'unfettered access' to the European Single Market. He has adapted his pre-Referendum pitch, repeatedly making the point that while the people of Wales voted for Brexit, they did not vote to be 'done over'.

He has defined his mission as seeking to retain full access to the Single Market while adapting free movement of labour rules so people seeking work would only have the right to move to the UK if they had a pre-existing job offer.

Whether those he hoped to influence before the referendum are any more aware of Jones' latest position on Brexit is doubtful. There is no evidence to suggest they are doing any more than reading the same English newspapers.

Notes
[1] Welsh Government White Paper Brexit: Securing Wales' Future, January 2017
[2] Ibid
[3] British Social Attitudes Survey 2013
[4] Ibid
[5] StatsWales June 2016
[6] International Passenger Survey, ONS 2016
[7] Ibid
[8] StatsWales June 2016
[9] ONS 2015
[10] Leanne Wood keynote speech Securing the Future, Cardiff and Vale College, July 4, 2016

Note on the contributor

Martin Shipton is Chief Reporter of the Western Mail. An ardent but not starry-eyed supporter of devolution, he has covered the National Assembly for Wales since its inception in 1999. He is the author of Poor Man's Parliament (Seren, 2011), a history of the Assembly's first decade. His biography of Viscount Tonypandy, In Search of George Thomas, will be published by Welsh Academic Press in September 2017. A graduate of York University and Cardiff's Centre for Journalism Studies, he has won many awards for his journalism including UK Reporter of the Year. shiptonmartin@yahoo.co.uk

Northern Ireland: Beyond Orange and Green?

Will the common challenge of Brexit prove to be the issue that finally helps break Northern Ireland's traditional political and sectarian impasse? A number of local commentators think so. Then again, it could simply represent one more area of continuing division, says Steve McGookin

On the morning of Thursday March 2, 2017, as the people of Northern Ireland were preparing to vote in what would turn out to be their most seismic election in a generation, the public policy magazine AgendaNI tweeted out a link to one of its stories.

Headlined 'EIB says no to Northern Ireland'[1] it explained how the European Investment Bank had stepped back from creating an infrastructure fund to assist large-scale improvement projects in the province using matched funding. "Following the Brexit referendum," the story said, "the bank, which represents the interests of European Union member states, wrote to the [NI] Department [of Finance] to state that it would not be offering direct support due to the 'non-EU origin' of the funding."

Even though the story wasn't new and may have appeared unremarkable – such an outcome could probably have been predicted under the circumstances – its resonance that particular morning and its relevance to events surrounding the election were far from lost. The headline also had something of a perfect sense of irony, intentional or not, in that usually it was Northern Ireland's politicians that had a reputation for saying 'no'.

Whatever else people were turning out to vote for – or against – that day, the spectre of Brexit and its catalogue of uncertainties loomed over everything, even if at times you might have been hard-pressed to realise it.

So before looking at where Northern Ireland might go from here and the role of the local media in covering the current debate, let's wind the clock back – not always a wise thing in these parts – to the 2016 EU Referendum. Like many things here, it's impossible to understand as a single event in isolation, without considering how it subsequently helped lead the province toward the challenges it faces after these most recent, and most potentially politically disruptive, Assembly elections.

The scene is set

In February 2016, Prime Minister David Cameron announced that on June 23, Britain would decide its future relationship with Europe. In May, scheduled elections to the Northern Ireland Assembly returned the Democratic Unionist Party (DUP) and Sinn Fein as the two largest parties and thus their two leaders – Arlene Foster and Martin McGuinness – as First Minister and Deputy First Minister respectively. Turnout across the six counties was 54.91 per cent, with just under 704,000 votes cast.[2] The DUP's share of first preference votes was 29.2 per cent, and Sinn Fein's 24 per cent.[3]

As the EU Referendum approached, the DUP – alone among the major parties – supported the Leave camp while Sinn Fein, the Ulster Unionist Party (UUP) the Social Democratic and Labour Party (SDLP) and the Alliance Party all backed the campaign to Remain.

It goes without saying that even without the likely significant economic implications,[4] the North of Ireland – as the only part of the United Kingdom to have a land border with the rest of the EU if separation went ahead – was always going to require special consideration, even if it wasn't formally acknowledged as such.[5] To add to the constitutional confusion, the then Secretary of State for Northern Ireland Theresa Villiers was one of the few members of Cameron's cabinet actively campaigning for Brexit, telling the FT in April: "It is the clear position of the Leave camp that we would not reintroduce border checks" and calling claims that Brexit would destabilise the peace process 'scaremongering of the … most irresponsible kind'.[6] In the same interview, she addressed the concerns of the province's farming community, saying: "We would not lose a penny of the EU grants and subsidies which flow into Northern Ireland. For example, with the money we save from leaving the EU we could continue with generous agricultural support payments."[7]

Nevertheless, warnings persisted from both Britain and Ireland over the implications of Brexit – and a UK withdrawal from the European Convention on Human Rights – for the 1998 Good Friday Agreement, the peace deal which provides the framework for how Northern Ireland is governed.[8]

Read all about it

As the province prepared to vote, the local papers geared up with extensive special coverage: the largest by circulation[9] and most influential being the three big Belfast dailies: the Belfast Telegraph and the News Letter from a broadly protestant/unionist perspective, and the Irish News reflecting a catholic/nationalist viewpoint. Like many local titles these days, their hard-copy circulations have been under pressure, leading them to ramp up their online offerings and all three provide informative rolling sections archiving the latest Brexit news and analysis (on the Telegraph – named the 2015 Website of the Year in the Regional Press Awards – and Irish News, the tab is 'Brexit', at the News Letter it's under 'Politics'. The Irish News is the only one of the three with a subscription wall.)

But somewhat strangely at the time, it was what happened at a paper in London and other mainland cities that was to prove particularly interesting.

Two days before the June 23 Referendum, the commuter freesheet Metro featured a wraparound ad urging readers to vote Leave, which was sponsored by the DUP. As the News Letter reported, there was speculation about how the ad in the 1.3m circulation paper had been paid for.[10] It wasn't until late February the following year that the party revealed it had received more than £400,000 from a donor group and had spent it on 'a variety of pro-Leave advertising media' including the Metro ad.[11] That figure far, far eclipsed total spending on the Referendum by all the other Northern Irish parties combined.[12] A DUP spokesman called the campaign 'a great success' and, as we now know, its national objective was narrowly achieved. Northern Ireland, though, voted to remain by 55.8 per cent to 44.2 per cent, on a turnout of 62.69 per cent with 790,523 votes cast.[13] Along with London and Scotland, it was one of just three regions with a Remain majority.

As people and politicians digested the results in various bigger and smaller pictures – one observer tweeted that watching Brexit from an Irish perspective is like 'seeing your neighbour torch their house and remembering your own roof is thatched'[14] – there were legal wranglings and what seemed like an impenetrable cloud of constitutional uncertainty; but there were also thoughtful and constructive considerations of what practical options were going to be open to Northern Ireland in the period ahead.[15]

The world turned upside down

As if that wasn't enough to deal with, Donald Trump's victory in the US presidential election and Leicester City winning the English Premiership title seemed to demonstrate that all bets were off, pundits weren't infallible and anything was, indeed, possible. Even if only one of those outcomes might have been attributed to the empowerment of the economically disenfranchised in an inevitable wave of national populism, we learned it was a year to be sceptical about what passed for conventional wisdom.[16]

On December 6, 2016, the BBC's Conor Spackman and the Spotlight team fanned new life into a story that had been on the proverbial back burner for a while, when they published fresh information related to the controversial Renewable Heat Incentive scheme, which became known as 'cash for ash'[17] and which had been overseen by Arlene Foster before she became First Minister.

The reporting by Spotlight – which won a Royal Television Society award for a previous investigation into property dealings by the Irish National Assets Management Agency or Nama[18] – started the ball rolling in the local media and as the RHI issue unfolded, a broader debate around official competence and accountability quickly grew. The News Letter's political editor Sam McBride wrote:

"Since [the Spotlight broadcast on RHI] there have been a deluge of revelations which paint an even darker picture of what went on and which raise fundamental questions about the ability of the Northern Ireland Civil Service, the actions of their political masters and the integrity of the entire Stormont edifice. The scandal has prompted a public outcry on a scale that is without precedent in Northern Ireland during my decade in journalism."[19]

Newspapers from both sides of the political divide highlighted the RHI scandal

Increasingly, that outcry and the debate surrounding it – not just on hot-button topics like Brexit or RHI but virtually every aspect of the province's political and social structure – was happening online at forums like Slugger O'Toole[20] with 'over 75,000 readers a month' or at the eponymous site run by veteran journalist and documentary filmmaker Eamonn Mallie,[21] both of which feature a broad range of insightful contributors. There are other online platforms too, like Northern Slant[22] which describes its mission as 'breaking a cycle of pessimism', as well as the public policy-focused ScopeNI[23].

In terms of driving the news of the day, broadcasters on Northern Ireland's TV and radio stations occupy a powerful position in defining the agenda, which then usually translates through to a vibrant conversation on social media. One personality, however, has been particularly influential. When the DUP's Jonathan Bell wanted to unburden himself over his role in the RHI scheme, he turned to the BBC's Stephen Nolan, host of both a TV show and a morning radio phone-in show, which can often be as infuriating as it is entertaining. In the week before Christmas, Bell came into the BBC studio where he was dramatically prayed over by his supporters before testifying to Nolan. The Belfast Telegraph called the show 'a compelling, incendiary and bizarre TV blockbuster that had us gripped'.[24] After that interview, and Arlene Foster's intransigent response to it, the countdown clock to an election was probably ticking.[25]

When it eventually came, triggered by Deputy First Minister McGuinness's resignation over Foster's refusal to step aside during an RHI inquiry, as well as frustration over other issues, Sinn Fein made dramatic gains, benefiting from an increased turnout (64.8 per cent). The DUP were returned as the largest party by one seat and fewer than 1,200 votes, even though unionists lost their overall majority at Stormont for the first time.[26] Arlene Foster – who had something of a Hillary Clinton moment during the campaign, but with 'crocodiles' rather than 'deplorables'[27] – still leads her party. Jonathan Bell, who ran as an Independent, was not elected.

The only certainty is uncertainty

At the time of writing – appropriately enough in the run-up to St Patrick's Day – the next steps, as they often are in Northern Ireland, are genuinely unknown. But they will be hugely significant.

Discussions are ongoing about re-establishing devolved government, with various demands, red lines and 'whataboutery' all part of the negotiations. In practice, there are several potential outcomes, none of which are easy, palatable or ultimately satisfying in terms of relationships within and between the UK, Ireland – which is undergoing its own political upheaval[28] – and the province itself.

But the longer the impasse continues, the further away any outcome of an inquiry into RHI appears. Meanwhile practical progress on legacy issues and discussions on crucial budget areas like health or education are on hold. And – particularly pressing – there's no discussion of how Northern Ireland can best protect itself as London prepares to push the button on Article 50.

As the broader debate continues – Stephen Nolan on his show the other morning said 'politics at the moment is highly reactive. I haven't seen as many calls come into this show as I have over the past few months'[29] – there's hope that common sense will prevail, but if we've learned anything over the past year, it's that anything can happen.

The *Independent's* correspondent Siobhan Fenton wrote: "Ireland looks set to join the roster of political shocks and upsets we have seen rippling across the world. Here's a sentence I never thought I'd utter: for the first time in my lifetime, a United Ireland is now credible – and perhaps even inevitable."[30]

Unionism, meanwhile, 'stands at a strategic crossroads'[31] with the DUP apparently looking to forge some kind of unity pact with the UUP, who were punished at the polls after their leader Mike Nesbitt proposed strategic voting to benefit the SDLP. In the wake of Scotland's move for a second independence referendum, however, it remains far from clear whether, in the longer run, there will actually be a union to pledge loyalty to.

Sinn Fein's renewal of its call for a border referendum notwithstanding, Vincent Boland, the Financial Times' Ireland correspondent, writes that the party, with 23 MPs in the Dublin parliament, 'is trying to make itself acceptable to voters in the Republic as a coalition partner. If it refuses to engage with the DUP in Belfast, it would contradict the wider instincts of a party with ambitions one day to govern a reunited Ireland'.[32]

Irish Times columnist Fintan O'Toole, in exploring the role of an emerging Northern Irish identity and considering pragmatic next steps, concludes that the election is 'the first example we have of the Brexit bubble being burst by sharp political realities'.[33]

Finally, given what we're facing, the last word should probably go to a humorist. American writer PJ O'Rourke said recently that last year's US election had prompted, rather than a civil war, a 'war of incivility' which was being fought 'between the frightened and what they fear'.[34]

Sounds about right.

Notes

[1] AgendaNI.com, February 2, 2017.

[2] Voter turnout at a glance, Belfast Telegraph, May 6, 2016.

[3] BBC.co.uk/news/election/2016/northern _ireland/results

[4] MacFlynn, Paul; The Economic Implications of Brexit for Northern Ireland, NERI Working Paper 2016/35

[5] Walker, Stephen; Brokenshire rules out special status for NI, BBC News NI, February 1, 2017.

[6] Parker, George; Irish border checks will not be restored after Brexit, says Villiers, Financial Times, April 14, 2016.

[7] Ibid

[8] Donnelly, Brendan; Troubles redux: Brexit would put the Good Friday Agreement in jeopardy, LSE Brexit Blog, April 28, 2016.

[9] Most recent ABC Circulation Figures July-Dec 2016 at abc.org.uk

[10] McBride, Sam; DUP: Party funded huge advertising campaign in paper not circulated in NI, News Letter, June 21, 2016.

[11] Rutherford, Adrian; Revealed: Group that funded DUP's £425,000 Brexit ad campaign, Belfast Telegraph, February 24, 2017.

[12] Hughes, Brendan; Brexit: Stormont parties spent under £19,000 backing Remain, Irish News, March 3, 2017.

[13] How NI voted in the EU Referendum, ITV News, June 24, 2016.

[14] Twitter; @josefoshea, January 17, 2017.

[15] Phinnemore, D., & McGowan, L. (2016). After the referendum: Establishing the Best Outcome for Northern Ireland, Centre for Democracy and Peace Building, Queen's University Belfast

[16] Inglehart, R., & Norris, P. (2016); Trump, Brexit, and the Rise of Populism: Economic Have-Nots and Cultural Backlash', Harvard University Kennedy School Faculty Research Working Paper Series RWP16-026

[17] Spackman, Conor; Renewable Heating Incentive 'wasted millions', BBC News, December 7, 2016.

[18] BBC Spotlight's Nama investigation wins RTS award, BBC News, March 1 2017.

[19] McBride, Sam; Voice of a public livid over RHI has been heard loudly within Stormont, News Letter, January, 7 2017.

[20] Sluggerotoole.com

[21] EamonnMallie.com

[22] Northernslant.com

[23] ScopeNI.nicva.org

[24] Meredith, Fionola; BBC's Nolan's Jonathan Bell interview a compelling, incendiary and bizarre TV blockbuster that had us gripped, Belfast Telegraph, December 16, 2016.

[25] Meagher, Kevin; Arlene Foster has led Northern Ireland into crisis – and Westminster is strangely quiet, New Statesman, January 11, 2017.

[26] A Warning To Brexit Britain, The Guardian editorial, March 5, 2017.

[27] Arlene Foster regrets Sinn Fein 'crocodiles' comment, Irish Times, March 9, 2017.

[28] Murray, Ken; Enda Kenny: Caught between a shamrock and a hard place, Politico, March 15, 2017.

[29] Nolan, Stephen; BBC Radio Ulster, March 9, 2017.

[30] Fenton, Siobhan; For the first time in my life the prospect of a united Ireland is not only credible but inevitable, The Independent, March 7, 2017.

[31] McBride, Sam; Reeling, unionism stands at a strategic crossroads, News Letter, March 11, 2017.

[32] Boland, Vincent; Northern Irish parties battle to save devolution, Financial Times, March 6, 2017.

[33] O'Toole, Fintan; After Brexit, the two tribes recede – and a Northern Irish identity emerges, The Guardian, March 12, 2017.

[34] O'Rourke, PJ; What to say about US politics in 2017, The Times, March 9, 2017.

References

Brodie, Malcolm (1995) The Tele – A History of the Belfast Telegraph, Belfast: Blackstaff Press.

McKittrick David, and McVea, David (2012) Making Sense of the Troubles, London: Penguin Books.

Oram, Hugh (1983) The Newspaper Book – A History of Newspapers in Ireland 1649-1983, Dublin: MO Books.

Rolston, Bill ed, (1991) The Media and Northern Ireland, London: Macmillan.

Note on the contributor

Steve McGookin was a journalist at the Financial Times for 20 years in London and New York, where he was part of the start-up team for FT.com and later its US News Editor. He recently returned to live in his native Belfast.

No son of the manse, nor anywhere else in the old country

The European debate never really took off in Scotland, says Maurice Smith, as a Remain result seemed certain. And no-one saw a President Trump arriving. Now the focus is on a renewed independence campaign – but neither side will be looking to recruit the nation's latest scion to make it big overseas

The leader of the free world is half-Scottish. Not a distant relative, of the type often claimed by the Irish, but a direct descendant of Mary Anne MacLeod, a Lewis girl who stepped off the boat in 1930 to stay with her sister on Long Island and went on to marry an up-and-coming property speculator, Fred Trump.

It is said that their infant child, Donald John, was hushed to sleep to the gentle airs of Gaelic lullabies, sung by his island-born mother. The billionaire speculator and reality TV star even owns businesses in Scotland, in the form of his golf resorts at Turnberry and in Aberdeenshire. He flies in regularly, and was even once on very matey terms with former First Minister Alex Salmond.

Mary Anne lived a long life in New York City, but not long enough to see her son move from Trump Tower to the White House. For the immigrant lass it might have been the supreme fulfilment of the American Dream. Certainly in any other circumstances she and her boy would be lionised back in the old country.

So what has gone wrong? Where was the great Scottish welcome to a new, genuinely Scottish-bred President? If it had been anybody but Trump, the Scottish body politic would have been falling over itself to be associated with his great victory. Trade missions would be jetting in and out of our airports. The media would be replete with happy images of joyous friends and relatives of Trump, whose mother's family still lives in the same home near Stornoway on the Western Isles. It has to be said they are not too welcoming of journalists who arrive there seeking to 'put a kilt' on the Trump story.

But this is modern Scotland, and Donald Trump is nobody's idea of the prodigal son. In fact, only days before his election, First Minister Nicola Sturgeon had publicly declared her support for Hillary Clinton, having earlier stripped

The Donald of some 'Scottish business ambassador' bauble and condemned his apparently misogynistic behaviour towards, well, lots of people. Scottish Labour leader Kezia Dugdale had even spent some time in the US working for the Clinton campaign – a move that some cynics joked probably sealed her candidate's fate, given the apparently terminal decline of Labour in Scotland. We hear a lot about the 'bubbles' of Washington and London, and Scotland has one of its own too.

Another country

Guto Bebb, a Tory Minister in the Wales Office, complained recently that visiting Scotland is more akin to being in the Republic of Ireland. Likening Edinburgh to Dublin – and not only for their Georgian architecture – he told readers of the North Wales Weekly News: "Read their papers, listen to talk shows and watch the news and it's clearly another country."[1]

He added: "My brief visit to Edinburgh left me somewhat despondent because I felt the same way as I do when I leave Dublin. For me Dublin is somewhere, which is recognisable but very different. That is fine in the context of the capital of an independent country but it should be a warning when visiting a city, which is a crucial part of the UK.

"The sense of nationhood in Edinburgh is palpable. For a long time it has been satisfied within the UK. Even in 2014 a majority saw themselves as British and Scottish. Is that changing though? My gut feeling is yes and that should be a cause for regret to all of us."

Good, think most Scots, even those who would vote to remain in the UK if a referendum were to be held tomorrow. We flaunt our difference. We have our own courts and legal system, our own devolved parliament, and lots of other symbols of nationhood (whether or not that nation is independent).

We can demonstrate that difference no more effectively than by pointing to the result of the 2016 Brexit vote. Yes, Northern Ireland voted to remain in the EU, as did London and most of the major English cities. But, while the UK as a whole voted Leave, the Scots backed the EU by a striking 62 per cent to 38. The vote in Edinburgh was 74 per cent.

The main political parties in Scotland had all supported Remain. UKIP has no representation in the Scottish Parliament. Earlier, the Scottish National Party (SNP) had won a third term in power, albeit with no overall majority. For key votes they rely on the Scottish Greens, against a three-headed opposition made up of the Conservatives, Labour and Liberal Democrats.

Campaign? What campaign?

Truthfully, the European Referendum campaign never really took off in Scotland. The TV coverage was dominated by the 'national' debate in London. Nicola and Ruth travelled south from Edinburgh to appear in TV debates with Boris, Nigel and the rest. The Brexit debate failed to ignite politics in Scotland, and therefore the media remained ambivalent to the whole idea.

Why should this be? First of all, there being so few Scottish dissenting voices, most commentators would have been forgiven for assuming the Referendum was a foregone conclusion for Remain. Scots found the prospect of Boris Johnson in Downing Street too ludicrous to contemplate. Surely voters would know how transparent it was that the bold Boris and his sidekick Michael Gove merely wanted to use the EU vote as a means of taking over their party?

So, in common with that much-vaunted 'metropolitan elite', Scottish opinion formers concluded that, while the EU vote was looking closer than might have been predicted a year earlier, Leave could not come close to winning. To be fair, this seemed to be a position shared by Nigel Farage, who conceded defeat hours before realising his side had actually won, before dawn broke on June 24.

Scottish politics, and its media, remains in thrall to the independence debate. From the SNP's achievement of an overall majority at Holyrood in 2011, to the independence poll in 2014, Scotland has been engaged in an intense debate about its future. Our politicians, commentators and media see other events – Brexit, maybe even Trump's election – through the constitutional prism.

This was heightened in the immediate aftermath of the Brexit vote. Then only one UK politician seemed able to emerge quickly from the shock of the result with some semblance of a plan: Nicola Sturgeon. As the Tories reeled from the result and David Cameron's speedy resignation, the First Minister of Scotland firmly stated her demands. Scotland voted to stay in Europe, and that vote should be respected by London, she insisted. Sturgeon seemed resolute as all around her scattered and flapped. For a while even those newspapers hostile to independence and the SNP seemed silent, almost admiring.

A changing media

It is worth stepping back to consider where the Scottish press has been on the constitutional question in Scotland these past years. Since the first devolution referendum campaign of the late 1970s, through to the creation of the Scottish Parliament in 1999 and today's independence-ready-or-not debate, the media has undergone fundamental change.

By the first devolution poll of 1979, every major Scottish newspaper – led by the Daily Record, The Scotsman and the Glasgow Herald – backed a Yes vote, with varying degrees of enthusiasm. The Tory election victory of that year, and the subsequent 18 years of party rule in Westminster, saw a real shift in Scottish politics. Tory support north of the Border had fallen to the point of collapse by 1997. The great media pro-devolution consensus seemed overwhelming. Even a right-wing interloper to the newsagents' shelves, The Sun, was badged the 'Scottish Sun'. In 1992 Rupert Murdoch's top selling tabloid – the paper of white van man and all blue collar English Tory voters – backed Scottish independence; but only in its Scottish edition, of course.

Two years later, in a book which sought to underline the cultural and commercial importance of appearing to be Scottish, I noted that whatever their provenance, any newspaper with the aim of improving sales north of the Border has to flaunt its 'Scottishness'. The Sun took that to its logical conclusion in 1992 with a famous Saltire-themed cover that screamed 'Rise Now and Be a Nation Again', echoing the unofficial anthem Flower of Scotland.

"The Scottish Sun has been thinking long and hard about what form of government would best serve our future," said a leader article that never saw the English sunlight. Sun-watchers will marvel at the newspaper's next comment: "We have come to the inescapable conclusion that Scotland's destiny lies as an independent nation within the European Community…for 300 years too long, we have thought of ourselves as a second class nation, somehow not worthy or capable of being an independent state. This is nonsense. With independence, Scotland could be one of the wealthiest small nations in Europe."

What has happened over the intervening two decades? Newspapers have lost sales to the Internet, and in a big way. But they are no less influential, both in terms of setting the news agenda for broadcasters, but also in their relevance to the political parties at Holyrood.

The essential thing that has changed, in terms of coverage, is that traditionally Scottish titles like the Herald, Scotsman, Daily Record, face sharp competition from well-resourced London-based rivals who now employ more staff and print full Scottish editions.

The Scottish Daily Mail started publishing in Scotland during the mid-1990s, following the Sun into the tabloid end of the market. Devolution has also attracted investment from The Times, Telegraph and Guardian. Perhaps ironically, although the majority are against Scottish independence, the fact of Scotland's heightened constitutional situation has been good for sales. The Times Scotland is said to be out-selling The Scotsman in Edinburgh. The Scottish Daily Mail has taken market share from several titles ever since setting up shop.

How Brexit nearly passed without notice

This is not all about politics. The London titles are highly competitive products. They carry a lot of content. Not everybody who reads the Mail is a Tory; arithmetic alone tells you that a considerable number must vote SNP, maybe even Labour.

Brexit almost passed the Scottish political and media scene by. Yes, it was there, mainly because the SNP signalled that a pro-Brexit vote would amount to the 'material change' that would justify a second independence referendum. Yes, the Scottish editions of the Mail and Express adhered to the Euro-scepticism of their Fleet Street parents. But the truth is so few people in Scotland – and certainly none of the commentariat, right or left, nationalist or unionist – expected a Brexit victory that it scarcely registered on the media Richter scale.

The absorption of political debate within the envelope of agitation for independence is almost complete. The SNP has won three successive elections, and still rides high in Scottish polls. Its supporters only possible point of disagreement is not whether there should be independence, but when. Even opposition parties, intent on portraying the SNP as a single-issue party that should be getting on with its day job in charge of health and education, have ended up talking about little else but constitutional change, albeit from the unionist perspective.

What next?

What happens next will depend largely on the progress and outcome of the UK's Brexit negotiations. Nicola Sturgeon might back down on her campaign for a new poll if a substantial concession is made to her government's demands for an exceptional deal for Scotland – remaining within the single market, somehow – but there is no evidence that Theresa May is likely to press for that.

Scotland watched unbelieving as her not-so-celebrated celebrity son persevered first in the Republican selection battle and later the race to the White House itself. Brexit carried something of the same disbelieving air. Apart from a few working class housing schemes and fishing ports, Scotland carried little sign of significant Leave support, and it came as a surprise that the pro Brexit vote reached even 38 per cent.

Brexit will have the biggest single impact on the progress of the independence campaign, for good or bad. It is likely that Nicola Sturgeon will have her new referendum, although whether it will be as soon as 2018 as she demands is another question.

There are signs of subtle change in the news media's attitude to constitutional change, and the SNP in particular. The pro-Labour, anti-independence Daily Record appears to have softened its line, and even has Ms Sturgeon as a weekly columnist. Since the last referendum, the SNP now has its own daily bugle in the form of The National, a small-selling tabloid that is unashamedly for 'Yes'. The rest of the Scottish press tends to be relatively even handed; papers that favour the status quo such as The Herald or Sunday Post also include a great deal of pro nationalist commentary.

Real opposition to independence is to be found in the Scottish editions of the Mail, Express, Telegraph, and to a lesser extend The Times and Guardian. None of that will change, as we gird ourselves for the next round of trench warfare and the unique brand of attrition that is a feature of Scottish politics.

Last time round both sides were keen to recruit international business figures and celebrities – from Sean Connery to J.K. Rowling – to their cause. It is safe to assume that Donald J. Trump, scion of the Western Isles and golf resort entrepreneur, will be among the absentees.

Notes

[1] https://www.gutobebb.org.uk/news/gutos-north-wales-weekly-news-column-wednesday-15-march-2017

Note on the contributor

Maurice Smith is a journalist, columnist and documentary producer based in Glasgow. He was previously Business Editor of BBC Scotland. He is the author of Paper Lions: The Scottish Press and National Identity (Polygon, 1994).

'It wasn't like a normal political campaign'. A snapshot of the Referendum in the regions

Regional journalism offered voters a much more balanced service than national newspapers in the EU Referendum, but with the benefit of hindsight, regional political reporters who thought it would pan out like normal election coverage, found it was a very different experience, for both journalists and voters, discovers Tor Clark

Many journalists in the UK regional media approached the EU Referendum as they would have any other, and all previous, election campaigns, with impartiality and as much balance as possible. Some regional newspapers did, unusually for the local press, advise their readers how to vote on June 23, 2016, but for virtually all, the actual coverage of campaign was as even-handed as circumstances allowed.

This was in stark contrast to the UK national press, most of which had already loudly declared their hands and ran coverage supportive of their own agendas. National newspapers with combined circulation of roughly 4.8m supported Leave and those with a combined 1.8m readers backed Remain. The pro-Leave papers were more numerous and more strident.[1]

But the Referendum didn't turn out to be like any previous electoral contest, and though they could not have known it at start, by the end of the campaign and in hindsight, some local journalists may have wished they had approached the binary referendum differently to a multi-party election.

Leicestershire was a good example of the EU Referendum in the English regions. At its heart was the multi-cultural, metropolitan, two-university, urban Labour-voting city of Leicester, which narrowly voted Remain. Surrounding Red Leicester were some of the most quintessential English rural districts – Rutland, Charnwood, Bosworth – all of which voted clearly to Leave.

Leicestershire is well served by well-established journalism, trusted and respected by its residents. The Leicester Mercury newspaper is based in the city but serves the whole county. It was launched in the 1870s and has swallowed up or seen off all its rivals over the intervening 140-odd years. At its height, its circulation topped 150,000 copies a night. It now sells 25,000 copies every morning, but with another 60,000 readers online[2]. It retains a dedicated political correspondent, Dan Martin, who has been covering that beat since 2012, but had previously spend a decade as a news reporter on the paper.

BBC Leicester was the UK's first BBC local radio station in 1967 and so in 2017 is marking its pioneering achievements with a series of 50th anniversary celebrations. It too has had a dedicated political reporter, in the form of experienced broadcaster Tim Parker, for the last five years.

Dan Martin is honest enough to admit, with hindsight, he might have covered the EU Referendum a little differently. But he clearly recalls at the time of the June poll, his paper's approach – like that of most of the rest of the media – was simply to approach this campaign like any other campaign. The approach was valid because it had worked at all previous elections. It was only after the result that political journalists began to realise it wasn't like a normal election campaign.

Indeed Martin is still an advocate for the usual ways of covering politics in the regional media – in contrast to most national newspapers – by offering both sides of an argument the chance to air their views and letting the reader decide. But looking back on the Brexit poll nine months later, he now realises the binary nature of the contest and the high stakes, made it a different kind of contest and perhaps required a different journalistic approach.

Tim Parker recalls how BBC Leicester took a typically BBC approach to the coverage, attempting to cover the issues that mattered to its listeners and always retain a balance. He notes how entrenched the views of committed voters were, but also how many voters, despite this were still making their minds up during the campaign.

Both Parker and Martin think the national press influenced the final result and while locally they tried to shine a light on issues that mattered in as balanced a way as was possible, the national press, largely just pushed for the outcome they wanted – and ultimately, perhaps surprisingly, achieved it.

Planning the coverage

Despite referenda being a relative rarity, both the Leicester Mercury and BBC Leicester approached the EU Referendum with confidence.

Martin recalled: "We were relaxed about it, our aim was to find a bit of balance. The Referendum was all-pervasive. Initially we did consider covering the campaign thematically but in the end we just let it develop rather than trying to force it in a particular direction. If something interesting was happening, we covered it. I still had my day job to do covering local politics, but increasingly that became all about Brexit too."

Parker added: "The BBC tends to try to look at issues, translate it all and make it relevant to our audience. We had access to a major BBC document, which was the result of a lot of research into what the issues might be. We had a major briefing session with one of the leading editorial people behind the report, which explained the buzzwords and key issues. It was expected the top issues would include immigration, the economy, impact on other services, food and agriculture. The idea was to lead the agenda with these issues and get both sides' views meshed into the coverage. On each issue, our aim was to seek the views of politicians, the public, academics and key people in each sector.

"We had gone into it with the kind of journalistic baggage you'd go into a normal election with but we were led by what our listeners were interested in."

The campaign

The Referendum campaign started normally enough for both Leicestershire's main news organisations, but then it developed and morphed into something unique, which was initially like general election coverage, but eventually showed itself to be distinctly different.

Martin remembered: "At the start it was no different to normal election coverage. It started a little later than a normal election campaign, but when it did kick in it really took off because people understood it was a binary choice and the stakes were really high. We had the luxury of choosing what to cover. Because I was personally Remain, I was concerned my own views might creep in so I found myself pushing balance the other way.

"Coverage didn't look balanced when we had a big political figure from one side visiting, so we had to work hard to make it look balanced, to find someone from the other side and get it in as soon as possible afterwards.

"I really enjoyed the campaign because people were so keen to talk to you. My phone was ringing all the time. It really invigorated you as a reporter. But people got tetchy more quickly. A lot of Leave supporters got very animated in the comments sections underneath my stories. They made accusations of bias which may have pushed me the other way to avoid those accusations because of my desire to remain balanced."

Parker started to notice the differences early on. He said: "There is a clear road map with general elections, but there wasn't a clear roadmap with this campaign. There was a national discussion but it didn't seem to trickle down to where we were. It felt like we were sometimes having to drive the agenda, I felt I was often coordinating the coverage into what I wanted, to get different subjects covered rather than following any politician's agenda which you do often do in general elections.

"Some organisations were very helpful. The NFU for example produced lots of useful information, but refused to be drawn into one campaign or the other because its members were evenly split. Plenty of high profile politicians visited our area, but when they did all they did was preach to the converted. I sometimes wished the Remainers would go to speak to people on the New Parks estate or the Leave politicians would go and talk at De Montfort University, where they would find more people opposed to their views, but they didn't."

The impact of the national press

Both the Leicester Mercury and BBC Leicester continually strive for balance and impartiality. They are both of course always accused of not achieving that goal by the partisan, but the audiences generally respect their neutral position and efforts to ensure it. But in the Referendum campaign, they were up against a national media which was arguably more biased than in normal election campaigns, and often led the news agenda with prominent stories, skewed to one side or another. The impact of national coverage on local voters was influential and not necessarily positive, the regional reporters agree.

Martin explained: "I tried not to read too much of the nationals' coverage at the time. I tried to talk to local people and get their unfiltered thoughts. The Leicester Mercury didn't take a line because we had an interim editor at the time who didn't want to commit the paper to one side or another knowing he was going back to his other job afterwards. And that was a good thing anyway. If you pick one side in a 50/50 contest you are in danger of irking half your readers, which is why local papers generally don't pick a side and why they shouldn't in my view.

"We tried to be a temperate as possible and tried not to be too inflammatory, especially on subjects like immigration. Our coverage wasn't bland but tried to avoid the worst excesses of the nationals. It was more measured, more factual, less agenda-driven than the nationals.

"The nationals are preaching to the converted. The nationals' coverage tended to reinforce their readers' prejudices. 50/50 voters would have found something I wrote more even-handed and useful than, say, something they read in the Express or The Guardian.

"Our approach was to honestly report what the campaigners said then find someone with a different view and report that. We reported what they said, presented the readers with facts and let readers decide how they felt. There was lots of scaremongering, sometimes more heat than light. We wanted to help people who weren't sure."

Parker recalls: "We tried to strip out all the hyperbole of the national press, which often led on the loudest politician. We tried to do what radio does best and explain to people in Leicestershire what the choice they were going to make would mean to them. But we couldn't ignore the national agenda being set – that was the over-riding noise people were hearing.

"Many people had decided how they were voting, but probably not as many as in a general election. Of the undecided voters, I'd say 80 per cent were influenced by the media, many by the national papers. Those papers have massive resources and were driving for the hearts of voters, not their minds. That's hard. On reflection, that was a very loud voice to counter.

"The BBC had to reflect what was being said elsewhere in the coverage, we couldn't ignore the debates started by the national press. You can't ignore great headlines like The Sun's 'Queen backs Brexit'."

The results

As with virtually all journalists, both Martin and Parker assumed Remain would win. The result surprised them both, but with hindsight they can see the signs were there during the campaign.

Martin said: "People were very keen to speak to us and get their message over. Pro-Leave readers were more vocal. I assumed the Remain supporters were just a quiet majority, but they turned out to be the minority.

"During the campaign I assumed people would to the 'sensible' thing, the 'cowardly' thing, the 'safe option' of what we already had, and vote Remain. I didn't see the frustration of many. I think it just simmered away."

Parker was genuinely surprised by how many voters hadn't decided in the campaign, but felt the campaign didn't do a lot to help them make rational choices.

He said: "There were many voters who had made up their minds, but probably assumed Remain would win. The biggest surprise was how many people realised they wanted to leave right at the end of the campaign, almost as they voted. Some even told me they would make up their mind at the polling station."

In retrospect

The biggest issue in Brexit for so much of UK journalism remains around whether they should have approached this rare and unusual poll in a different way, especially given the outcome, a slap in the face for liberal, metropolitan, establishment Britain. Martin and Parker divide on this issue.

Martin says: "With hindsight, I should have spoken to more of our readers and fewer politicians and maybe I regret that I didn't, but I didn't like the shoutiness of some of the Leave campaigners. People didn't necessarily use us or other media as much as they would have in a normal election. I think they paid more attention to what their friends and neighbours were saying.

"I think we achieved being scrupulously fair, what we didn't achieve was to debunk some of the stranger claims, such as spending £350m a week on the NHS. We just reported it and thought readers would realise it was a bit of a fib and people would work it out.

"If I had my time again I would challenge politicians more on their claims. When I did do this I was accused of scaremongering and it could feel as if I was being partisan. They made their case and it was my job to find someone else to provide the balance."

Parker was happy with the overall local coverage, but in a different world admits he might have at least had a go at greater interrogation of some of the more questionable arguments put forward.

He says: "In hindsight, I might have taken on some of the national arguments head-on, possibly using more fact checks. But fact checks were ignored by both sides. People would not change their minds. Otherwise, I don't think I would have approached it differently.

"Some Brexit claims were just dismissed as silliness, for example the claim to spend £350m on the NHS. It was lazy national journalism and lazy politics, but the journalism was a lot less lazy than the politics. Both sides of the argument acted with swaggering arrogance. Even at national level there wasn't much proper argument. Most debates were just shouting matches between the two sides who had already made up their minds."

In the end…

So regional journalists, in this fairly representative area, approached the Referendum like a normal political campaign and found it was different. They justify their balanced and impartial approach to trying to serve their readers but are honest enough to admit some of the most spurious arguments perhaps ought to have had greater interrogation. They believe they served their own audience in the way they normally do, but both feel uncommitted voters were more plentiful than normal and were definitely swayed by the very partisan coverage of the national press, which they feel was very influential on the campaign itself and on voters' final choices.

Whatever the regional media might do to retain their local reputation for balance and fairness, in the end, in a tight contest, the national press, with all its partiality and inaccuracy, can be – and perhaps was in this instance – the deciding factor in the UK's decision to leave the EU.

Notes

[1] Figures calculated from published Jan-Jun 2016 ABC figures. Leave papers were The Sun, the Daily Star, the Daily Express, the Daily Mail, and the Daily Telegraph. Remain papers were the Daily Mirror, The Guardian, The Times and the Financial Times.

[2] Jul-Dec ABC figures for circulation and daily unique users. http://www.holdthefrontpage. co.uk/2017/news/yorkshire-post-tops-abc-league-but-all-dailies-see-sales-decline/?utm_ source=emailhosts&utm_medium=email&utm_campaign=Feb27Mailout

http://www.holdthefrontpage.co.uk/2017/news/abcs-two-thirds-increase-sees-jp-daily-top-the-web-charts/?   utm_source=emailhosts&utm_medium=email&utm_ campaign=Feb27Mailout

Note on contributor

Tor Clark is Associate Professor in Journalism at the University of Leicester and co-editor of this book. Previously he was Principal Lecturer in Journalism and a Teacher Fellow at De Montfort University, in Leicester, where he taught political journalism, the regional media, and the history and context of journalism. He was also co-editor of this book's predecessor, Last Words? How Can Journalism Survive the Decline of Print? He is a political journalist and was editor of two UK regional newspapers. He is a regular contributor to the Leicester Mercury and BBC Leicester.

Why Asian voters backed Brexit in surprising numbers

Asian people emigrated to Britain in significant numbers from the 1960s and many voted for Brexit. Did the media miss a trick by not focusing enough on the 'Eastern Exiters', asks Professor Barnie Choudhury

Premiership champions come and Premiership champions go. That's one possible interpretation of Leicester's fortunes in the past year. But one thing remains a constant in Leicester city's legacy – 'interculturalism'[1]. At the time of the next census, we can expect in Leicester the ethnic minority will have become the ethnic majority[2]. It's evident around the city today, where lights and bunting hang from the lamp posts with symbols acclaiming one religious festival, being swapped for another faith, more often than the changing seasons. The Belgrave area of Leicester, a stone's throw from the bustling city centre, is the perfect case study of what was to be a main Brexit talking point: immigration. It's here that between 10,000[3] and more than 20,000[4] East African-Asians settled in the late 1960s and early 1970s. And it's here that, thanks to mass immigration, an area was economically rejuvenated and culturally enriched[5]. Yet over the decades the media has failed to report on a self-evident truth: after a period, many immigrants, no matter their colour, begin to share the same values, assumptions and thoughts as the native population, on most issues.

Media failures

The media failed to report on people like Kam Patel, an IT consultant in banking and former Leicester Mercury journalist. It failed to understand how Asians consume their news and have therefore misjudged and misrepresented their diverse thinking. His three-generation family still live together, 'down the road' from where his parents bought their first home in Belgrave. Kam's parents came from East Africa before the Kenyan and Ugandan expulsions. Once, news was passed through the community via the 'community leader', usually an educated and respected man who spoke English. What happens today is that news comes from several media platforms, social, digital and analogue – and, of course the so-called community leader.

198

"We didn't talk about Brexit much before or during the referendum," he said. "But I had to challenge my Dad when he was going to vote Leave because a community leader down the pub had convinced him the immigrants had taken jobs meant for him. Once I'd pointed out he was an immigrant and people said the same thing about him and he was retired, he began to think differently."[6]

Asian perspectives

Perhaps the most influential publisher for Asian businesses is the Asian Media Marketing Group (AMG). It was founded in 1968 and now has offices in America and India as well as the UK. Among its publications is the Eastern Eye, which badges itself as 'Britain's number 1 leading weekly Asian newspaper'. Like most media, Brexit was a recurring story and the paper's position was firmly in the Remain camp, reflecting the views of its readership and Asian businesses. The newspaper tested claims being made by Brexiteers. For example, when a prominent campaigner for Brexit, Priti Patel MP, told Asian restauranteurs leaving the EU would be good for them, the paper rejected that thesis[7]. Shailesh Solanki, AMG's executive editor and firm remainer, argues there are particular topics, issues and stories which are of interest to Asian communities which the mainstream media misses time and again. He believes this gives his paper a special standing among decision-makers, such as prime ministers, by bringing them information which would otherwise be inaccessible to them.

What his paper found on immigration, said Mr Solanki, illustrated the changing views of the different generations of British-Asians, and it surprised him.

"They went through exactly the same thing 30, 40 years ago, when our parents first arrived here. And exactly the same things which were said about our parents, (about) taking their jobs, we don't like their food and how it smells, and the rest of it, they were saying about the Eastern Europeans. Unfortunately, they have short memories."[8]

Opportunities missed

Experiential and empirical evidence suggest the mainstream media deals in shorthand and clichés. So, even today, after more than five decades of mass immigration, the media continues to portray Asians as a homogenous entity, when the truth is more nuanced. The award-winning writer, broadcaster and former BBC sports editor, Mihir Bose, believes the media missed an opportunity to put the immigration debate into historical perspective. Bose thinks the media failed to understand and question the motives of those 'coloured immigrants', as they were then called, who arrived in the 1960s and 1970s.

"If they had, they would have found the younger generation of immigrants, like those who were non-immigrants, were against leaving the EU, while some in the older generation, who'd done well, broadly agreed with the older white generation who felt these new immigrants were not desirable," he said. "Nobody now wants to admit they're anti-immigrant and certainly don't want to admit they have any racial views. We don't want to talk about race, we don't want to be identified in any way as racist and therefore we don't discuss the subject. There was no proper analysis of immigration. Most modern journalists would rather not talk about it."[9]

One exception to that observation was the Channel 4 News programme from Leicester's De Montfort University which invited Black Asian Minority Ethnics (BAME) to discuss issues which were important to them, including immigration. Among the guests was Leicester-based international businessman Kulvinder (Vic) Sethi who welcomed the opportunity to make the case for Remain. Like many, he feels the mainstream media ignores views from minority ethnics and suggests a two-pronged approach.

"The media needs to do both specials and general programming," he argues. "The single forum approach was a good idea because some British-Asians didn't understand the issues. They needed to realise this vote was important to them because the outcome would affect them. But the media also needed to make sure British-Asians were part of the general mix because white-Britons needed to realise what impacts them impacts British-Asians. We're part of the same society and we're no different."[10]

Target audiences
Some media experts believe television's previous grip on the nation's attention, where the family and neighbours would gather around a set to see a big news story, such as the death of Princess Diana, is over. Yet in an email[11], the BBC contended: "TV remained the best way of reaching audiences – including young audiences – with 26m people overall tuning in for coverage of the result. We also devoted lots of primetime coverage to the referendum. BBC reached over 17m viewers on TV with its results night coverage – significantly ahead of competitors that evening. More than 20m people watched at least three minutes of one of the debate programmes on the BBC. Online was the second most-used platform for news about the referendum, with 48.4m global browsers on 24th June."

The implication that the BBC reaches a wide-ranging mass of audiences is clear but what specifically did it do for British-Asians? The email suggests it relied on Asian Network (AN) to feed into mainstream programming. In it, Bill Mostyn, deputy editor of Asian Network said:

"Asian Network treated Brexit like any other major news story - looking for angles specific to an Asian audience (immigration, for example) - and that given it's a young audience we attempted to break down the different issues and explain the different arguments.

"In the week before the referendum vote we hosted a panel and audience debate in Slough largely from the local Asian and eastern European communities - to focus on the issue of immigration.

"We also had standalone interviews with Chris Grayling and George Osborne and two in depth, 45 minute long interviews with Priti Patel and Seema Malhotra - during which listeners were able to put their questions to them."

ITV[12] was clear that its policy was not to target Asians per se. Its acting head of newsgathering is Julie Hulme:

"ITV News decided against producing pieces specifically targeting minority voters, instead treating Asian voters as any other voters around the UK. The team behind ITV News' coverage of the EU Referendum aimed to reflect the views of every voter, making a commitment to consistently reflecting the make-up of Britain in our output.

"In one strand, 'Your Choice', the ITV News editorial team included Asian voices as part of a voter tracking on-air project, where four groups of three connected people were selected from regions spanning the UK. They were spoken to each month during the campaign and on the night before the vote, illustrating how different elements of the campaign were playing out across the country. Of the four groups, one comprised three Asian co-workers from Leicester. Similarly, the group in Scotland included an Asian woman who was working as a hairdresser."

Sky News, on the other hand, took a different approach, specifically targeting different demographics. Head of Sky News, John Ryley said: "In the run up and after the Referendum Sky News reflected the issues and views of multiple sectors of the British population ranging across ethnicity, age, social group and geography. In particular, our Nation Divided series examined the concerns of Asian communities from around the country including London, Lancashire and Glasgow, and our set piece live events ensured communities were fairly represented. Sky News endeavours to avoid painting any one particular group as a voting bloc and reflects views and issues across multiple factors."[13]

These statements do not surprise Uday Dholakia, who chairs the National Asian Business Association, but they do disappoint him.

"Throughout the past 30 years, I've been arguing diversity is all about the business case. Sky News gets it," he said. "It has the commercial savvy to know its customer base and serve it accordingly. Yet the BBC and ITV, especially with their public service remit, don't seem to understand what Sky does. It makes business sense. The BBC and ITV did not inform or target Asian voters enough, putting them in a category marked 'Bollywood interest only'."[14]

Conclusion

During my time as a journalist, spanning 35 years, I have seen the coverage of BAME issues fluctuate. Sometimes it is the 'flavour of the month', with an apparent push on 'ethnic stories and ethnic contributors'. This schizophrenic, inconsistent, approach is frustrating and does a disservice to BAME audiences. As the Baby-Boomer generation is replaced by the Millennials via Generation Z, we will logically see a shift in emphasis of news consumption and audience atomisation. Social media, YouTube, text alerts, push announcements and new digital technology are content providers. Despite the prevalence of 'fake news', this appears to be the way ahead for future generations.

But at this moment, the media is missing a trick by deliberately trying to homogenise news. While British-Asians do integrate, they have yet to assimilate and so, axiomatically, they have diverse viewpoints which need to be reflected properly and seriously, not least because, in broadcast terms, they pay their licence fee. That remit for public service to all, regardless of race, religion or gender, is not being serviced adequately.

This was clearly shown during the Brexit coverage and, no matter what mainstream media says, it can be seen every day by the lack of differentiation of viewpoints among our different communities. What the Brexit coverage has illustrated, once again, is an argument so often espoused by BAMEs – the mainstream media has given up on covering topics which are important to them. In doing so, it misses out on different and interesting perspectives, such as, when it comes to immigration, those who were once immigrants may indeed hold the same views as indigenous Britons – and may just interest and surprise listeners, viewers and readers in the process.

Notes

[1] Cantle, T. (2015) *Interculturalism: 'Learning to Live in Diversity'*. Available from http://www.bristol.ac.uk/media-library/sites/spais/documents/Cantle%20-%20Modood%20Debate_Ethnicities-2015.pdf [Accessed 11 February 2017]

[2] BBC News. (2012) *Census 2011: Leicester 'most ethnically diverse' in region*. Available from http://www.bbc.co.uk/news/uk-england-leicestershire-20678326 [Accessed 11 February 2017]

[3] Leicester Mercury. (2012) *Forty years ago today: A tyrant's whim boosted our city's fortunes*. http://www.leicestermercury.co.uk/years-ago-today-tyrant-s-whim-boosted-city-s/story-16647839-detail/story.html#HAzxt48dUgDfWuH6.99 [Accessed 11 February 2017]

[4] Panasar, J. (2005) *A history of Leicester*. Available from http://www.bbc.co.uk/leicester/content/articles/2005/10/10/al_leicester_backgrounder_feature.shtml [Accessed 11 February 2017]

[5] Hardill, I. (2002). *Diasporic Business Connections: An Examination of the Role of Female Entrepreneurs in a South Asian Business District*. Available from http://www.egrg.rgs.org/wp-content/uploads/2013/12/egrg_wp-Hardhill.pdf [Accessed 11 February 2017]

[6] Patel, K. (2017) *Questions on Brexit coverage among Asian communities* [interview] Interviewed by Barnie Choudhury, 11 February

[7] D' Souza, S. (2016) *Curry crisis hots up Brexit debate*. Available from https://www.easterneye.eu/news/detail/curry-crisis-hots-up-brexit-debate [Accessed 26 February 2017]

[8] Solanki, S. (2017) *Questions on Brexit coverage among Asian communities* [interview] Interviewed by Barnie Choudhury, 29 January

[9] Bose, M. (2017) *Questions on Brexit coverage among Asian communities* [interview] Interviewed by Barnie Choudhury, 29 January

[10] Sethi, K. (2017) *Questions on Brexit coverage among Asian communities* [interview] Interviewed by Barnie Choudhury, 11 February

[11] Pratt, J. (2017). *Asian Brexit coverage.* [email]. Sent to Barnie Choudhury, 23 February & 7 April.

[12] Brander, L. (2017). *Asian Brexit coverage.* [email]. Sent to Barnie Choudhury. 10 February.

[13] Ryley, J. (2017). *Asian Brexit coverage.* [email]. Sent to Barnie Choudhury. 9 February.

[14] Dholakia, U. (2017) *Questions on Brexit coverage among Asian communities* [interview] Interviewed by Barnie Choudhury, 22 January & 4 March

Note on contributor:

Barnie Choudhury has been a broadcaster for more than 35 years. He worked for the BBC for 24 years. He is the University of Buckingham's first professor of professional practice in communications, and honorary secretary of the Royal Television Society Midlands. He is a member of Ofcom's Advisory Committee for England and currently the director of media and PR for the Commonwealth Secretariat

Giddens

Furlong + Cartmel

Hickerntoff

{ Lupton + Tullock - 9

Lupton Tullock - 6   ONLINE

Pilkngton

Section five

The 2016 air war

***

Balance in an unbalanced world

John Mair

Modern elections (referendums even) are fought on the airwaves, much to the chagrin of the printed press. Television is the master medium here.

Political parties spend much of their campaign time creating 'TV opportunities' in suitable locations with the major dramatis personae speaking (or in reality offering sound bites) to an often small cast of supporting activists' posters in hand. Go wide angle and you will see how artificial these are – David Cameron in the corner of a Cornish barn in 2015 filling the TV frame but only filling a tiny bit of the available space!

The parties fight for television space on the major prime-time bulletin programmes, especially on the terrestrial channels. They argue like hyenas over the format and casting of leaders' debates (which should in 2017 surely now be called 'deputy or deputy to the deputy leaders' debates'. The careful format evolved seven years ago having been sabotaged by Sir Lynton Crosby).

Parties recognise the importance of the goggle box to their image, profile and chances with the electorate. Voter involvement is now electronic.

The 2016 Referendum campaign presented special problems for the 'pop up' 'Remain' and 'Leave' campaigns but more so for the broadcasters. There was a binary 'yes/no', 'remain/leave' choice for voters. Traditional parties were split several ways vertically and horizontally.

In many senses, it became little more than a 'Blue on Blue' contest (Tory Remainers vs Tory Leavers) especially once Boris Johnson had defected to Leave. Applying the normal broadcast rules of balance and impartiality proved a conundrum (maybe one too far) for broadcasters. Did they get it right?

This section attempts to answer that question with contributions from academics, journalists and those sitting on the scales of broadcasting balance.

First, Professors Justin Lewis and Stephen Cushion of Cardiff University in their content analysis of the output –'Impartiality in an age of confusion' – find that by trying to be 'fair' the broadcasters skewed to the right of the political spectrum; they left questions of balance too much to the campaigns themselves.

They needed simply to be braver. 'In short, broadcasters could be bolder in debunking popular myths and informing the public where the weight of evidence lies.' The result was that overall 'the clear political skew of television news coverage of the EU Referendum campaign… raises serious questions about the way in which impartiality is interpreted and delivered.'

What of those at the coalface of TV reporting of the Referendum? Gary Gibbon is the distinguished political editor of Channel Four News. In his contribution 'Turbo-charged pop-up politics: Lessons from 2016' he admits they got it wrong. Badly wrong,

His mea culpa on behalf of the electronic press: "Most newsrooms, let's be honest, were surprised by the result. We failed to track the new political forms of engagement and still don't fully understand them. We lent on high impact gladiatorial contests and ghettoised fact checking when it should have coursed through all we did. We slipped into our comfort zone of big Tory beast fights."

In short, they reported but did not help understanding.

His ITN colleague, the equally eminent James Mates, North America and Now Europe Editor for ITV News, puts the blame fairly and squarely on a media fascination with American and a studied ignorance of European politics.

"European politics has been treated as if it was largely irrelevant, a conspiracy to thwart us and, the biggest sin of all, insufferably dull," he opines. The British media finally woke up to our nearer neighbours – but, alas, too late. "The biggest irony of all is likely to be we finally gave Europe the attention it deserves only after we decided to leave it."

In the 2016 Referendum, facts were not at a premium on both sides of the argument. 'Alternative facts' were. The biggest 'whopper' of them all – the claim on the side of the 'Vote Leave ' battle-bus that Europe cost the UK £350m per week and re-patriated that could build a new hospital each and every week. It was, at best, inaccurate, at worse a simple porkie.

Professor Richard Tait has shouldered editorial responsibility for two big broadcasters – the BBC and ITN. He has fought many TV election campaigns. In his contribution – 'Get that Lie off Your Bus!' Accuracy, the Broadcasters and the Referendum Campaign' – he uses the £350m false claim as a portent for the future relationship between broadcasters, politicians and the public.

"They should themselves have a fresh look at how they report politics: the balance between the Westminster 'bubble' and the nations and regions; the balance between reporting the arguments and analysing them; and the balance between interviewing political figures and talking to non-politicians who may have different perspectives and relevant expertise," he says.

"As the 'phoney war' ends and the negotiations begin, the broadcasters, while building on their strengths and resisting bullying from whatever quarter, should also bear in mind that those who fail to learn from their mistakes are doomed to repeat them."

Fact checking has crossed the Atlantic from US journalism to Britain. Both Channel Four and BBC News have fact-checking pages on their websites. Critics say this is simply a ghetto that should be part of the mainstream bulletins.

Patrick Worrall is a fact-checker for Channel Four News. He is forthright in his analysis in his contribution, 'Keep calm and carry on fact-checking'. "The night of November 8, 2016 was a painful one for just over half the people who voted in the US Presidential election. Many fact-checking journalists – even the ones who managed to stay impartial – had their heads in their hands too. Because for the second time in a year, a major world political event had ended with victory for the side that told the most lies."

Yet he is despondent about just how (and if) alternative facts can be connected and corrected with the truth: "...fact checking proved to have very little answer when confronted with naked shamelessness. The campaigners knew their veracity was being questioned, and took no effort to correct themselves or even offer a coherent defence. Statements that had been proved blatantly untrue became central to both the Trump and Brexit campaigns."

Professor Jay Blumler is the doyen of media researchers in the UK. In many ways he invented the discipline and has been practising it for more than half a century. Blumler has observed and analysed scores of election campaigns. In 'How the broadcasters did – and what they did not do', Blumler is left less than impressed with the British broadcasters' performance in 2016 .

"...what about the broadcasters' role in the Referendum campaign? 'Not us guv' seems to have been their predominant reaction to its shortcomings. It was as if they felt they had done the best they could with the hands they had been dealt by the Remain and Leave campaigns."

Professor Ivor Gaber is a poacher turned gamekeeper; a former TV Election producer (for ITN and the BBC) who now analyses them and their motivation for an academic audience. He argues in 'Did the BBC fail its Brexit balancing act?' that 'balance' – which he labels 'phoney balance' – meant lack of analysis of the weight of arguments.

As he points out: "On the day before the Brexit vote 1,280 business leaders signed a letter to The Times backing UK membership of the EU. Not only within the body of the story, but within the very headline, the BBC 'balanced' the letter with a quote from one – repeat, one – entrepreneur, Sir James Dyson, who had said he was in favour of Leave..."

Gaber pleads for the BBC to learn lessons from this deviation from normal good practice. "If trust in the Corporation begins to diminish then we are all diminished. The BBC needs defending, but that task is that much easier when the defending is clearly merited. We need more good journalism and less phoney balance."

Finally , it is left to the BBC to stoutly defend itself. David Jordan and Ric Bailey are the most senior editorial policy figures in the Corporation. They make the rules on balance, impartiality and fairness. Jordan/Bailey pull few punches in 'Impartiality and the BBC: 'Broad balance' in a two-horse race.'

They see no evil, no lack of balance and impartiality with the BBC and the Referendum coverage. They admit it was difficult in a binary vote but the programme makers, under their guidance, were impartial. They say: "Nonetheless, the BBC should be open to those who may challenge a consensus – not all such conventional opinions stand the test of time, as those many economists who banged the drum for the Euro or who failed to anticipate the financial crash might now attest" – which does not really answer the question of the balance of ten Nobel Prize winners in economics saying 'Vote Remain' being given equal air time with a rogue 'Leave' economist.

Jordan and Bailey give the BBC's critics short shrift. "This has meant much of the research and criticism of broadcasters which followed the EU Referendum was too often based on an unspoken and partial, but deadly, assumption: that the British people had made a monumental mistake in the way they voted."

Leave won the vote but by a small margin. This surprised both the leaders of that campaign and the broadcasters on the night of June 23. How much a part the air war and the seeming partiality of some of the broadcast news coverage played in that victory is open to question. This section may have provided some clues to an answer.

Broadcasting, balance and Brexit: the role of impartiality in an age of confusion

Justin Lewis and Stephen Cushion analyse a year of bad press and bendy bananas

Before the EU Referendum campaign in the UK began, information about the European Union was both threadbare and lop-sided. Most people's understanding of the EU was hazy: a knowledge survey, conducted across all 28 EU countries, put the UK public second from bottom (above only Latvia), with only around a quarter able to answer three basic questions about the EU (Hix, 2016). How far journalists were aware of this democratic deficit remains unclear. But any attempts to provide information about the EU, both its limits and its possibilities, its benefits and pitfalls, have often been drowned out by narrow party political debates at Westminster in which UK interests were invariably pitched against the EU (Wahl-Jorgensen et al, 2013).

Sections of the popular UK press (notably The Sun, Daily Mail and Daily Express) have played a leading and overtly adversarial role in promoting Euroscepticism, captured by the Sun's famous 'Up Yours Delors' headline ('Sun readers are urged to tell the French fool where to stuff his ECU')'. The tone of this coverage, reinforced by a determined group of Eurosceptic politicians, has often shaped how broadcasters report EU affairs. So, for example, Media Tenor's analysis of BBC coverage over the last 15 years found negative stories about the EU – in which their institutions were portrayed as interfering, bureaucratic and undemocratic – outnumbered positive stories by more four to one. To put this in perspective, in 2015 they found the EU had the same proportion of negative coverage on BBC news as Syria's dictator Bashar al-Assad (Media Tenor, 2016).

Why does the EU get such a bad press? Part of the problem is that while its detractors are persistent and vocal UK politicians, its supporters have less incentive to sing its praises: even those politicians who are supportive of the EU are not in the business of giving kudos to other political institutions. They prefer to take the credit for popular initiatives, while anything less popular can be blamed on Brussels. Indeed, a headline saying 'PM gives credit to membership of the EU for jobs growth' is unimaginable, even for a Europhile Prime Minister like Tony Blair. The EU may be one of the most benign political unions ever created, but since most politics is conducted at the national level, it has, in PR terms, a structural disadvantage.

So when the EU Referendum campaign began, it would be fair to say most people didn't know much about European institutions, their power or perhaps even the very point of their existence. What they did know, or thought they knew, given the mischievous spate of misleading news stories about renaming sausages or banning straight bananas (BBC News Channel, 2007), invoked images of overpaid, meddling bureaucrats foisting pointless regulations on a long-suffering British public. While the Eurosceptic press has been vociferously negative, pro-EU outlets been far more dispassionate and even-handed, meaning few stories ever painted a favourable image of the European Parliament or other European bodies. In other words, well before the EU Referendum campaign had even begun the Remain side were at a disadvantage. The Leave campaign was able to draw upon a well-established narrative about waste, bureaucracy and interference, while the Remain campaign began with little more than an apologetic acceptance of the status quo. This was particularly the case in the Conservative Party, whose leadership felt obliged to adopt an attitude of critical engagement with the EU – one that did little to challenge the Eurosceptic narrative but asked people to put their faith in their ability to broker a better deal.

A bewildering use of balance: tit-for-tat reporting and the bias against understanding

Loughborough University's analysis of UK press coverage of the EU Referendum campaign (Deacon et al, 2016) suggested a continuation of a lop-sided news landscape which favoured Leave, as well a framework in which the main adversaries were all on the political right (principally David Cameron and George Osborne versus Boris Johnson and Nigel Farage). Firmstone's (2016) research also suggested this quantitative imbalance was compounded by a qualitative imbalance, her 'tenacity index' demonstrating Leave newspapers were far more tenacious than Remain newspapers in their support.

But for news about politics and public affairs, most people rely on broadcast media, which has both a legal obligation to be impartial and a public service mission to inform. In order to assess broadcast coverage we examined the main evening bulletins over ten weeks of the EU Referendum campaign on Channel 5 (5pm), Channel 4 (7pm), the BBC, ITV and Sky News (10pm) (Cushion and Lewis, 2017). Our aim was to look at basic measures of impartiality, but also to consider the role the evening flagship bulletins played in informing the public during the Referendum, whose apparent simplicity of response (in or out) rested on a complex cost-benefit analysis, weighing up a series of benefits and disadvantages.

The dismal state of public knowledge about the EU could, and perhaps should, have been the starting point for broadcasters. As Justin Webb, presenter of the BBC's Radio 4 Today programme, put it: "One of the clearest messages during the Referendum campaign was that audiences were hungry for real knowledge. People wanted to go beyond claim and counter-claim so they could work out what was true" (cited in Plunkett, 2016b). Broadcasters may also have been aware a well-intentioned commitment to balance opposing views had, in the past, helped create misleading impressions when the weight of evidence clearly lay on one side – notably in coverage of the MMR vaccine (Lewis and Speers, 2003) and climate change (BBC Trust, 2011).

Broadcasters were also in a unique position: as the UK's most trusted and most used news sources they were able to use the Referendum campaign to educate the public about the EU, while seeking to present the best available information about the likely impact of leaving or remaining. As we shall see, in the main news bulletins they largely chose, instead, to place responsibility for educating the public squarely on the campaigns themselves. This decision was compounded by a failure to consider impartiality within the campaigns (as well as between them), rooting the debate firmly on the right of British politics.

The focus on the two campaigns meant television news coverage of the Referendum was dominated by politicians. As Table 1 shows, the only other group to get any significant airtime were members of the public, who mostly echoed the campaigns or expressed uncertainty or bemusement. Independent experts who might have been used to enhance the informational landscape, such as academics or economists, were marginal voices.

Table 1: Sources used in coverage of the EU Referendum campaign on UK news bulletins

Politicians (Leave/Remain campaigns)	62.2%
Public	15.5%
Foreign Leader or diplomat or institution	5.2%
Business	3.7%
Financial institution	2.6%
Economist	1.9%
Academic	1.6%
Celebrity	1.2%
Thank tank	1.1%
Other	4.9%
Total	**100%**

The coverage was so remorselessly partisan that when non-political sources were used, they tended to be absorbed into the campaigns. This worked to nullify one of the Remain side's main advantages, which was support from most of those with relevant expertise (such as economists), or from a wide cross section of civil society (hence Michael Gove's famous dismissal that 'people have had enough of experts'). Accordingly we found a significant proportion (42 per cent) of the reported claims favouring Remain came from outside politics, from business, the academy, trade unions, financial institutions or other professions, compared to only two per cent of claims on the Leave side, who were heavily reliant on politicians. But in the broadcast coverage these voices were simply absorbed onto the Remain side of the ledger, independent economists 'balanced' by dismissals of cronyism or 'Project Fear' by Leave campaigners.

So, for example, the weight of macroeconomic expertise suggested leaving the single market was likely to have a negative effect on the UK economy and would leave most people worse off, with less money available to spend on public services like the NHS. For most economists, the question was not whether people would be worse off, but by how much. The rubric of balance adopted by most broadcasters, however, meant this informed opinion was countered by – usually less independent or well-qualified – campaigners on the Leave side. Just as we saw in the coverage of MMR and climate change, this left many people confused and unsure who, or what, to believe.

Indeed, one of the main criticisms levelled at broadcasters by senior journalists like Justin Webb, John Simpson and others, was the way in which claims and counter claims of the campaigns were simply repeated rather than evaluated or assessed. So, for example, the UK Statistics Authority criticised the Leave campaign for its repeated use of the misleading claim the UK government sent £350m to the EU every week. Yet the sheer weight of repetition of this claim meant it became one of the statistics people were most likely to remember and believe (when Ipsos Mori asked people late into the campaign whether they believed this claim, 47 per cent said yes and only 39 per cent said no).

Following our analysis for a review of statistics in news reporting commissioned by the BBC Trust (Cushion, Lewis and Callaghan, 2016), we examined every statistical claim made on the bulletins in our sample during the ten week campaign, 517 in total. We found (see Table 2) most claims were neither challenged nor contextualised. When they were challenged, it was generally – in around two thirds of cases – by members of the rival campaign. This also left little space for more independent sources with expert knowledge to verify claims or contextualise information.

Table 2: The proportion of statistical claims challenged or contextualised in television news coverage of the EU Referendum.

	BBC	ITV	Ch 4	Ch 5	Sky	**Total**
Percentage of statistical claims challenged	20.4%	27.0%	18.6%	13.2%	13.7%	**21.0%**
Percentage of statistical claims contextualised	25.5%	23.6%	18.6%	23.7%	9.4%	**19.4%**

In relying so heavily on campaigners without journalistic arbitration or expert opinion, audiences were often left with little more than a statistical tit-for-tat between rival camps, with no independent voices to give claims weight and proportion. This was a campaign, in short, which generated considerably more heat than light. And it was, in significant part, a consequence of the decision by broadcasters to adopt a fairly passive approach to impartiality, relying largely on the in or out campaigners to create a well-informed British public.

More than 40 years ago, John Birt and Peter Jay wrote an essay about 'TV's bias against understanding' (1975). Their critique was, in some ways, a call for a return to Reithian values, and, like the BBC's first Director General, they did not really deal with the need for television to both address and engage with a popular audience, many of whom might not be especially well-informed or interested in what is often referred to as 'hard news'.

Our analysis of EU Referendum campaign coverage suggests a more contemporary version of the 'bias against understanding'. We knew, at the start of the campaign, the British public were not well informed about the EU. Justin Webb's statement that people were 'hungry for knowledge' may have been, in many cases, an overstatement, but it caught the mood of an electorate feeling ill-equipped to answer a complex question, and frustrated by being offered a series of claims and counter-claims.

In defending BBC coverage, James Harding, Head of BBC News, pointed out its editorial rules about 'due impartiality' and 'broad balance' allowed journalists plenty of freedom to make judgements about the relative merits of campaign claims and, where appropriate, challenge their veracity. This may well have been true on Newsnight, The Daily Politics or the BBC's fact-checking website, Reality Check, but these news formats attract relatively small audiences and cater to the most politically engaged section of the electorate. On all channels, the flagship evening bulletins have far more reach and influence, attracting millions of viewers and representing the gold standard of news output.

Indeed, shortly before the vote, Ipsos Mori published a report about public understanding of issues surrounding the EU (Ipsos Mori, 2016). It suggested despite weeks of lengthy news coverage, high levels of ignorance and misinformation persisted. One of its authors, Anand Menon, suggested this was 'troubling, so close to the Referendum. However, it is not so surprising, given the lack of accurate information provided to the public, as well as the mistruths, exaggerations, and scaremongering that have taken place during this campaign'. The broadcasters' decision to focus their coverage on the battle between two adversarial camps was understandable, but it exacerbated the problem of public confusion and misperception about the EU.

The blind-spot of broadcast impartiality: the blue on blue battle for Brexit

The BBC, commendably, issued specific EU editorial guidelines which asked editors to pursue a 'broad balance' approach to reporting the campaign. According to the guidelines:

> referendums are seldom fought purely on the basis of just two opposing standpoints – on each side, where there is a range of views or perspectives, that should be reflected appropriately during the campaign.

Beneath the central binary – in or out – lay a series of cross-cutting debates: between international cooperation and national sovereignty, unfettered free trade versus regulated trade (to protect employment rights and the environment), or the free movement of labour versus controls on immigration. A left-wing case for Remain might stress the EU's success on protecting the environment and workers' rights, as well as the economic benefits of immigration in increasing money for public services. A right-wing case for Remain might focus on the economic benefits of free trade and the EU's role in fostering market competition.

Our study suggested the BBC, along with other broadcasters, failed to reflect this range of perspectives – dramatically so. Like the press, the broadcasters privileged right-wing (mainly Conservative) voices on both sides of the argument. Conservative and UKIP politicians received, between them, four times as much coverage as Labour, the Lib Dems, the SNP, Plaid, the Greens and all other parties combined (see Figure 1). A left-of-centre case for Remain was thereby side-lined in a blue-on-blue battle for the nation's future.

The decision to portray the country's two leading Conservatives, David Cameron and George Osborne, as the principle flagbearers for the Remain side meant a focus on the issues closer to Conservative hearts: principally the importance of the single market to the British economy. In marginalising Labour, the Liberal Democrats, Plaid and the SNP, pro-EU membership issues such as employment rights, consumer protection or the environment fell down the agenda. It also muted the strong economic case for immigration, on which (ironically, given the Government's pledges to reduce immigration) most UK growth in recent years has depended.

Left-of-centre pro-EU voices were not hard to find. On the contrary, while the Conservative Party was divided about the EU, UK parties of the centre/centre-left were overwhelmingly in the Remain camp. While the Labour leader's support for

Remain may have been lacklustre, there was no shortage of Labour 'big beasts' on the campaign trail, as well as fulsome support for Remain from the other centrist or left-of-centre parties. Their absence from the broadcast campaign undoubtedly narrowed the debate.

POLITICIANS APPEARING ON TV NEWS OVER THE TEN-WEEK EU REFERENDUM CAMPAIGN

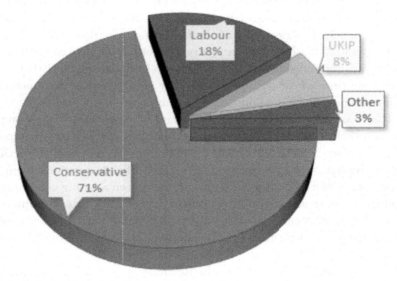

Figure 1: The political balance of politicians during the campaign

This narrowing was reflected in the topics covered during the campaign. Indeed, much of the broadcast coverage – nearly 40 per cent – was simply about the hurly burly of the campaign itself, often referred to as 'horse race' coverage (see Cushion and Thomas 2017) rather than matters of policy. Just two issues, the economy and immigration, dominated coverage, with significant and relevant areas of policy given little or no time. Loughborough's study of EU Referendum coverage found a similarly narrow focus at the expense of most other issues, 'including the environment, taxation, employment, agricultural policy and social welfare', as well as the potential consequences of a Leave vote, not least on the possible departure of Scotland from the United Kingdom (Deacon et al., 2016).

The consequences of this imbalance may well have been significant. It seems plausible at least some of those living in those Labour heartlands which voted heavily to leave were responding, in part, to a predominantly Conservative case for remaining. The Remain camp, after all, appeared to be led by a Conservative Prime Minister and Chancellor, both of whom had, in the past, been highly critical of the EU while stressing the importance of reducing immigration. This interpretation of 'due impartiality' was, in this sense, both even-handed and one-sided: the Leave and Remain camps received equal time, but we ended up with an argument that privileged Conservative arguments on both sides.

Can broadcast news play a role in restoring deliberative democracy?

It is easy, in hindsight, to be critical of the broadcast news coverage: broadcasters, after all, made efforts to be impartial in a way much of the press coverage did not (Deacon et al, 2016; Firmstone, 2016). But there are lessons to be learned, not just for covering the Brexit negotiations ahead, but for news coverage of public affairs more generally. It is clear, first of all, in an era of fake news and 'alternative facts' audiences want (and need) more clarity of information, derived from independent and well-informed sources (Cushion, Lewis and Callaghan, 2016). While it is important people hear arguments about key political issues, too much reliance on a tit-for-tat approach does not serve the public well.

It is, of course, much more straightforward for news editors to rely on politicians to communicate truths than seek out independent and well informed perspectives and construct a balanced discussion based on the best available evidence. To report through a more independent lens raises difficult questions about truth and expertise, as well as dealing with grey areas between a strong consensus of expert opinion (as in areas like MMR or climate change) and areas of genuine debate. It also raises fundamental questions about the relationship between public service broadcasters and mainstream politicians and the broader duty of broadcasters to inform.

So, for example, a key issue in the Referendum was EU immigration. Overall, research suggests EU immigration overall has a positive impact on the UK economy, with EU immigrants paying more to support public services than they receive back (e.g. Dustmann and Frattini, 2014), and yet the idea EU immigration was a drain on public services like the NHS and schools was often voiced (both during and before the Referendum period) without reporters questioning this assumption. Part of the problem, in this instance, was the extent to which pro-EU politicians saw immigration as a negative issue, and thus preferred to talk about other things rather than champion its economic impact, allowing anti-EU campaigners a clear field. In our view, broadcasters should not passively allow parties to set the terms of the debate, but be bold in assessing the weight of evidence about claims and assertions.

The failure to do this has meant the weight of public discourse rather than the weight of evidence has shaped misconceptions about immigration. Surveys show most people think immigration costs rather than benefits public services. In this instance, we would suggest, regardless of the volume of anti-immigration voices on the issue (notably in sections of the popular press[1]), broadcasters have a public service duty to rely on evidence rather than opinion. There may be various reasons to oppose EU immigration levels, but providing relief for public services is not one of them. In short, broadcasters could be bolder in debunking popular myths and informing the public where the weight of evidence lies.

This brings us to the second related point. The public deserved a wide-ranging debate with right and left more evenly represented. The broadcasters' tendency to present the Referendum largely as a battle between two shades of Conservative opinion ran counter to the BBC's own editorial guidelines as well as falling foul of broader principles of impartiality. There are a number of explanations for this: the fact the battle within the Conservative Party was seen as a 'good story', the equivocal support by the Labour leader for Remain, the news value accrued to the Prime Minister and Chancellor (who, while not leaders of the Remain campaign, appeared to be so in news coverage) and the agenda-setting role of a right-leaning national press. None of these, however, should justify the clear political skew of television news coverage of the EU Referendum campaign, which raises serious questions about the way in which impartiality is interpreted and delivered.

References

BBC News Channel, 23rd March, 2007 'Guide to best Euromyths', available at http://news.bbc.co.uk/1/hi/world/europe/6481969.stm

BBC (2011) 'BBC Trust review of impartiality and accuracy of the BBC's coverage of science', available at http://downloads.bbc.co.uk/bbctrust/assets/files/pdf/our_work/science_impartiality/science_impartiality.pdf

Birt, J. and Jay, P. (1975) 'The radical changes needed to remedy TV's bias against understanding', The Times, 1 October: 14

Cushion, S. and Thomas, R. (2017) Reporting Elections: Rethinking the Logic of Campaign Coverage. Cambridge: Polity Press

Cushion, S. and Lewis, J. (2017). Impartiality, statistical tit-for tats and the construction of balance: UK television news reporting of the 2016 EU referendum. European Journal of Communication

Cushion S, Lewis J and Callaghan R (2016) Data journalism, impartiality and statistical claims towards more independent scrutiny in news reporting. Journalism Practice. Epub ahead of print 22 November. DOI: 10.1080/17512786.2016.1256789.

Deacon D, Downing J, Harmer E, et al. (2016) The narrow agenda: How the news media covered the referendum in Jackson D, Thorsen I and Wring D. EU Referendum Analysis. 2016: Media, Voters and the Campaign, Bournemouth: Centre for the Study of Journalism, Culture and Community. http://www.referendumanalysis.eu/

Dustmann, C and Frattini, T (2014) 'The Fiscal Effects of Immigration to the UK' The Economic Journal, Doi: 10.1111/ecoj.12181, Royal Economic Society.

Firmstone J (2016) Newspapers' editorial opinions during the referendum campaign. In Jackson, D; Thorsen, E; Wring, D (2016) EU Referendum Analysis 2016: Media, Voters and the Campaign, Bournemouth: Centre for the Study of Journalism, Culture and Community. http://www.referendumanalysis.eu/

Hix S (2015) Brits know less about the EU than anyone else. In: LSE Blog. Available at: http://blogs.lse.ac.uk/europpblog/2015/11/27/brits-know-less-about-the-eu-than-anyone-else/ (accessed 14 August 2016).

Ipsos MORI (June, 2016) European Union: The Perils of Perception, at https://www.ipsos-mori.com/researchpublications/researcharchive/3742/The-Perils-of-Perception-and-the-EU.aspx

Lewis, J. and Speers, T. (2003) 'Misleading Media Reporting? The MMR story', Nature Reviews Immunology, 3 (11), pp. 913-918.

Plunkett J (2016b) Media should rethink coverage in wake of Brexit vote, says Justin Webb. The Guardian, 5 July. Available at: https://www.theguardian.com/tv-and-radio/2016/jul/05/media-should-rethink-coverage-in-wake-of-brexit-vote-says-justin-webb (accessed 2 August 2016).

Wahl-Jorgensen K, Sambrook RJ, Berry M, et al. (2013) Breadth of Opinion in BBC Output. London: BBC Trust.

Note

[1] Journalist Liz Gerard has monitored anti-immigration stories in the UK press, and found the UK's mid-market tabloids, the Mail and the Express had, between them, printed five pages a day of overwhelmingly negative stories about immigration during 2016. As she points out, laid next to each these stories would stretch for a third of a mile. http://www.sub-scribe2015.co.uk/whitetops-immigration.html#.WNt4GKLauM8

Note on contributors

Justin Lewis is Professor of Communication at Cardiff School of Journalism, Media and Cultural Studies, and Dean of Research for the College of Arts, Humanities and Social Sciences. He has written widely about media, culture and politics. His books, since 2000, include Constructing Public Opinion (New York: Columbia University Press, 2001), Citizens or Consumers: What the media tell us about political participation (Open University Press, 2005), Shoot First and Ask Questions Later: Media Coverage of the War in Iraq (Peter Lang, 2006), Climate Change and the Media (Peter Lang, 2009) and The world of 24 hour news (Peter Lang, 2010). His latest book is Beyond Consumer Capitalism: Media and the Limits to Imagination (Polity, 2013). He has also written books on media audiences, cultural policy and media and race.

Dr Stephen Cushion is a Reader at Cardiff University School of Journalism, Media and Cultural Studies. He is co-author of Reporting Elections: Rethinking the Logic of Campaign Coverage (Polity, 2018), sole author of News and Politics: The Rise of Live and Interpretive Journalism (Routledge, 2015), The Democratic Value of News: Why Public Service Media Matter (Palgrave, 2012) and Television Journalism (Sage, 2012), and co-editor of The Rise of 24-Hour News Television: Global perspectives (Peter Lang, 2010) and The Future of 24-Hour News: New Directions, New Challenges (Peter Lang, 2016). He has also published many academic journal articles and book chapters about journalism, news and politics, and co-authored several BBC Trust impartiality reviews.

Turbo-charged Pop-up Politics – Lessons from 2016

The EU Referendum has generated many lessons for TV's political journalists to learn, says Channel 4 News Political Editor Gary Gibbon

The EU Referendum was a contest like no other: conducted in unique times by unconventional political forces and driven by data not used to the same extent before. The broadcast media coverage, I think it's true to stay, didn't keep up.

There were some continuities in this campaign. There's often a shrill tone to political campaigning. This wasn't our first encounter with implausibly precise, eye-boggling sums being bandied about in political messaging. Political journalists were, as so often, drawn to 'blue on blue' attacks and the divisions amongst big name Tory politicians. But there were some novel challenges layered on top.

One of the biggest novelties in the 2016 EU Referendum was, instead of established, traditional, political parties we had the political equivalent of 'pop-up stores'[1] two multi-party campaigns, though both dominated by Tory politicians. Another new development was after decades of reporting on parties chasing a segment of swing voters in marginal seats we had Vote Leave chasing those who don't normally vote and who don't identify with the main political parties[2].

There were false demons raised and undeliverable promises sprayed at the voters. Both camps were in an almighty race to win and the normal, already strained inhibitions of political life were abandoned. As Nick Timothy, now the Prime Minister's Joint Chief of Staff, wrote after voting Leave, this was a campaign full of 'poison'[3]. Mr Timothy identifies one of the central ploys of the campaigns, not new but developed to new depths in the Referendum campaign: deploy ever more 'violent rhetoric' and a new aggressive turn of phrase will be rewarded by journalists with the front page or the top of the bulletin.

Pop-up Politics

Pop-up campaigns can pose a special threat to public understanding and trust in politics. They're entitled, under Ofcom rules[4], to dominate the coverage of the political battle, their campaign lines and promises command most of the campaign news agenda. But to adapt Sir Robin Day's phrase, there have never been more 'here today, gone tomorrow' forces. It breeds a recklessness to campaign claims and broadcasters struggled to deal with that.

After purdah came into force and the Government machine was silenced, Vote Leave moved into full bombardment mode. They behaved like a shadow government announcing a manifesto[5]. Many of them thought if they won they would take power and many of them still struggle to believe they are now scattered across the backbenches and public affairs companies, while a non-combatant like Theresa May inherited the highest office.

In these strange times, the broadcasters needed to call out the disingenuousness of a political offer the Vote Leave campaign was in no position to make. Take the 'Australian points system' for immigration, offered to the voters as a natural consequence of voting Leave. It was nothing of the sort. When Leave had won and Britain had a new Prime Minister, Theresa May acted quickly to rule out the APS approach as irrelevant to the UK's needs. In bulletin after bulletin, Vote Leave's pledge was taken on its own merits and the pop-up campaign's lack of any credentials to make major policy commitments would not have been the viewer's main take away from most bulletins.

In the 2014 Scottish Referendum, the Yes campaign anticipated these issues and their prospectus for an independent Scotland laid out what powers independence would bring to Scotland and, separately, what an SNP administration might do with those powers[6]. Some campaigning, no doubt, blurred the lines between these but the distinction was made and was highlighted in broadcast media. In 2016, the distinction was lost.

Newsrooms ferociously self-policed their adherence to the Ofcom rules but the duty of 'balance' does not over-ride other responsibilities to provide 'due impartiality' and "due weight"[7].

When the rigorously independent Institute for Fiscal Studies attacked the economics of leaving the EU[8], Iain Duncan Smith was deployed to slur its credentials and suggest EU money was dictating its slanted analysis. It was, he raged, 'a paid-up propaganda arm of the EU'. On some bulletins that attack was mocked by the reporter. But I heard bulletins which put the Iain Duncan Smith attack ahead of the painstaking research by the IFS. I wonder what I would've heard if I had tracked all the shorter bulletins on music-based or regional outlets?

Broadcasters were seduced by the vigour of the attack, exactly as they were meant to be. Programme editors want to 'freshen up' a running order, keep their audiences engaged and get some light relief from what no doubt feels like yet another dry set of numbers. And, after all, the rationale might run, we are under a duty of balance so why not switch the top of the story round?

Talking politics

Gladiatorial television debates have, in the space of a few years, come to dominate much broadcast coverage of political moments. The Referendum programmes absorbed a lot of broadcasting executives' energy. They are obsessed with getting one over on their rivals. The 'fight night' build-up might help audience share but helps to shape programmes in which studied attack lines and focus-grouped soundbites are deployed relentlessly to the enlightenment of nobody.

Sky News' extended interviews with David Cameron and Michael Gove conducted by Faisal Islam were more forensic, testing the lines deployed by the two campaigns. This was combative stuff, charged and pokey. But the politicians have it within their power to lower the pressure on these occasions. They should subject themselves to more, longer form interviews by broadcasters both in political peace-time and when voting is pending. That would reduce the intensity of what have become rare encounters to challenge at length.

The leading figures in Remain contributed to an environment in which longer interviews (and regular press conferences) were strictly limited (or abolished altogether). David Cameron deleted press conferences from his No. 10 diary. If the British Prime Minister of the day is subjecting himself to them it is harder for others to skip them. Mr Cameron also stripped longer interviews out of his diary when he was at No. 10. If these were still part of the expected access a free media is entitled to from major political figures you might get a better standard of political conversation. You might also avoid one of the more pernicious off-shoots of interview rationing. Both campaigns, knowing how competitive the broadcasters are with each other, offered 'exclusive' interviews on special terms. These would sometimes be on a 'no approach' basis[9] which means a campaign secures the 'twofor' deal of winning a place at the top of one main broadcaster's bulletin and ambushing the other side who've had no advance warning allowing them to get a retaliation in place.

I was granted one extended interview in the campaign with David Cameron and was encouraged to feel very grateful for that. At short notice, as panic set in on the Remain side, I was told Jeremy Corbyn was willing to talk to me if I could get myself up to West Bromwich. It was the first interview he had granted me since becoming leader in September 2015.

Reporting our country

I was very glad for the trip to West Bromwich. You didn't have to spend long on the high street there to discover just how little Labour identifiers knew about the party's official position on the EU. I found the majority of people I stopped either couldn't say which side Labour was on in the EU Referendum or were convinced it was supporting Leave. On another trip to the West Midlands, I found a local Labour Party was not bothering to canvas white working-class estates, effectively 'no go areas' for the purposes of the Referendum campaign.

Getting out of Westminster more and earlier would have improved my own coverage and I suspect some colleagues in the parliamentary lobby, with hindsight, feel the same. In a referendum campaign, in which every vote weighs the same, more than ever you cannot rely on the fixed points of the constituency map and the polling companies' dashboard to understand the political scene.

Most newsrooms were surprised by the result in 2016. If they reflected the country a little more maybe we wouldn't have been so blind-sided. There are exceptions – some would surprise you – but the main broadcast newsrooms reflected the pro-Remain views of their own governing demographic: city-dwelling, under 50s with university degrees. If we want to understand the country we report on better maybe we need to represent it better. Perhaps we should focus not only on gender and race when trying to balance our recruitment but on economic and geographical background too?

And if we want to know what's really going on we should ration our obsession with the nation's newspapers. I've known a number of political broadcasters who, ahead of their own late evening bulletins, check in with high circulation newspapers like the Daily Mail and The Sun to know what their headlines are going to be the next morning. There is a natural tendency not to want to get too far out of the mainstream in your take on the day's events. There's also a sense amongst public service broadcasters (and senior politicians) that these successful commercial products have a feel for public opinion which eludes the rest of us. But even if that were true, when these newspapers are in full campaign mode, weaponised and more partisan than ever, they're not the best tool for helping you shape a television news report.

Dominic Cummings has written[10] of how broadcast journalists in particular didn't have a clue what his campaign was up to mining data on voters and to this day don't have the newsroom skills to keep up with modern campaign methods. He may have a point.

For years, television bulletins have conducted their own quantitative and qualitative polling in part to help their viewers understand what the politicians are doing. If the politicians, as they were in Vote Leave, are using data on voter preferences in a more advanced and skilled way than ever before[11], the newsrooms need to understand that. Vote Leave was pursuing voters who are detached from politics and didn't normally join in the democratic process. The UK media generally didn't follow this part of the plot and that played a big part in the big surprise many of us experienced on polling day night.

Chasing facts

Broadcasters worked tirelessly in the Referendum campaign on their duty to inform. There were strands on issues, much vox popping and special features on all the issues at play in the Referendum campaign. That said, I suspect an awful lot of voters began the Referendum unclear on what the Single Market was and ended it in the same state. The details of trade negotiations and World Trade Organisation terms, visa policy and tariffs, are outside the normal stuff of political debate, a challenge to convey in simple terms and a challenge to grasp.

Several newspapers added specialist trade and Brexit correspondents to their staffing in the aftermath of the vote. It raised the quality, depth and range of reports. It generated many more stories about the impact of Brexit and authoritative challenges to Remain and Leave assertions alike. I wonder whether the better resourced broadcasters could have tried something similar before the vote?

We need to internalise 'fact checking' and 'reality checks' which have increasingly been parked in silos on the news channels or websites of major broadcasters. Checking facts should permeate everything the broadcaster does in the lead bulletins of the day, whether it is challenging the spuriously specific mega numbers which George Osborne claimed were the cost of Brexit or the £350m a week number which Vote Leave pushed into the public consciousness to massive effect.

The result

Most newsrooms, let's be honest, were surprised by the result. We failed to track the new political forms of engagement and still don't fully understand them. We lent on high impact gladiatorial contests and ghettoised fact checking when it should have coursed through all we did. We slipped into our comfort zone of big Tory beast fights. We did our best in the mission to inform but, even allowing for some people not listening, we didn't succeed.

Our obligations require us to do more than just balance one voice from one side with one voice from the other. And the only way organised, funded journalism survives is if we act as filters, professionally sifting the gems from the slag, researching the context, doing the stuff our readers and viewers are too busy doing something else all day to do for themselves.

Notes

[1] Simon Kuper, Financial Times, 26.1.17. He writes: "Like pop-up stores selling fake Rolexes, they were only ever aiming to convince the public once."

[2] Understanding the Leave Vote, by Kirby Swales, Nat Cen, 2017

[3] Conservativehome.com, 14.6.16

[4] Section 6, Ofcom Broadcasting Code, Ofcom.org.uk

[5] Tim Shipman, All Out War (2016) p 289-290; Gary Gibbon, Breaking Point (2016) p28-9

[6] Scotland's Future, 2013 p. xii – xiii, Scottish Government

[7] Ofcom Code, op cit

[8] Institute for Fiscal Studies, 25.5.17

[9] Craig Oliver, Unleashing Demons (2016), p266-7

[10] Dominic Cummings's Blog (9.1.17)

[11] Dominic Cummings's Blog (29.10.16)

Note on contributor

Gary Gibbon has been Political Editor of Channel 4 News since 2005. He was nominated for the Royal Television Society Specialist Journalist award for his coverage of the EU Referendum. In 2016, he published Breaking Point (Haus Publishing), a diary of the campaign.

In love with America, indifferent to Europe – UK journalism's westward squint

James Mates has covered the United States and Europe in detail for ITV News for many years, but argues whilst we are fascinated by life on the other side of the Atlantic, we have very little knowledge of or interest in what goes on in the organisation we have been a part of for 40 years just across the Channel. And journalism is much to blame for it

It comes around every leap year, in the dog days of summer, as if carried on a westerly breeze blowing in off the Atlantic. There's a friskiness in the air around a dozen foreign desks and editorial offices: a US Presidential election is in the offing, and a hundred journalistic nostrils catch the scent of the immigration queue at Washington Dulles, the debate spin-rooms, the balloons and ticker-tape as the fate of the free world is decided once again. In the newsroom the alpha males and females are strutting and asserting, establishing precedence, seniority and the right to this quadrennial plum assignment.

There's nothing quite like the obsession with US politics among journalists of a political bent. It's so much more glamorous and sophisticated than boring old Westminster and, most importantly, it matters. The stroke of a presidential pen can change the world.

Sadly the same has never been said of the European equivalent. Compared to the US, with its constitution and separation of powers and party conventions and electoral college tallies and inauguration day parades and state of the union addresses, how mysterious and opaque are the workings of the EU? Who is even in charge? Who put them there? Why are there so many of them? Why does so much of it happen in a foreign language?

For decades we have covered every jot and tittle of the US political landscape while ignoring the politics of our own continent, except to gleefully report on scandal, civil disturbance or outbreaks of anything with echoes of fascism. The UK media will descend on Atlanta on a cold February weekend to cover a Republican primary, and yet treat a General Election in Spain as if it were as interesting as a parish council result on the Isle of Wight. Hundreds of thousands of Britons live in Spain; as many more own holiday homes there. Spanish Government policy can have a profound effect on the UK economy and the UK's ability to get things done in Brussels, and yet... 'No', say foreign editors in dozens of national newsrooms. 'America's the place'.

The Supreme Court vs the 'Brussels Court'

Another example: the make-up of the US Supreme Court is a staple of our coverage of US politics. The battle by each successive president to swing the balance of the court from right to left or back again, the confirmation battles in the Senate, the possibility of overturning Roe vs Wade. Exciting stuff, and vital to a full understanding of power in Washington DC, but what about our coverage of the European Court of Justice? Or... hang on... do I mean the European Court of Human Rights? I never can remember. Are they even different? If I just refer to them generally as 'the Brussels Court' will that do?

I wish I was making that last bit up, but it represents a fairly standard level of reporting in the UK about judicial decision-making in Europe. The ECJ is a part of the EU. The ECHR is nothing to do with the EU. The former can be found in Luxembourg, the latter in Strasbourg. Neither is in Brussels. But how many times do we hear that 'the Brussels court' is insisting we give prisoners the vote or blocking the deportation of Abu Qatada? Damn the EU telling us what to do again!

In five years as Washington Correspondent for ITV News, requests from London to report US Supreme Court decisions were frequent enough that I certainly knew my way around the building. In the last five years as Europe Editor of ITV News I have been assigned to cover either the ECJ or the ECHR precisely zero times. Does this matter? Well, when Theresa May promises 'freeing' this country from decisions being handed down by the ECJ is a red-line in our Article 50 negotiations, shouldn't we have at least some idea what we are freeing ourselves from? Are we unshackling ourselves from the oppressive yoke of 'unelected judges' (is there another kind?) or are we damaging our prospects of free trade with our biggest market because we will not accept a disputes resolution mechanism?

Do we like it when a foreign court overrules our own? No. Do we like it when the same court over-rules some other country's judges and makes them do what we want? Yes. But without informed and reasonably regular reporting of this sort of stuff, how can a voter possibly judge whether sacrifices in some areas are more than made up for by gains in another? I would make a small wager that if you asked a thousand people in the UK to name a single judge on the ECJ you would get nothing more than blank looks. Any British judge, past or present? Do people even know there are British ECJ judges? That's how bad it is.

British neediness and the 'Special Relationship'

The difference is not just the volume, but the tenor of the way we cover US and European politics. The UK media reports America as if it's our much-admired (if occasionally baffling) older brother, doing great things in the world and from time to time letting us join in, while rewarding us with a friendly, but hopefully not patronising, pat on the head when we do well. At least once a year during my time in Washington, usually on the occasion of a Prime Ministerial visit, the foreign desk would commission a piece on 'the state of the Special Relationship'. We would call up some of our regular commentators well versed in this peculiar manifestation of British neediness, who would dutifully appear and tell us we are, indeed, still 'special'. And then, at a joint press conference, the President, standing next to the PM, would be asked just how special we were, and he'd look benignly at Fleet Street's finest and say 'very special indeed'.

The Europeans, in contrast, are just hopeless. Really not a clue how to run a country or an economy, so what gives them the right to tell us what to do in our own country, or on a continent we had to 'save' (with the help of our big brother) not once but twice in the last century? The attitude was summed up by International Trade Secretary Liam Fox declaring recently the UK is 'one of the few countries in Europe that doesn't have to bury its 20th century history', giving voice to an idea of British exceptionalism which so colours our press coverage.

It is all revealed in the language. Every interaction is a confrontation, every summit a showdown, every policy suggestion a demand, every time we don't get precisely what we want, a snub. In the UK officials who work for the Government to implement policy are civil servants. In the US they are 'administration officials'. In Europe they are 'unelected bureaucrats'.

Diplomacy by ultimatum

It was brought home vividly to me in late June 2016, just days after the Brexit vote, when a chastened David Cameron was making his final appearance at an EU summit. The press were briefed by his official spokesperson that, among the usual goodbyes, he would be saying to his fellow leaders he hoped the UK and EU would be able to forge the closest possible relationship once we had gone, but, in his view, just how close would depend on how much flexibility London and Brussels were going to show on freedom of movement.

More details were requested by an inquiring press corps. "I won't say any more because you're all going to write whatever you want anyway," said the spokesperson, wearied by experience. How right that turned out to be. The front pages of two broadsheet papers the next day spoke of 'Cameron's migrant ultimatum!'   Some mild valedictory observations on the future had suddenly become an ultimatum. Would a similar conversation in Washington have ever been characterised in such a way? I suspect the last British Prime Minister to present an 'ultimatum' to a US president was Hugh Grant.

So is it any wonder there is a widespread perception in the UK that 'we never get our way in the EU'? This is something which baffles my European colleagues. Suggest to a French journalist or politician the UK lives in a state of semi-permanent subjugation, beholden to the whims of a 'continental cabal' in Brussels and they would laugh in your face. The French complain of an EU that was a cosy, semi-statist club before the British came along and created the single-market and the globalisation that came with it. London insisted on, and got, enlargement into Eastern Europe and the migration flows that followed. And as for the Common Agricultural Policy so beloved of French farmers, Britain fought tooth and nail to reduce agricultural spending from 70 per cent of the EU budget, down to 40 per cent (and falling) today. Don't try telling a Frenchman we never get our own way!

This is why the way things are reported matters. Because however much politicians deny it, the tone and content of day-to-day coverage has a profound impact on policy-makers. Consider the health debate in the UK. When discussing the strengths and weaknesses of the NHS, journalists and policy-makers should surely be asking how others do it? To an extent we do, but we look almost exclusively across the Atlantic rather than closer to home across the Channel. We have heard plenty about Obamacare, and more recently have been given chapter and verse about the failure of Trump's plans to replace it. We know about the numbers of uninsured Americans and the perils of unrestrained capitalism when let loose on the sick and infirm. We know that's not what we want, but do we ever look at Europe? The Dutch system anyone? How do they do things in Germany, where they seem to avoid the British state of perma-crisis without impoverished Germans being left to die in the streets? It would be good to know how they do it, wouldn't it? We may even learn something.

When we steadfastly refuse to engage with European politics, even when so much of it is actually our politics, we get to the point where a UK Government White Paper can contain these words: "The sovereignty of Parliament is a fundamental principle of the UK constitution. Whilst Parliament has remained sovereign throughout our membership of the EU, it has not always felt like that." Astonishing, isn't it? We have just taken the biggest decision in our post-war history based on a 'feeling', moreover a feeling they now confirm had no basis in fact. That we could have reached this point is a failure of politics, certainly, but it is also a failure of journalism.

The Knowledge Illusion

There is a subtler point at play here as well: cognitive scientists have studied how we react in conditions of imperfect knowledge? As a species, we humans think we know a great deal more than we actually do, which, because it allows us to rely on other people's knowledge (a Community of Knowledge), has been an essential requirement of technological progress. We don't need to know how everything works in order to make use of it, which has allowed us to move on to new and more advanced technologies. So far so evolutionarily beneficial. Our weakness is we don't always grasp how much we don't know. It is only when asked to explain, in detail with a pencil and paper, how some complex process actually works that we come to realise we don't know as much as we thought. This, it turns out, applies not just to technology, but to public policy.

All very interesting, but these same cognitive scientists have identified a secondary effect alongside this 'knowledge illusion'. Evidence from numerous studies suggests our strength of feeling about an issue stands in inverse proportion to our understanding of it – the less we know, the more robust our opinions. The more we discover about the complexity of an issue, the more we moderate our views on how it could or should be tackled. And when you understand that, you understand why those who try to sell us simple solutions to difficult and often intractable problems urge us not to listen to 'experts'.

For 40 years we have not paid attention. European politics has been treated as if it was largely irrelevant, a conspiracy to thwart us and, biggest sin of all, insufferably dull. Historians may debate how much that had to do with the result of June 2016, but looking ahead we had better start to take notice now.

We know almost nothing about the European Parliament (except it's a place that 'wastes' our money and allows Nigel Farage to be rude to foreigners) but it is a body which will have a crucial voice in deciding whether we get a deal from the Article 50 talks. Not just the big one, either. We have heard (perhaps too late?) that tiny regional assemblies can wield a veto on a future free-trade deal between ourselves and our biggest market.

European politics is not going to be dull any more. Still complex, yes, but it is going to decide so much about our future prosperity that we won't be able to take our eyes off it.

The biggest irony of all is likely to be that we finally gave Europe the attention it deserves only after we decided to leave it.

References
HMSO White Paper Cm 9417 February 2017
Sloman and Fernbach, The Knowledge Illusion: Why We Never Think Alone.

Note on contributor
James Mates is Europe Editor of ITV News who has been covering events and crises (mostly crises) in the EU and the Eurozone since the Greek crisis broke out in 2011. For more than three decades he has been covering global hotspots, including postings to Tokyo and Moscow. For five years at the end of the last century he was Washington Correspondent, watching the Clinton administration implode under the Lewinsky scandal, the US Supreme Court make GW Bush president, and then the world change on 9/11.

Keep calm and carry on fact-checking

Should readers and viewers become a fully integrated part of the news process? Patrick Worrall argues that it may be an answer to journalism's woes

The night of November 8, 2016, was a painful one for just over half the people who voted in the US presidential election. Many fact-checking journalists – even the ones who managed to stay impartial – had their heads in their hands too. Because for the second time in a year, a major world political event had ended with victory for the side that told the most lies.

Whatever you felt about the case for and against Brexit, or the relative merits of Donald Trump and Hillary Clinton, there can be little dispute that the campaigns did not play by the same rules of truthfulness.

Without the firepower of Treasury number crunchers and economics think-tanks on their side, Vote Leave built the Brexit campaign around one big, resounding number: Britain was sending the EU £350m a week, which could be spent on the NHS instead. This was of course, nonsense, as everyone from the UK Statistics Authority to the Treasury select committee pointed out (fact-checkers saw this one coming a long way off: it was a variation of an old canard circulated by UKIP years before the Referendum).

In America, the country that invented fact-checking journalism, reporters started nailing Trump's frequent falsehoods from day one of his campaign. By election night, news desks buckled under the weight of bulging dossiers of mendacity.

But fact-checking proved to have very little answer when confronted with naked shamelessness. The campaigners knew their veracity was being questioned, and took no effort to correct themselves or even offer a coherent defence. Statements that had been proved blatantly untrue became central to both the Trump and Brexit campaigns. This wasn't supposed to happen. Fact-checking had been around for a decade or so but came into its own last year, regularly breaking into prime-time TV on both sides of the Atlantic for the first time. It should have made a difference.

The concept of fact-checking rests on a number of assumptions: lying is a bad thing; we can generally agree that certain things are demonstrably true or false; the public don't like being lied to; prominent people don't like being called liars and will therefore be more careful in the future. In their most high-minded moments, fact-checkers like to think that they are raising the standard of public discourse, encouraging politicians to be more honest and promoting evidence-based thinking. All of these assumptions came under extreme pressure in 2016. Did fact-checking fail as a concept, then? Should we all give up?

The challenges

First of all, we have to be honest about the scale of the challenges we face.

What do fact-checkers actually do? We take the statements, claims and narratives that shape public debate and we check them against the best evidence available. Very often, this means consulting experts. How else do you sensibly tackle questions of climate science, international law, epidemiology and other highly specialised fields? If, as Michael Gove put it, people really have "had enough of experts", there is very little fact-checkers can offer them. We have no real answer to anti-intellectualism.

It's also hard for us to reject the criticism that we are part of a loosely-defined "liberal elite" class that is being attacked by populist political movements and punished by voters around the world. In a sense, journalists are reaping what we sowed here. After all, fact-checking is predicated on the idea that politicians are habitually dishonest and often lie to voters for self-serving reasons. It served our purpose to promote this kind of mistrust in authority, but now readers are extending the scepticism to include the media too.

For journalists who joined the profession for idealistic reasons, we liked to think that we were holding the establishment to account. It is painful to realise that viewers and readers increasingly see us as being part of the establishment.

Look at the big fact-checking organisations in Britain and America and you see a pattern. Who funds these operations? Universities, NGOs, media organisations with ties to the state, newspapers and broadcasters that are widely perceived to have a liberal bias. For a great deal of people, organisations like Channel 4 News, the BBC, the Washington Post and Politifact personify the liberal elite. The accusation often levelled against us that we are sanctimonious and superior. It is particularly hard to refute this when you are do journalism that points out other people's errors and falsehoods.

It's also hard to say for sure whether fact-checking works. Academics, mostly in the US, have started to try to measure the effects on readers and politicians but the evidence is a mixed bag so far. Researchers have found that some politicians watch their words more carefully if they fear being fact-checked – but others twist the findings of fact-checkers dishonestly to attack their opponents.

The extent to which fact-check articles are widely read and believed is still being investigated. Different studies have disagreed on whether fact-checking can even backfire by reinforcing false beliefs in some readers.

Reasons to be cheerful

I'm going to suggest why fact-checkers should keep calm and carry on after their annus horribilis, and a potential way forward that might answer some of our critics.

The main reason to carry on exposing falsehoods is that there are people who obviously want us to stop, and those people may not have our best interests at heart. Donald Trump's presidential campaign saw an onslaught on the truth from both the campaign itself and from counterfeit news sites peddling an outlandish string of hoaxes and fabrications, most of them rabidly pro-Trump.

"Fake news" became the phrase of the moment – a problem over which politicians, journalists and internet giants began to wring their hands. The phrase quickly became devalued through overuse – and twisted and weaponised by some, notably Trump himself. But fact-checkers know what we mean by fake news: fabrication, hoax and propaganda that masquerades as honest reportage, and cloaks itself in some of the trappings of traditional journalism.

If you spend time reading news sites that peddle outright hoaxes or crazed conspiracies, tracing the connections between them and paying attention to the obsessions of the army of online trolls who help spread disinformation, then the question of foreign state involvement inevitably arises.

Why would the websites, which promote enormous numbers of apparently unconnected conspiracy theories, all happen to share a dislike of Nato and a respect for Vladimir Putin?

Is it plausible that there are hordes of real people out there waiting to descend on stories about the Syrian civil war and leave hundreds of comments heaping abuse on the enemies of Russia and her allies? This might sound paranoid, but then spreading mistrust and self-doubt is part of the propagandist's art. It's hard to discuss the problem of fake news seriously unless we know the extent to which agents of foreign powers are pulling the strings.

I found it frightening to see how quickly a sense of hopelessness spread around newsrooms at the end of 2016, fuelled by a nihilistic strain of commentary. We were now living in a "post-truth" age where facts didn't matter, or where the evidence of the eyes could be disputed with Orwellian "alternative facts". Some of my colleagues rushed to embrace this pessimism with indecent haste, as though the ascent of a celebrity property developer to the US presidency was a good reason to abandon concepts of truth and objectivity that had served western civilisation for millennia.

But until we know whether we are really dealing with a genuine organic loss of faith in our traditional standards of democracy and journalism or a determined campaign to undermine that faith and warp our perception of the public mood, we would do well to hold our nerve. Why else should we carry on with fact-checking initiatives in particular? Because we know that there is a growing public appetite for it.

Channel 4 News ran a string of video explainers in the run-up to the EU Referendum that was some of our most widely shared and watched content, racking up millions of views on Facebook, our main social media platform. Experimenting with different formats paid off: there was a huge demand for informative journalism that debunked myths and falsehoods.

In the US, fact-checkers reported similar success. Both new formats like live-blogs written to comment on televised debates, and traditional long-form articles, attracted record numbers of readers. At the very moment when fact-checkers were plagued by existential doubts about our usefulness, we found that the public were more interested in our work than ever.

The most pressing reason to carry on pointing out falsehoods, even when politicians and voters don't appear to care, is that it's the right thing to do. Stop meticulously detailing Trump's falsehoods, and lies become the new normal. Fail to point out that some people who called for Brexit did so on a false prospectus, and you embolden those individuals.

Of course it's possible to be pessimistic about the current state of the world, but this is often based on an assumption that things can't change. The journalist's habitual pessimism is usually wrong. Wars and famines come to an end eventually. Conflicts that appear intractable get resolved. No president stays in the White House forever and no political trend remains in the ascendant for long. There's no inherent reason why the public's lost faith in the media cannot be restored, with a big collective effort.

How does fact-checking in particular move forward now? One answer I am groping towards as I sit at my desk is that we need to radically change our relationship with readers and viewers, becoming enablers of the public rather than informers. The most successful recent video we made at Channel 4 News was one telling people how to do their own fact-checking, spotting fake news stories using simple internet search techniques. The message was: we are not asking you to trust us a brand or claiming to have access to secret information or skills. We are sharing the tools we have with you.

A new kind of journalism based on this kind of humility is an attractive but challenging idea: more guides, fewer splashes. More open source investigations, less privileged access to power. We would be educating and empowering people, rather than dazzling them with exclusives from secret sources. We would have to be more candid about the limits of our knowledge and resources.

It will be a tough transition to make, but the prize is a world where fact-checking stops being a niche pursuit for journalists and becomes a reflexive habit for everyone. And that's how we kill lies and fake news.

Note on contributor

Patrick Worrall is a senior producer at Channel 4 News, where he is currently most associated with the programme's FactCheck section.

'Get that lie off your bus!' Accuracy, the broadcasters and the Referendum campaign

Political debating point' – or blatant lie? The £350m claim on the side of the Vote Leave battlebus convinced the voters. It also bamboozled the broadcasters. Richard Tait thinks no one has heard the last of it

David Nicholas, that greatest of television news editors, used to send his ITN troops into election campaigns with the cheerful warning "just remember, the losing side will go down to defeat with its fingers wrapped around the testicles of the broadcasters". That has certainly been the case with the 2016 referendum. The broadcast coverage of the campaign, particularly at the BBC, has been identified by some of the Remain campaign (Oliver, 2016: 380-1) and by academic critics (including some of the authors in this book) as partly responsible for the result.

Tim Shipman, in his brilliant account of the referendum, identifies a host of key political moments that could have swung the campaign either way. It is hard to quarrel with his conclusion, shared by many of those who fought on different sides, that Leave won not because of any failings of the broadcasters but because its campaign had a more powerful emotional appeal (Shipman, 2016, 579-607).

The BBC, ITN and Sky can point to plenty of good political journalism, lively debate programmes and inventive use of online (Shipman, 2016: 306-317). However, the campaign itself marked a new low point in British political communications. The Treasury select committee, with pro Leave and pro Remain members, found in May 2016 "the public debate is being poorly served by inconsistent, unqualified and, in some cases, misleading claims and counter-claims" (House of Commons 2016). Polls showed 46 per cent of the public thought politicians in both campaigns were mostly telling lies (Ipsos Mori, 2016).

'A new hospital a week'
The committee was particularly appalled by the Leave campaign claim that on quitting the EU there would be a £350m a week windfall to spend on the NHS. Vote Leave's first billboard said "Let's give the NHS the £350 million the EU takes every week" (Bennett, 2016: 245). The campaign's red battle bus carried the slogan

"We send the EU £350 million every week, let's fund our NHS instead". Vote Leave's website, wiped the day after the vote, talked of a new hospital a week (Vote Leave, 2016).

The committee saw this in a different category from other dubious claims by both sides. It calculated that once you deducted the UK's rebate and the money that came back to the UK the true figure for the UK's net contribution to the EU was about £110m a week. The committee was scathing about the £350m figure: "The public should discount this claim. Vote Leave's persistence with it is deeply problematic" (House of Commons, 2016). Sir Andrew Dilnot, chair of the UK Statistics Authority, tried twice to get the Leave campaign to change its figure, saying "the continued use of a gross figure in contexts that imply it is a net figure is misleading and undermines trust in official statistics" (UK Statistics Authority, 2016).

'Due accuracy' vs 'Fake news'

The issue for the broadcasters in reporting the £350m was that they have an obligation to report with due accuracy as well as due impartiality. The debate about how the broadcasters interpreted impartiality in the referendum is covered elsewhere in this book, but I believe the duty of accuracy is at least equally important. It is now even more significant in an age where fake news seems to be on the verge of swamping the truth on the digital platforms which are rapidly becoming the public's main sources of news.

The BBC guidelines say 'our output must be well sourced, based on sound evidence, thoroughly tested' (BBC, 2016). The Ofcom guidance (which now applies to the BBC as well as commercial broadcasters) is crisper – 'accuracy means getting the facts right' (Ofcom, 2017). Stronger In tried to get the BBC to stop showing the bus with its claim (Shipman, 2016: 311) – the broadcasters opted for trying to challenge the figure and letting Remain politicians attack it – "Get that lie of your bus!" was Angela Eagle's challenge to Boris Johnson in the ITV debate on June 9. Nick Robinson probably got it right when he said "anybody looking at BBC News could find many examples of where we questioned and queried the £350m figure...I suppose I wish we had been a bit ballsier about it" (Bell, 2017: 16). Ironically, a BBC Trust review of the BBC's use of statistics conducted before the campaign but published after found "the BBC needs to get better and braver in interpreting and explaining rival statistics and guiding the audience" (BBC Trust, 2016: 11).

'Bullshit on a bus'

A number of Vote Leave's supporters also expressed doubts; some withdrew from its campaign in protest (Bennett, 2016: 271-6). Leave.EU's Arron Banks thought it was 'bullshit on a bus' a 'daft promise' and a 'blatant lie'. He feared 'these exaggerated claims undermine the credibility of our entire case' (Banks, 2016:

261). But Vote Leave rejected all criticisms of the figure – with good reason. It was winning them the referendum. Dominic Cummings, their campaign director, concluded:

> "Would we have won without immigration? No. *Would we have won without £350m/NHS? All our research and the close result strongly suggests no*" (Cummings, 2017).

While the media thought Stronger In won the economic argument, Leave knew differently. As Dominic Cummings put it: "For millions of people, *£350m/NHS was about the economy and living standards – that's why it was so effective.* It was clearly the most effective argument not only with the crucial swing fifth but with *almost every demographic*" (Cummings, 2017).

The rows about the figure consolidated public awareness. The MP Bernard Jenkin, who had doubts about it, saw the benefits: "I remember one Six O'Clock News with one broadcaster saying 'but how do you justify that?' with a picture of the bus with £350m for the NHS on it – you couldn't pay for that publicity!" (Bennett, 2016: 273-4). A week before the election Ipsos MORI found that 78 per cent of the public had heard of the claim; 47 per cent believed the figure to be true; only 39 per cent knew it was false. (Ipsos Mori, 2016).

Pop-up campaigns

Is the £350m just an 'overcooked' claim (Shipman, 2016: 607) or as John Whittingdale put it, simply 'a political debating point' (Bell, 2016: 16)? British politicians rarely tell outright lies – the consequences of being found out later are usually an effective deterrent. The fact that the two campaigns were pop-ups, dissolved the day after the result, may have encouraged a certain recklessness with the facts (Kuper, 2017).

But there will come a point over the next two years when it will become clear to the 47 per cent who took the figure on the bus literally that £350m a week extra will not be available to come back from the EU into the NHS. The 'new hospital a week' will not happen. It is unlikely to increase those people's faith in the integrity of the political process that such an important claim will be proved by events to have been inaccurate. They may also wonder whether the broadcasters, as their most trusted source of news, did enough to warn them.

And what if 'the lie on the bus' is the start of a new phase of British politics? The last thing in the world the UK broadcasters want to be is the electoral referee but they do have a duty of accuracy in their own reporting. The jaw-dropping events in the US, with CNN baldly contradicting Trump statements with graphic straplines such as 'Trump: I Never Said Japan Should Have Nukes (He Did)' shows you where this could all end.

One of the reasons why the £350m claim was so well known is, as the Loughborough and Cardiff content analysis has shown elsewhere in this book, that the campaign, as covered by the broadcasters, was very narrow in its scope, with non-politicians virtually excluded and each of the two camps focusing relentlessly on a very short list of issues. Jay Blumler, the doyen of UK election scholars, comparing the 2016 referendum campaign with 1975, was struck by absence of background reports – such as ITN in 1975 devoting '18 films, totalling 72 minutes of viewing time, in which different features of Common Market workings were explained' (Blumler, 2016).

Putting the boot into Dave and George

Dominic Cummings himself accused the broadcasters of showing little interest in complex issues such as the Eurozone " *'Sounds boring. Who's fronting it? Got any new names? Any chance of Boris putting the boot into Dave and George?'* is the first question from the BBC TV producer who has no interest in 'the arguments'" (Cummings, 2017).

The debate over the priorities between covering the political horse race and analysing the issues is not new (Tait, 2002). At a session at the NewsXchange Conference in November 2016, Jon Williams, then managing editor, international news of ABC News (whose chapter on Trump and Brexit is elsewhere in this book) argued that in their enthusiasm for the moment the broadcasters ran the risk of losing sight of the issues that matter for the audience.

A very senior BBC executive, Katy Searle, the BBC's head of political news, was not quite so sure: "I accept that and I think we should do more and we try and do more, in the end, it's just a bit boring. The more exciting stuff is the argument between the top politicians…and in the end I just don't think that's going to change"

Williams shot back: "But if in the end of the day all we've covered is do the exciting and we've got it wrong our reputation is massively damaged" (NewsXchange, 2016).

That debate will play itself out over the next two years' coverage of the Article 50 process. There will certainly be plenty of scope for 'arguments between top politicians'; EU negotiations can always provide late-night sessions with stressed participants. But there will also need to be sharp analysis of the issues, from what happens in future at the UK border, to how industries such as cars, financial services and airlines will operate, to the reciprocal rights of expatriates. Asking well-informed questions of experts as well as politicians is not to be an 'embittered remoaner'. It is to be a professional journalist, trying to hold power to account.

Learning from your mistakes

I began this chapter with a wise David Nicholas principle, so let me end with another one – "No former editor should say anything that makes life more difficult than it already is for the poor bastards who are still in the newsroom". The broadcasters have always been in the front line in the bitter battles over Europe –

the intimidatory attack (copy to the incoming chairman) on the BBC's journalism for not being sufficiently enthusiastic about Brexit by 70 MPs the day after Theresa May announced the Article 50 notification date is, sadly, the shape of things to come (Cowburn, 2017). So I hope these modest suggestions for the future will not add to their pressures.

The main news organisations, BBC, ITN and Sky, together with ITV, Channel 4 and Channel 5, need to agree with their regulator, Ofcom, how they should interpret their obligation to report the news with due accuracy in an era of fake news in general (quite easy) and occasionally mendacious politicians in particular (a bit trickier). The broadcasters need to know what they can do on air if faced with demonstrable falsehoods, what the regulator will do to support them if the source of the lie is a powerful politician or party and how far impartiality should take account of the credibility of claims and counter-claims.

And they should themselves have a fresh look at how they report politics: the balance between the Westminster 'bubble' and the nations and regions; the balance between reporting the arguments and analysing them; and the balance between interviewing political figures and talking to non-politicians who may have different perspectives and relevant expertise. As the 'phoney war' ends and the negotiations begin, the broadcasters, while building on their strengths and resisting bullying from whatever quarter, should also bear in mind that those who fail to learn from their mistakes are doomed to repeat them.

References

Banks, Arron (2016) The Bad Boys of Brexit, London: Biteback.

Bennett, Owen (2016) The Brexit Club, London: Biteback.

BBC (2016) Editorial Guidelines. Available online at http://www.bbc.co.uk/editorialguidelines/guidelines/accuracy/principles, accessed March 26, 2017.

BBC Trust (2016) Trust impartiality review of the BBC's reporting of statistics, 27 August 2016, London: BBC. Available online at http://www.bbc.co.uk/bbctrust/our_work/editorial_standards/impartiality/statistics, accessed on March 26, 2017.

Bell, Mathew (2017) 'The Fight against Fake News', Television, March 2017, pp 14-17.

Blumler, Jay (2016) EEC/EU campaigning in long term perspective, Jackson, Daniel, Thorsen, Einar, Wring, Dominic (eds), EU Referendum Analysis 2016: Media, Voters and the Campaign, Poole: Bournemouth University p. 11.

Cowburn, Ashley (2017) BBC accused of Brexit bias by more than 70 MPs in open letter, Independent, 21 March 2017. Available online at http://www.independent.co.uk/news/uk/politics/over-70-mps-write-open-letter-to-bbc-accusing-broadcaster-of-bias-a7640756.html, accessed on March 27, 2017.

Cummings, Dominic (2017) How the Brexit Referendum was won, Spectator, January 9, 2017. Available online at https://blogs.spectator.co.uk/2017/01/dominic-cummings-brexit-referendum-won/

House of Commons (2016) The economic and financial costs and benefits of the UK's EU membership, May 27, 2016. Available online at https://www.publications.parliament.

uk/pa/cm201617/cmselect/cmtreasy/122/12202.htm, accessed on March 26, 2017.

Ipsos Mori (2016) June 2016 Political Monitor, Topline Results, June 16, 2016. Available online at https://www.ipsos-mori.com/Assets/Docs/Polls/pm-16-june-2016-topline.pdf

Kuper, Simon (2017) The age of broken promises, FT.Com/Magazine, January 28-29, 2017.

Ofcom (2017) Broadcasting Code, Guidance Notes. Available online at https://www.ofcom.org.uk/__data/assets/pdf_file/0033/99177/broadcast-code-guidance-section-5-march-2017.pdf, accessed March 26, 2017.

Oliver, Craig (2016), Unleashing Demons, London: Hodder & Stoughton.

NewsXchange (2016). Available online at https://www.youtube.com/watch?v=dQ1WgAgF2Dg, accessed on March 27, 2017.

Tait, Richard (2002), The Parties and Television, Some Antidotes to Apathy in Bartle, John, Mortimore, Roger, Atkinson, Simon (eds) Political Communications: The General Election Campaign of 2001, London: Cass pp 236-245.

UK Statistics Authority (2016) UK Statistics Authority statement on the use of official statistics on contributions to the European Union, May 27, 2016. Available online at https://www.statisticsauthority.gov.uk/news/uk-statistics-authority-statement-on-the-use-of-official-statistics-on-contributions-to-the-european-union/, accessed on March 27, 2017

Vote Leave (2016) Cached Version of Wiped Website. Available at http://voteleave-eu.com, accessed on March 27, 2017

Note on the author

Richard Tait is Professor of Journalism at the School of Journalism, Media and Cultural Studies, Cardiff University. From 2003 to 2012 he was Director of the School's Centre for Journalism. He worked on business magazines and then at the BBC where he was editor of The Money Programme and Newsnight. He moved to Independent Television News (ITN) where he was editor of Channel 4 News from 1987 to 1995 and editor-in-chief from 1995 to 2002. He wrote a weekly column on media policy for the Creative Business section of the Financial Times from 2002 to 2004. He was a BBC governor and chair of the governors' programme complaints committee from 2004 to 2006, and a BBC trustee and chair of the trust's editorial standards committee from 2006 to 2010. He is a Fellow of the Society of Editors and the Royal Television Society and Treasurer of the International News Safety Institute.

How the broadcasters did – and what they did not do

Jay Blumler says broadcasters were jointly responsible, with politicians, for the poverty of the campaign – and makes suggestions for future referendum coverage policy

On the face of it, a referendum is a unique instrument of popular sovereignty. Whereas at general elections voters choose the representatives and parties that will enact policies into laws, in a referendum they decide for themselves what should be done over the matter in question.

And in the 2016 EU Referendum, that 'matter' was of supreme constitutional importance. Evidence indicates many Britons valued the opportunity to decide whether their country should remain in or sever ties with the European Union. Levels of public interest in the question and of turnout at the polls on June 23 were both quite high. And yet, for their part, many voters felt the campaign itself had been uninformative, even ugly at times (Brett 2016); while for their part, leading broadcasters (e.g. Laura Kuenssberg, Jeremy Paxman and Anne McElvoy) looked back on the event in post-mortem programmes through predominantly critical eyes.

Why was that? At bottom, the explanation may turn on what is meant by 'democracy' – or what is required for democracy to be efficacious. This is measurable not merely by giving people a vote but by providing materials that will enable them to vote sensibly on behalf of their interests and values.

Democratic self-governance pivots, then (as I have put it elsewhere), on a 'norm of meaningful choice', which 'is best understood in terms of a clarification of what is at stake in how an important issue might be tackled or a problem addressed' (Blumler and Coleman, 2015). Or in Banducci and Stevens' (2016: 22) words:

> Referenda function as legitimate instruments of democracy if (1) voters are informed about the issues at stake in their vote, (2) they vote on the basis of those issues once informed, and, finally, (3) they turn out to vote in sufficient numbers.

Although in their opinion, the last criterion was met by the EU Referendum, the other two on the whole were not.

Five grounds of a critical verdict on the political campaign

First, in contrast to the wide-ranging ramifications and likely impacts of the decision, was the narrowly constricted set of issues on which the campaign was actually fought. According to Glencross (2016: 19), "Once campaigning began in earnest, the EU debate bifurcated between the Government's dogged economic argument about the risks of Brexit and the anti-EU's camp's relentless politicization of immigration" – plus of course the latter's demand that the UK should rule itself free from control by Brussels.

Second, there was the narrowness of argumentation on behalf of the opposed positions – with the Remain case based predominantly on a cost-benefit calculus of overwhelming risk, leading in all probability to economic collapse, and lacking a positive stress on the shared interests and values inherent in EU functions and roles (e.g. of peace and security, international clout, over global warming, etc.); and with the Leave case seemingly based on blithe assumptions that reducing immigrant numbers, striking trade deals with non-EU countries, earning a monetary windfall for public service betterment (through elimination of the UK's allegedly huge contribution to Brussels budgets), and independently exercising national sovereign power effectively – would all be a cakewalk!

Third, there were the oft-repeated enunciations of the opposed positions in short, sharp slogans. Quirk (2016: 72-73) points out, for example, that during the BBC's blockbuster debate at the Wembley arena:

> Remain repeated the maxim that there could be no 'silver bullets' (for immigration Control) while Leave leant back on their platitude: take back control. Three words on either side were intended to stick in the memory: the tactic presumed that audiences would seek reductive approaches to a complicated matter.

As Quirk concludes, "The Referendum highlights the simplistic mode of address that has come to dominate political discourse, and its inadequacy."

Fourth, there was the engagement of leading spokespersons in what Wheeler (2016: 78-79) has termed 'a race to the bottom' of a newfound, uninhibited, sometimes snide, aggressiveness of attack upon and intolerance of opponents' stances – not entirely unlike Trump's rhetorical excesses in the US primary and general election campaigns.

According to Wheeler, 'making numerous outrageous statements [to command] media attention' was the rhetorical stock in trade of Boris Johnson, who happened to be the most frequently quoted leader of the Leave campaign. Examples among many include his equation of the EU 'superstate' with the ambitions of Nazi Germany's Fuhrer, Adolf Hitler, and his suggestion that statistical analyses by the

242

Institute for Fiscal Studies could be discounted since it was funded in part by the European Commission.

Fifth, there was the tendency for leading politicians to play fast and loose with their factual assertions, ushering in what has come to be called an age of 'post-truth politics'.

According to Yuratich (2016: 79), 'half-truths and untruths abounded' during the Referendum campaign, as with Leave's charge that Turkey was on course to join the European Union. The most egregious was the £350m bounty which Leave claimed the National Health Service could enjoy after Brexit. This was not only blazoned on its tour bus; one of its Referendum Campaign Broadcasts was devoted to it, featuring a film that showed "the difference between an old lady's experience of the NHS inside the EU – queues, waiting, not getting treated – to Leave's vision of outside the EU – empty waiting rooms, immediate service, and being cured" (Campbell, 2016: 68-69).

The broadcasters' provision: Some positive features?

But what about the broadcasters' role in the Referendum campaign? 'Not us guv' seems to have been their predominant reaction to its shortcomings. It was as if they felt they had done the best they could with the hands they had been dealt by the Remain and Leave campaigns.

In their view, they had laid on a fully responsible provision of campaign news and current affairs programming in line with UK general election standards and with the principles of public service journalism. In support, they could point to the extensiveness of their campaign coverage with relatively long and prominent reports in the morning, lunchtime, early evening and prime-time news programmes.

According to a detailed analysis by Cushion, Lewis and Campbell (2016) spanning ten weeks before polling day, as many as 571 reports on the campaign appeared in the prime-time bulletins alone of BBC1, ITV, Channel 4, Channel 5 and Sky News (somewhat more so on BBC1 than on the other channels). Moreover, this involved a commitment to do justice to the campaigners' activities and announcements. Cushion, Lewis and Campbell also said that 62 per cent of on-screen sources were politicians, mainly from the Remain and Leave camps (62 per cent ITV and 61 per cent BBC1).

The broadcasters could also maintain their campaign coverage had fulfilled their legal obligation to report impartially (with 'due' impartiality in BBC guidelines). According to Cushion, Lewis and Campbell's findings, 'actors representing the Leave and Remain campaigns were fairly well balanced in UK television news' – with 42 per cent of total minutage given to Leave spokespersons and 46 per cent to Remain ones.

How these contestants squared up to each other was also fully dealt with in campaign news. As Cushion, Lewis and Campbell say, "the coverage was generally adversarial (with arguments pitched between Leave and Remain camps)".

Ample attention was also paid to the campaign as a battle of facts and figures. Blumler (2014: 38-39) has noted how present-day political communication is continually fed by a 'rationalization stream – a flooding of the public sphere by a great deal of systematically gathered evidence, some of it quantitative' on institutional performances, social problems and trends. And according to Cushion, Lewis and Campbell as much as 37 per cent of the prime-time campaign news items included at least one statistical claim.

Blumler (2016a: 11) mentions another feature of their campaign provision, in which broadcasters could take pride: "In 2016 there were debates galore all over the television schedule, often organised around pointedly challenging questions from members of studio audiences."

What the broadcasters did not do

So far, so good...or was it? Despite their apparent public service fidelity, the broadcasters were jointly responsible with the politicians for the poverty of the Referendum campaign.

For one thing, they did precious little to broaden its issue lens beyond those on which the campaigners concentrated. An audit of seven weeks of news coverage by the Loughborough University Centre for Research in Communication and Culture in the national newspapers and the five television services showed a:

> ...remarkable consistency in coverage across the media (i.e. TV, and pro-in and out newspapers), with three issues dominating media debate: the economy, immigration and the conduct of the campaign itself...the marginalization of many other issues including the environment, taxation, employment, agricultural policy and social welfare was striking (Deacon, et al 2016: 34-35).

In a campaign lasting seven weeks, no excuse of time and space constraints could possibly apply. In postwar general elections, the BBC deliberately 'took steps to ensure that all the main issues were dealt with (Blumler, 2002: 215). The Corporation mounted nothing like a similar effort during the 2016 Referendum campaign.

For another, in normative respects, the broadcasters' news coverage sometimes seemed to have been governed less by 'due impartiality' than by 'impartiality carried to an extreme'! It was as if they considered that 'every claim by or piece of evidence for Remain [had to] be balanced by something from or for Leave' (Blumler, 2016b).

According to Cushion, Lewis and Campbell (2016), "The campaign was dominated by statistical tit-for-tat reporting in which the two campaigns traded statistical claims". By their calculation over a third of all news items about the EU included a statistical tit-for-tat between the two sides – and 42 per cent on BBC news.

Gaber (2016: 54) illustrates the point with two examples – when on a day before polling, the BBC balanced the fact that 1,280 business leaders had written a letter to The Times backing UK membership of the European Union with a contrary quote from a single entrepreneur (Sir James Dyson); and when it balanced a warning by ten Nobel Prize-winning economists of the dangers of a Brexit with a contrary quote from a single economist. Not only is such 'regulated equivocation' (Starkey's, 2016: 42) term a recipe for confusion over what to believe.

After reviewing surveyed voters' patterns of acceptance and rejection of certain factual claims made during the campaign, Banducci and Stevens (2016: 22) suggest that "if they were not motivated by accuracy…perhaps they were encouraged not to do so by a media that treated all claims as equivalent".

The broadcasters' performance was noticeably lacking in another factual area. They made no attempt to speak of to inform audience member/voters about the European Union, its component institutions, their powers and functions, and the range of policy areas in which they operate.

That it embraced the free movement of EU citizens, thereby enabling unrestricted flows of migrants; that it ran a customs union within a tariff-free single market area, as well as regulating a lot of other things; and that the UK made a large contribution to its budget – these were just about the sum total of what voters could glean about the EU from the coverage.

That contrasts sharply with how broadcasters pulled out all the cognitive stops during the 1975 referendum campaign. At that time, ITN news, for example, presented a series of 18 short films, totaling 72 minutes of screen time, explaining different aspects of Common Market workings. World in Action went on a 'Voyage of Discovery' throughout Europe (3,000 miles overall) in 'Search of the Common Market'. But it was as if in 2016, "Voters were… being asked to decide whether to stay in or leave an institution about which they could know very little" (Blumler, 2016a: 11).

Also noticeable was how the broadcasters tethered their coverage to the campaigners' ploys. Of course, they reported each side's challenges of their opponents' claims. And at times in interviews and debate moderation, they vigorously pursued the inadequacies of those claims.

According to Cushion, Lewis and Campbell (2016), however, reporters rarely probed, far less questioned, the factual assertions (even when patently unfounded or misleading) made by the two sides. As they put it, "Journalistic challenges to statistical references were not routine", having occurred in only 18 per cent of the statistically based items. Although as Starkey (2016: 42) points out, "Often the BBC referred listeners to a 'fact-checking' service online, its findings were rarely broadcast in the news."

Bound so tightly to what the Leave and Remain teams were saying and doing, the broadcasters never really moved the argument on. And in consequence they failed to prepare the electorate in advance for the momentous depth and breadth of the host of challenges, complexities and uncertainties of Brexit policy and negotiations, which only after the Leave fact are they depicting now.

How to do better in the future

Three major implications follow from this assessment for future election/referendum coverage policy.

First, broadcast journalists should take on board the inescapable fact that they play a part in defining what is at issue in public debate. Bruggemann (2014) usefully points out that this sits on a continuum between passively passing on interpretations provided by other actors and providing the audience with journalists' interpretations of a situation. In other words, they engage both in agenda-<u>sending</u> and agenda-<u>setting</u> to different degrees. The 2016 Referendum experience shows the need for more of the latter, albeit not at the expense of the former.

In addition to presenting campaigners' arguments about their pet issues, public service journalists should strive to ensure that responsible attention is also being paid to other issues a) of concern to many voters and/or b) that will evidently have to be addressed by governments once in power.

Second, there is a case for reconsidering (not jettisoning) the standing of the norm of impartiality in broadcast journalism, especially its supremely elevated role (as if a 'be-all' and 'end-all`) in election campaign coverage. Perhaps it should be regarded more as a means than as an end of such coverage – the latter being to ensure that individual citizens, without being propagandised by some dominant viewpoint, are offered bases for making informed choices on issues that matter for themselves and society at large.

Third, public service broadcasters should adopt and implement a new norm. In addition to those of impartiality, objectivity and holding power to account for its activities, policies and failings – to hold political advocates to account for the factual accuracy of their claims. They should put routines in place to serve that norm effectively – e.g. refusal to report falsehoods altogether or to give them top-line coverage; to challenge false claims within news reports; and to establish rapid response units to detect and rebut falsehoods immediately.

References

Banducci, Susan and Stevens, Dan (2016) Myth Versus Fact: Are We Living in a Post-factual Democracy? In Jackson, Dan, Thorsen, Einar and Wring, Dominic (eds) EU Referendum Analysis 2016: Media, Voters and the Campaign, Poole: Bournemouth University.

Blumler, Jay G. (2002) Public Service in Transition? Campaign Journalism at the BBC, 2001 in Bartle, John, Mortimore, Roger and Atkinson, Simon (eds) Political Communications: The General Election Campaign of 2001.

Blumler, Jay G. (2014) Mediatization and Democracy in Frank Esser and Jesper Stromback (eds) Mediatization of Politics: Understanding the Transformation of Western Democracies, Houndmills Basingstoke: Palgrave Macmillan.

Blumler, Jay G.(2016a) EEC/EU Campaigning in Long-term Perspective in Jackson, Dan, Thorsen, Einar and Wring, Dominic (eds) EU Referendum Analysis 2016: Media, Voters and the Campaign, Poole: Bournemouth University.

Blumler, Jay G. (2016b) Some Fundamental Problems of British Political Journalism, presentation to annual conference of the International Association of Mass Communication Research, Leicester.

Blumler, Jay G. and Coleman, Stephen (2015) Democracy and the Media Revisited, Javnost: The Public, Vol. 23, No. 2.

Brett, Will (2016) It's Good to Talk: Doing Referendums Differently after the EU Vote, London: Electoral Reform Society.

Bruggemann, Michael (2014)   Between Frame Setting and Frame Sending: How Journalists Contribute to News Frames, Communication Theory, Vol. 24 , No. 4: 61-82.

Campbell, Vincent (2016) Interaction and 'the floor' in the Televised Debates of the EU Referendum Campaign in Jackson, Dan, Thorsen, Einar and Wring, Dominic (eds) EU Referendum Analysis: Media, Voters and the Campaign, Poole: Bournemouth University.

Cushion, Stephen, Lewis, Justin (2017) Impartiality, statistical tit-for-tats and the construction of balance: UK television news reporting of the 2016 EU referendum campaign, European Journal of Communication, DOI: 10.1177/0267323117695736.

Deacon, David, Downey, John, Harmer, Emily, Stanyer, James and Wring, Dominic (2016) The Narrow Agenda; How the News Media Covered the Campaign in Jackson, Dan, Thorsen, Einar and Wring, Dominic (eds) EU Referendum Analysis, Media, Voters and the Campaign, Poole: Bournemouth University.

Gaber, Ivor (2016) Bending over Backwards: The BBC and the Brexit Campaign in Jackson, Dan, Thorsen, Einar and Wring, Dominic (eds) EU Referendum Analysis: Media, Voters and the Campaign, Poole: Bournemouth University.

Glencross, Andrew (2016) The Great Miscalculation: David Cameron's Renegotiation and the EU Referendum Campaign in Jackson, Dan, Thorsen, Einar and Wring, Dominic (eds) EU Referendum Analysis: Media, Voters and the Campaign, Poole: Bournemouth University.

Quirk, Sophie (2016) Comedy Clubs Offered a Better Quality of Debate than the Political Stage in Jackson, Dan, Thorsen, Einar and Wring, Dominic (eds) EU Referendum Analysis: Media, Voters and the Campaign, Poole: Bournemouth University.

Starkey, Guy (2016) Regulated Equivocation: The Referendum on Radio in Jackson, Dan, Thorsen, Einar and Wring, Dominic (eds) EU Referendum Analysis: Media, Voters and the Campaign, Poole: Bournemouth University.

Wheeler, Mark (2016) Celebrity Politicians and Populist Media Narratives: The Case of Boris Johnson in Jackson, Dan, Thorsen, Einar and Wring, Dominic (eds) EU Referendum Analysis: Media, Voters and the Campaign, Poole: Bournemouth University.

Yuratich, David (2016) The Referendum Campaign and the Public's Constitutional Understanding in Jackson, Dan, Thorsen, Einar and Wring, Dominic (eds) EU Referendum Analysis; Media, Voters and the Campaign, Poole: Bournemouth University.

Note on contributor

Jay G. Blumler is an Emeritus Professor of Public Communication at the University of Leeds and an Emeritus Professor of Journalism at the University of Maryland. A past president and Fellow of the International Communication Association, and a founding co-editor of the European Journal of Communication, his numerous writings on political communication include: The Crisis of Public Communication (with Michael Gurevitch, 1995); The Third Age of Political Communication: Influences and Features (with Dennis Kavanagh, 1999); The Internet and Democratic Citizenship (with Stephen Coleman, 2009): Core Theories of Political Communication: Foundational and Freshly Minted (2016).

Did the BBC fail its Brexit balancing act?

The Corporation certainly covered both sides of the EU Referendum campaign, but in its slavish devotion to 'balance', did it fail to truly interrogates the arguments advanced by the politicians, asks Professor Ivor Gaber

A long time ago in a galaxy far, far away – at least that's how it feels – there was a terrific row about the BBC's coverage of the Falklands War and the Corporation's alleged 'lack of patriotism'. The causus belli – of the row, not the war – was the BBC (rightly in my view) describing the British solders as, just that, 'British soldiers', rather than, as some Conservatives MPs were demanding, 'our soldiers' or, in Sun-speak, 'Our boys'. At the time I was one of the producers of ITN's Falklands coverage and I remember thinking, "Oi what about us?" But of course the BBC is different and in times of national emergency, or at least great national events, the public and the opinion formers put the BBC under far a greater intensity of scrutiny than that used to monitor the other broadcasters. And so it was with the Brexit campaign, which is why the BBC's failings were so much more significant than the failings, real or imagined, of the others, and those failings largely hung around the notion of 'balance'.

Search the estimable BBC's Editorial Guidelines for the word 'balance' and you will search in vain. As someone who has been involved in the BBC's regulatory operation I know this word has long been eschewed because it is unhelpful in seeking to produce news coverage that is as fair, impartial and accurate as possible (note in passing the Guidelines also do not contain the word 'objectivity' and the only reference to 'truth' is 'post-truth'). However, the BBC's Brexit guidelines, when referring to the Corporation's gold standard of 'due impartiality', invoked the formula of seeking: "a broad balance between the arguments" in navigating the choppy Brexit waters. Unfortunately, this 'balance between the arguments' quickly became 'balance between the facts', and led the BBC ship of state to head widely off compass. There cannot be a 'balance of facts' it is a tautological nonsense – but this did not deter BBC News on radio and TV, from approaching their coverage with this as, apparently, their guiding principle; two, of many examples, will suffice.

On the day before the Brexit vote 1,280 business leaders signed a letter to The Times backing UK membership of the EU. Not only within the body of the story, but within the very headline, the BBC 'balanced' the letter with a quote from one – repeat, one – entrepreneur, Sir James Dyson, who had said he was in favour of Leave. In fact, Dyson's support for Leave had already been broadcast two weeks before, hence this was hardly 'news', let alone balance. Nor was there any mention, in the more extensive web report of the fact Dyson had moved some of his production, not just out of the UK but out of the EU altogether, to Malaysia, a background fact highly relevant to the overall story.

Another example of this 'phoney balance' came on June 20 when ten Nobel prize-winning economists warned of the dangers to the British economy of a Brexit; the BBC 'balanced' this story with a quote from just one economist, Professor Patrick Minford. Indeed, the professor was one of the Corporation's clear favourites – he had been quoted two days before in a story about the IMF issuing a similar warning, and again the previous month when a poll found 88 per cent of UK economists were against Brexit. As eminent as Professor Minford might be, didn't the absence of any other leading economists supporting the Leave campaign ring even the tiniest of alarm bells within New Broadcasting House?

Roger Mosey, the BBC's former Editorial Director reported on a conversation with a senior BBC presenter at the time who had observed to him: "Balance has too often been taken to mean broadcasting televised press releases... Instead of standing back and assessing arguments, we have been broadcasting he says/she says campaign pieces, which rarely shed any light on anything."

Simple balance is an anathema to good journalism. It is a bolt hole for lazy journalists and, more importantly, can be unethical and misleading. It is a bolt hole because 'bothsidedness' requires little thought in producing news packages that consist simply of: introduction, brief quotes from both sides and a non-committal summary. But it is also unethical and misleading. Is it right to balance serious holocaust historians with holocaust deniers or climate change scientists with climate change deniers? Of course not, it is both unethical and misleading. Brooke Gladstone who edits National Public Radio in the US has talked about a 'Fairness Bias' which she defines as "...when the media tries to show two sides, even when they aren't equal." The result of this phoney balance was the BBC (and here we are essentially talking about news) produced coverage that was boring and confusing and drove the debate away from a meaningful discussion into a sterile chorus of he said/she said.

Another aspect of the BBC's coverage which came in for criticism was that (presumably because of fears of being accused of bias) they were perceived not to have challenged, sufficiently robustly, the Leave campaign's claim the UK 'sent' £350 million a week to Brussels and, somehow, this sum could be spent on the NHS instead. Leave campaigners have subsequently rowed back from this claim arguing this was just part of the rough and tumble of politics. They also counter-claimed that the BBC allowed itself to be equally 'conned' by the Remain campaign by publicising George Osborne's claim that leaving would cost the average family more than £4,000 a year. But this too is a 'false equivalence'. First because, perhaps due to the broadcasters' fear of being seen as unbalanced, the Leave campaigners' bus, with the £350 million claim displayed on the side, was prominent in almost every bulletin throughout the campaign. Remain had no such bus. And second, once the paucity of the evidence behind the £4,000 claim was clear the Remain campaign quietly dropped it, but the Leave campaigners continued to push £350m from Day One through to polling day.

The BBC hierarchy was not slow in seeking to rebut the torrent of criticism that came their way after the referendum. The BBC's Director of News, James Harding, wrote in The Observer: "The fundamental charge – that BBC reporting resulted in a false balance in which fanciful claims got the same billing as serious insights – is not true." He claimed Leave campaigners were challenged by BBC journalists throughout the campaign: "Go back and look at Evan Davis take on Douglas Carswell over the claim voting Leave would bring £350m a week back into UK coffers; watch David Dimbleby take on Michael Gove's dismissal of the IFS; read what Reality Check said about George Osborne's forecast that voting Leave would cost each home £4,300; watch Andrew Neil pick apart Nigel Farage's numbers on immigration. Or Kamal Ahmed on the 6pm and 10pm bulletins saying: 'The economic consensus is on one side of this debate'."

What is significant about Harding's refutation is that he mainly highlights programmes (or websites) with small audiences, or programmes not seen as part of the mainstream news output. He does mention Kamal Ahmed's comments on the main news bulletins, but for the most part the BBC's radio and television news bulletins – the most trusted sources of news – largely allowed the claims of the Leave campaign to go unchallenged. As former BBC presenter Robin Lustig has observed in his autobiography (Is Anything Happening): "It is no good the BBC replying to complaints about skewed coverage on the Ten O'clock News or the Today programme by pointing to a much better item on the website or on the Radio 4 statistical analysis programme More or Less. It would have been far better if it had embedded its excellent online Reality Check material in its mainstream broadcast output." Lustig goes on to argue: "The problem, as I see it, is that the BBC hates generating complaints – it is, by its nature, a cautious, almost timid, creature, craving love and affection and terrified of causing offence."

One BBC reporter who defended the BBC's coverage – assistant political editor, Norman Smith – justified the Corporation's approach on its Radio 4 Feedback programme by explaining: "We are there to report what the main combatants in this referendum say, do, argue. I don't think it's up to us to, as it were, go AWOL and say well, fine, but we're actually going to talk about this because we think that's what voters are interested in." To the contrary. I would argue journalists, particularly political journalists, have an obligation, not to go AWOL but certainly to go beyond simply reporting what the combatants have to say. He dismisses the notion of journalists responding to what they believe "the voters are interested in" – surely giving the voters what they are interested in is precisely what BBC journalists should be doing? The result of simply covering what the combatants said, and ignoring the audience was condemned by journalism professor Angela Phillips who, writing on The Conversation website, observed: "The decision to cover the referendum as though it were a cricket match, rather than a complex event in which every viewer and listener was actually a participant, rather than an observer, meant that in the days before the vote, fewer than a third of voters felt well, or very well, informed about their vote."

One justification for the BBC's he said/she said focus came from the Corporation's, former political editor and now Today presenter, Nick Robinson, who claimed there was a paucity of facts available and therefore one campaigner's opinion was as good as another's: "… for potential voters wanting a fact, the truth is there isn't a fact here … it's a guess, it's a judgment about what happens in the future." This augment was effectively refuted by commentator Timothy Garton Ash who wrote in the Guardian "Well, yes and no. There are facts about the past: as [Gus] O'Donnell pointed out, Greenland took three years to negotiate its comparatively simple exit and Canada spent seven years trying to get a deal with the EU. Strictly speaking, I suppose everything we say about the future is a guess. That apple might miraculously rise from your hand back to the tree, instead of falling to the ground. But even in the far from scientific field of politics, there are well-informed guesses and less-informed guesses."

Most of the BBC journalists I have spoken to when researching this subject have given an 'off-the-record' cringe when asked about the Corporation's Brexit coverage. Although a number have raised the question as to what does one do when the exigencies of 'impartiality (not to mention 'balance') requires one to try and be even-handed. News coverage does not offer the journalist the possibility of a ten-minute interrogation of a politician. As former Today programme editor Phil Harding has written in a recent article in the British Journalism Review: "What do you do about a politician who is lying though his teeth? Do you report something that isn't true? If you don't, are you censoring the news? If you do, how do you report it?"

It's an important question for all news media but particularly for the BBC; for to conclude where we began, the BBC is important, very important. According to the most recent Ofcom research, 57 per cent of the public trust the BBC most as a source of impartial news, next was ITV News with 11 per cent and Sky on seven per cent. The highest score for any national newspaper was two per cent for the Guardian. The concern is, that in an age of 'alternative facts' and 'fake news', the fact that in the UK we have a source of news which still commands such a high level of trust is a great plus for the BBC, the British media and for our democracy. If trust in the Corporation begins to diminish then we are all diminished. The BBC needs defending, but that task is that much easier when the defending is clearly merited. We need more good journalism and less phoney balance.

Note on contributor:

Ivor Gaber is Professor of Journalism at the University of Sussex. He was an independent editorial advisor to the BBC Trust and prior to that worked as a political journalist for BBC TV and Radio, ITN, Channel Four and Sky News.

Impartiality and the BBC – 'broad balance' in a two-horse race

Opinion is polarised during a binary vote and broadcasters face a particular structural challenge in their commitment to impartiality. It has led some to question whether impartiality itself needs an overhaul. That would be to risk throwing the baby out with the bathwater. Overall, impartiality served the electorate better than some partisan views would suggest, say the BBC's David Jordan and Ric Bailey

There were those, some inside the BBC, who scoffed when we suggested the EU Referendum could be the greatest impartiality challenge the Corporation had ever faced. The General Strike? The scraps with the governments of Wilson and Thatcher? The Iraq War, the Middle East? Most general elections, for goodness sake! But there is something about referendums which poses a particular challenge for an impartial news organisation. The single focus on one issue, the passion and the partisanship, the win-or-die mentality of the one-off battle (notwithstanding indyref2) where the polarised arguments become entrenched. And that was just the AV Referendum.

We are never keen on the argument that being attacked by both sides shows you must be getting it right. It's quite possible to be wrong in two different ways, so we always take such criticisms seriously. In any case, few issues only have two sides, so teetering in the middle of the proverbial see-saw is seldom the right place. After all, the centre is itself a political position in normal politics. It is why we normally prefer to talk about 'impartiality' rather than 'balance'; the editorial judgements for programme-makers are invariably far more complex and nuanced than a simple 'on the one hand this, on the other that' neutrality. And yet, that is what a referendum campaign, at heart, presents to us: a binary choice, in this case between Remain and Leave, increasingly shouted from those entrenched positions. There is no middle ground, no compromise, no overlap. If you are not with us, you are against us. When the issue is as fundamental as the UK's membership of the European Union, impacting directly on every part of the UK, impartiality is not valued, or even recognised, from the perspective of the trench; but that is the very moment it is even more vital for the voters.

Referendums are not like elections

It is this dilemma which the broadcasters have to confront when people are deciding how to vote (rather different, incidentally, after the vote, when one side has lost and we are once again faced with far more intricate judgements, such as the subsequent proper scrutiny of the execution of Brexit). How are we to avoid the simplistic stopwatch notion that impartiality – or proper 'balance' – is achieved by giving an 'equal' number of minutes and seconds to each side and yet somehow impose a rigorous test of fairness and consistency on those complex and nuanced editorial judgements made by many different people across multiple genres and timescales? Contrary to received wisdom, there is no general set of onerous rules corseting the broadcasters into a 'false balance', thus enforcing perfect equality of time, inhibiting the exposure of untruths and generally failing to inform the electorate of what it needs to know before entering the voting booth. The obligation, of course, is for 'due' impartiality; that is, take specific account of the particular circumstances of the vote in reaching judgements about fairness, accuracy, appropriate scrutiny, allowing the audience to hear all the relevant different perspectives before they make their decisions.

So in each referendum (and each election for that matter) the BBC draws up for its programme-makers a specific set of guidelines[1], which complement and supplement the normal editorial guidelines[2]. With a binary question, such as the EU Referendum, each part of the output had to achieve 'broad balance' – a disarmingly bland phrase which actually gives editors the freedom to make judgements rather than be ruled by maths, whilst recognising there had to be an overall similarity and consistency in the levels of coverage for Remain and Leave.

The second key element is that the broad balance must be between the two sides of the argument, not necessarily between the two formally designated campaign groups. This is especially important, after all, unlike elections, voters are actually being asked to answer a specific question, not just put their cross next to someone who they trust to answer the question on their behalf. The designated campaigns hone their own strategies, but do not necessarily straddle the full range of views. And the campaign groups are also very different from political parties in that – when it comes to promises to the voters – they don't really exist after polling day. A winning party has its manifesto held to account for the promises, as Chancellor Philip Hammond discovered after the 2017 Budget. Referendum campaign groups – as against individuals within them – do not have to worry about whether their speculative claims turn out to be true; they just have to win. But these designated groups are still part of the formal furniture of the referendum: their recognition, their rights and their obligations are set down in law and to win such an accolade, they must meet the criteria laid down by the Electoral Commission[3]. So whilst it is absolutely the journalistic duty of the broadcasters to scrutinise their claims, it is also appropriate we provide a platform so the electorate knows what they are saying. Imagine, as some would have it, the broadcasters refused to allow an officially designated campaign group to use certain figures or statistics during a referendum campaign; we would be in the dock before you could say the words 'judicial review'.

This approach allowed editors to use proper journalistic judgement in telling the story of the Referendum campaign; it does not, for instance, as some argued it should, impose any sort of separate matrix on coverage of the political parties in the way that happens during an election campaign. That would distort the story and certainly not help the voter.

Statistics and Lies

The most contentious issue in terms of coverage of the EU Referendum was the unprecedented allegation and counter allegation over the statistics used by both sides. These arguments were accompanied by widespread assertions we have entered a 'post truth' world, fed by a diet of internet and social media exaggeration and untruths. Of course, it has not been unknown for politicians to use statistics selectively on many previous occasions. It was ever thus. Think back to various disputes over whether spending on specific programmes has gone up or down. This illustrates well the contention that, though there are some exceptions, politicians rarely use figures to support their arguments that have no basis at all in reality. Whether spending had gone up or down depended on which years you were comparing. Neither side of the argument is telling an untruth, they are just selecting whichever part of the truth best suits their contention. The EU Referendum campaign saw a barrage of claims made by both sides: the Leave campaign's persistence in claiming the UK would regain control over £350m from EU coffers; the Remain side's focus on speculation about what might happen, especially the macro and micro economic effects of Brexit, dubbed by the Leave campaign as Project Fear.

The problem with much of the EU Referendum debate about the economy was it was about forecasts more than facts. At times we were told a vote to leave would mean the economy and public finances would deteriorate, mortgage rates would go up, more specifically house prices would decline by up to 18 per cent, each family would be £4,300 a year worse off, and so on. On the other hand, it would free us from red tape, curtail immigration and save us a fortune which could be spent on the health service.

What is the BBC's duty faced with each campaign's claims in the context of a referendum? It is not, as some have suggested, to banish some facts, or one of the campaigns, to the outer darkness, a contention usually based on who is making the argument rather than the argument itself. Nor is it to indulge 'false balance', that is, to give opposing arguments equivalence whatever the weight of opinion on either side.

It has sometimes been suggested this is what happened. But the BBC was abundantly clear, for instance, that the overwhelming weight of expert economic and business opinion was advising people to vote Remain. Nonetheless, the BBC should be open to those who may challenge a consensus – not all such conventional opinions stand the test of time, as those many economists who banged the drum for the Euro or who failed to anticipate the financial crash might now attest. Different voices must be heard from time to time, though not necessarily given the same weight or exposure.

In the binary setting of a referendum, the poor public – some of them anyway – simply plead for the BBC (which, when asked to name a single provider, they still trust more than any other medium by a country mile[4]) to just say who is telling the truth and how, therefore, they should vote. That cannot be the right role for a public service broadcaster. Whether leaving the EU is a good or a bad thing depends for each voter on their own position, what their own priorities are, their own job, economic circumstances, lifestyle, family background and so on.

Debate and Scrutiny

The BBC's job is to enable the debate; it is to interrogate, to challenge, to contextualise and to analyse the claims made on each side. Being a platform for the democratic argument, allowing the two sides to engage directly, is a fundamental purpose of our political coverage, offering the opportunity to cross-examine each other's claims. Most notably in the big debate at Wembley, just days before the vote took place, each of the big beasts present had every opportunity to challenge the wilder and dodgier assertions of the other. But throughout the campaign, there were also dozens of debates up and down the country on BBC local radio, and national and regional TV as well as on the UK networks.

Nor did the BBC shirk its responsibility to analyse the competing claims of both sides. Extensive use was made of Reality Check[5], the BBC's fact checking brand, in TV news bulletins, as well as online. Voters could find out whether it was true £350m a week could be repatriated to the UK if it left the EU[6]. And there too the assumptions and statistical underpinnings of the Remain side's claims about the future were dissected and laid bare. The notion that these claims were not scrutinised is simply untrue. Where claims were misleading or wrong, the BBC called it.

Indeed by the end of the campaign some spokespeople had become rather more shy of these claims, faced, as they were, with continuing challenge from interviewers in the big set pieces and in the day to day news coverage on the Today programme, Five Live, the Andrew Marr Show or in a series of Andrew Neil interviews with representatives of each side on BBC One.

The squeakier claims made by politicians were challenged again and again by BBC presenters and correspondents. Go back and look at Evan Davis take on

Douglas Carswell over the £350m claim[7]; watch David Dimbleby take on Michael Gove's dismissal of the IFS[8]; read what Reality Check said about George Osborne's forecast that voting Leave would cost each home £4,300[9]; watch Andrew Neil pick apart Nigel Farage's numbers on immigration[10] or Kamal Ahmed across the main bulletins stating in terms that the economic consensus was on one side of the debate. There is example after example, not just on more specialist programmes on Radio 4, such as More or Less, but primetime on BBC One, where Nick Robinson, days before the vote, clearly set out and tested the arguments of both sides[11].

Eye of the beholder

What many academics and disappointed campaigners (perhaps some in this book) present either as a 'false' or 'phoney' balance, or claim a failure on the part of the broadcasters to inform the public properly, is often rooted in their own misunderstanding of impartiality in the context of this Referendum. They fume at the failure to expose the 'lies' of one side of the campaign, and ignore the plank obscuring their own vision. Even more than in normal party politics, it seems to be much harder in a polarised referendum to self-perceive personal prejudices and then acknowledge others will have a different view. This has meant much of the 'research' and criticism of broadcasters which followed the EU Referendum was too often based on an unspoken and partial, but deadly, assumption: that the British people had made a monumental mistake in the way they voted.

Interestingly, the audience seemed to take a rather different view of the coverage, with a majority of both Remain and Leave voters believing BBC coverage was fair and balanced. The numbers on both sides for those who thought the BBC was biased were actually lower than normal, in other words, even some of the people who sometimes think the Corporation biased, in either direction, did not believe that was the case during its Referendum coverage.

So suggestions the notion of impartiality itself needs to be re-thought in the so-called 'post-truth' world and in the wake of the EU Referendum may themselves need reconsideration. The BBC's contribution followed the Referendum Guidelines about how to achieve due impartiality and a broad balance between the Referendum arguments; the evidence suggests, by and large, it succeeded, with no substantive complaints from either campaign. Before future elections or referendums, the guidelines will be looked at afresh, but then they always are, because that is precisely the requirement of judging the 'due' in 'due impartiality'.

Notes

[1] BBC Guidelines for the EU Referendum, BBC Trust http://www.bbc.co.uk/editorialguidelines/news/referendum-guidelines-feb-2016 retrieved April 13 2017

[2] BBC Editorial Guidelines http://www.bbc.co.uk/editorialguidelines/guidelines retrieved April 13 2017

[3] Electoral Commission: The Designation Process; updated March 3 2016, retrieved April 13 2017 http://www.electoralcommission.org.uk/__data/assets/pdf_file/0005/194594/Designation-process-for-the-EU-referendum.pdf

[4] 'Public Perceptions of the Impartiality and Trustworthiness of the BBC' June 2015, retrieved April 13 2017 http://downloads.bbc.co.uk/aboutthebbc/insidethebbc/howwework/reports/pdf/bbc_report_trust_and_impartiality_jun_2015.pdf

[5] http://www.bbc.co.uk/news/live/uk-politics-eu-referendum-35603388 retrieved April 12 2017

[6] http://www.bbc.co.uk/news/uk-politics-eu-referendum-36040060 updated April 26 2016, retrieved April 12 2017

[7] http://www.bbc.co.uk/news/uk-politics-eu-referendum-36380980 May 25 2016, retrieved April 12 2017

[8] Question Time; BBC One June 15 2016, retrieved BBC iPlayer April 12 2017

[9] http://www.bbc.co.uk/news/uk-politics-eu-referendum-36073201 April 18 2016, retrieved April 12 2017

[10] The Andrew Neil Interviews: Leave or Remain; BBC One June 10 2016, retrieved BBC iPlayer April 12 2017

[11] The Big EU Reality Check; BBC One June 20 2016, not currently available on BBC iPlayer

Note on the contributors

David Jordan is the BBC's Director of Editorial Policy and Standards, responsible for the development and implementation of the Corporation's Editorial Guidelines. He is a former Editor of the weekly political programme On The Record and established Radio 4's The Westminster Hour.

As Chief Political Adviser, Ric Bailey drafted the BBC's Referendum guidelines. A former lobby correspondent and Executive Editor of Question Time, he is Visiting Professor in Political Journalism at the University of Leeds. Instrumental in setting up TV election debates, his paper 'Squeezing out the Oxygen – or Reviving Democracy?' was published by the Reuters Institute in 2012.

Section six

Over here, over there

***

A belated awakening of what the media should be doing

Raymond Snoddy

The gradually emerging paradox – and consensus – is that it was members of the media who helped create the Presidential phenomenon that is Donald J. Trump and who have now emerged – some argue belatedly – as robust critics of his Presidency.

Bill Dunlop, president and chief executive of Eurovision Americas, the US subsidiary of the European Broadcasting Union, argues bluntly that there "would have been no President Trump today had it not been for the US media." Months before a single vote was cast every move Trump made, every word he spoke were given blanket coverage and carried largely unedited and unchallenged because he 'got great ratings.'

As CBS chairman Les Moonves put it: "Who would have thought this circus would come to town. It may not be good for America, but it's damn good for CBS. The money is rolling in and this is fun…Bring it on, Donald keep going." Estimates put the value of the free coverage Trump obtained in the nine months after his candidacy was announced at more than $2bn.

Then, Dunlop observes, after a year of 'giving a leg up' to the Trump campaign, the American media turned incredulous that such a person might actually be able to win.

Trump's distaste for journalists, which would later develop into open warfare, was established in the months between his nomination and the November election. "The same unregulated networks, which had allowed such an imbalance in exposure for Trump, now almost universally turned against him," says Dunlop.

After Trump's election the President's fierce attacks on the media was matched only by his unfailing ability to create fresh material for them. The result has been an injection of vigour into the mainstream media, which has awakened the interest of a public that had apparently been abandoning traditional journalism.

261

"More than any other single factor, it was the mainstream media that turned Donald Trump into a credible political force. Now Donald Trump is returning the favour, giving the mainstream media new life, as a credible, robust and truly essential journalistic force," says Dunlop.

Professor Philip John Davies, director of the David and Mary Eccles Centre for American studies at the British Library, agrees that thanks to the media Donald Trump had no problem with name recognition. It also became clear later that the public would accept his widely observed experience on The Apprentice, as well as his business career, as a reasonable substitute for having served in any public office.

It was however his skilful use of social media that was a significant characteristic of his campaign.

"He (Trump) used new technology to deliver his message direct to supporters without the intervention of political party or political journalists," Davies argues.

In fact Michael Glassner, one of the Trump team, quoted his candidate's opinion on the use of Twitter: "It was like owning the New York Times without the overhead or debt."

Davies also highlights comments from the Clinton campaign that Trump got all the coverage and that Hillary Clinton was only mentioned by the media when she talked about Trump. He notes that President Trump is antagonistic to spending public money on cultural outreach, and other aspects of soft power such as national public radio, even though he is "a genius at using soft power himself."

He says: "He has used modern and relatively untried forms of communication to shift and dominate the campaign debate and the political agenda. It is not yet clear whether he can use the same methods in a permanent campaign to government the nation he nominally leads."

Helen Boaden, former BBC Director of News, highlights the comments by the Washington Post's Margaret Sullivan that the media's blindness to the rise of Donald Trump was 'an epic fail.' The media didn't believe that someone who 'spouted misogyny, racism and anti-Semitism' could become President of the country they thought they knew. But Trump played to the journalistic love of a controversialist and as a result fairness and balance flew out the window as Trump was allowed to grab nearly two thirds of the coverage in the Primaries.

"CNN took the initiative, live streaming almost all his rallies, largely without comment or challenge. His Republican rivals barely got a look in. Trump served up conflict, outrage, headlines and tremendous ratings and the rest of the media piled in," Boaden argues.

She believes, along with academics who have studied the subject, that journalists fell into the trap of 'ping pong' reporting – creating a false moral equivalency between the two candidates. There was little attempt to stand back and test the veracity or credibility of what each was saying. But in the end the media simply didn't get what was going on, Broaden believes.

Damian Radcliffe from the University of Oregon argues that a Trump presidency is in part a reflection of the status and evolution of the media and technology industries in 2016. He sets out ten ways that they combined to help Donald Trump capture the White House in a way that was not previously possible. "Without them, Trump might not have stood a chance," he says.

The ten elements include the fact that fake news can spread more quickly than real reporting, that tech doesn't automatically discern fact from fiction and that the tech companies have helped pull away resources from the sources of real reporting. The role call, according to Radcliffe, continues with the fact that the unparalleled airline given to Trump helped him build momentum, while many journalists were out of step with the mood of the country.

Radcliffe argues that journalism has still a long way to go to rebuild public trust and to understand what journalism in the age of Trump should look like. "That's a journey that has only just begun," he argues.

In my chapter, I argue my belief that the rise of fake news and alternative facts can be countered by the vigorous pursuit of journalism and could ultimately turn out to be a blessing in disguise. As the legendary American newsman Dan Rather put it, part of the answer is to step up and say simply and without equivocation that a lie is a lie.

"Those who know that there is such a thing as truth must do everything in their power to diminish the liar's malignant reach into our society," Rather argues. Faced with barefaced lies and the noisy repetition of what is demonstrably false could create a new age of opportunity for the mainstream media where valid information will be increasingly valued. It could even help to ease the current serious pressures on the funding of that professional journalism.

Jon Williams, Managing Director, News and Current affairs of Ireland national broadcaster RTE, emphasises the extent to which the UK's vote to leave the European Union became entwined with Donald Trump's rise to the Presidency.

The parallels are many and include increasing anti-immigrant sentiment in both countries and attacks on 'experts' on both sides of the Atlantic. Trump tweeted he would soon be called Mr Brexit and former Ukip leader Nigel Farage came to America to campaign for Trump. And at a rally in Michigan Trump said that election day would be Brexit plus, plus plus.

"Two campaigns on two continents, defined by one message: the very reverse of former Guardian editor, C.P. Scott's construction – comment is free, but facts are sacred," Williams believes.

By way of contrast Doug Saunders, international affairs columnist for the Canadian newspaper The Globe & Mail asks whether Canada has become a lone safe harbour from the populist flood as the rest of the Western world took a sharp turn towards angry intolerance in 2015 and 2016.

Canada, Saunders believes, has been spared the worst – so far – because the country had an outbreak of conservative populism in the 1980s and 1990s but the wave had been successfully incorporated into mainstream conservatism. Canada also largely missed out on the painful effects of the 2008 recession.

He fears that anger, fear and paranoia could spread in the future and was just as likely to entrap minority Canadians as the white population.

"Canada has traditionally avoided extremism by offering hope – if you start on the bottom rung you can make it higher. But the second and third rungs are no longer so secure. If they fail Canada could make history by electing the world's most diverse form of self-destructive intolerance," he argues.

Trumped: the American institutional media and the new president

Helen Boaden details how US journalists forgot a few basics tools of the trade in their run-up to a reporting fail of epic proportions.

'An epic fail' was how the Washington Post's Margaret Sullivan described American reporters' blindness to the rise of Donald Trump.[1] Despite saturating him with coverage, they couldn't believe that someone 'who spouted misogyny, racism and anti-Semitism' could become President in the America they thought they knew.[2]

In 2016, The San Diego Union Tribune made history by endorsing a Democrat candidate for the first time in its 148-year history. So too the Detroit News –143 years, and the Arizona Republic, 126 years. Of the hundred top circulation print newspapers, only two endorsed Trump. The rest plumped for Hillary Clinton.[3]

Journalists and media organisations didn't want Donald Trump as President but they found him irresistible.[4] He played directly to their love of a controversialist. Fairness and balance flew out of the window as he grabbed nearly two thirds of the coverage in the Primaries. CNN took the initiative, live streaming almost all his rallies, largely without comment or challenge. His Republican rivals barely got a look in. Trump served up conflict, outrage, headlines and tremendous ratings and the rest of the media piled in.

He claimed the language of the campaign. 'Lock her up' and 'make America great again' were heard far more often in the news than 'he's unqualified' and 'stronger together'.[5] From the moment Trump announced his candidacy until he received his party's presidential nomination, he received 63 per cent of the media's coverage compared to 37 per cent for his nearest rival. In the general election period, he received 15 per cent more coverage than Hillary Clinton.[6]

That coverage was literally worth a fortune. The media measurement firm, mediaQuant, has calculated that over the course of the campaign, Donald Trump received the equivalent of $5.8bn in free media advertising from news organisations, nearly $3bn more than Clinton.[7]

Not that the coverage was positive. Quite the reverse. Tonally it was relentlessly negative, the most negative campaign since 2000 when the media decided Al Gore was too sly and George W Bush too stupid to deserve the presidency.[8]

After analysing the election content of the major daily newspapers and TV nightly news shows Professor Thomas Patterson, of the Shorenstein Center at Harvard, said journalists fell into the trap of false balance, a 'he said, she said' ping pong of opposing claims which created a moral equivalency between the two candidates. There was little attempt to stand back and test the veracity or credibility of what each was saying.[9] The writer Joan Didion once described this kind of balance as "a scrupulous passivity, an agreement to cover the story not as it is occurring but as it is presented."[10]

Some journalists later claimed that the polls misled them. In fact the 2016 presidential polls were as accurate as they had been, on average, since 1964.[11] The polls were not the problem. It was the people looking at them.

Social scientists have documented over many years our natural tendency to pay more attention to things we already agree with – our confirmation bias.[12] Margaret Sullivan sniffed it in the media's 'epic fail' of 2016. Most of Trump's swing voters are not college educated, while 92 per cent of American journalists have a degree.

For Sullivan, the cultural gap between the two explained a great deal. With their higher education, their liberal attitudes and their urban lifestyles, journalists were victims of their own confirmation bias, which, just like their audiences on social media, they almost certainly reinforced by checking and rechecking the news on their favorite election sites.[13]

If Sullivan is right, it's an irony to make the great American journalist, Walter Lippmann, wince. A hundred years before, he'd seen how wishful thinking had blinded American reporters to the realities of the Russian Revolution. He'd argued for an objective methodology to help reporters combat their natural bias. It was the key element of their newly professionalised training. Fairness and balance were norms added later to help reporters explain, as well as report, a complex world.

Critics often confuse Lippmann's idea with an all-knowing objective journalist, exactly the opposite of what he meant. Some believe objectivity is inherently implausible but its supporters point out that society accepts other roles based on an idea of impartial professional practice: judges, juries and scientists, for example, so applying it to journalism is not so outlandish.[14]

In 2016, not every American journalist forgot the basics. The Washington Post's David Fahrenthold won a Pulitzer Prize for his in-depth reporting into how Donald Trump manipulated his charities and has explained how he started his investigations acutely aware of his own potential for bias.[15]

He worked against it by actively seeking out evidence that might have knocked down his hunches about his story. It was a classic piece of objective methodology rooted in Fahrenthold's genuine open mindedness. Walter Lippmann would have been proud.

But in the intensity of a highly emotional election campaign, many journalists collectively failed to apply their old fashioned professional norms of impartiality, fairness and balance to get to what Carl Bernstein has called 'the best obtainable version of the truth.'[16] They couldn't see the importance of Trump's swing voters or how those voters really felt about Trump and Clinton. They gave them airtime but they just didn't take them seriously. As Margaret Sullivan ruefully summed up: 'They just didn't get it'.[17]

Notes

[1] Margaret Sullivan, 'The Media Didn't Want to Believe Trump Could Win. So They Looked the Other Way.' Washington Post, November 9, 2016, https://www.washingtonpost.com/lifestyle/style/the-media-didnt-want-to-believe-trump-could-win-so-they-looked-the-other-way/2016/11/09/d2ea1436-a623-11e6-8042-f4d111c862d1_story.html.

[2] Ibid.

[3] 'EBU - 11th News Assembly,' accessed May 9, 2017, https://www.ebu.ch/events/2016/11/11th-news-assembly.

[4] Thomas E. Patterson, News Coverage of the 2016 General Election How the Press Failed the Voters, Faculty Research Working Paper Series / Harvard Kennedy School, John F. Kennedy School of Government, RWP16, 52 (Cambridge, MA, 2016), 7.

[5] Ibid.

[6] Ibid.

[7] Jonathan Mahler, 'CNN Had a Problem. Donald Trump Solved It,' The New York Times, April 4, 2017, https://www.nytimes.com/2017/04/04/magazine/cnn-had-a-problem-donald-trump-solved-it.html?_r=0.

[8] Patterson, News Coverage of the 2016 General Election How the Press Failed the Voters, 4.

[9] Ibid.

[10] Thomas E. Patterson, Informing the News : The Need for Knowledge-Based Journalism (New York, 2013), 52.

[11] Nate Silver, 'The Real Story Of 2016,' FiveThirtyEight, January 19, 2017, https://fivethirtyeight.com/features/the-real-story-of-2016/.

[12] Anne Kim, 'Do Partisan Media Add to Political Polarization?,' Republic 3.0, June 26, 2014, http://republic3-0.com/partisan-media-add-political-polarization/.

[13] Sullivan, 'The Media Didn't Want to Believe Trump Could Win. So They Looked the Other Way.'

[14] Bill Kovach and Tom Rosenstiel, Elements of Journalism (Three Rivers Press, 2014).

[15] 'David Fahrenthold: Reporting on President Trump,' Shorenstein Center, February 7, 2017, https://shorensteincenter.org/david-fahrenthold-reporting-president-trump/.

[16] Eric Black, 'Carl Bernstein Makes the Case for 'the Best Obtainable Version of the Truth' | MinnPost,' Minn Post, April 17, 2015, https://www.minnpost.com/eric-black-ink/2015/04/carl-bernstein-makes-case-best-obtainable-version-truth.

[17] Sullivan, 'The Media Didn't Want to Believe Trump Could Win. So They Looked the Other Way.'

Note on contributor

Helen Boaden, former Director of BBC News and BBC Radio, was a Fellow at the Shorenstein Center on Media, Politics and Public Policy at Harvard University in 2017. Her Fellowship coincided with Donald Trump's first 100 days as president. Her full paper will appear on the Shorenstein Centre website later this summer.

The soft power of President Donald J Trump

Trump's success should not surprise us, says Professor Philip John Davies. He used the media to establish his familiarity to the US public and continued to use it incredibly effectively during his victorious campaign to generate publicity, his success at 'unfiltered communication with the electorate' via Twitter and disregard for bad publicity chiming perfectly with the 21st century media's insatiable appetite for news

Donald Trump's election as 45th President of the United States of America was greeted by many commentators with surprise, accompanied by much discussion of the perceived uniqueness of the winner, his candidacy, and the campaign that took him to victory. Trump, it has been argued, broke the mould in many ways. He became the Republican candidate without the support of any significant sector of the party hierarchy and against the strong opposition of many in the Republican elite. He used new technology to deliver his message direct to supporters without the intervention of political party or political journalists. His campaign was relentlessly and unapologetically negative.

Candidate Trump appeared to have a less well developed ground operation than that of Hillary Clinton. His campaign was substantially outspent by his Democratic opponent. Alone among holders of America's highest office he had no previous experience of elected office or public service. In a reaction that may possibly be self-examination, self-importance, or perhaps the latter disguised as the former, some journalists speculated whether they, cumulatively, had been the Frankenstein responsible for creating the monstrously successful candidacy that took Donald Trump to the White House.

Every presidential candidate's campaign provides a lens through which the American electoral process can be observed. Each team will adopt a strategy aimed at delivering their electoral objectives. Such factors as the attributes of the candidate, the contemporary issue agenda and the resource package available to the campaign operation will help determine the strategy and structure the campaign takes. Candidate campaigns assemble the elements in various individual formations, but the roots of most campaign operations lie in observation and experience of previous elections together with the regular introduction of innovations imported from every corner of US culture and life.

I capture the party
Presidential candidacy in the USA has always been an entrepreneurial business, and elections have often been bitterly contested. The US Constitution was written by men who were both wary of overbearing monarchical authority and unconvinced of the quality of unfettered democracy, especially if participants were tempted to organise into factions. Factions nevertheless emerged.

Party political structures, election regulation, the size and diversity of the electorate and the nature of campaign management and communication have evolved considerably in more than two centuries, but the USA has continued to choose its national leaders in open combat at scheduled quadrennial intervals. The language of presidential campaigns in the USA has regularly been one where candidates capture the nomination, followed by a rapid period of internal party healing, bringing factions back inside the party tent to work together on behalf of the champion nominated to compete for the White House. The ability of party political stalwarts to control the situation is limited, the potential for maverick candidacies is ever present, and the drive to discover innovative and powerful forms of political communication is critical.

Some attention has been given to the very low levels of public trust in government and other large institutions during the 2016 election campaign. The slide in public confidence among Americans that government and public officialdom could be relied on to act in good faith has been evident for half a century. This public scepticism has spread to encompass an increasing range of major institutions. Upbeats in public trust have proved temporary and attacking government even while competing to be part of it has become part of the context of US politics. Ronald Reagan opined: 'Government is not the solution to our problem; government is the problem,' in his Inaugural address. An apprenticeship in government may provide valuable experience, but comes with a track record. Opposition research is a key feature of modern campaigning, and will pick up and exploit any potential liabilities. In this atmosphere distance from the federal government and maverick status can be an advantage. Barack Obama was the first sitting US Senator to win the presidency since John F Kennedy in 1960, and Obama was such a junior US Senator that his main experience was at the local and state level in Chicago and Illinois, and his main exposure one televised convention speech. In the same period four presidents emerged from state governorships – Carter, Reagan, Clinton and George W. Bush – whose campaigns made a virtue of their unfamiliarity with Washington DC. Nixon had considerable experience in federal government but his 1968 presidential victory was the culmination of return from political oblivion. There were notable mavericks too among losing candidates – Barry Goldwater, George McGovern, John McCain.

The candidacy of Donald Trump builds on this recent history of outsider success, but takes it further. While others may have fought to capture the nomination from competing factions within their party, none had so varied a party-political history. Trump's party allegiance includes a period as a registered Democrat, sandwiched by time registered as a Republican, and peppered by a brief flirtation with Ross Perot's Reform Party. Roxanne Roberts of the Washington Post claims Trump had been considering a run for the presidency since the 1980s. He came to the campaign then not wholly inexperienced in the politics of national elections, but with a strong claim to fulfil the role of anti-establishment candidate, just as, in the estimation of Harvard scholar Theda Skocpol, 'the GOP became ripe for a Trump-style hostile takeover'.

Nominee Credentials
The Democrats' nomination of Hillary Clinton served to emphasise Trump's insurgent status. Having seen off an unexpectedly powerful challenge for the Democratic nomination from former Socialist Party member Bernie Sanders, Clinton brought to the candidacy an embarrassment of establishment credentials. Arkansas state politics, the White House, the US Senate and the State Department provided Mrs Clinton with unmatchable political experience, and a rich history to be picked over by opposition researchers.

Trump has been on the American cultural scene for decades. His abrasive style is well known. He first featured in Gary Trudeau's Doonesbury cartoon in September 1987, when he was thought to be contemplating a run for the presidency. Since starting in business he has concentrated on being front and centre of the Trump brand. The American version of The Apprentice made him a star of a hit TV programme which normalised his abrupt and dominating behaviour in an entertainment format which has the virtue of matching reality game humiliation with apparent rewards for entrepreneurship, and might even claim to have some value as business education. Name recognition was not a problem when Trump declared his candidacy for the 2016 race, though it only became clear later the public would accept his widely observed experience in reality television as a reasonable substitute for having served in any public office.

The media is the message: Or not
The Republican field in its early stages included up to 22 candidates. Trump's name recognition helped him achieve poll ratings that justified a place in the 'first tier' of candidates included in debates and similar campaign coverage. Media outlets also found Trump would reliably provide interviews, join in long radio call-in programmes, and generally make himself accessible. This continued a practice Trump had followed in his business and celebrity life. Apparently unafraid of bad

coverage, and predictably ready to hit back hard against any challenge, Trump provided media content at a time when the demand from 24-hour coverage and multiple outlets has increased massively.

Trump's complex relationship with the media was evident at the quadrennial conference for presidential candidate campaign managers, media executives and their colleagues, hosted by the Kennedy School at Harvard University in December 2016. The Trump campaign was keen to stress their distress at the bias they perceived in the coverage received from the mainstream media. Under these circumstances, it was claimed, fighting the media was a necessary and inevitable part of their campaign strategy. At the same time, public distrust of the media, especially in voting groups that might be favourable to Trump, made anti-media strategies a good campaign option. It was an option incorporated by the Trump campaign from early days. "We actively picked fights with the Union Leader," said one-time Trump campaigner Corey Lewandowski, referring to the Republican-leaning major newspaper in New Hampshire.

Lewandowski, who left the Trump team and was hired by CNN in the latter part of the campaign, also recognised the power of the Trump tweet, marvelling his candidate could 'change the narrative with 140 characters'.

Michael Glassner, also on the Trump team, quoted his candidate's opinion: "It was like owning the New York Times without the overhead or debt." Trump's tweets themselves became news – opinions expressed bluntly and often overnight that added character and entertainment value to the first and defining newscasts of the day. The news day that followed would be diverted by discussions, telephone interviews and responses and possibly further tweets, all focussed on Trump and creating a kind of media multiplier effect which kept him always in view.

The Kennedy School conference tapped the depth of dismay in other campaigns about the amount of coverage afforded to Trump. President of CNN, Jeff Zucker, was loudly heckled when he claimed Trump's famed media accessibility made him a particularly good participant in the many evening and Sunday political phone-in programmes. Campaign managers representing other Republican hopefuls did not recognise this relatively benign narrative. Denying their candidates were inaccessible, they claimed the lack of access was a consequence of decisions made within media corporations. It was a feeling shared not just by other Republicans. Hillary Clinton's director of communications, Jennifer Palmieri shared her conclusion: "He gets all the coverage and you guys only covered her when she was talking about him."

Traditionally all hopefuls make themselves very accessible early in the campaign when they need the coverage to ensure they get traction. Further into the campaign candidates often become less open as they try to control any risk factors. The Trump campaign appeared to remain more direct and high risk throughout the campaign.

Lewandowski insisted Trump's decisions on political communications – such as his attack on former Republican presidential candidate John McCain's military service, or his questioning the motivations of Judge Gonzalo Coriel – were made personally and often against the more moderated strategic recommendations of his staff. When response is negative Trump generally takes his own advice: "Anybody who hits me, we're gonna hit them 10 times harder."

Testing the limits and counting the costs

Trump pushed the boundaries of political debate. Kathleen Carroll former executive editor of Associated Press, was 'not sure middle America was ready for a candidate as loud and obnoxious as Chris Christie' at the start of the campaign. Her concerns for moderation in political rhetoric and for Christie himself were soon eclipsed. The Trump campaign also expanded the boundaries of modern social media use in campaigns, and emerged proud of their success in finding ways to bypass the mainstream media with Facebook and Twitter.

While the Trump campaign may well be remembered as powerfully innovative, there are two entirely traditional things going on here. Campaigns have always searched for new media through which to spread their message, and incumbent politicians as well as candidates in the USA have often looked for ways of communicating direct with the electorate without the encumbrance of intervening and potentially distorting messengers.

Trump made statements during the campaign about Mexicans, Muslims and women that drew general disapprobation, but did not seriously disrupt his progress to the White House. Kellyanne Conway, a campaign staffer who has become Counselor to President Trump, claimed this was because 'People don't vote on what offended them, they vote on what affected them', and it is important to remember Trump issues such as immigration, the loss of manufacturing jobs, America's overseas commitments were important matters differentiating the candidates in the eyes of the Trump electorate. Additionally, the critics taking the moral high ground when responding to Trump generally came from inside the Beltway groups and their allies, including traditional media leaders. Their criticism confirmed his outsider status, and his position as champion of everyone who professed a belief in turning out the existing elites, living up to his 1989 Chicago Tribune headline: 'Trump: The people's billionaire.'

Presidential campaigning was relatively decorous until 1828, when Andrew Jackson, feeling he had effectively been cheated of the office four years earlier, won an election where medallions, handbills and similar materials emerged as a considerable feature of the campaign.

Technological advances steadily increased the range of materials that could carry messages and be inexpensively mass produced. Whitehead and Hoag of New Jersey produced the first modern campaign buttons in the 1890s. Button vendors still may have their fingers on the pulse of the American electorate as firmly as any pollster. In 1896 William McKinley's campaign manager reached into ethnic populations often ignored by the national parties, reportedly distributing 200 million leaflets in at least ten languages. Railways brought candidates and news of candidates to voters for more than half a century. Radio was a powerful political medium from the 1920s. Self-adhesive bumper stickers were developed at about the same time television took centre stage and brought candidates visually into the American living room.

The Obama campaigns were respected for their skilful use of the internet. Campaign organisations are not necessarily cutting edge developers of communications tools, but move rapidly to adopt any new and powerful applications that become available. The 2016 campaign appeared to provide the perfect opportunity for a relatively new campaign resource to find a worthy champion. Donald Trump was a champion whose outsider status was enhanced when he could reach his constituency other than through the establishment media. His creative use of social media formats, especially of Twitter, fits into an historic pattern of incorporating relatively new technologies to create candidate-driven, unfiltered communication with the electorate.

The Trump social media campaign, and the multiplier effect of news and public affairs journalism coverage also provides a plausible explanation for the fact that, unusually in US politics, the higher spending campaign was defeated. The Center for Responsive Politics reports the Clinton campaign and other groups favouring Clinton spent between them just under $770m. The figure for Trump is just over $408m. Trump seeded his campaign with around $66m of his own money, which reduced his campaign's fundraising burdens and eased his path to the nomination. The Clinton campaign faced a longer, more expensive and more bruising nomination campaign than expected, and usually the candidate with the most damaging nomination campaign does go on to lose the election. But the most likely compensating factor for this apparent Clinton funding advantage is the free media achieved by Donald Trump. During the campaign the Internet Television News Archive recorded Trump as receiving about twice as many mentions as Clinton on TV News networks. Clinton outspent Trump on media by $262m to $126m, but the Center for Responsive Politics estimates Trump received around $5bn worth of free media attention.

President Trump is reported to be antagonistic to public expenditure on cultural outreach, national public radio and similar elements of soft power. But his route to the presidency suggests he is a genius in the use of soft power even if his messages can be harsh. He has used modern and relatively untried forms of communication to shift and dominate the campaign debate and the political agenda. It is not yet clear whether he can use the same methods in a permanent campaign to govern the nation he nominally leads.

Note on contributor:

Professor Philip John Davies is Director of the David and Mary Eccles Centre for American Studies at the British Library. Previously he was Professor of American Studies at De Montfort University in Leicester. He has written extensively on American politics and society and has been a regular observer and sometime participant in US presidential elections over the last 50 years.

How the mainstream media created President Trump – and President Trump saved the mainstream media

American TV networks and newspapers were in the doldrums, struggling to hold on to viewers and readers in the digital age, says Bill Dunlop. Then along came Donald Trump

Finally it was happening. After years of speculation, on June 16, 2015 Donald Trump made probably the most famous escalator descent in history to announce his candidacy for President of the United States.

The American media could not contain themselves. An impending election campaign, which had looked like a slam dunk for Hillary Clinton as she faced down a ragbag of mediocre Republican candidates, suddenly came to life. What was to follow in the next two years showed the American media at their worst – and its best: unregulated and shameless in the pursuit of ratings and profit, but ultimately fiercely defensive of its crucial role as a pillar of American democracy.

There would be no President Trump today had it not been for the US media. From that summer's day in 2015, for months before a single vote had been cast, every move Trump made, and every word he spoke, was given blanket coverage. Speeches and rallies were carried unedited, and it was no secret why. As Trump himself might have put it, he got great ratings.

CBS Chairman Les Moonves was among the media executives who could not believe what was happening to the moribund revenue streams of their news divisions. "Who would have thought this circus would come to town?" he asked in early 2016. "It may not be good for America, but it's damn good for CBS. The money is rolling in and this is fun...Bring it on, Donald, keep going!"[1]

The value of the coverage for Trump was enormous. Estimates put the worth of the free exposure in the nine months after he announced his candidacy at almost $2bn.[2] And it wasn't just on cable news: Trump was also dominating coverage in the terrestrial networks' evening news programmes, which have a far higher combined audience. From January to November 2015, ABC, NBC and CBS combined gave Trump 234 minutes of primetime coverage. At the same time Hillary Clinton got less than half that, at 113 minutes. And Bernie Sanders, despite already showing signs of becoming a populist phenomenon, received just 10 minutes of network news coverage in the crucial period when the electoral race was being shaped.[3]

When Trump started winning

Then, in early 2016, as voters finally went to the polls in primary elections, something unexpected happened: the man who was dominating the airwaves because of his entertainment value, actually started to win.

First in New Hampshire, then South Carolina, Florida and New York: Trump cast aside the challenge from one establishment candidate after another as he powered towards the nomination at the Republican National Convention in July. As his delegate count at the Cleveland event rose, his son Donald Junior had the honour of announcing to the Convention, in strangely appropriate terms, that his father had gone 'over the top'.

After a year of giving a leg up to Trump's campaign, now the American media were incredulous. Trump's distaste for journalists, which would later develop into open warfare, was established in the months between his nomination and the November election. The same unregulated networks, which had allowed such an imbalance in exposure for Trump, now almost universally turned against him.

During the final months of campaigning in the autumn of 2016, the narrative became that the extreme views which had appealed to Republican primary voters would be unacceptable to the wider electorate. The dark view of America articulated in Trump's Convention speech was deemed a turn-off. In short, Trump was not a fit person to be President.

That standpoint was bolstered by the release in October of the 'pussygate' tape, in which Trump infamously discussed how being a celebrity gave him licence to sexually assault women.[4] It wasn't just for the media that this moment was especially significant: the Republican Speaker of the House of Representatives, Paul Ryan, declared himself sickened by what he'd heard and said he would no longer campaign for candidate Trump.[5] And Jason Chaffetz, the Republican Chair of the House Oversight Committee, stated, "I'm out. I can no longer in good conscience endorse this person for President."[6]

As he sought to contain the damage, the candidate made a personal appearance in front of a cheering crowd at Trump Tower in New York. The media might have paused to reflect on the fact that despite the scandal, Trump still appeared to have vocal support, but they did not. "It is over for him," opined Mark Preston, Executive Editor for CNN Politics, alongside video of Trump engulfed by supporters. "This is by far the worst chapter in Donald Trump's life."[7]

Little wonder, perhaps, that Trump ended his campaign with open contempt for journalists. He took to pointing them out at the back of his rallies, describing them and their work as dishonest, false, a fabrication and part of a pro-Hillary rigged system. Journalists were met with jeers of 'disgrace' and 'traitors' from foot-stomping crowds.

When, despite all indications, Trump went on to victory on November 8, 2016, it seemed his grievances about the way TV networks and newspapers had treated him were vindicated. The media, in their collective assumption that Hillary had done enough to overcome last-minute obstacles and win the election, had been guilty of at best downplaying the evidence before their eyes. They had reported from huge Trump rallies and done colour pieces from midwest towns where front gardens were awash in Trump signs. But their conclusions were shaped not by what they'd seen, but rather by polling data, which failed to take account of how America's electoral college system might distort the outcome of the popular vote. Coupled with that was an apparent mental block over the possibility that Trump's support might be wider than a hardcore rump, which was assumed by the media not to be enough to carry him to the White House.

Tension mounts

In the wake of Trump's victory, there was no attempt at détente. Two weeks after the election, the now President-elect called leading editors and TV presenters to a meeting at Trump Tower at which they were expecting to discuss access to his administration. Instead, he reportedly let fly about what he called the 'dishonest media', singling out MSNBC and CNN as "the worst". CNN would not comment on an off the record briefing, but according to the New York Post's sources, Trump told the network's President Jeff Zucker, "Everyone at CNN is a liar and you should be ashamed."[8]

With any other President, the media might have been humbled by such treatment, licking their wounds over their inaccurate assumptions about the election and giving the new administration a chance. But Trump's fierce beating down of the media was matched only by his unfailing ability to create fresh material for them.

First and foremost, there were the tweets. Freewheeling, ill-informed, comically misspelt and often based on nothing more than what he'd seen on the breakfast shows of Fox or MSNBC; yet, since January 20, forming part of the official presidential records of the United States.

Then there were the potential conflicts of interest. On taking office, Trump refused to divest himself of his businesses; and in contrast to past practice of establishing a fully independent blind trust, he handed control of the Trump organisation to his children.

It was just the kind of thing that the legislative branch might have taken an interest in; but Paul Ryan, the House Speaker who had been sickened by Trump in October, had staged a full recovery by December. Asked how President-elect Trump should address potential conflicts of interest, he responded: "However he wants."[9] And Jason Chaffetz, the oversight chairman who earlier could not in good conscience endorse Trump, now saw no need to look too closely. "The President is exempt from conflicts of interest, so it's kind of a non-issue," he told Wolf Blitzer on CNN.[10]

As the opening weeks of the presidency progressed, the unconventional actions and statements of questionable accuracy mounted. By February 26, the Huffington Post was able to publish a list of what it called 'The First 100 Lies: the Trump Team's Flurry of Falsehoods'. Everything from the Trump camp's claim that the Inauguration crowd on the National Mall was the largest ever to the allegation that he would have won the popular vote had it not been for voter fraud, were in there.

But the media were doing more than just having fun at Trump's expense. On Monday February 13, 2017, the Washington Post, a paper with an illustrious history of exposing administration wrongdoing, reported that the acting Attorney General had warned the White House in December, 2016 that its pick for National Security Adviser, Michael Flynn, had misled officials over his conversations with the Russian ambassador and was vulnerable to blackmail. By the end of the day, Flynn had resigned.

Sensing a growing scandal over the Trump campaign's links with the Russian government, the Post, the New York Times and CNN competed to reveal new angles. All reported and analysed extensively the revelation that the new Attorney General, Jeff Sessions, had met the same Russian ambassador twice during 2016, but had denied any meetings during his Senate confirmation hearing.

This unrelenting pressure from the mainstream media annoyed Trump intensely. On February 24, as he was describing the media to a conservative gathering as "fake, phoney, fake" and saying they had no real sources, they simply made them up,[11] his Press Secretary made an unusual move. Instead of holding a regular briefing in the White House press room, Sean Spicer that day called selected journalists into his office for what was described as an 'extended pool' briefing. Barred at the door from entering the briefing were CNN, the New York Times and the BBC, among other outlets.[12]

If this was intended to intimidate media outlets which had been at the forefront of revelations about Trump, it had no effect. Jake Tapper, a distinguished former White House correspondent for ABC News who had become a presenter on CNN, was making a name for himself as a measured but forthright commentator on the behaviour of the new administration. He launched his 4pm programme that day with this statement:

"Let's not make any mistake about what's happening here. A White House that has had some difficulty telling the truth and that has seemed to have trouble getting up to speed on the basic competent functioning of government, and a President who seems particularly averse to any criticism and has called the press 'the enemies of the American people'; they are taking the next steps in attempting to avoid checks and balances and accountability.

"It's not acceptable; in fact, it's petulant. And it's indicative of a lack of basic understanding of how an adult White House functions."[13]

A reinvigorated media

This new vigour in the mainstream media awakened the interest of a public that had long been assumed to be abandoning traditional journalism. In the face of brashly partisan networks and a youthful preference for trivial clickbait, channels like CNN had seemed in terminal decline. But for both TV and newspapers, the first weeks of the Trump presidency brought a clearly quantifiable revival in fortune.

According to the US Neilsen ratings, in February 2017 Jake Tapper's 4pm CNN programme showed a 60 per cent rise in total viewers over the same month in 2016, and a 108 per cent rise in the elusive 18-54 age group, which advertisers covet.[14] This was despite the fact that February of 2016 had included the early primary elections, which in themselves had generated considerable interest.

Trump was reported to be a voracious consumer of late evening cable news and at his press conference on February 16, 2017, he fulminated against CNN's 10pm programme, hosted by Don Lemon. "You just take a look at that show," he told the assembled journalists. "The panel is almost always exclusive anti-Trump. The good news is he doesn't have good ratings." More accurately, he didn't have good ratings. When the Neilsen figures were published at the end of that month, Don Lemon's programme had risen 80 per cent in total viewers and 103 per cent in the 18-54 age group compared with February 2016.[15]

And it wasn't just serious news programmes that were benefitting. America's late night entertainment programmes had been going through a tough time since the departure of David Letterman from The Late Show on CBS and Jon Stewart from The Daily Show on Comedy Central.

By introducing a prolonged and sharply written monologue satirising Trump's daily activities, Stephen Colbert's lukewarm ratings soared, and in the week of February 13-18, 2017, The Late Show attracted 3m viewers, overcoming the long-standing dominance of NBC's more entertainment-oriented Tonight Show at 2.71m.[16] On Comedy Central, The Daily Show touched 1m the same week, after languishing around 800,000 since the departure of Stewart in 2015.[17]

Most famously, NBC's somewhat tired 42-year old institution Saturday Night Live, through the inspired casting of Alec Baldwin as Trump and Melissa McCarthy as the explosive Press Secretary Sean Spicer, attracted a peak of 10.84m viewers on February 11, 2017, its best performance for six years.[18] And on YouTube, McCarthy's first appearance as Spicer a week earlier topped 25m views in hardly more than a month.[19]

Serious print journalism also benefitted. Trump's obsession with what he called 'the failing New York Times' was doing the title no harm at all. On February 2, 2017, CEO Mark Thompson said: "President Trump was once again busy tweeting this weekend that our audiences and our subscribers were, to use his word, 'dwindling'. Well, not so much, Mr. President." The paper reported that it had added 276,000 paying digital subscribers and 25,000 print subscribers in the fourth quarter of 2016, bringing its total subscriber base to more than 3m.[20]

Executive Editor Dean Baquet backed his CEO, stating: "Every time he tweets, it drives subscriptions wildly." But for Baquet, the Trump effect was about more than revenue growth.

"There was a long time when the press wondered about its place in society," he told CNN's Reliable Sources programme on February 26, 2017. "I think what's happened in the last couple of months has been tremendous for news organisations. Our mission is clearer than it's ever been. We're covering a dramatic revolution in how the country is governed, and it feels like all the things that bothered us and made us lose a little bit of confidence in the last few months have gone away. It is so clear what our mission is."

The checks and balances in American society are supposed to be between the three branches of government. The actions of the executive branch, headed by the President, are supposed to be restrained by the oversight of the legislative branch, and by the constitutional interpretations of the judicial branch.

We have already seen that the legislative branch, dominated by Republicans who see a dream opportunity to push through a conservative agenda, is showing little sign of performing meaningful oversight of the Trump White House.

The courts, openly derided and insulted by Trump, have been more dutiful, blocking the administration's hasty attempt at a travel ban, which had focused on Muslim-majority countries. But long-term questions about judicial oversight remain, given the likelihood that the retirement or death of a Supreme Court justice will give Trump the opportunity to swing the balance of the nation's high court to the right.

Into this situation has stepped the American mainstream media.

From the ratings grab of the early days to its misjudgement over the election outcome, its record had not been great. But now, constitutionally protected by the free speech provision of the First Amendment, motivated by the regular diet of administration falsehoods and missteps, and heartened by the boost in ratings and revenue, the mission to which Dean Baquet referred has been embraced with enthusiasm.

The media are fulfilling the rôle of fourth arm of the system of checks and balances; what the British would call the 'fourth estate'. To its great credit, it has not shied away from its responsibilities, nor in any way been intimidated by the barrage of abuse and obfuscation from the new administration.

More than any other single factor, it was the mainstream media that turned Donald Trump into a credible political force. Now Donald Trump is returning the favour, giving the mainstream media new life as a credible, robust and truly essential journalistic force.

Notes

[1] Interview at the Morgan Stanley Technology, Media and Telecom Conference, San Francisco, February 29, 2016

[2] New York Times, mediaQuant and SMG Data, March 16, 2016

[3] The Tyndall Report, December 6, 2015

[4] "Trump recorded having extremely lewd conversation about women in 2005", Washington Post website, October 8, 2016

[5] Statement issued by the office of Paul Ryan, October 7, 2016

[6] Interview on FOX 13, Salt Lake City, October 7, 2016

[7] CNN, October 8, 2016

[8] New York Post, November 21, 2016

[9] Interview on CNBC, December 7, 2016

[10] Interview on CNN, February 8, 2017

[11] Speech to Conservative Political Action Conference, February 24, 2017

[12] "White House blocks CNN, New York Times from press briefing hours after Trump slams media", Washington Post, February 24, 2017

[13] "The Lead", CNN, February 24, 2017

[14] CNN press release quoting The Neilsen Company, February 28, 2017

[15] CNN press release quoting The Neilsen Company, February 28, 2017

[16] The Neilsen Company, late night ratings February 13-17, 2017, quoted by TV by the Numbers website.

[17] The Neilsen Company, late night ratings February 13-17, 2017, quoted by the TV by the Numbers website.

[18] The Neilsen Company, live + same day ratings, quoted by Deadline Hollywood, February 14, 2017

[19] YouTube views tally as at March 11, 2017

[20] New York Times earnings call, February 2, 2017

Note on contributor

Bill Dunlop is President and CEO of Eurovision Americas, Inc., the US subsidiary company of the European Broadcasting Union. He is a former Senior Programme Editor of Channel 4 News and Editorial Director of the pan-European channel Euronews. He has served as a judge at the Royal Television Society Journalism Awards and on several occasions at the International Emmy Journalism Awards in New York. He is author of an EBU report on the issues facing public service news providers in the digital age.
dunlop@eurovision-us.net

Brexit and Trump: A special relationship

A year before Britain voted to leave the EU, across the Atlantic, another election campaign had begun that was to change the course of politics in the New World, and the Old. Jon Williams explores how Donald Trump and Brexit became so closely interwoven, and each reinforced the other to deliver an extraordinary one-two punch to politics-as-usual on two continents

At 9.25am on June 2, 2016 – just hours after the UK voted to leave the European Union – a Sikorsky S-76 helicopter touched down on the West Coast of Scotland. On board, was the man who, in part, had made Brexit possible. Where once the Royal Flying Corps had trained to defend the British Empire from a continental assault, that summer morning, Donald J Trump stepped out at his newest luxury golf resort, rechristened Trump Turnberry, to hail another famous victory, and a defeat of Europe few had thought possible:

> "I think it's a great thing that happened, an amazing vote, very historic... People are angry. All over the world they're angry... They are angry over borders, they are angry over people coming into the country and taking over and nobody even noticing. They are angry about many, many things... The UK, the US, many other places. It will not be the last."[1]

A year before Britain voted for Brexit, Trump had sailed down a golden escalator in New York to launch one of the most unlikely Presidential bids in the 239-year history of the United States. On June 16, 2015, Donald Trump – property developer, reality TV star, Master of 'The Apprentice' – stood in the lobby of the Manhattan tower block that bears his name, and declared his intention to 'Make America Great Again'. It wasn't the first time the slogan had been used in a Presidential election campaign. A generation earlier, Ronald Reagan had ridden to the White House on the back of a similar pledge. But in the Internet age, Trump saw a recycling opportunity. At a rally in the country music capital, Nashville that summer, the ultimate showman told a crowd: "This is a movement... I don't want it to be about me. This is about common sense. It's about doing the right thing."[2]

For over a year before he landed at Turnberry, Trump rode a rollercoaster of hypotheticals. He declared on a presidential debate stage that he knew a two-year-old who developed autism from a vaccination.[3] He appeared on the radio show with the conspiracy theorist Alex Jones, who has suggested that the US government played a role in the 9/11 terrorist attacks. Famously, the man who was to become America's 45th President questioned the 44th President's birthplace. In 2011, Trump repeatedly demanded that Barack Obama produce his US birth certificate.[4] In 2016, he used similar questions to try to inject doubt about the qualifications of one of his GOP Presidential rivals, Senator Ted Cruz of Texas, who was born in Canada to a United States citizen.[5]

On a winter day six months before his trip to Scotland, and before a single vote had been cast in the election campaign, Trump told a crowd in Sioux Center, Iowa: "I could stand in the middle of Fifth Avenue and shoot somebody and I wouldn't lose any voters."[6] None of the controversies seemed to affect his popularity. Quite the reverse. Just four weeks before he landed in Turnberry, he had passed the target of 1,237 pledged delegates, the minimum to secure the Republican presidential nomination. His insurgent campaign had taken him from outsider to presumptive nominee.

Trump had launched his unlikely Presidential campaign just a month after David Cameron had won an equally unlikely victory in Britain's General Election. Two years earlier, besieged by an increasingly assertive Eurosceptic wing of the Conservative Party, Cameron made a promise intended to keep a short-term peace among the Tories before the 2015 General Election. He promised, if re-elected, he would hold an in-or-out referendum on continued British membership.[7] It seemed like a relatively low-risk ploy to deal with a short-term political problem. But Cameron hadn't bargained for what one of his predecessors, Harold Macmillan, once described as 'events, dear boy, events'.

No sooner had Cameron been returned to Downing Street than every night a modern day exodus began appearing on Britain's TV screens. In the third quarter of 2015 (July-September), nearly half a million people claimed asylum in the EU, a third of them refugees fleeing the war in Syria.[8] In August 2015, the German government announced that it expected to receive 800,000 asylum applications by the end of the year.[9]

For Cameron, it presented a real challenge. He'd pledged to cut net immigration into 'the tens of thousands'.[10] But just as the refugee crisis was reaching its peak, net immigration into Britain reached record levels. Official data showed a net 330,000 people moved to Britain in the year to March 2015, up 40 per cent on the same period the year before.[11]

While the rest of Europe was confronting the consequences of war in the Middle East, just a fraction of those coming to the UK were seeking asylum. Fewer than one in ten of those arriving in Britain did so, seeking protection. Some 186,000 new UK residents were from the EU. China and India accounted for the largest share of those granted visas to come to Britain from outside the EU, followed by the United States. But, coupled with the images on TV of bedraggled families fleeing conflict, it fed a perception that Britain was unable to control its own borders.

It had a parallel across the Atlantic. Right from the start, Donald Trump had made immigration a key part of his campaign to become President, promising to build a wall on America's southern border with Mexico, to keep out the illegal immigrants he blamed for crime in the United States. "Thousands of Americans have been killed by illegal immigrants," Trump told a rally in October in Springfield, Ohio.[12]

He offered a range of anecdotes in different cities. In Springfield, Trump mentioned a 90-year-old Minnesota farmer 'brutally beaten by illegal immigrants and left to bleed to death in his home'. In North Carolina, Trump told the story of a 21-year-old 'viciously murdered in cold blood, shot point blank by an illegal immigrant with a long and vicious criminal record'.[13] In Florida, he spoke about a 25-year-old shot dead by a man who had been deported four times and 'had a lengthy criminal record'.[14] He message was clear. But in fact, The American Immigration Council, a pro-immigrant nonprofit, says only 1.6 per cent of immigrant males between 18 and 39 years old were incarcerated, compared to 3.3 per cent of the native-born population in that same age group.[15] No matter. Trump was adopting Einstein's theory: "If the facts don't fit the theory, change the facts."

Three thousand miles away, immigration was continuing to prove a headache for David Cameron. With Britain heading for an in-out referendum, in February 2016, Cameron went to Brussels to renegotiate the UK's position in the EU. He'd made the Government's position on Brexit dependent on getting a new deal – and returned, Chamberlain-like, hailing if not 'peace in our time', then a deal, he claimed, gave Britain 'special status'.[16] At its heart was an 'emergency break' on welfare payments. But in truth he returned from Brussels with very little to show on the hypersensitive immigration issue. The EU simply couldn't compromise on a single market that includes labour mobility. A Prime Minister, who pledged at a General Election, just nine months before, to reduce net migration into the UK, had agreed a deal that confirmed his inability to achieve his objective.

When Cameron set the referendum date for June 23, the Ukip-backed Leave.EU campaign seized on immigration to rally support for Brexit. While Trump presented a nightmarish vision of America overrun by Mexican felons and Muslim terrorists, a week before election day, Ukip leader Nigel Farage unveiled a poster which depicted hordes of migrants — mostly of apparent Middle Eastern origin — as if lining up to enter Britain under the label 'breaking point'.[17] In fact, the photograph had been taken in Slovenia[18] – and even the leader of the official Vote Leave campaign, Michael Gove said he "shuddered" when he saw the poster, telling the BBC's Andrew Marr: "I thought it was the wrong thing to do."[19] Others went further, saying the poster had 'echoes' of 1930s' literature. But it wasn't the anti-EU campaign's only stunt to borrow a leaf from the Trump playbook.

In May, Vote Leave launched its campaign battle bus designed to take its message to all parts of the United Kingdom. Emblazoned on the side was a key campaign claim: "We send the EU £350m a week. Let's fund our NHS instead". The campaign's 'rock star', Boris Johnson criss-crossed the country, photographed alongside the (Polish-built) coach.[20] The only problem was it soon became clear, Vote Leave's sums didn't add up. The UK's Statistics Authority made an unprecedented intervention in the campaign.[21] It suggested Britain UK did not send £350m a week to Brussels – the maths, subsequently done by the BBC, showed the rebate of £74m, secured by Margaret Thatcher, is deducted before the money is sent, which takes the contribution down to £276m a week. That figure includes £88m a week spent in the UK on things like regional aid and support for farmers. Then there's another £27m a week that goes to support things like research projects in UK universities and companies, leaving £161m.[22]

Journalists went as far as accusing Vote Leave of 'importing the 'post-truth' politics of Donald Trump to the UK'.[23] When challenged on the figure by Sky News in one of the campaign's more memorable televised exchanges, Vote Leave's Michael Gove told Faisal Islam that people 'have had enough of experts'.[24] In truth, he was making Islam's point for him. If Gove's throwaway line sounded familiar, it should have done. A month earlier, in Wisconsin, Donald Trump had told an audience 'the experts are terrible'. In remarks on foreign policy, he told the crowd in La Crosse: "Look at the mess we're in with all these experts that we have. Look at the mess. Look at the Middle East. If our presidents and our politicians went on vacation for 365 days a year and went to the beach, we'd be in much better shape right now in the Middle East."[25]

If those pushing Brexit had been borrowing a leaf from Trump's playbook in the run-up to the referendum, in the aftermath of the result, it was Trump who sought to use the halo of Brexit to bolster his credentials as the underdog.

As Britain was voting on its future, a WSJ/NBC News poll had Hillary Clinton leading the Presidential race 46 per cent to 41 per cent.[26] In August, Trump tweeted out that he would soon be called 'Mr Brexit'[27] - confirmation that an usual political marriage was underway. Nigel Farage had resigned the Ukip leadership following the referendum. But a week after Trump sent his tweet, the future President was introducing Farage on stage in Jackson, Mississippi.[28] Trump described Brexit as a bid for independence and drew parallels to his own campaign, declaring a Trump presidency would bring about 'American independence'.

He introduced Farage as the man who stood up to the EU 'against all odds'. Farage, in turn, told a crowd of thousands they in voting for Trump, too 'could take back control of their country, take back control of their borders and get back their pride and self-respect'.[29] It was a theme Trump would repeatedly return to in the run-up to election day on November 8. On the eve of the election, at a rally in Grand Rapids, Michigan, Trump told the crowd; "It will be an amazing day, it will be called 'Brexit plus plus plus'."[30]

In the early hours of November 9, less than five months after Britain had voted to leave the EU, Donald Trump pulled off an equally unlikely victory to become the 45th President of the United States. On the eve of his inauguration, Nigel Farage hailed Brexit as a rare moment when Britain had set the course for America to follow: "I would like to think, in my own little way, that what we did with Brexit was the beginning of what is going to turn out to be a global revolution and that Trump's victory is a part of that."[31] Two campaigns on two continents, defined by one message: the very reverse of former Guardian editor, C.P. Scott's construction 'comment is free, but facts are sacred'.

Notes

[1] http://www.telegraph.co.uk/news/2016/06/24/donald-trump-visits-uk-republican-presidential-hopeful-to-reopen/

[2] http://www.politico.com/story/2015/08/donald-trump-2016-movement-213160

[3] http://www.cbsnews.com/news/fact-check-gop-debate-on-vaccines-and-autism/

[4] http://edition.cnn.com/2016/09/09/politics/donald-trump-birther/

[5] https://www.washingtonpost.com/politics/trump-says-cruzs-canadian-birth-could-be-very-precarious-for-gop/2016/01/05/5ce69764-b3f8-11e5-9388-466021d971de_story.html?utm_term=.1665b6c86223

[6] http://abcnews.go.com/Politics/donald-trump-jokes-shoot-losing-support/story?id=36474145

[7] http://www.bbc.com/news/uk-politics-21148282

[8] http://ec.europa.eu/eurostat/documents/2995521/7105334/3-10122015-AP-EN.pdf

[9] https://www.ft.com/content/1099e22c-467e-11e5-b3b2-1672f710807b

[10] http://www.telegraph.co.uk/news/politics/6961675/David-Cameron-net-immigration-will-be-capped-at-tens-of-thousands.html

[11] https://www.ons.gov.uk/peoplepopulationandcommunity/populationandmigration/internationalmigration/bulletins/migrationstatisticsquarterlyreport/2015-08-27

[12] https://www.c-span.org/video/?417557-1/donald-trump-campaigns-springfield-ohio

[13] https://www.c-span.org/video/?417502-1/donald-trump-campaigns-kinston-north-carolina

[14] https://www.c-span.org/video/?417446-1/donald-trump-campaigns-tallahassee-florida

[15] https://www.americanimmigrationcouncil.org/research/criminalization-immigration-united-states

[16] http://www.reuters.com/article/us-britain-eu-idUSKCN0VS153

[17] https://www.theguardian.com/politics/2016/jun/16/nigel-farage-defends-ukip-breaking-point-poster-queue-of-migrants

[18] https://www.buzzfeed.com/jimwaterson/these-refugees-in-ukips-anti-eu-poster-are-actually-in-slove?utm_term=.xsMN1RxDR#.rpYnk2m52

[19] http://www.telegraph.co.uk/news/2016/06/19/michael-gove-ukips-poster-made-me-shudder/

[20] http://www.telegraph.co.uk/news/2016/05/11/boris-johnson-began-his-vote-leave-campaign-on-bus-made-in-germa/

[21] https://www.statisticsauthority.gov.uk/news/uk-statistics-authority-statement-on-the-use-of-official-statistics-on-contributions-to-the-european-union/

[22] http://www.bbc.com/news/uk-politics-eu-referendum-36040060

[23] http://www.mirror.co.uk/news/uk-news/post-truth-politics-michael-gove-8111335

[24] https://www.ft.com/content/3be49734-29cb-11e6-83e4-abc22d5d108c

[25] http://www.politico.com/blogs/2016-gop-primary-live-updates-and-results/2016/04/donald-trump-foreign-policy-experts-221528

[26] http://www.nbcnews.com/meet-the-press/nbc-wsj-poll-clinton-leads-trump-5-points-n598716

[27] https://twitter.com/realdonaldtrump/status/766246213079498752?lang=en

[28] http://www.reuters.com/article/us-usa-election-trump-idUSKCN10Z2PU

[29] http://www.telegraph.co.uk/news/2016/08/25/nigel-farage-tells-donald-trump-rally-i-wouldnt-vote-for-clinton/

[30] http://www.independent.co.uk/news/world/americas/us-elections/donald-trump-latest-us-election-day-votes-results-rally-brexit-plus-plus-plus-north-carolina-a7404051.html

[31] http://www.dailymail.co.uk/video/news/video-1396235/Nigel-Farage-says-Trump-s-victory-global-revolution.html

Note on contributor

Jon Williams is Managing Director, News & Current Affairs of Ireland's national broadcaster, RTE. During the EU Referendum and US election campaigns he was based in News York as Managing Editor, International News at the American broadcaster ABC. He was previously World & UK Editor at the BBC, and serves on the board of the New York-based Committee to Protect Journalists.

Ten ways the tech industry and the media helped create President Trump

In late 2016, after Donald Trump became President-elect, Damian Radcliffe wrote an article[1] for The Conversation, highlighting how the media and tech industries had helped to make a Trump presidency a reality, contributing to a communication landscape unlike previous elections. This landscape remains unfamiliar post-election, Radcliffe argues, as journalists and others aim to make sense of the implications of a Trump Presidency on their trade and tradecraft. His piece is republished here, with a coda updating the story of Trump's relationship with these sectors

December 2016

Three weeks after Donald Trump won an historic victory to become the 45th president of the United States, the media postmortems continue.

In particular, the role played by the media and technology industries is coming under heavy scrutiny in the press, with Facebook's role in the rise of fake news currently enjoying considerable coverage.[2] This represents a shift from earlier in the campaign, when the volume of media airtime given to Trump was often held culpable for The Apprentice star's political ascendancy (Media Matters Staff 2016).

In truth, a Trump presidency is – in part – a reflection of the status and evolution of the media and tech industries in 2016. Here are ten ways that they combined to help Trump capture the White House in a manner not previously possible. Without them, Trump might not have stood a chance.

Inside the tech industry's role

1) Fake news looks a lot like real news. This is not a new issue (Love 2016), but it's a hot topic, given the social media-led explosion of the genre. As BuzzFeed found, fake news can spread more quickly than real reporting (Silverman 2016).

President Obama has weighed in on the problem, as have investigative reporters. And the New York Times found that fake news can 'go viral' very quickly, even if it's started by an unassuming source with a small online following – who subsequently debunks their own false story (Maheshwari 2016).

2) Algorithms show us more of what we like, not what we need to know. Amazon, Netflix and Spotify demonstrate how powerful personalisation and recommendation engines can be. But these tools also remove serendipity, reducing exposure to anything outside of our comfort zone.

Websites like AllSides[3], and the Wall Street Journal's Red vs Blue feed[4] experiment – which let users 'See Liberal Facebook and Conservative Facebook, Side by Side' – show how narrow our reading can become, how different the 'other side' looks, and how hard it can be to expose ourselves to differing viewpoints, even if we want to.

3) Tech doesn't automatically discern fact from fiction. Facebook doesn't have an editor and Mark Zuckerberg frequently says that Facebook is not a media company. It's true that Facebook content comes from users and partners, but Facebook is nonetheless a major media distributor.

More than half of Americans get news from social media (Greenwood, Perrin and Duggan 2016); Facebook is the 800-pound gorilla. "The two-thirds of Facebook users who get news there," Pew notes, "amount to 44 per cent of the general population" (Gottfried and Shearer 2016). But its automatic algorithms can amplify falsehoods, as happened when a false story about Megyn Kelly trended on Facebook this summer (Meyer 2016).

4) The rise of robots. It's not just publications and stories that can be fake. Twitter bots (Kollanyi, Howard and Woolley 2016) can look the same as real Twitter users, spreading falsehoods and rumors and amplifying messages (just as humans do). Repeat a lie often enough and – evidence suggests (Hasher and Goldstein 1977) – it becomes accepted as fact. This is just as true online as it is on the campaign trail.

My mother always warned me not to believe everything I read in the papers. We need to instill the same message in our children (and adults) about social media.

5) Tech has helped pull money away from sources of real reporting. Google, Facebook, Craigslist and others have created new advertising markets (Baekdal 2016) diverting traditional ad revenues from newspapers in the process.

Meanwhile, programmatic advertising, which uses computer algorithms to buy – and place – online ads (Marshall 2014), is changing the advertising dynamic yet again. This can mean companies unintentionally buy ads on sites – such as those from the alt-right – which don't sit with their brand or values; and that they would not typically choose to support (Benes 2016).

The media played its part, too
1) Fewer ad dollars means fewer journalistic boots on the ground. Data from the American Society of News Editors show that in 2015 the total workforce for US daily newspapers was 32,900, down from a peak of 56,400 in 2001 (ASNE ND). That's 23,500 jobs lost in 14 years.

Though some of these roles have migrated to online outlets that didn't exist years ago, this sector is also starting to feel the cold (Doctor, 2016). A reduced workforce has inevitably led to less original journalism, with fewer 'on-the-beat' local reporters, shuttered titles and the rise of media deserts. Cable news, talk radio, social networks and conservative websites – channels that predominantly focus on commentary rather than original reporting – have, in many cases, stepped in to fill these gaps.

2) Unparalleled airtime helped Trump build momentum. A study by The New York Times concluded (Confessore and Yourish 2016) that in his first nine months of campaigning, Trump earned nearly US$2bn in free media. This dwarfed the $313m earned by Ted Cruz and the $746m secured by Hillary Clinton. The Times noted this was already "about twice the all-in price of the most expensive presidential campaigns in history" (ibid).

Wall-to-wall coverage wasn't just beneficial to Trump. "The money's rolling in," CBS Chairman Les Moonves told an industry conference this year noting that a Trump candidacy "may not be good for America, but it's damn good for CBS" (Bond 2016).

3) Did all the investigative journalism and fact-checking make a difference? Great work by NPR, The New York Times, the Atlantic, the Washington Post and others didn't slow Trump's momentum. Just two of the country's 100 largest newspapers endorsed Trump (Willson 2016), but more than 62m people voted for him anyway.

We need to understand whether these journalistic efforts changed any opinions, or simply reinforced existing voter biases. As Fortune journalist Mathew Ingram observed: "Trump supporters and the mainstream media both believed what they wanted to believe" (Ingram 2016).

4) Many journalists were out of step with the mood of much of the country. We need a greater plurality of voices, opinions and backgrounds to inform our news coverage.

A 2013 study from Indiana University's School of Journalism revealed that journalists as a whole are older, whiter, more male and better-educated than the American population overall (Indiana University Bloomington 2014). This means journalists can be disconnected from communities they cover, giving rise to mutual misunderstandings and wrong assumptions.

5) The jury's out on whether Trump is a master of deflection. But despite his fabled short attention span, too often it's the media that is distracted and dragged off-course.

In March 2016, the Washington Post's editorial board (Post Opinions Staff 2016) astonishingly allowed Trump to play out the clock when he ducked a question on tactical nuclear strikes against Isis by simply asking – with just five minutes of the meeting remaining – if people could go around the room and say who they were.

More recently he led the press corps and Twitterati[5] on a merry dance, after his 'Hamilton' tweet got more coverage than the $25m settlement against Trump University. He repeated the trick when tweets alleging illegal voters turned the spotlight away from discussions about potential conflicts of interest between his presidency and his property empire.

The next four years

There were other factors, of course, that helped Republicans win the Electoral College. These include a desire for change in Washington, Clinton's ultra-safe campaign and Trump's ability to project the image of 'blue-collar billionaire' who understood economically and politically disenfranchised communities.

Trump capitalised on these opportunities, prospering despite myriad pronouncements and behaviours (accusations of assault, unpublished tax returns, criticism of John McCain's war record, feuding with a Gold Star family, mocking a disabled reporter and routinely offending Muslims, Mexicans and women) that would have buried any other candidate.

Trump's use of media and technology means his presidency promises to be like no other.

In the past few days we've finally started to see discussions emerge about how the media should respond to this (Drenzer 2016). Suggestions include focusing on policy, not personality (Yglesias 2016); ignoring deflecting tweets (Shafer 2016); and a raft of other ideas (Kramer 2016). To these, I would add the need to promote greater media literacy, a more diverse media and tech workforce and improving the audience engagement skills of reporters.

Journalists and technologists will need to redouble their efforts if we are to hold the White House accountable and rebuild trust across these two industries. This promises to be a bumpy ride, but one that we all need to saddle up for.

April 2017 coda: Where are we now?

In the four months since this original article was written, the prediction that a Trump 'presidency promises to be like no other,' looks like something of an understatement.

Clashes between the White House and the mainstream media have been frequent, with the commentary pages – and news cycle – often dominated by these dynamics[6]. The volume of incidents can be both dizzying and dazzling, so it's helpful to be able to take a step back and chart some of the most significant confrontations.

Of these, perhaps the prominent example is the appropriation of the term fake news to represent stories that the Trump White House disagrees with; or which the President, his surrogates and supporters, feel show the President in a bad light (Alderman 2017). Fake news is a charge that's been used to challenge the veracity of individual stories and entire institutions, most notably CNN.

As a rhetorical device, it's already proved to be astonishingly effective; a recent poll found that more than half of Americans believe that traditional media outlets produce fake news (Sutton 2017). That figure, Monmouth University's Patrick Murray noted, increases among GOP supporters. "If you are a Republican, Trump is a font of truth," he said. "For other Americans, not so much" (Monmouth University 2017).

Meanwhile, a number of journalists, politicians[6] and other commentators have expressed concern about the implications of talking down the media[7].

Interestingly, 'fake news' is not a term that the press itself has used to challenge errors or deliberate falsehoods propagated by the Trump administration. Indeed, the industry remains unsure about how to address these concerns (Boehlert 2017).

This is despite the fact that there have been high profile incidents – ranging from unproven accusations about wiretapping through to disputes about the size of Trump's inauguration crowd, and unsubstantiated claims that it was only because of illegal voters that Trump failed to win the popular vote – where there appears to be a clear disconnect between the available evidence and the lines propagated by the White House.

As a result, we've not only seen the emergence of fake news as a catch-all label for unfavourable reporting, but also the idea of alternative facts being espoused – and derided – as the mainstream media has been pilloried for being the enemy of the people and labelled the main opposition by the White House's Chief Strategist, Steve Bannon.

With the Trump Presidency, at the time of writing, not even 100 days old, it's clear – unless you work for a few select Trump-supporting outlets – that this tumultuous relationship will only continue.

Journalists continue to challenge the competency of the administration, ask questions about conflicts of interests (Venook 2017), and question the role – and influence – of Trump's close family in government affairs.[8] In going about their day-to-day business, seeking clarifications on policy, or trying to fact-check key officials, journalists are already finding that established rules, norms and behaviours do not apply.

We can, therefore, expect to see plenty of on-going discussions about how the journalistic profession should best address this (Greenberg 2017, Rosenstiel 2017). Whether, as LSE's Charlie Beckett predicts, 'Fake news [is] the best thing that's happened to journalism' (Beckett 2017), it's too early to say. But, certainly the uptake in subscriptions to the New York Times, donations to ProPublica and on-going discussion about the future of the industry offer some signs of positivity.

Nonetheless, there's a long way to go to rebuild public trust and understand how what journalism in the age of Trump should look like. That's a journey that has only just begun.

Notes

[1] See: https://theconversation.com/10-ways-the-tech-industry-and-the-media-helped-create-president-trump-69609, accessed on April 7, 2017.

[2] See for example: https://www.google.com/search?q=fake+news+facebook&source=lnms&tbm=nws&sa=X&ved=0ahUKEwjQ1bX4_7zQAhVX1mMKHcGnA8gQ_AUICygE#spf=1, accessed on March 28, 2017.

[3] See https://www.allsides.com/, accessed on March 29, 2017.

[4] See http://graphics.wsj.com/blue-feed-red-feed/, accessed on March 29, 2017.

[5] See https://en.oxforddictionaries.com/definition/twitterati, accessed on March 29, 2017.

[6] See, for example, http://fortune.com/2017/02/24/white-house-bars-nyt-cnn/, http://www.usatoday.com/story/news/politics/2017/02/24/donald-trump-cpac-media-enemy-of-the-people/98347970/ and http://www.realclearpolitics.com/video/2017/01/22/stephanopoulos_vs_conway_it_is_completely_unacceptable_for_media_to_call_trump_press_secretary_a_liar.html, accessed on April 3, 2017.

[7] See for example: http://www.businessinsider.com/trump-is-gaslighting-america-heres-how-to-survive-2017-3 and https://www.theatlantic.com/magazine/archive/2017/03/how-to-build-an-autocracy/513872/, accessed on April 5, 2017.

[8] See for example: https://www.washingtonpost.com/news/the-fix/wp/2016/11/18/why-donald-trumps-family-being-in-the-white-house-is-problematic-explained/ and http://www.mercurynews.com/2017/03/30/ivanka-trump-still-doesnt-get-it-statement-about-new-white-house-role-wont-ease-public-concerns/, accessed on April 5, 2017.

References

ASNE (ND) Minority employment in daily newspapers, ASNE, ND. Available online at http://asne.org/content.asp?pl=140&sl=129&contentid=129, accessed on March 30, 2017.

Alderman, Julie (2017) Trump Has Called Dozens Of Things Fake News. None Of Them Are, Media Matters, February 13, 2017. Available online at: https://mediamatters.org/research/2017/02/13/trump-has-called-dozens-things-fake-news-none-them-are/215326, accessed on April 19, 2017.

Baekdal, Thomas (2016) What Killed The Newspapers? Google Or Facebook? Or...? Baekdal blog, 21 September. Available online at https://www.baekdal.com/blog/what-killed-the-newspapers-google-or-facebook-or/, accessed on March 30, 2017.

Beckett, Charlie (2017) Fake news: the best thing that's happened to journalism, LSE, 11 March. Available online at http://blogs.lse.ac.uk/polis/2017/03/11/fake-news-the-best-thing-thats-happened-to-journalism/, accessed on April 6, 2017.

Benes, Ross (2016) Why site blacklists often fail in programmatic ad buying, Digiday, November 29. Available online at https://digiday.com/marketing/site-blacklists-often-fail-programmatic-ad-buying/, accessed on March 30, 2017.

Boehlert, Eric (2017) Media must choose: If Trump's not a liar, he's delusional, Media Matters, 29 March. Available online at https://mediamatters.org/blog/2017/03/29/media-must-choose-if-trumps-not-liar-hes-delusional/215857, accessed on April 5, 2017.

Bond, Paul (2016) Leslie Moonves on Donald Trump: "It May Not Be Good for America, but It's Damn Good for CBS", Hollywood Reporter, 29 February. Available online at http://www.hollywoodreporter.com/news/leslie-moonves-donald-trump-may-871464, accessed on April 18, 2017.

Confessore, Nicholas and Yourish, Karen (2016) $2bn worth of free media for Donald Trump, New York Times, March 16. Available online at https://www.nytimes.com/2016/03/16/upshot/measuring-donald-trumps-mammoth-advantage-in-free-media.html?smid=tw-share&_r=1, accessed on March 30, 2017.

Doctor, Ken (2016) Newsonomics: With new roadblocks for digital news sites, what happens next? NiemanLab, April 13. Available online at http://www.niemanlab.org/2016/04/newsonomics-with-new-roadblocks-for-digital-news-sites-what-happens-next/, accessed on March 30, 2017.

Drenzer, Daniel (2016) Is there an optimal response to the provoker-in-chief? Washington Post, November 30. Available online at https://www.washingtonpost.com/posteverything/wp/2016/11/30/is-there-an-optimal-response-to-the-provoker-in-chief/?utm_term=.381082567966, accessed on March 30, 2017.

Gottfried, Jeffery and Shearer, Elisa (2016) News Use Across Social Media Platforms 2016, Pew Research Center, May 26. Available online at http://www.journalism.org/2016/05/26/news-use-across-social-media-platforms-2016/, accessed on March 30, 2017.

Greenberg, David (2017) The perils of calling Trump a liar, Politico, January 28. Available online at http://www.politico.com/magazine/story/2017/01/the-perils-of-calling-trump-a-liar-214704, accessed April 6, 2017.

Greenwood, S., Perrin, A., Duggan, M. (2016) Social Media Update 2016: Facebook usage and engagement is on the rise, while adoption of other platforms holds steady, Pew Internet, November 11. Available online at http://www.pewinternet.org/2016/11/11/social-media-update-2016/, accessed on March 30, 2017.

Hasher, Lynn and Goldstein, David (1977) Frequency and the conference of referential validity, Journal of Verbal Learning and Verbal Behavior, Vol. 16, No. 1, February 1977, pp 107-112. Available online at http://www.sciencedirect.com/science/article/pii/S0022537177800121, accessed on March 30, 2017.

Indiana University Bloomington (2014) IU survey: U.S. journalists say they are less satisfied and have less autonomy, Indiana University Bloomington, 01 May. Available online at http://archive.news.indiana.edu/releases/iu/2014/05/american-journalist-in-the-digital-age.shtml, accessed on March 30, 2017.

Ingram, Matthew (2016) Facebook Still Has a Fake News Problem, Fortune, October 12. Available online http://fortune.com/2016/10/12/facebook-fake-news/, accessed on March 29, 2017.

Ingram, Mathew (2016b) Here's why the media failed to predict a Donald Trump victory, Fortune, November 9. Available online at http://fortune.com/2016/11/09/media-trump-failure/, accessed on March 30, 2017.

Kollanyi, Bence; Howard, Philip; and Woolley, Samuel (2016) Bots and Automation over Twitter during the U.S. Election, Politicalbots, November 17. Available online at http://politicalbots.org/?p=787, accessed on March 30, 2017.

Kramer, Melody (2016) Here are 28 ideas for covering President-elect Donald Trump, Poynter, November 29. Available online at http://www.poynter.org/2016/here-are-28-ideas-for-covering-president-elect-donald-trump/440532/, accessed on March 30, 2017.

Love, Robert (2016) Before Jon Stewart: Fake news is back, but our tolerance for it isn't what it was before journalism donned the mantle of authority, Columbia Journalism Review, March/April. Available online at http://archives.cjr.org/feature/before_jon_stewart.php, accessed on March 29, 2017.

Maheshwari, Sapna (2016) How fake news goes viral: A case study, New York Times, November 20. Available online at https://www.nytimes.com/2016/11/20/business/media/how-fake-news-spreads.html?_r=1, accessed on March 29, 2017.

Marshall, Jack (2014) WTF is programmatic advertising? Digiday, February 20. Available online at http://digiday.com/media/what-is-programmatic-advertising/, accessed on March 30, 2017.

Media Matters Staff (2016) Harvard study confirms media's role in Trump's political rise, Media Matters, June 14. Available online https://mediamatters.org/blog/2016/06/14/harvard-study-confirms-media-s-role-trump-s-political-rise/210955, accessed on March 29, 2017.

Meyer, Robinson (2016) Facebook Purges Journalists, Immediately Promotes a Fake Story for 8 Hours: Why did the company trend a false article about Megyn Kelly? The Atlantic, September 3. Available online at https://www.theatlantic.com/technology/archive/2016/08/facebook-steps-in-it/497915/, accessed on March 30, 2017.

Monmouth University Polling Institute (2017) POTUS less trusted than media, "Fake News" comes from all sources, Monmouth University, March 29. Available online at https://www.monmouth.edu/polling-institute/reports/MonmouthPoll_US_032917/, accessed on April 3, 2017.

Post Opinions Staff (2016) A transcript of Donald Trump's meeting with The Washington Post editorial board, Washington Post, March. 21. Available online at https://www.washingtonpost.com/blogs/post-partisan/wp/2016/03/21/a-transcript-of-donald-trumps-meeting-with-the-washington-post-editorial-board/?utm_term=.35b31795060c, accessed on March 30, 2017.

Rosenstiel, Tom (2017) What the post-Trump debate over journalism gets wrong, Brookings, December 20. Available online at https://www.brookings.edu/research/what-the-debate-over-journalism-post-trump-gets-wrong/, accessed on April 6, 2017.

Seipel, Arnie (2016) Trump makes unfounded claim that 'millions' voted illegally for Clinton, NPR, November 27. Available online at http://www.npr.org/2016/11/27/503506026/trump-makes-unfounded-claim-that-millions-voted-illegally-for-clinton, accessed on April 5, 2017.

Shafer, Jack (2016) The new rules for covering Trump, Politico, November 28. Available online at http://www.politico.com/magazine/story/2016/11/donald-trump-media-coverage-new-rules-214485, accessed on March 30, 2017.

Silverman, Craig (2016) This analysis shows how viral fake election news stories outperformed real news On Facebook, Buzzfeed, November 16. Available online at https://www.buzzfeed.com/craigsilverman/viral-fake-election-news-outperformed-real-news-on-facebook?utm_term=.wg2z7DddK#.fvl4ljwwn, accessed on March 29, 2017,

Sutton, Kelsey (2017) Poll: 6 in 10 Americans think traditional news outlets report fake news, Politico, March 27. Available online at http://www.politico.eu/blogs/on-media/2017/03/poll-6-in-10-americans-think-traditional-news-outlets-report-fake-news/, accessed on April 1, 2017.

The Wall Street Journal (nd) Blue Feed, Red Feed: See Liberal Facebook and Conservative Facebook, Side by Side. Available online at http://graphics.wsj.com/blue-feed-red-feed/, accessed on March 30, 2017.

Venook, Jeremy (2017) Trump's interests vs. America's, Mar-a-Lago edition, The Atlantic, April 5. Available online at https://www.theatlantic.com/business/archive/2017/04/donald-trump-conflicts-of-interests/508382/, accessed on April 6, 2017.

Willson, Reid (2016) Final newspaper endorsement count: Clinton 57, Trump 2, The Hill, November 6. Available online at http://thehill.com/blogs/ballot-box/presidential-races/304606-final-newspaper-endorsement-count-clinton-57-trump-2, accessed on March 30, 2017.

Yglesias, Matthew (2016) The case for normalizing Trump, Vox, November 30. Available online at http://www.vox.com/policy-and-politics/2016/11/30/13767174/case-for-normalizing-trump, accessed on March 30, 2017.

Note on contributor:

Damian Radcliffe is the Carolyn S. Chambers Professor in Journalism at the University of Oregon, a fellow of the Tow Center for Digital Journalism at Columbia University, an honorary research fellow at Cardiff University's School of Journalism, Media and Culture Studies, and a fellow of the Royal Society for the Encouragement of Arts, Manufactures and Commerce (RSA).

He is an experienced digital analyst, consultant, journalist, and researcher who has worked in editorial, research, teaching, and policy positions for the past two decades in the UK, Middle East, and USA.

Damian is a regular contributor to the BBC Academy, CBS Interactive (ZDNet), Huffington Post, MediaShift, and TheMediaBriefing, where he writes about digital trends, social media, technology, the business of media, and the evolution of journalism.

Find him online: www.damianradcliffe.com or @damianradcliffe on Twitter.

The perilous times that might just become better times

The spread of online fake news and rise of alternative facts may, counter intuitively, be saving graces for the traditional media as it finds a new role in life, argues Raymond Snoddy

It was like a scene from an old-fashioned black-and-white film about the reporter as hero. Joe Sonka, a staff writer for the Insider Louisville website, was having a beer in the Backdoor bar when someone texted him that Trump advisor Kellyanne Conway had just said something 'insane' about violent events in Kentucky where he used to work.

Conway had cited 'the Bowling Green massacre' on television as justification for the Trump imposed travel ban from seven Muslim countries. Sonka checked and found that two Iraqi refugees had been arrested in Bowling Green and accused of plotting to send money and arms to Al Qaeda in Iraq. They were never charged with any offence in the US although they may have been involved in Islamic terrorism in Iraq.

At 9.34pm on Thursday February 2, 2017 Sonka wrote on Twitter "@KellyannePolls says that 2 Iraqi refugees were the masterminds behind the Bowling Green massacre (there was no such massacre)"

The story of Joe Sonka and what happened next was told by New York Times columnist Jim Rutenberg.

The modest Tweet was retweeted 2.4m times and then followed up by Vox, The Washington Post, CNN and even Fox News, the Trump news channel of choice, and then into the television mockery of Saturday Night Live. Eventually Conway was forced to retract although she only admitted to having "misspoke one word". She had meant to say Bowling Green terrorists. The record showed Conway had referred to the 'Bowling Green massacre' that never was on a number of previous occasions.

Rutenberg hopes the affair marks a turning point in the battle against fake news and a boost for the credibility of mainstream media." In the end, social media and journalistic scrutiny aligned with comedy to right a wrong pretty definitively. That it happened so organically showed that false 'facts' might not always be the stubborn things so many people fear they are becoming," he argues.

What is clear is that the American media – perhaps belatedly in the case of television – has renewed its efforts to check and triple check everything that Trump says and does – the difference between covering a 'colourful' and ratings driving candidate and the US President.

Obviously Twitter is a double-edged sword. Trump lives by Twitter and could yet have his credibility undermined by millions of disgruntled citizen Tweeters. There is little that Trump would hate more than becoming a ridiculous figure outside the ranks of his most diehard supporters. A culture of rebuttal is coming from up from the crowd and is magnified by the mainstream media which is benefiting mightily from the poisonous attentions of Trump and his staff.

Watching television news in the US just after the inauguration on a family visit was to enter a parallel Trump universe. Whether CNN or Fox News it was wall-to-wall Trump – except briefly for the Super Bowl – and even that was Trump packaged with a long interview with Bill O'Reilly on Fox News. It was noticeable, however that even O'Reilly pushed back firmly on some of the Trump views such as why he respected President Putin – producing replies which caused outrage by apparently equating US and Russian behaviour.

The vigorous American media response to fake news has highlighted the importance of the issue, which has also been taken up in the UK, France and the EU.

A Channel 4 survey showed that only 4 per cent of Britons could correctly identify six true or false stories, with those who used Facebook as their primary source of news being the least able to tell the difference. A surprising 36 per cent thought that a story made up in Macedonia, that the Pope had endorsed Trump, was true.

In France news organisations have linked with Google News Lab and Facebook to run a CrossCheck project aimed at catching falsehoods and the EU has been threatening action unless Facebook and Google take greater responsibility for their websites.

The momentum to do something about truly fake news – made up possibly for financial gain – has spread to the House of Commons Media, Culture and Sport select committee.

Dealing with mere fake news where there can be a difference of opinion, is more difficult and ultimately people believe what they want to. But the case of Conway's Bowling Green massacre, Joe Sonka and Twitter is a hopeful sign of what can be achieved in the vital arena of 'genuine' political fake news.

Former Prime Minister Harold Wilson was vilified for cynicism when he declared more than 50 years ago that 'a week is a long time in politics'. With President Trump it's come down to just a day or an afternoon. Include Twitter and the political window collapses to seconds.

What have we learned about Trump, the media and journalism on the roller-coaster ride since inauguration day?

Trump has always been obsessed by the media, and loved the papers and the news channels while they publicised his business 'triumphs'. Now he is obsessed by how he is portrayed and the inconvenient Trump truths the media is reporting.

It is a sign of unhealthy vanity and priorities that Trump's first vicious attack on the media was in response to those reports that many more people attended President Obama's inauguration eight years ago than his. Official transport records show the reverse was true in the face of Conway saying she had her own 'alternative facts' on the issue claiming that the turnout was the biggest ever.

Trump also can't stop lying about small things. God, no less, had held off the Washington rain until after inauguration speech was over. God didn't. The rain started as he began his speech. However, much larger problems loom for the media and journalism than the size of the inauguration crowds and the willingness of President Trump to make things up.

If last year was the year of 'post-truth' and 'fake news' then Conway had already, before January was out, produced what will turn out to be the Zeitgeist term of 2017 – 'alternative facts'.

Assume that the concept of alternative facts is not a one-off but a marker for the Trump presidency. They will do it in the full knowledge that true Trump supporters will believe what their hero says and that doubt will enter the minds of millions of others who do not follow the details of politics and policy. With the help of Facebook and Google it could easily be possible to assemble an American majority who accept alternative facts rather than those provided by the vilified traditional media.

The new world of post-truth, fake news and alternative facts is a problem not just for journalism but also for society. The legendary American newsman Dan Rather has a large part of the answer: "What can we do? We can all step up and say simply and without equivocation: 'A lie, is a lie is a lie!'"

Those who know that that there is such a thing as truth must do everything in their power to diminish 'the liar's malignant reach into our society'. Rather even proposed terminating interviews with senior Republicans if they equivocate and refuse to combat lies from the White House. Ultimately advanced democracies cannot function on a tissue of lies no matter however many times they are repeated on Facebook.

There is a danger that the British will be too smug and believe that La La Land is solely an American manifestation. Who said in April 2016: "We export more to Ireland than we do to China, almost twice as much Belgium as we do to India, and nearly three times as much to Sweden as we do to Brazil. It is not realistic to think we could just replace European trade with these new markets"?

The answer is the lady who is prepared to turn her back on the single market and the European Customs Union – Prime Minister Theresa May. The UK too, it seems, has alternative facts, although not so risible as those emanating from the Trump administration.

Apart from being counted with Dan Rather there are a few hopeful signs.

The BBC has assembled a team to fact check and counter misleading and false information. It may be a response to criticisms that the BBC should have produced more analytical and robust journalism to combat the myths of the referendum campaign. And Channel 4 News has had a fact-checking team for years but at least, in current circumstances, the BBC has taken a small positive step.

Facebook has also woken up, at least partially, to the reputational damage it could suffer from hosting echo chambers for the transmission of lies, however high their origin. It promised it would begin highlighting fake news stories relying on users and outside fact-checking organisations.

Readers will draw Facebook's attention to possible fake stories and they will be sent to fact-checking organisations such as ABC News and Associated Press, which will not be paid for their work. If a problem is encountered then Facebook will flag up that the story is disputed by a third party. How many Trump true believers will go through that process – or even Brexiteers?

In the year of alternative facts the only hope for optimists is to do everything possible to ensure that in the brutal battle for the truth real facts prevail.

Recently the former editor of the Sunday Times, Sir Harold Evans, argued that this is a 'uniquely perilous time for journalism' when in Trumpland journalists are described as the opposition and when in the UK judges are denounced as 'enemies of the people' by the Daily Mail.

The situation appears perilous and unprecedented, but what if the opposite is true? What if the craziness of Trump and growing Brexit uncertainties provide a major boost to the traditional media?

Faced with barefaced lies and the noisy repetition of what is demonstrably false, is professional journalism about to enter a new age of opportunity where valid information will be increasingly valued? There could be a flight towards quality, combined with a better understanding that investigative reporting has to be funded and that there are limits to free lunches. There might a better understanding that unverified, and often unverifiable, information on social media could be a snare and delusion.

The Oscar ceremony will be forever remembered for the accidental fake news that La La Land had won best picture. But anyone watching the ad breaks would also have seen the first television advertising the New York Times has done for five years and first brand advertising for a decade. The main copy line said it all: "The Truth is...Hard...Hard to find...Hard to know...More important now than ever".

Trump's attacks on the 'failing New York Times', which carried the leaks on Trump's tax affairs, are the best thing that has happened to the paper in years. New subscribers are signing up in the hundreds of thousands and are at a record 2.5m – but it's not just the New York Times; The Washington Post, the paper of the 'grab 'em by the pussy' video, is up more than 70 per cent and the Boston Globe noticed a tripling of its new subscriber signings following the Presidential election.

Every word that comes out of the mouth of President Trump and his spokespeople produces not just another story but a further opportunity for journalistic fact-checking.

'Obamacare covers very few people', President Trump insisted recently. Actually, the press replied, more than 20m have received health insurance through the Affordable Care Act. Former president George W Bush weighed into the overall debate by insisting that the American people need answers on any contacts between the Trump campaign and the Russian government. It is entirely possible that before the Trump years in power are over 'the enemy' may well be queuing up to cover Trump: The Impeachment.

Will there be a Brexit equivalent to the Trump effect on the British media? The slow-motion leaving of the European Union over the next two years will be a huge story and, if the opponents of Brexit are right, it will be a story of uncertainty and possible chaos for years. It will not be the same as Trump in the US where the newspapers are in effect turning into a near united opposition in the pursuit of facts.

The UK media is much too split for that with the pro-Brexit press determined to keep the anti-EU arguments going at all costs – preaching positive information to the true believers however uncomfortable the facts. They will benefit from the stridency of their case.

There should also be a significant boost for those publications that deal in facts and analysis rather than emotion and pre-ordained coverage. The pro-Remain *Financial Times* has already seen a surge in subscriptions as its largely business audience tries to work out what leaving will mean for them. And the pop-up *New European*, the paper of the 48 per cent, is still with us as an example of publishing innovation.

For *The Times*, which backed Remain, former Premier Sir John Major's intervention was a perfectly arguable warning that the expected hard Brexit outside the single market would hurt those least able to protect themselves and could lead to the dismantling of the welfare state. To the *Daily Mail* Sir John was 'a vengeful doormat' who was also intensely vain. 'Treachery of Remoaner Major', screamed the *Mail*'s headline.

Perilous times? Perhaps. Interesting times? Certainly. And maybe even the best of times for journalism on both sides of the Atlantic and just possibly better times for the funding of that journalism in the battle against fake news and alternative facts.

This chapter is based on articles written for Mediatel.

Note on contributor

Raymond Snoddy OBE, after studying at Queen's University in Belfast, worked on local and regional newspapers, before joining The Times in 1971. Five years later he moved to the Financial Times and reported on media issues before returning to The Times as media editor in 1995. At present, Snoddy is a freelance journalist writing for a range of publications. He presented NewsWatch on the BBC from its inception in 2004 until 2012. His other television work has included presenting Channel 4's award-winning series Hard News. Snoddy is the author of a biography of the media tycoon Michael Green, and of the acclaimed book on the British press, The Good, the Bad and the Ugly. He was awarded an OBE for his services to journalism in 2000. He is co-editor of this book.

The Canadian exception: Better than everyone else, or just lucky?

Canada prides itself on being neither America nor Britain. Which means a Trump-like politician or a Brexit-style movement could never happen. Or could it? Doug Saunders examines the state of the nation that has long been perceived as allowing populism to pass it by

As the Western world took a sharp turn toward angry intolerance in 2015 and 2016, it seemed to many that Canada had become a lone safe harbour from the populist flood. As Americans turned to Trump and Britons cast their ballots for Brexit, America's northern neighbour moved decisively in the opposite direction, giving a sizeable majority to a moderately social-democratic Liberal Party government led by the youthful Justin Trudeau, who campaigned on a platform of increased immigration, greater numbers of refugees, open embrace of ethnic diversity and more free-trade agreements with the wider world.

As other countries of Europe and North America were threatening to shut their borders to people and commerce, Canada opened its gates further than ever. And Canadians seemed uniquely uninterested in the ideas of populism. Polls repeatedly show that strong majorities of them – including majorities of ideologically conservative Canadians – continue to embrace multiculturalism, immigration and free trade.

Is there something we might call Canadian Exceptionalism at play? Is one country, for some reason, immune to the temptations of populism, isolationism, protectionism and exclusion?

Many observers seemed to think so. A few days after the catastrophic US election in November 2016, an elected German state politician told me: "It looks like it is now just Germany and Canada holding down the Western world." And even that declaration was built on his hope that the right-populist Alternative For Germany party wouldn't earn more than token seats in the Bundestag in the 2017 elections.

There was plenty of this sentiment within Canada, too. The national newsmagazine The Walrus declared in a 2016 feature editorial that "Canadians Are Better than Other People," in which its editor-in-chief made the case that Canada's ethnic, linguistic and religious diversity, its tendency to political moderation and its hearty embrace of anti-Americanism mean that Canadians "increasingly have come to embrace the outward rejection of narrow-minded nativism as a defining feature of our national brand."

Is Canada really the anti-populist exception? Or does its smug posturing hide some ugly political trends whose looming presence make it considerably less unique? On closer examination, it appears that Canada does indeed face populist and nativist threats that could quite conceivably become powerful national forces (though not likely in the next couple years). On the other hand, those forces of intolerance could quite possibly turn out to be uniquely Canadian in important ways – not least because they might be embraced by a uniquely multi-ethnic and multi-racial group of voters. Canada's contribution to the world of politics could turn out to be rainbow populism.

Who votes for populist parties?

Canada is not as unique as it might first appear. We now have a fairly clear idea what sort of people vote for populist parties of ethnic and religious intolerance. Now that we have several years of data from elections and referendums in the United States, Britain and a good number of Western European countries, a clear pattern has formed.

They tend, almost everywhere, to be voters who are older and lacking in education beyond secondary school. They are not generally people who are in absolute poverty or long-term unemployment, but they aren't people who are part of the 'new economy' of information. And they tend, everywhere, to be people who don't live in districts with high levels of immigration or ethnic and cultural diversity (or if they do, it tends to be very recent) – in other words, it's a movement that appeals to people who are made to feel insecure and excluded (and resentful of 'elites') by age, economic change and geographic segregation. Another thing: In Britain and the United States and Western Europe, such voters have almost exclusively been white people of European descent.

Canada certainly has substantial numbers of voters who fit that profile. And their numbers may be growing, as rising property prices, a changing and less secure labour market and an ageing population create pools of separation, exclusion and alienation.

Its effects are registering on the radar. In the early months of 2017, the marketing agency Edelman released its annual "Trust Barometer" survey of the Canadian public; its pollsters concluded that the country "can no longer count itself immune from the global trend of populism and sinking institutional trust". That might be an overstatement, but their numbers do show a rise in the same factors that have led Americans, French and Britons to support Trump, Le Pen and the Brexit politicians.

Most notably, it showed for the first time that more Canadians distrust their institutions than trust them. The survey found large and growing numbers (8 in10) believing that distant 'elites' are out of touch with regular Canadians and are causing harm; almost half believe that 'globalisation' is hurting Canada; more than a quarter fear immigrants rather than regarding them as neighbours (a figure that is only high by Canada's very tolerant standards). And, tellingly, when it came to trust in institutions (government, media, business) the pollsters registered a 15 per cent gap – twice as high as in 2016 – between the 'informed public' (that is, the university-educated elite population) and the 'mass population' (everyone else).

Many observers assumed that this alienated 'mass public' must be the core Trump constituency of angry, older, under-educated, non-urban, middle-income white people. And, in fact, such voters have flexed their political muscle in recent years in Canada.

Canada's moment of populist revolt has, by one argument, already occurred. A populist movement first entered mainstream politics during the decade of governance by the centre-right Progressive Conservative party in the 1980s, when Prime Minister Brian Mulroney found himself challenged on social-policy matters such as abortion and immigration by an outspoken circle of his own party's MPs calling itself the Family Caucus. With the collapse of his party's parliamentary seats in the 1993 election, that caucus turned into the right-populist Reform Party, which by 1997 had become Canada's official opposition party. After changing its name to the Canadian Alliance, in 2003 it merged with the remains of the Progressive Conservatives to become a united Conservative Party. Its leader, Stephen Harper, had been a right-wing populist Canadian Alliance activist for the previous decade, and led the party to minority-government victory in 2006.

However, the realities of Canada intervened. In order to achieve that victory, and to remain in power through eight years and three elections, Mr. Harper's Conservatives had to back away from their most typically populist platforms and messages. Beyond a few symbolic gestures to the party's populist rank-and-file (such as making the census optional and imposing very tough prison sentences on some crimes), Mr. Harper governed from a conventional conservative position – his party did not challenge free trade, abortion or same-sex marriage, and most significantly it embraced immigration and multiculturalism to an extent never before seen in a conservative party.

Mr. Harper and his ministers eagerly courted religious and racial-minority voters in mosques, temples and community events, and in the 2011 election they achieved a key symbolic breakthrough. For the first time more racial-minority Canadians voted for the Conservatives than for the Liberals. They did not achieve this, however, by turning leftward. Rather, they recognised that minority and immigrant Canadians tend to be more religious than average, and therefore are socially conservative; and they tend to be small businesspeople, and therefore economically conservative.

Mr. Harper's ethnic-pluralist conservatism would prove a popular export. It was eagerly adopted in Britain by David Cameron's Conservatives shortly after their 2010 electoral victory (which was followed by a flurry of exchanges between Downing St and Ottawa, and a distinctly multi-ethnic message from Britain's Conservatives) and by Angela Merkel's Christian Democrats. This was in sharp contrast to France and the United States, where the mainstream conservative parties turned against, not toward, minority groups.

That multi-hued conservatism would collapse somewhat in the 2015 election, where Conservative MPs proposed outlawing Islamic headcoverings and vaguely defined 'barbaric cultural practices' – but those gestures would contribute to a large-scale electoral defeat.

Can a populist movement occur in Canada?

Mr Harper became a multi-hued conservative by abandoning core populist messages – especially intolerance of minorities and immigration. But could a full-scale right-wing populist movement find a foothold in Canada's polyglot terrain? There is strong evidence that it could.

Canada's most dramatic recent triumph of Trump-style politics occurred in Toronto – half of whose metropolitan population of 6m are foreign-born. Despite this, half the city's voters cast a ballot for a wealthy, unpredictable, far-right, anti-immigration, anti-elite, racist-slogan-uttering politician named Rob Ford in 2011, and a third voted for his movement in 2014. Mr Ford gained a certain sort of worldwide recognition after phone videos emerged of him smoking crack cocaine with known Somali-Canadian drug-gang members. Those videos, and his subsequent admission of regular crack use, did little to harm his popularity in the polls, which seemed only to diminish with his death, by cancer, in 2016.

Many noted the ideological, rhetorical and behavioural similarities between the late mayor and Donald Trump. Others pointed out the big difference – Mr Ford's voters weren't generally, or even mainly, white. His very popular campaign rallies were seas of black and brown faces.

This was not coincidental. An analysis by University of Toronto geographer Zach Taylor found that the Torontonians who voted for Mr. Ford overwhelmingly lived in inner-suburban wards whose populations were mainly racial and ethnic minorities, mainly lacking university education, and mainly getting by on family incomes of less than $100,000. Those voters are what the journalist Naheed Mustafa, in an analysis of their backgrounds, called 'the non-white suburban poor', whom Mr Ford pitted against an unseen well-paid downtown elite (and sometimes against newer immigrants) – "Despite his personal wealth, he gave the impression that he spoke the language of the marginalised." In other words, his voters were Donald Trump's, except that they replaced an older white man's anger at minorities with an older brown-skinned man's anger at privileged elites (and, sometimes, also at other minorities).

Since the 1980s, immigrants to Canada have been increasingly educated and sophisticated. Almost 60 per cent of the nearly 300,000 immigrants Canada receives every year have university degrees, a rate far higher than that of native-born Canadians. But those immigrants have also been forced, by an increasingly unaffordable housing market, to live in communities far removed from the Canadian mainstream. Since the 1990s, recently-arrived Canadians and their families have tended to live in the low-cost, poorly transit-connected suburbs; they are more likely to be excluded from the housing boom and the secure new-economy jobs that have buoyed Canada; they are generally not white. Mr Ford spoke their specific language of outsider resentment; he stoked the anger felt by many marginal Caribbean, African, South Asian and East Asian Canadians, and he was manifestly adept at working their Evangelical and Pentecostal churches. He knew their sense of exclusion could be turned into angry intolerance, and he gave his voters a mythic 'them' to be angry about.

This doesn't mean minorities in Canada have turned to the far right – they haven't, any more than anyone else has. It does mean that anger and exclusion and paranoia in Canada, and even racial intolerance and xenophobia in Canada, are just as likely to entrap minority Canadians. And it means that there is an constituency capable of electing a right-wing populist movement on a national level – a constituency that would have to include both a substantial number of angry, older, insecure-feeling white people and also a good number of angry, insecure, over-educated, under-employed, isolated non-white people.

Canada may have avoided the populist surge through economic good fortune. It was comparatively unharmed by the 2008 global economic crisis (Canada's big crisis, comparable in scale to Ireland's, occurred in the middle of the 1990s), and its middle class saw continuously rising incomes through the 1990s. So the ingredients for a populist revolt haven't been as potent in Canada as elsewhere in the West – but that doesn't mean Canada lacks a population capable of being seduced by populist ideas.

Canada has traditionally avoided extremism by offering hope – if you start on the bottom rung, you can make it higher. But the second and third rungs are no longer so secure. If they fail, Canada could make history by electing the world's most diverse form of self-destructive intolerance.

Note on contributor
Doug Saunders is the international-affairs columnist for the Canadian newspaper The Globe and Mail and is the author of several books on migration, cities and population, including Arrival City: How the Largest Migration in History is Reshaping Our World.

Section seven

Post-truth Politics and Journalism

***

A slow-changing media in a fast-changing world

Raymond Snoddy

Where does journalism go from here in the era of 'post-truth' politics when public esteem of the mainstream media appears to be languishing at historic lows, not least because journalism failed to predict the seismic shifts involved in the rise of Brexit in Britain or the triumph of Trump in the US? Can anything be done?

Mark Thompson, chief executive of the New York Times, is against censorship, legislation or regulation as cures for fake news. Instead citizens should put their money where their mouth is and help to pay for the real journalism that is vital to democracy.

At the same time the big search and social media groups who are inadvertently making money by 'enabling malign and destructive forces' must do more to sustain the economics of real journalism.

Apart from being prepared to pay for 'the real thing,' consumers should expose themselves to multiple sources, including properly funded, professional news organisations and always include a source whose editorial perspective is different from theirs.

In the end the battle against fake news is not one of right against left or between traditional and digital media but, Thompson argues, a battle 'between facts and lies.'

The only answer for Bill Wheatley, former executive vice president of NBC News who now teaches at Columbia University's Graduate School of Journalism, is to get back to basics – and facts.

In the face of fake news and alternative facts, journalists have to major anew on accuracy, relevance, clarity, the avoidance of hype, and promoting balance while reporting vigorously the affairs of their communities.

Wheatley argues that the media has to try to get as close to objectivity as possible, must remember there can be bias in story selection as well as coverage and should always endeavour to separate fact from opinion. For publishers who operate across multiple platforms, standards should be consistent across all of them, and those who would hold others to account, must in turn be prepared to be held to account themselves.

Trust can only be won over time and can be quickly lost. But, says Wheatley, "if you care deeply about what you do, cover the news energetically and fairly, and apply high standards consistently, your chances of winning the public's trust stand to improve appreciably." Yet let there be no misunderstanding: there are no shortcuts. "In the end trust must be earned," the former NBC executive believes.

Journalist and broadcaster Phil Harding saw 2016 as a great year for news but not such a good year for journalism. According to Harding, on both sides of the Atlantic editors and journalists were in turns bewildered, cowed and overwhelmed by the new age of post-truth politics and fake news.

The former editor of BBC Radio 4's Today programme believes that fact checking lies at the heart of dealing with half truths and lies but that the process has to be bold and carried out in real time as much as possible.

During the EU referendum debate in the UK too many dubious claims and counter-claims were allowed to stand unchallenged. "The British media needs to be far bolder and blunter in pointing out official falsehoods and lies. It needs to take a leaf out of the American media's book, which after the failures of the early campaign coverage really seems to have got the bit between its teeth," he argues.

Above all else journalists on both sides of the Atlantic, and television as well as newspapers, need to spend less time talking to each other and more time getting out of the office listening to the public.

"The media can and must play a vital role in providing the facts and calling out the lies. But it needs to do a far better job than it has managed so far," he says.

Channel 4, which had a system of fact checking in place before the arrival of the latest post-truth era, decided at the beginning of 2017 to see whether people could tell the difference between fake and factual news.

Dan Brooke, in charge of marketing and communications at Channel 4, found the results disturbing.

When 1,684 British adults were asked to assess six headlines— three fake, three true – nearly half said they were confident they could tell the difference. In reality only 4 per cent got all six right. Half thought at least one fake story was true and the percentage rose to 71 per cent for those citing Facebook as their primary source of news.

In a world of fake news the importance of trusted sources becomes paramount, Brook believes, and the aim of good journalism must be truth telling rather than sensation.

'If all publishers took the same view then the problem of fake news would be significantly alleviated,' argues Brooke, who also believes that the major technology companies of the social media have to admit that they too are publishers and behave as such and admit their responsibilities.

Peter Preston, former editor of The Guardian finds Brexit a highly personal matter, both as an individual and a journalist and, for him, the result of the referendum has been 'damned hard to swallow.'

Understanding the European Union, Preston concedes is 'a symphony, not a gavotte' but certainly for journalists there ought to be some gasp of how and why the European Union works.

"Europe may seem a forbidding home base: too many tongues, too many impenetrable back stories, too many damned complications and bits of bureaucracy. But it is who we are and where we are, especially if our job, as journalists, is finding the ties that bind and define us,' insists Preston.

And when he tries to explain it all to his Spanish grandchildren and sees the confusion on their faces he says at least he understands one thing: "It's personal."

One possible explanation why journalists missed the Brexit story may be more fundamental than failing to get out of the office enough: They are simply too metropolitan and too middle class.

Mark Spilsbury, a freelance economic researcher, has had a detailed look at who journalists are as an occupation and found a lack of diversity and disparities between them and the overall workforce.

Journalists are older and less ethnically diverse than the workforce as a whole and tend to have parents in higher-level occupations. While the balance between male and female is nearly even, women are more clustered in lower level jobs.

Earlier research showed that 72 per cent of journalists had a degree or higher-level qualification but of those becoming journalists in the last three years, 98 per cent had a degree. And 43 per cent of all journalists lived in London.

Would it have made any difference to the Brexit vote if journalists had been more evenly spread across the UK? "Perhaps not. But they might have seen it coming," he concludes.

Trump, Brexit and the broken language of politics

The use of misinformation is taking the Western world in to unchartered waters, says New York Times' CEO Mark Thompson, and there is no clear destination in sight

Why did the established language and conventions of political debate, the established relationships between politicians and public and media, relationships which had delivered relative political stability and at least adequate levels of public trust for many decades, break with such apparent suddenness in Britain and America in 2016?

In 2012, I gave a series of lectures on 'rhetoric and the art of public persuasion' at St Peter's College, Oxford. In them, I made the case that a set of political, cultural and technological forces had come together to cause a crisis in the language of politics, and in the relationship between politicians, media and public.

I argued that, as a result, the political language, which the public actually hears, was becoming more compressed, instrumental and extreme, gaining rhetorical impact at the price of explanatory power.

I added that wild exaggeration and outright lies had become routine, that the authority of science, medicine and other kinds of special knowledge and expertise were so widely disputed and denied that ordinary people were struggling to discriminate between facts and fantasies.

I said it was becoming harder and harder for us to find words to bridge the gap between different cultures and belief-systems, and that mutual tolerance was becoming more difficult to sustain. And I warned that some governments seemed to be having doubts about the wisdom of free and open public discourse, and that in many parts of the world – including our own – freedom of the press was under attack.

So how is my thesis holding up four and a half years later? It doesn't give me much pleasure to say: pretty well.

In 2012, it was still possible to argue that rhetoric didn't really matter – especially when compared to apparently more fundamental matters like economics, ideology and social change. But political language was clearly at the centre of the discontinuities of 2016. Other Republican hopefuls laughed at Donald Trump's idiosyncratic and impromptu style of speaking to the American public. Hillary Clinton did the same. When Trump refused to change or moderate his style, most commentators said he was doomed. In fact it was the key to his success.

There were linguistic winners and losers during the Brexit debate too. Remain had any number of economic arguments – and any number of experts prepared to back their case. But it was the Brexiters who came up with the two best political phrases of the campaign: 'Take back control' and 'Independence Day'.

The Brexiters also took active steps to undermine the rhetorical advantages of their opponents. If you are faced with rivals who boast more expert witnesses than you, why not undermine the whole idea that people with specialist expertise and knowledge should carry extra weight in an argument?

When Michael Gove said, "I think the people in this country have had enough of experts" (adding, to be fair, "from organisations with acronyms"), he was not just accusing economists of failing to predict the financial crisis, but advising his listeners to dismiss the *language* of these experts and its privileged status. Aware that he himself would be seen by many as a member of the technocratic elite, Gove also said:

"I'm not asking the public to trust me. I'm asking them to trust themselves."[1]

Now this is very artful: I accept that you can't trust me because I'm one of *them* – but I'm just voicing the instinct that *you yourselves* have about experts, namely that they speak gibberish, make you feel stupid and are usually wrong.

Unfortunately, it turns out that an absence of knowledge is not an unmitigated blessing when it comes to a referendum. Unlike general elections – where broad political instincts play a central and legitimate role – a single-topic referendum demands a minimum level of understanding of the issues and trade-offs involved.

By this standard, the 2016 Brexit Referendum was a disaster. Low levels of pre-existing knowledge of the EU and a chaotic and evasive debate left many people voting by gut, or for a series of essentially imaginary propositions – millions more for the NHS, no more Syrian refugees, the end of fishing quotas, whatever you wanted really – or alternatively on the basis of claims by one authority figure after another that the ten plagues of Egypt would immediately descend if the public had the nerve to vote Leave. Whatever the long-term impact of Brexit, the failure of the frogs and locusts to turn up on cue didn't exactly help the reputations of those battered experts.

Public confusion, of course, is not limited to UK. In early 2017, it became clear a significant percentage of Americans did not realise it was impossible to abolish Obamacare, which they had been taught to hate, without *also* abolishing the Affordable Care Act, on which many of them had come to rely, because it turned out they're the same thing. "Nobody knew healthcare could be so complicated," as Donald Trump put it.[2]

It's difficult to disagree with the harsh judgement on the quality of the Brexit campaign which Andrew Tyrie MP, the chairman of the Treasury Select Committee, delivered a few weeks before the vote:

> "What we really need is an end to the arms race of ever more lurid claims and counterclaims made by both sides on this."[3]

I want to endorse Tyrie's reference to 'both sides'. Many disappointed Remainers would like place all the blame for the woeful quality of the debate on the Leavers.

There was indeed plenty to criticise on that side: comically exaggerated claims and promises; outrageous opportunism on the part of some of the key leaders followed by an instant denial of accountability once the votes were cast; and an ugly undertow of nationalist xenophobia or worse, best exemplified by Nigel Farage and Ukip's 'Breaking Point' poster which, with its depiction of a teeming snake of refugees, took us straight back to the playbook of Josef Goebbels.

But, at least to my eye and ear, there was almost as much cynicism in the way advocates of Remain made their case and attacked their opponents. The Conservative and Labour leaders of the Remain campaign seemed scarcely more enthusiastic about the UK's membership of the EU than their opponents. Instead they opted for those over-heated warnings – 'Project Fear' was fairly named. The campaign as a whole sounded negative, instrumental and complacent. No wonder it failed.

Many Americans and Europeans used to look to Britain for a better kind of political debate: at least as feisty as their own, but with greater underlying common sense; less poisoned by ideological division, and with a shared sense of responsibility across right and left to debate issues in ways which help rather than hinder public understanding; at its best, more eloquent, more witty, more courteous, more intelligent.

But last year British political debate was exposed to the cold light of day and turned out to be the same as everyone else's, or worse – small-bore, bitter, inward-looking – and Britain itself looked less like a nation than a grab-bag of feuding classes and regions and generations.

Yet this dismal picture still pales in comparison to events on the other side of the Atlantic. In 2016 I published Enough Said, a book about public language based on those 2012 lectures. I was just able to reflect the Brexit decisions, changing the final proofs a few days after the vote. But the US election was still months away.

Even back then though, I thought Donald Trump had a much better chance of winning than most people did – precisely because I believed he had stumbled on a rhetorical formula which, though incredibly high risk, was potentially an almost unstoppable disruptive force.

This story is still far from over, but we know a good deal more today than we did last June, so let's now analyse some key features of the Trump rhetorical revolution. The first is a paradox. Donald Trump claims he doesn't use rhetoric. On

Inauguration Day, he told America:

"The time for empty talk is over. Now arrives the hour of action."[4]

Some of Donald Trump's enemies, especially those who look back fondly to the stately oratory of past presidents, might be tempted to agree that his public speaking doesn't add up to rhetoric. But they'd be wrong – and so is he. Despite its protestations, anti-rhetoric is itself just another form of rhetoric. So let's open the bonnet and take a closer look at the Trumpian variety.

The strong man, the general, the dictator, nowadays the CEO who's trying his hand at politics, wants to keep it short and sweet.

"We have to build a wall, folks. We have to build a wall. And a wall works. All you have to do is to go to Israel and say how is your wall working? Walls work."[5]

That was Donald Trump addressing supporters in Dallas back in September 2015. As I note in my book, consciously or unconsciously he's using a style which students of rhetoric call *parataxis* – short, simple sentences which emphasise certainty and determination and can be layered up like bricks in a wall.

Whatever you think of this style of rhetoric, it was effective enough to win a presidential election. But it clearly has drawbacks. You can't convey sophisticated thought or conduct a sophisticated debate – indeed, even to attempt to do so would be a betrayal of the style.

Most presidents delegate the majority of their messaging to surrogates. Given how much of his political credibility with his supporters depends on his unique style of political speech, Donald Trump may well find that he largely has to speak for himself.

But perhaps he's up to the task. Because right now this one man army is assaulting America's eardrums with what amounts to a 24/7 rhetorical blitzkrieg of presidential speeches, press conferences, campaign-style political rallies, tweets and impromptu one-liners.

Exaggeration, distortion, the reckless deployment of baseless rumours and conspiracy theories as if they were facts. Today they are central features – not just of Donald Trump's early morning tweets – but of his formal rhetoric as president.

In his inaugural address, he described his own country, one of the most successful and prosperous in the world notwithstanding its problems, in apocalyptic terms: "This American carnage stops right here and stops right now."[6]

'American carnage' is a supreme example of President Trump's tendency, implicitly or explicitly to argue fallaciously from the particular to general. If one Mexican immigrant is a rapist, they all are. If some Americans have lost their jobs or been the victims of crime, then every American, or at least every 'real' American, lives in poverty and fear and carnage. "Mass propaganda," Hannah Arendt wrote about the totalitarian regimes of the 20th century:

"discovered that its audience was ready at all times to believe the worst, no matter how absurd, and did not particularly object to being deceived because it held every statement to be a lie anyhow."[7]

But there are some important features of Donald Trump's rhetoric, which I did *not* foresee. A good example is what could politely be called *indeterminacy* – his tendency to say different or even contradictory things about the same policy area, within days or even hours each other, or to flip from praise and warmth to blame and fury, without appearing to trouble his own supporters in the slightest.

Conventional politicians place great emphasis on consistency. They only change tack when they feel they have to and only then after careful thought and risk analysis. They also dutifully suppress their emotional mood, or distill it into a carefully calibrated and politically useful essence.

Neither Donald Trump nor his base feel bound by these conventions. Trumpian policy is plastic, reshapeable to almost any degree at any time. If he says one thing and then another, the second doesn't so much replace the first, as co-exist alongside it.

Many observers are still parsing his rhetoric as if he was a traditional politician. Thus his address to Congress in January 2016 was talked of as if it might be a considered 'turn' to a more presidential approach in substance and style. Not a bit of it: within days he was angrily tweeting about how his predecessor Barack Obama – a 'Bad (or sick) guy!' – had supposedly wiretapped him, a claim for which no evidence has been offered. The shifts in style are not strategic, merely additional new voices generated by a rhetorical multiple personality.

And much of what he says is not really about policy at all, but is part of a stream of real-time bulletins about his emotional state. Thus those exclamation point sign-offs on Twitter: 'Sad!', 'Jobs!', 'Not!', 'Very dishonest!', 'SO DANGEROUS!', 'Enjoy!'.

For a large swathe of America, this emotional candour, the informality, the spontaneity, even the willingness to self-contradict, speaks to Donald Trump's *authenticity* – and they like and admire it.

Indeterminacy was in the air when Donald Trump came to lunch at The New York Times a few weeks after his election victory, and spent 75 minutes answering our questions on the record. Would he bring back torture? His pick as Defence Secretary, General Jim Mattis, had told him it didn't work, so maybe not. Since then, it's been back on the table and then off again at least once.

Donald Trump sees contemporary politics as a Manichaean struggle between two opposing worldviews, that of the liberal elite establishment, which seems to include many Republicans as well as Democrats, and that of 'real' Americans, whose 'voice' he claims to be. So to him, facts cited by the establishment are necessarily lies because of their source, whereas any claim, which fits his own worldview, no matter how fanciful or demonstrably false, is by definition a 'fact'.

One of Mr Trump's sayings is that 'everything is negotiable'. It turns out that this 'everything' includes reality. If you don't like the facts, here are some alternative ones.

"I want you all to know that we are fighting the fake news," he told the Conservative Political Action Conference, CPAC. "It's fake. Phoney. Fake."[8] It tells you everything about the new president's intuitive rhetorical facility – and his lack of scruple – that he should have so adroitly turned the phrase 'fake news' into a stick to beat news organisations like The New York Times, organisations which, whatever else they do, take immense care to make sure that they report what has actually happened.

Donald Trump has repeatedly claimed that The Times is losing audiences and subscribers. At it happens, exactly the opposite is happening – in the last three months of 2016 we added more new digital subscribers than in the *whole* of 2013 and 2014 combined. Other serious news providers are also seeing larger audiences and more subscribers.

But we should be under no illusion: in America a tradition of fact-finding and truth-telling which, with all its inevitable frailties, is second to none in the world, is now under fundamental attack.

Misinformation aims to level, to disrupt and to divide. There was misinformation aplenty in last year's Brexit debate, and anger about it persists to this day. But to me at least it felt like an irresponsible means to an end in the heat of a political campaign.

Perhaps the same could have been said of Donald Trump if the misinformation had stopped once the electoral battle was over. But it hasn't. Instead it looks as if deliberate misinformation is to be a central feature of Mr Trump's presidency.

That would be an unremarkable if we were talking about Vladimir Putin's Russia. The fact that this is happening in America takes not just America but the whole Western world into unknown territory.

Nor do we know where the President's hatred of what he thinks of as establishment media will lead to. When he visited The Times, I asked Donald Trump whether, given what he'd said about tightening America's libel laws, he supported the First Amendment, in other words freedom of the press. "I think you'll be OK," he said, "I think you're going to be fine".

Then he left the building telling the rest of the world's media that the organisation he'd described the same morning as the 'failing nytimes' was a 'jewel' for America and the world. Make of that what you will.

An extract from the 2017 John Donne Lecture, organised by Hertford College, University of Oxford, and given at the Sheldonian Theatre Oxford in March 17, 2017.

Notes

[1] Michael Gove MP, speaking on Sky News, June 3, 2016.

[2] President Donald J. Trump, speaking to Governors at the White House, February 27, 2017.

[3] Andrew Tyrie MP, speaking on BBC News, May 27, 2016.

[4] President Donald J. Trump, Inaugural Address, September 14, 2017.

[5] Donald J. Trump, speech to supporters in Dallas, January 17, 2017.

[6] President Donald J. Trump, Inaugural Address, September 14, 2017.

[7] Hannah Arendt, *Totalitarianism: Part Three of The Origins of Totalitarianism*, Houghton Mifflin Harcourt, New York, 1968, p. 80.

[8] Donald J. Trump, speech to CPAC, January 24, 2017.

Note on contributor

Mark Thompson is CEO and President of The New York Times. Previously he was Director General of the BBC 2004-2012 and Chief Executive of Channel 4 2002-2004.

Earning and keeping the public's trust: Thoughts for mainstream media

The polls might have been wrong on the Brexit Referendum and on the US presidential election – but every gloomy survey on what people feel about the media seems to be correct. Bill Wheatley suggests some back-to-basics practice might not go amiss

'In God We Trust' may be the official motto of the United States, but when it comes to having the confidence of the American public, even God's earthly representatives would appear to be falling short these days. Organised religion, like many other institutions in society, is experiencing a sharp decline in public trust: a 2016 Gallup Poll found that only 41 per cent of Americans surveyed had 'a great deal' or 'quite a lot' of confidence in the churches.

If trust in organised religion seems low, consider what the same poll had to say about trust in the American news media: only 21 per cent of those questioned expressed substantial confidence in television news; for newspapers, the figure was 20 per cent. The only major US institutions in the poll with lower trust ratings were big business (18 per cent) and Congress (6 per cent). (In other studies, confidence rises when people are asked about the specific media outlets they rely on as opposed to the news media overall. But even in these more narrowly focused surveys, levels of public distrust are sizable.)

It is not only in America, of course, that the trustworthiness of the media is being questioned. The 2017 Edelman Trust Barometer, an annual global survey by the Edelman public relations firm, found a lack of trust in mass media in 20 of the 28 countries surveyed. While confidence was understandably lowest in authoritarian countries, it was also less than abundant in democracies: in the US, Germany, France, the United Kingdom, and Japan, more than 50 per cent of those surveyed lacked such confidence.

Why is the public's trust in the media at such historically low levels? Some say it is a natural consequence of an ongoing worldwide populist revolt against traditional institutions; others feel that it stems from readers, viewers and listeners sensing that journalists no longer share the values of the public at large; still others believe that it is a result of the media becoming increasingly politicised; and some say that years of attacks on the news media by both conservatives and liberals have inevitably taken their toll.

The list doesn't end there. Some claim that staff and budget cutbacks caused by falling revenues resulting from Internet competition have diminished overall journalistic quality; others believe that misinformation spread by 'fake news' impresarios and social-media prevaricators has led to less public confidence in news and information generally; still others say that we have entered a 'post-truth' era in which one person's facts are deemed by many people to be every bit as reliable as another's, including the media's. Finally, there's the matter of the media itself sometimes failing to be on top of things, as in the failure to anticipate the pro-Brexit vote and Donald Trump's election.

Whatever the causes – all of the above and others might well be in play – the waning of the public's faith in news media shows no sign of abating. For journalism organisations that value the public's confidence, the big question is whether the slide can be halted or perhaps even turned around.

Various efforts are underway to explore that question. Among them, the City University of New York has announced that it will oversee the News Integrity Initiative, a global consortium of concerned parties wishing to foster news literacy and trust in the media. This project, which has attracted considerable initial funding from the technology industry and major foundations, will pursue a comprehensive review of existing research on the media, commission some of its own, and sponsor events and projects to help news consumers make informed decisions about what they read and pass on to others.

While these and other endeavours may well prove helpful in understanding what is happening and developing ways to address it, mainstream media organisations surely need not wait to take steps to shore up public confidence in what they do; indeed, some organisations are already hard at work on this.

There are numerous ways to proceed. Some approaches are tried and true, obvious to some but perhaps not to others. Some measures are newly possible. While each outlet will need to chart its own way, here are some suggestions that point in the right direction:

Be aggressive in covering your community:

Vigorous reporting of your community is what your readers/viewers/listeners expect of you. If you don't do it, they'll soon lose confidence in your work. This is true whether the community you cover is a small town or a large city or an entire nation or the whole world. People come to you to find out what is happening and how it may affect their lives. You have to deliver this to them, even if you don't have the financial resources that you once did. Doing your job well is fundamental to earning and keeping the audience's trust.

Maintain standards:

For generations the news media has employed values like accuracy, clarity, timeliness, balance and relevance to cultivate the public's respect. At a moment when standards are under assault and anyone with a digital device can claim to be a journalist, such time-honored professional values remain critical to inspiring faith in your product. If ever there were a time to double down on these attributes, it is now.

Accuracy, in particular, has renewed importance as news consumers are confronted with 'fake news' and 'alternative facts.' With more and more bad information circulating, your audience is counting on you to separate fact from fiction. This includes not only testing the claims of public figures but also making sure that every bit of your content is reliable. Now more than ever, the reporter's adage holds true: 'If your mother says she loves you, check it out.'

Avoid bias:

We all know that there is no such thing as complete objectivity. But the audience for your news coverage expects you to try to get as close to it as you can. This means insisting not only that your news stories reflect high standards of probity but also that they not be an outlet for the personal views of writers, editors or management.

Remember that bias can display itself in the selection of stories as well as in the coverage of them. If your news assignments deal heavily, for example, with liberal causes, it's not likely that news consumers who have a conservative point of view are going to trust your judgment. It's important that your journalism displays a broad balance of ideas and interests. No one likes to be spoon-fed what to think, least of all news consumers.

Consider also that one of the best ways to promote balance in your overall product is to support diversity in your staff. Hiring competent journalists from differing economic, racial and ethnic backgrounds will help rid your newsroom of the 'groupthink' that historically has driven so many uninspired editorial decisions. It will also invigorate your coverage and better inform your audience.

Separate fact from opinion:

Many mainstream media outlets offer their audiences both news and opinion. To encourage trust it's important that such content is clearly separated, using careful positioning and appropriate labeling. Similarly, in situations in which news and opinion staffs operate independently, don't assume that everyone in your audience understands this. Underscore the distinction daily by stating it in a prominent position in your publication or on your website.

If your brand operates on multiple platforms, be sure that your standards are consistent across all of them: a reporter expressing opinions on one platform can undermine his or her neutrality on another. If, for example, your reporters use

Twitter or other social media, insist that their communications stick to facts, avoiding commentary and speculation.

Remember that televised discussion panels offer special challenges in separating fact from opinion. This is especially the case when a panel includes both reporters and partisans. How is the public to distinguish between the two? Doesn't this play into the conceit that journalists are intertwined with the political establishment? To avoid these questions, limit your reporters to panels that include only journalists.

Try some transparency:

To further encourage trust, let your audience in on how you do what you do. In this, you almost certainly have a good story to tell, so why not tell it?

Find ways to let your audience know about your codes of ethics and best practices, demonstrating how these important standards inform and govern your newsgathering and presentation. Post the codes online; mention them in editor's notes, show how they were applied in particular stories; bring them up in panel discussions. Your organisation can only benefit when the public knows how seriously you take your work.

Also, don't hesitate to let reporters, photographers and editors present first-person accounts of how they deal with particularly difficult journalistic challenges. Not only will members of your audience find the stories interesting, they are also sure to appreciate the extra effort your staff goes to regularly to ensure that they are well informed.

Engage and be accountable:

The arrival of the digital age has given you numerous opportunities to engage electronically and quickly with members of the public. You can post their comments, solicit their story tips, display their news photos, and even seek out their cooperation and expertise as you work on investigations. In addition to assisting your journalism, engagement like this sends a strong message that you value your audience beyond the contribution it makes to your financial bottom line. This can only help gain their trust.

Accountability is another public confidence builder. Just as journalists work to hold accountable public figures and institutions, they need to be accountable themselves. This means disclosing possible conflicts of interests, owning up publicly and rapidly to errors and making sure that employees guilty of unethical journalistic conduct are disciplined. Respect for you will follow.

Reject hype:

Shrink from any tendency to make more of the news than it demands. As the number of media outlets has increased dramatically, so, too, has the competition for advertising revenues. In the process, hyperbole has been increasingly working its way into headlines, news copy, and, especially, promotion.

In some places, the use of overblown words like 'bombshell,' 'shocking ' and 'stunning' has become the order of the day in describing news developments. Relatedly, the designation 'Breaking News' has become ubiquitous, used even after a story has been reported on for hours and sometimes when a development barely qualifies as news. And the label 'Exclusive,' once reserved for notable stories that your organisation alone possessed, is now applied routinely to stories of modest importance; it is also used often to describe interviews with readily available newsmakers and ones interviewed elsewhere as recently as the day before. How can you expect your audience to trust your reporting if you wrap it in such exaggeration? These actions serve only to convince audiences that journalism is more a business than it is a public service.

If you ardently and persistently follow these and other worthy practices is there any guarantee that your news organisation will gain and hold the public's confidence? Not necessarily, because trust is fragile and keeping it is sometimes beyond your control: a single notable slip-up can tarnish a strong reputation years in the making; bad conduct by a few news organisations can weaken confidence in them all; even when criticism aimed your way is unjustified, it sometimes sticks.

Still, if you care deeply about what you do, cover the news energetically and fairly, and apply high standards consistently, your chances of winning the public's trust stand to improve appreciably. But let there be no misunderstanding: there are no shortcuts. In the end, trust must be earned.

Note on contributor

Bill Wheatley is a former executive vice president of NBC News. He teaches at Columbia University's Graduate School of Journalism and is an editorial consultant to news companies.

Journalism versus lies and fake news: Time for a rethink

The era of post-truth and fake news has left many journalists and media organisations very confused about how to deal with these new challenges. Journalist and broadcaster Phil Harding suggests some of the steps that should be taken

2016 may have been a good year for news – the big stories certainly came fast enough and thick enough – but it wasn't a good year for journalism. On both sides of the Atlantic, editors and reporters were in turns bewildered, cowed and overwhelmed by the new age of post-truth politics and fake news. It has been a new era for which journalism seems to have been singularly ill-prepared.

While politicians have often had a tenuous relationship with the truth this was the year in which the half-truths became outright lies and the ordinary lies became brazen whoppers. It was perhaps no surprise that in the aftermath the New York Times ran its first TV ads for seven years under the slogan: "The truth is alternative facts are lies".

Many journalists remain very unsure about how they should cover powerful people who lie. Do you report something that isn't true? If you don't, are you censoring the news? If you do, how do you report it? Is the use of the word 'lie' justified? Many media organisations have been playing a game of belated catch-up in dealing with this new style of politics.

So if the media has done a bad job of covering the politics of 2016, what lessons can be learnt? What can it do better next time?

Fact-checking

This has to be at the heart of dealing with the half-truths and lies. But it's not just what you do; it's also how you do it.

There is no shortage of fact-checking websites and organisations. According to the Duke Reporter's Lab there are now 114 dedicated fact-checking teams operating in 47 countries across the world. But too often fact-checking operates in its own silo. Either the checking comes from a separate organisation with its own identity and website or if it is part of a larger media operation it is relegated to a separate unit in the newsroom. To be effective fact-checking needs to be a daily part of the mainstream news team. In broadcasting it needs to be in the middle of the Ten O'Clock News report, not just a script afterthought from the presenter. In print fact-checking needs to be part of the main article and not shoved to a side box on the inside pages or on the website.

Fact-checking also needs to be bold and blunt and done in real time or as near instantaneous as possible. Late in the American Presidential campaign CNN tried to put fact-checking supers on a few of Donald Trump's speeches. National Public Radio (NPR) did something similar on its website during the Presidential debates. Now the Washington Post has introduced its RealDonaldContext app to act as an instant check on the President's tweets. Full Fact, the British charity, is working on a mobile app for journalists to instantly check and question statistics they hear spouted at press conferences. Speed is of the essence for fact-checking to really work but that takes effort, very good judgement and nerve.

Lies and untruths

Too often during the EU referendum debate in the UK dubious claims and counter-claims were allowed to stand unchallenged. Too often Boris Johnson was not quizzed about the £350m a week to the NHS claim. George Osborne's proposed 'emergency budget' was not treated sceptically enough.

The British media needs to be far bolder and blunter in pointing out official falsehoods and lies. It needs to take a leaf out of the American media's book, which after the failures of the early campaign coverage really seems to have got the bit between its teeth. When senior White House aide Kellyanne Conway appeared on NBC's Meet The Press to talk about the figures for the attendance at Trump's inauguration, the host Chuck Todd told her bluntly 'alternative facts are not facts, they are falsehoods'. In January the New York Times put on its front page the headline: "Trump Repeats Lie About Popular Vote in Meeting With Lawmakers". That in turn has provoked a debate about the use of that word 'lie'. NPR doesn't use it arguing that to conclude that someone is lying; you have to know their intent. The Wall Street Journal has expressed a similar view.

Fake news

Social media is playing an increasing role in elections and political campaigns especially as older, more politically active voters have taken to Facebook. While the role of social media in recent elections can be over-stated (for example most Americans did not get their news from social media, they got it from television) the trends are unmistakable. This in turn has brought a new set of concerns about the phenomenon of fake news. Research by Buzzfeed found that in the final three months of the American presidential campaign, the top-performing fake election news stories on Facebook generated more engagement than the top stories from major news outlets such as the New York Times, Washington Post, Huffington Post and NBC News.

The deliberate manufacturing of news stories to amuse or mislead is nothing new. But the speed and make up of social media means that nowadays the lie gets half way round the world before anyone can think to challenge.

The recent row about ads appearing next to anti-semitic material on Google's YouTube service, which caused some advertisers to pull their ads, shows that it is no longer possible for tech companies to deny editorial responsibility for the content they are hosting.

Facebook has been at the centre of many of the rows. Having started out by saying that they did not see themselves as editors, the company now appears to be beginning to belatedly acknowledge that it does have editorial obligations and is not just some value-free technology enabler. It has announced that for a test period it will invite users to flag fake news stories. If enough of Facebook's users report a story, the social network will pass it on to ABC News, AP, FactCheck.org, Politifact or Snopes to check it out. If a story is deemed to fail, it will be publicly flagged as "disputed by 3rd party fact-checkers". Users will then be able to click on a link to understand why the story is disputed. Stories that have been disputed may also appear lower in the news feed. It will be interesting to see if this new system can cope with the volume of disputes.

However, this idea of flagging 'disputed stories' may bring in its wake its own set of problems. Stories about Israel and the Middle East notoriously attract many complaints about distorted facts and biased coverage. Is every such disputed story going to be flagged? Who is going to decide? This may be a system that satisfies nobody.

Twitter's new system of allowing people to apply for 'verified accounts' 'of public interest' – a sort of white-listing of sources regarded as reasonably reliable – may offer a better way forward. All solutions will require money and resources. But then Silicon Valley is not exactly short of those.

If Facebook and the other social media companies do not grasp this nettle firmly soon there will be increasing calls for them to be regulated. In Germany the Justice Minister has said he will introduce a bill to fine internet companies as much as €50 million if they don't remove material regarded as fake news or hate speech.

But the problem of fake news is not just confined to the social media companies. Mainstream media has a responsibility here too. Beguiled by the prospect of a sensational headline, it can be all too easy for a reporter or editor to give publicity to a story when they suspect or indeed know that it comes from an unreliable source. Reporting every false statement ends up rewarding lies with publicity. That is not to say of course that false news cannot be news in its own right. Otherwise we would never report on Donald Trump's tweets. But the context description and language that surrounds such reporting is all important.

Search engines

Put into Google the question 'Who was the first black president of the United States' and prominently displayed in a box near the top of the search will be an article telling you that there were seven black presidents before Barack Obama including Thomas Jefferson and Dwight D Eisenhower. Put the same question into Bing and you will also get bizarre results. Search engines claim they are merely providing a route for the user to search the Internet. Google says its aim is "to provide the most relevant and useful results for our users". But of course it's not that simple because the search engines use secret and complex software algorithms to determine the ranking of news stories. It looks as though the search engines are going to have to work a lot harder to ensure that the consumer can distinguish between the real and the fake. Otherwise again the prospect of regulation looms.

Coverage

Journalists on both sides of the Atlantic need to spend less time talking to themselves and more time getting out and listening to the public. There is too much group-think. The media missed a lot of the anger voters were feeling because it didn't spend enough time on the ground. Newspapers spend too much on competing columnists and not enough on sending reporters out of the office. There is too much desk-top journalism. According to the Press Gazette more than 6,500 jobs in regional journalism have disappeared since 2006.

Television should get out more too. The expertise of senior television correspondents in the studio can be invaluable in helping us understand the story, but the news networks now spend too much time interviewing each other. Especially in America, the rise of the in-house political analyst has often produced much more heat than light. On CNN's election coverage the normally excellent Anderson Cooper was reduced to chairing eight-way shouting matches between Trump-supporting and Clinton-supporting 'CNN analysts'.

In the future broadcasters will have to think a lot harder about live coverage of candidates. Covering hours of Donald Trump speeches and giving an uncritical live platform to his outrageous claims may have been good for ratings on the US news channels but was not necessarily good for democracy. Breaking news coverage makes real-time fact-checking hard. Putting Nigel Farage frequently on the panel on Question Time because he's 'good value' may make for a lively programme but it also skews the political process.

At press conferences it's become all too easy for politicians to shut down a topic by restricting correspondents to one question each. There needs to be greater collaboration between news organisations and a willingness to follow up on each other's questions.

Coverage of immigration

Some British newspapers seriously need to ask themselves whether their coverage of immigration has been responsible and proportionate. Yes immigration raises some serious questions that need to be debated but sensational reporting out of context is not good journalism. We need to ask ourselves why Britons think 24 per cent of the population are immigrants when the real figure is 13 per cent. The regulator Ipso should take more of a lead here, as could the Society of Editors. The rejection by Ipso of the complaint against Katie Hopkins' cockroaches column in the Sun means that at the very least the Editors' Code urgently needs revising.

Broadcast regulation

Broadcast news in Britain is required to be duly impartial. That obligation needs to stay. In America the abolition of the Fairness Doctrine ushered in the start of one-sided news channels such as Fox and MSNBC coupled with the rising talk radio anger of the shock jocks. It is a process that has continued unchecked all in the name of free speech. You can now watch or listen to news 24 hours a day in the States and never encounter a view contrary to your own. Such a polarised media is not healthy for democracy. You now have large groups of blinkered voters for whom the facts have been fixed to fit the argument.

Impartiality and false balance

While a continued commitment to impartiality in broadcast news is vital, it is a concept that should be neither misunderstood nor misused. In the hands of bad editors impartiality can lazily lapse into false equivalence. As my former colleague Allan Little shrewdly remarked, if you have two men arguing in a pub and one says two plus two equals four and the other says they equal six, the truth does not lie somewhere in between. Too often in the EU referendum campaign broadcasters cautiously went for spurious balance rather than a serious weighing of the facts. The more vigorous and questioning stance adopted by the broadcasters in the 2017 General Election suggests that some lessons have been learnt.

Media literacy

Finally in the new media era, with its ever widening choice of sources of news we all – but particularly the next generation – need help to make sense of the bewildering array of information on offer; to enable us to pick our way through the facts and the fakes. A recent survey for Channel Four suggested that 96 per cent of Britons have trouble distinguishing between fake news and true reports. Media literacy is a subject much talked about but where tragically little has been done.

In 2004, the then Culture Secretary Tessa Jowell predicted that '…in the modern world, media literacy will become as important a skill as maths or science. Decoding our media will become as important to our lives as citizens as understanding literature is to our cultural lives'. How prescient those words sound today. She pointed to the need for media literacy to be embedded in the National Curriculum. After that, unfortunately, the idea became lost in various changes in government media policy. Sadly very little happened. Today the idea seems more important than ever. A proper programme of digital media literacy alongside active civic literacy could be a large part of the answer to many of the risks of fake news and without the need for restrictive and expensive regulation.

Journalism and democracy

Why does all this matter? It matters because it matters for democracy. The effective functioning of a democracy crucially depends on being able to give the electorate enough reliable information for it to be able to make an informed choice between platforms, parties and candidates. That in turn depends on there being enough of a consensus on the basic facts to be able to establish a baseline for debate.

When politicians foment misinformation and citizens are left uninformed, democracy falters. As Marty Barron, the editor of the Washington Post (and the real-life hero of the film Spotlight) puts it: "How can we have a functioning democracy when we cannot agree on the most basic facts?" It is that consensus that the pollution of fake news and the relativism of post-truth politics wilfully seeks to destroy. The media can and must play a vital role in providing the facts and calling out the lies. But it needs to do a far better job than it has managed to so far.

Note on contributor

Phil Harding is a journalist and broadcaster. He is a former editor of Radio Four's Today programme and was Controller of Editorial Policy at the BBC.

On guard for fake news

The dissemination of news has changed dramatically with the internet's freedom to allow anyone to pronounce anything on any subject. Which means the truth sometimes gets forgotten, deliberately. Channel 4's Dan Brooke looks at what can be done

During the 2016 US presidential campaign an extraordinary story broke. Pope Francis came out to endorse Donald Trump as the best choice for President of the United States. The story received more than a million engagements on social media. There was only one problem with this brilliant piece of news, which any broadcaster or newspaper would have led on. It was complete nonsense. It was fake. By the time that message got out, though, the damage had been done. The story was half way around the world while the truth was still strapping its boots on. Global technology available to us all has changed the relationship of the publisher and the reader, of the broadcaster and the viewer. While there is a great deal about that for democracies to celebrate, the prospect of falsehoods being cast as facts is not one of them. We need to be on our guard for fake news.

What is fake news?

The first task is to define what is meant by fake news. There have always been stories, which are partial, both in the sense that they are incomplete or that they are partisan. There have also been stories which, though published in good faith, turn out not to be true. Some stories are faithful representations of untruths that one person is telling about another and wants to see in the public domain. We should be complacent about none of these instances but none of them is what we mean when we use the term "fake news".

Fake news is a lie. It is a story that is invented, in the full knowledge that it is not true. It is passed off as if it were true and published with the intent to create a truth that does not exist, with either a financial or a political motivation. Fake news is a new phenomenon, a child of the internet and it takes one of three forms.

First, fake news takes the form of websites, which offer nothing but invented stories such as the one that produced the imaginative fiction about the Pope and the President.

Second, there are the websites, which are so entirely partisan that their reporting simply cannot be relied upon. When the political point precedes the reporting then news has given way to commentary and should be labelled as such. The line between the two is never a hard one but there are now websites where the distinction is totally obliterated.

Third, there is a species of website in which fact and fiction are freely mixed. These are sites that lack the traditional function of editorial curating and discretion. Some of their stories are true, some are not, but it is usually impossible to tell the one from the other.

At Channel 4 we decided to test the idea that people can tell the differences. In January 2017 we asked 1684 British adults to assess six headlines that had appeared, three fake, three true. The results were alarming. Although almost half of all respondents (49 per cent) said they were fairly or very confident that they could distinguish between a fake news story and a true on, just 4 per cent of people got all six right. Half of those asked thought that at least one fake story was true and, for those who stated that Facebook was their primary source of news, the numbers were worse. Seventy one per cent of that group believed one of the fake stories to be true.

It can be difficult to tell whether a story is true or false. People do not have the time to start checking out the origins of every story. This is meant to be one of the function of media brands, many of which try to become repositories of trust. The reader, listener or viewer should know that, by taking a news feed from this source, that it can be relied upon to be trustworthy. The source of news is crucial if we want to arrest the spread of fake news. The survey showed that if news organisations are cavalier about their own standards of truth it is possible to purvey fake news in the public realm and turn fiction into conventional wisdom.

There is a real danger too of an echo-chamber in which the range of opinion is never heard. The proliferation of information paradoxically leads to a reduction in the diversity of views that are heard. When people retreat online behind the tariff walls of their own prejudices the conversation that takes place is not very enlightening. This was a feature of the EU Referendum campaign.

Check your sources

The multiplicity of providers of news in a world wired all the way round has, of course, changed broadcasting beyond measure. Newspapers are struggling to adapt to a new world in which information is now more freely, and more rapidly, available than ever before.

However, the changes have not swept the traditional providers away. Ofcom's data shows that it is still the case that around two thirds of people (67 per cent) get their news from broadcasters, and that they are highly trusted. But Channel 4's own YouGov survey found that less than a fifth of people said that their principal source of news was the newspapers. Thirteen per cent of people go first to websites other than the online operation of the established newspapers for their news. Six per cent said that Facebook was their main source and 2 per cent cited Twitter, though in both of the latter cases, of course, the original source of the news they consume may derive from somewhere else.

Reuters conducted a survey across 26 countries, which found that 51 per cent of those asked used social media as a source of news each week. Twelve per cent said it was their main source. For the 18-24-year-old age group more than a quarter cited social media as their main source of news, with Facebook being by far the most popular place. In the US the number of people saying they use social media to find their news has almost doubled since 2013.

The first answer to the problem of fake news, therefore, is to trust those organisations that have proven themselves worthy of that trust. There is more than the word of their advocates to go on. Broadcasters and newspapers are subject to regulatory oversight on questions of truth that are vastly tighter than the lawless internet. Indeed, the only news content online that is probably actively regulated is that which is regulated under the old media guidelines and placed on line by newspapers and broadcasters. The problem is not yet so acute in the UK. Half of all people trust news in the UK compared to 33 per cent in the US. That may be at least in part because we rely on news online less than the US and because less of the available news outlets are overtly ideological or partisan.

News and current affairs is a major part of Channel 4's remit. Channel 4 airs more long-form news and current affairs programmes in peak time than any other main public service channel. We are proud that we show more in-depth investigative and international programmes than any rivals. We are not, however, free to air whatever we want and neither should we be.

Channel 4's standards of truth are set externally through regulation. As a public service broadcaster Channel 4 has a remit, enshrined in Parliament, to show alternative viewpoints. It does not have a remit to show alternative facts. We are also subject to Ofcom's Broadcasting Code, which is the gold standard in the TV world. Everything we broadcast is subject to challenge and we go to great lengths to establish the veracity of what we put out. These are the standards that should be required of any organisation exercising the privilege of taking part in the democratic conversation.

None of this is to say that social media is therefore a medium to be frightened of. Social media has become more important for us at Channel 4. Channel 4 News videos had 2bn views on Facebook in 2016. We publish 60 videos a week, each of one to three minutes in duration, which are created specifically for a Facebook audience. Channel 4's best ever performing video, from inside an Aleppo hospital, has achieved around 70m video views to date.

Digital media, properly used, can be a boon for democracy. The potential for engaging with citizens in new ways is considerable. Channel 4's digital record is very good. Over half of all 16-34 year-olds in the UK have registered with All 4, our online video on demand service, and Channel 4 has become one of the most popular UK news broadcasters on Facebook. The opportunities this presents are real. Jon Snow's short video imploring people to register and vote in the EU referendum reached 1m views in just 24 hours. Digital can and does involve people in democratic debate, especially the young who might otherwise be harder to reach.

The problem is real, though, and sometimes the consequences are real. A fake news story about Hillary Clinton's ties to a paedophile ring resulted in a gunman discharging his firearm in one of the alleged ringleader's Washington pizza restaurants. Analysis by Buzzfeed of the top 20 real and fake news stories during the US election found that Facebook engagement with fake news stories was greater than it was with legitimate ones.

The public is, rightly, worried. Of the people that Channel 4 asked, half said they were worried about the effects of fake news. Among the younger cohort of 18-24-year-olds, 57 per cent express concern. With respect to Facebook and Twitter specifically, two thirds of the British public believe they are not doing enough to tackle fake news. More than half of those asked think that the Government is not doing enough to tackle fake news. This raises the two crucial questions about fake news: whose responsibility is it to address the question and what can they do about it?

What can be done?

The regime under which Channel 4 and the other established broadcasters operate is a clue to what can be done to ensure that news obeys basic standards of truth. It is notoriously difficult to regulate the sprawling eternity of the Internet but we should not allow a counsel of despair. There is no need to accept that fake news is inevitable. There is plenty that can be done.

The first and most important point is that the veracity of the work of Channel 4 and the other public service broadcasters does not derive just from the regulators. It comes from our sense of journalistic ethics and our commitment to truth. Good journalism is a search for the truth that may not otherwise be revealed. The purpose is not sensation; it is truth telling. If all publishers took the same view then the problem of fake news would be significantly alleviated. In order for that to be possible the major tech companies have to admit their responsibilities. They have become publishers, whether they like it or not, and should behave as such.

There are some signs that they are belatedly starting to do so. Google has announced that it will restrict advertising on fake news web sites. Google has also announced it is changing its policies to restrict sites that contain misinformation from using Adsense, its lucrative click-per-view ad tool.

And Facebook says it is working on its ability to detect misinformation, by making better use of third party fact-checkers such as Snopes, and by including warning flags on stories known to be false. Mark Zuckerberg announced in November that Facebook has a number of projects trying to tackle fake news. They include stronger detection of misinformation, making it easier for people to report fake stories, using third party fact-checking sites to adjudicate on stories, and adding warning flags to dubious stories and by seeking to disrupt the flow of advertising revenue to fake news.

It is salutary too that Facebook has introduced measures to tackle fake news in the UK, France and Germany in light of elections this year. In France, Facebook and Google have collaborated with 17 newsrooms, including Le Monde and AFP, to introduce CrossCheck which offer users the option of identifying and flagging news stories as "real", "satire" or "fake".

News organisations will be able to see the articles which have been flagged by users as odd and verify them, or not, accordingly. If two of the media partners agree that a report is false it will appear in feeds with a flag attached, and if users then want to share the content a fake news alert will spring up.

In Germany, Facebook has also announced plans to work with third parties to verify and flag disputed sources. In addition, the parliamentary chief of the Social Democratic Party, Thomas Oppermann, said that ministers would introduce a Bill in 2017, which would require social media sites to establish a legal production unit to address issues of defamatory or fake news. The proposal could also include fines if Facebook does not remove the offending posts within 24 hours.

Social media platforms could also flag news from sources known to be consistently true and the same for those that are regarded as unreliable. They could pioneer kite-marking of known and trusted sources. Within the algorithms of the social media platforms it is possible to punish repeat offenders. Independent third party fact-checking websites are a good option and the digital giants should embrace them as a matter of urgency.

In the UK, Facebook announced several measures to address fake news ahead of the General Election in June 2017. This included changes to reduce the spread of misinformation by fake accounts; support for fact-checking site, Full Fact – the detail of which is yet to be confirmed – as well as adverts in national newspapers with tips on how to identify fake news. It remains to be seen whether these measures alone will be effective.

As part of these measures, Facebook is also trialling a new system whereby news posts which aren't shared widely will appear lower on newsfeeds. This is based on the assumption posts which aren't shared, but have been read, may come from dubious news sources. However, this runs counter to the evidence from the US election where there was wide dissemination of fake news stories, often outperforming legitimate journalism. This sets a dangerous precedent. It not only has the potential to drown out legitimate journalism, but also reinforces the echo-chamber effect where users are only exposed to popular stories shared by those around them. So it is important to be vigilant about the unintended consequences of these measures, particularly in upholding the important principle of plurality.

Self-regulation is not always easy. There is a valid question about where the sanctions should be applied. Should the punishment be visited upon the social media players as the disseminators or on the sites and the authors of the fake news? However, voluntary approaches have worked before with online players and ISPs on complex issues such as copyright infringement and child protection. But there should be no doubt that if self-regulation fails there will have to be a more onerous intervention by the state. As difficult and undesirable as that is, there would be no other option.

Conclusion

The major technology companies have responsibilities they are not properly discharging. Stanley Baldwin once famously said that the press exercised "power without responsibility…. the prerogative of the harlot throughout the ages". It is not good enough to allow fake news to go unchecked. It has to be stopped before it does serious damage to the democratic process. The process is not as far advanced in the UK as it is in the US but it may be that the US is the canary in the coalmine. We need to be vigilant. The snap General Election in the UK this summer will be an important first test in whether these new initiatives from Facebook hold any water.

Free speech is a crucial principle but free speech is threatened if the parties to the conversation cannot be relied upon to tell the truth. Newspapers and broadcasters all exercise their free speech vigorously while also submitting to clear guidelines on truth and falsehood. All platforms already have to abide by the criminal and civil law in respect of defamation, libel and incitement. They now need to be held to the same standards of truth.

News is one of the cornerstones of an argumentative democracy. There can be no democracy without argument and no argument is possible if one side suspects the other side is not capable of telling the truth. A democracy depends on the quality of information in its public domain. Just as money is the currency of its economy, information is the currency of a democracy. It needs to be trustworthy and it needs to be true.

Note on contributor

Dan Brooke is Chief Marketing and Communications Officer and Board Champion for Diversity at Channel 4. He heads up Marketing, Press and Publicity, 4Creative and Corporate Relations across the Channel 4 group. He joined from documentary producer Rare Day, where he was Managing Director. Previously, he was Managing Director of Discovery Networks UK. He also worked at Channel 4 from 1998 to 2005. Under Brooke, Channel 4 has been awarded the Marketing Society's Brand of the Year 2016, Best Diverse Company at the National Diversity Awards 2016, Campaign's 2015 Advertiser of the Year and Creative Review's 2012 Global Agency of the Year.

The trade of journalism: out of step with the real world?

Many Brexit supporters claimed the media missed the eventual outcome of the vote because most journalists are metropolitan and middle class with no understanding of what 'real' people think and do. So how diverse are journalists in the UK? Mark Spilsbury looks at who are they and from where they come

Concern about the diversity of the journalism workforce in the UK is not a new issue. It was first identified in the 2002 Journalism at Work research[1] and this has been supported by others in more recent times. The research shows, on balance, when compared to the UK population and the rest of those working in the UK, journalists are more likely to be older, white, from higher social classes and be educated to high levels (i.e. have a degree or higher level of qualification) with more senior journalists tending to have been privately educated.

Analysis undertaken by the National Council for the Training of Journalists (NCTJ) and published in Journalists at Work in 2012[2], more anecdotal evidence from the Sutton Trust[3] and new research from City University[4] have all added weight to the question of a skewed diversity.

This says nothing about why journalists failed to anticipate the result of the referendum. After all, nearly everyone else did, too. But it does pose the question of whether the trade of journalism is out of step with the real world? And if it is, does it matter?

Personal characteristics

Broadly, the characteristics of journalists differ from the overall workforce in:

- **Age:** journalists tend to be older than the UK workforce as a whole with only four per cent aged under 25 compared to 13 per cent for the whole UK workforce. This is driven by the need for high-level entry qualification. Journalism has become a graduate-only entry profession so entrants can only start work until they are beyond 21. This raises the age structure compared to other jobs where work can still be entered from age of 16 onwards.

- **Ethnicity:** journalists are less ethnically diverse than the workforce as a whole. Around 94 per cent of journalists are white – slightly higher than the proportion for the UK workforce as a whole (91 per cent). However, the lack of diversity in journalism is less positive than even this would suggest. The concentration of journalism in London and the Southeast and (when not in these areas) in urban centres, where ethnic minorities live in greater numbers, suggests that ethnic minorities are significantly under-represented in journalism. For example, the 2011 Census indicates that 60 per cent of London's population is white, with 19 per cent being Asian/Asian British and 13 per cent Black.

- **Gender:** the 2012 Journalism at Work report suggested that the balance of jobs between men and women was relatively equal. National data (the ONS's Labour Force Survey) analysis for this research suggests that there are only slightly more male than female journalists (52 per cent compared to 48 per cent). The NCTJ's research shows no apparent difference in the distribution of jobs on a sex basis – women appear to be as likely to occupy the more 'senior' roles of editorial management and section heads as men, suggesting at this level that there are no issues with sex discrimination.

However, Thurman et al[5] in the more recent City University research found that women may be more clustered in lower level jobs, which attract lower levels of pay. This research suggests that women appear to remain in junior management roles, whereas men are more likely to progress into senior management.

Table 1: Personal characteristics of journalists

	All UK employment	UK Journalists	
	Labour Force Survey	Labour Force Survey	Journalists at Work
	%	%	%
Age			
Under 25	13	4	4
25-29	11	14	12
30-39	22	32	26
40-49	26	20	27
50 and over	28	31	20
			13
Sex			
Men	54	52	57
Women	46	48	42

Ethnicity			
White	91	95	94
Asian/Asian British	1	1	1
Black/Black British	4	1	1
Chinese	2	1	*
Other	0	1	4

Source: *Journalists at Work Surveys, 2012 and Labour Force Survey, 2012*

Social background

Does journalism remain an occupation where social class impacts on the likelihood of entering the profession? The Journalism at Work research found that in 2012, as in 2002, young people entering journalism are likely to need financial support from their families. As a result, higher than would-be expected proportions of journalists have parents or carers in higher-level occupations, particularly managers and directors (17 per cent compared to 10 per cent of all employed in the UK) and professionals (48 per cent compared to 19 per cent across the UK). Relatively few new entrants have parents or carers from lower occupational groups.

Table 2: occupation of new entrants' parents and of all employed in the UK

	JaW, 2012	Occupational distribution of all employed in the UK
Managers, directors and senior officials	17	10
Professionals	48	19
Associate professional and technical	7	14
Administrative and secretarial	17	11
Skilled trades	5	11
Caring, leisure and other service	2	9
Sales and customer services	3	8
Process, plant and machine operatives	1	6
Elementary occupations	2	11

Source: *Journalists at Work Survey, 2012 and Labour Force Survey, 2012*

This is confirmed by research into social mobility[6], including journalism, that uses data from the Labour Force Survey to compare an individual's background (i.e. parental occupations) and their current occupation. This uses the National Statistics Socio-economic Classification (NS-SEC) to describe parental classification, with four categories:

- NS-SEC 1, higher managers and professionals;
- NS-SEC 2, lower managers and professionals;
- NS-SEC3, 4 and 5, intermediate and clerical occupations, occupations which are normally self-employed and technically skilled and craft occupations; and
- NS-SEC 6 and 7, routine and semi-routine occupations, which are often called the 'working class'.

The data below shows that 39 per cent of journalists come from NS-SEC 1compared to 15 per cent of the overall population, while a further 24 per cent come from NS-SEC 2, compared to 16 per cent of the overall population. At the other end of the scale, only one in ten journalists (11 per cent) come from NS-SEC 6 and 7 (*i.e.* a 'working class') background compared to a third (32 per cent) of the entire population.

Table 3: Social class of Journalists

Social class of parents		All population	Journalists
		%	%
NS-SEC 1	Higher managers and professionals	15	39
NS-SEC 2	Lower managers and professionals	16	24
NS-SEC3, 4 and 5	Intermediate and clerical, self-employed and technically skilled and craft occupations	35	26
NS-SEC 6 and 7	Routine and semi-routine occupations	32	11

Source: Laurison and Friedman, 2016

This pattern of social background is also reflected in journalists' education. Whilst private schools educate only a small population of the population - about seven per cent – the Sutton Trust[7] found that in 2015 more than half (51 per cent) of the UK's '100 top journalists' attended private, fee-paying schools.

This is, of course, not a true sample of all journalists in the country. But it is a subjective list chosen because of its perceived influence on the 'public debate' and so is weighted towards the 'commentariat' in national newspapers, as well as newspaper editors.

Furthermore, all the research now suggests that journalists are highly qualified, in that:

- Journalists at Work in 2012 suggests that 73 per cent of people working as journalists had a degree or higher level qualification 2012;
- Thurman's research suggests that 86 per cent of UK journalists now have a degree.

The clearest relationship with regard to qualifications is with age, with the likelihood of holding a degree-level qualification decreasing significantly as individuals get older. Thurman's research shows that if you look just at those who have entered recently (in the last three years), 98 per cent have a degree, with 38 per cent having a postgraduate degree. All the evidence suggests that journalism is now an occupation that requires a degree.

Given that entry into university is socially skewed, then it follows that entry into journalism from university will also be equally biased.

Personal views

Thurman explores the political stance of journalists by asking them to choose a point on a scale that was closest to their own political stance from 0 to 10, where 0 was left and 10 was right, with five being the centre. The single most chosen point of the scale was the central point of 'five' (24 per cent), with half choosing a point to the left of centre and 23 per cent to the right of the centre.

This pattern varies between journalists of different ranks and levels of responsibility. The proportion of journalists with a 'centre' position stays fairly steady; there are more right-of-centre journalists in more senior roles, and more left-of-centre journalists in more junior roles.

Table 4: Political affiliation of UK journalists

	Left	Centre	Right
	%	%	%
All journalists	53	24	23
Rank and file journalists	56	26	18
Junior managers	55	22	23
Senior managers	42	27	31

Source: Thurman et al, 2016

Where they work

A final concern about journalists is not a personal characteristic or demographic as such, but a frequent criticism of the reporting is that it is based in a 'London-bubble' and fails to be in touch with what the majority living elsewhere really thinks. This has been exacerbated by the decline in regional and local newspapers, further weakening the airing of 'local' (i.e. non-London) points of view.

There would be expected to be some concentration of journalists in London – it is after all a large part of the UK's economy. However, the data shows that the concentration of journalists in London is far greater than this, with 43 per cent of all journalists working in the capital (compared to 16 per cent of all in employment in the UK). A further 15 per cent work in the south east.

Whilst certainly significant whether this justifies the 'metropolitan-bias' that has been raised is debateable – there are still substantial numbers of journalists working in the regions and devolved administrations outside London. This may be an issue where the approach taken by the Sutton Trust, with its emphasis on a subjective list chosen because of its perceived influence on the 'public debate' may actually provide better information, although this is not available as yet.

Table 5: Region of work

	Journalists	All UK employment
	%	%
South West	8	9
South East	15	14
London	43	16
East of England	8	9
West Midlands	3	8
East Midlands	3	7
Yorkshire & Humberside	4	8
North West	3	11
North East	3	4
Wales	3	4
Scotland	6	8
Northern Ireland	1	3
Outside UK	1	0

Source: Labour Force Survey

And in the end

Concerns have existed about the diversity of journalists in the UK for 15 years and the most recent research suggests that these concerns remain. So the Brexiteers may be right.

On balance, when compared to the UK population and the rest of those working in the UK, journalists are more likely to be older, white, from higher social classes and be educated to high levels (i.e. have a degree or higher level of qualification). Data suggests that among the ranks of senior journalists a far greater proportion have been privately educated than across the UK population as a whole.

But in the end, does it matter? And would the referendum vote have been different if the ranks of journalists across the UK had been more diverse? Perhaps not. But they might have seen it coming.

Notes

[1] Journalists at Work, 2002, NCTJ. As a result of this work, the industry set up the Journalism Diversity Fund , managed by the NCTJ.

[2] Journalists at Work, 2012, NCTJ, 2012

[3] Leading People 2016, the educational backgrounds of the UK professional elite, the Sutton Trust

[4] Journalists in the UK, Thurman N, Cornia A and Kunert J, LMU Munich, City University and Volkswagen Stiftung, 2016

[5] Journalists in the UK, Thurman N, Cornia A and Kunert J, LMU Munich, City University and Volkswagen Stiftung, 2016

[6] Introducing the Class Ceiling: Social Mobility and Britain's Elite Occupations, Laurison and Friedman, LSE Sociology Department Working paper Series, 2015

[7] Leading people 2016: the educational backgrounds of the UK professional elite, Kirby P, The Sutton Trust, 2016

Note on contributor

Mark Spilsbury is a freelance economic researcher who works frequently in the creative industries. He was responsible for the underpinning work on defining the creative industries on behalf of the Department for Culture, Media and Sport, Creative Skillset. Mark has studied the changing employment patterns of journalists over a number of years in a series of research projects for the NCTJ, including Journalists at Work (2012), the developing skills journalists will require in the future (NCTJ, Emerging Skills for Journalists, 2014) and the emerging freelance journalism market (Exploring Freelance Journalism, NCTJ, 2017).

Brexit and before

Brexit denies who we are, as journalists and as people, says former Guardian editor Peter Preston

We know it's the most visceral issue in contemporary British politics. We know it turns red tops into attack dogs and Tory backbenchers puce with rage. So we ought to know that it's personal. Individual and personal. Europe isn't just one more tick on some routine policy list. It is history and emotion... even for newspaper editors.

Take me, and one personal route. I grew up in the East Midlands through the 40s and 50s. Sundays featured a grandparents' vigil at the local Baptist church. Holidays featured Hunstanton and Skegness. Europe? Well, there was always the Hotel de Paris, Cromer. It was a warm, loving family time (scarred by my father's death and my polio). But there were no far horizons. I look at my grandchildren now, veterans long before they left school of South East Asia, America, Europe from Norway to Romania, three of them Spanish in Barcelona, and pinch myself. Their worlds began early at Heathrow or El Prat. My world ended at Dover.

So, for me, the lands over the Channel assumed an almost exotic fascination, an escape; and university was a bridge to the future. I did a summer vac French course in Lausanne; I drove right across to Zagreb a year later with three friends in a 1924 Morris, cheered as we wound through countless village streets. I discovered French and Italian movies, as well as Wajda, Bergman and Bunuel. It was a personal journey, shared by many around me.

I didn't renounce those years of growing up, the Saturdays on the touchlines watching Barrow Old Boys play Midland Woodworkers, the table tennis nights at the Baptist youth club. But I was on a voyage of discovery, to tuna fish and tomato baguettes on the road south of Lyon, to the beer halls of Munich and the cafes of St Tropez, to pizzas, lasagne and kebabs, to new experiences that seemed to define a different existence.

And that didn't stop fifteen or so years later when I became editor of the Guardian. On the contrary, the learning process accelerated. You were invited to a weekend conference in Rome and saw, for the first time, how Europe instinctively divided north from south as the Italian delegates made long, rhetorical speeches and you sat hunched at the back with the Danes and the Dutch, muttering. You were directly involved as the fledgeling editors of El Pais in post-Franco Madrid came and asked for a little help getting started in freedom, and, later, when one berserk colonel tried a Cortes coup and you found yourself standing in front of the El Pais presses, alongside editors from far and wide, as though defending that freedom.

Of course you couldn't forget America, the new Atex systems, the fact checkers, the huge staffs and stately style books. There was plenty of necessary immersion there. But Europe, because so politically charged, so full of different cultures and traditions, because so various in its journalism, held a special fascination. Those new Spanish papers, El Pais and El Mundo, showed the world, and me, what a neat, clear, totally upmarket tabloid could do. La Repubblica in Rome amplified that feisty message. Dagens Nyheter's techniques with facsimile publishing – when the presses rolled there were sudden waves cresting on the Swedish lake nearby – put distribution together. A daily in Lausanne, mixing section sizes on its presses, gave me the idea for the Guardian's G2 features section.

And there were the people there, too. Juan Luis Cebrian and Pedro Horto Ramirez from El Pais and El Mundo (which the Guardian helped finance), two brilliant talents and the best of enemies. Hasan Cemal, the dean of upright Turkish editors. Harry Lockefeer, guiding De Volkskrant. Christina Jutterstrom, a commanding voice in Swedish journalism. Friends.

When I ploughed deep into editing trouble back home – feeling oddly alone as the critics closed in – I joined the International Press Institute and learned how the strength of cross-border solidarity can make even hostile governments stop and think. When Helmut Schmidt, former German chancellor, summoned potential collaborators from far and wide to Die Zeit in Hamburg and outlined his dream of a European newspaper that would underpin discussion about ideas and ways forward, I went home and devised Guardian Europe which, flying solo, strove to fit Helmut's bill. (Until it and much else fell with the ERM).

Do these lists of people, contacts and initiatives recited here appear a touch obsessive? Maybe, if you strip out the rest of British editing life. But in fact they were just another dimension tacked round the side of a hectic working week. They were just one path to the future.

And now that future is here, either as a road ahead or a cul de sac. After I packed up editing, there was the Guardian Foundation to explore, new demands and new friends in Croatia, Bulgaria, Slovenia, Macedonia and more. Plus, in the last five years, a founding role in the European Press Prize network that spans all 47 nations in Council of Europe membership.

Pause for a moment over that prize and that horizon. Journalism reveres the Pulitzer Prizes as some kind of editorial Oscars. It was, and is, foolish to think as the

European Prize as a competitor in that area – so many languages to be translated, so many different styles of writing. Five years of life backed by major foundations in Amsterdam, Copenhagen, Prague and London can only be a beginning.

But the number of entries increases almost exponentially, up nearly fourfold since launch. The Innovation area has already brought us Blendle, a subscription model the New York Times has put on its investment roster, as well as hugely influential news websites such as De Correspondent in Holland and el.diario.es in Spain. Where do the big scoops start worldwide? Munich and Suddeutsche Zeitung this year for the Panama Papers. Data journalism picks up speed as it crosses the Atlantic. And entry after entry stakes a claim to the highest quality, not just via word-spinning, but by the toil and bravery involved. 2016's German collection of refugee-tracking pieces is truly amazing for its punctilious research and eloquent description. Work at the highest level.

I'll always remember Elena Kostyuchenko, a tiny Russian in her mid-twenties, winning the writing palm for her amazing exploits on the Ukraine border. Were Russian soldiers active within Ukraine? A tale of fervent Moscow denial. Then how was the soldier husband of a grieving young widow killed in action? Where was his body? Why were the authorities full of outright hostility? Gallant Elena took the widow's arm. She found her the husband, hidden in a morgue. She published, in Novaya Gazeta, this first proof positive of Putin involvement. She blew official mendacity to smithereens.

Which, over and over again, is the trademark of East European journalism. It was impossible to read this year's investigative entries without your jaw dropping over a Moldovan inquiry into the illicit trade in anabolic steroids (made in Moldova, fast forwarded to you by the Moldovan post office). As for Serbia, and the Serbian Centre for Investigative JournalIsm, there's a whole batch of exemplary delving, turning over the stones of community life. You can't find a more consistent dedication to cleaning up a grubby world.

And here, amongst so much first-class digging, is a deeper truth, one that, for me, reaches right to the heart of Brexit.

Our world is full of communities – heart surgeons who meet in Capetown or Chicago to discuss new techniques, lawyers in conference from Boston to Brussels. These communities of professionals transcend national boundaries. Their disciplines define their borders. And if that applies to doctors or barristers then it applies many times over to the humble tradesmen of journalism.

Our job is not to deliver tiny fragments of reportage carved out of a wider picture. Our job is to add context to events, to see and show how one thing fits with another. Our job, in short, is to help understanding.

Far, far easier said than done, of course. Journalists come from all kinds of backgrounds with all kinds of experience. You don't have to mingle with Westminster lobby correspondents very long without scenting a strong corporate antipathy to

Brussels and Strasbourg, for instance. Why should these alien institutions get in the way of my fantastically important job, chronicling the greatest democracy on earth? Time and again, hidden or manifest influences shape the role. The Telegraph didn't send Boris Johnson to Brussels to do some rigorous 'I am a camera' stint. Rupert Murdoch doesn't cherish total independence of mind when he appoints a new editor for the Sun. But this does not mean the role itself, the fundamental job of understanding, is redundant.

Now, of course, there are many different variations on the theme: 'Understanding the European Union' is a symphony, not a gavotte. Yet logic and history still impose duties.

There ought to be some grasp of how and why the European Union works (at least sufficient, once in a while, to avoid the classic mistake of dumping the Convention of Human Rights and attendant court in Brussels' lap). There ought to be some comprehension of the forces that drive ever closer union. There ought to be some effort to see how countries, over-run time and again in war, have a different order of priorities for partnership. Economics? Pounds sterling, euros, profits and losses? Naturally. But don't for a second think this is all you need to know.

When I read the journalism of Spain, Germany, Norway, even Moldova, I hear a common voice. One that puts itself at odds with the rich, powerful and corrupt. There's a belief in the people who matter most, the readers. There's an anger on behalf of the oppressed. There is also, often enough, a proud resistance to anyone – prime ministers or owners – telling reporters what to do.

It's the authentic voice of British journalism too, operating just a few hundred miles from our door. Yet how many editors and correspondents in the UK stop to listen? Long ago the great training ground for British editors was America. The Daily Mail was rebuilt by David English and cemented by Paul Dacre, both US correspondents in their time. The FT uses New York as its global training ground. Rupert Murdoch is an American citizen who fills his Dow Jones with Brits and Australians. And, of course, the great media companies of Silicon Valley now overshadow every scene. The future seems American.

But is that a definitive reason for pulling up the anchor off Land's End and heading away, as though Calais, and all that lies beyond it, didn't exist? It's easy to make the bland assumption. The weight of Netflix, Sky, Amazon and the rest can feel irresistible. But it's not where history – British history – truly lies. It's not where the great wars we religiously commemorate happened. It's not where our most immediate rivalries grow, or where our most obvious trade and political ties exist. It's not what my predecessor in the Guardian chair thought as he fashioned Die Welt in Hamburg from the ashes of defeat. It's not where we are. Nor, when you look at its underlying assumptions about the safety nets of society, is it where we want to be.

Europe may seem a forbidding home base: too many tongues, too many impenetrable back stories, too many damned complications and bits of bureaucracy. But it is who we are and where we are, especially if our job, as journalists, is finding the ties that bind and define us. That's why the result of this referendum has been so damned hard to swallow. It deals in roots, not convenient refuges. It pretends – as the stories from Syria and Iraq and Libya sweep in – that we're somehow elsewhere. It seeks to paint us as something we're not: would-be masters of understanding who don't realise that we understand very little.

And when I attempt to explain it all to my Spanish grandchildren and see the confusion on their faces I at least understand one thing. It's personal.

Note on the contributor
Peter Preston is the media commentator for The Observer. He was the editor of The Guardian for 20 years from 1975 to 1995 and is widely considered one of the most distinguished journalists in Europe.

The 2017 General Election

***

The beginning of the end or the end of the beginning?

Richard Tait

When Theresa May called a general election on 18 April 2017 the polls put her 21 points ahead of Labour and heading for a landslide. The media-fuelled expectations of a massive victory only made the eventual result seem all the more humiliating. The Conservatives lost their overall majority and Mrs May her long-term political future. This section tries to make sense of one of the most dramatic and unexpected election results in British political history, and explores the role of the media, much of which, as in the 2016 EU referendum, failed to spot significant political and social changes – in this case resentment of austerity and a new engagement among younger voters - and ended up looking out of touch with significant strands of public opinion.

Ironically, the first indication that much of the media had got the election horribly wrong came from the one unchallengeable media success story of 2017 – the broadcasters' exit poll which at 10 o'clock on the night of 8 June accurately forecast a hung parliament. Professor John Curtice's work for the BBC has made him the best-known psephologist in the UK and on election night he had to both have the courage to make the prediction for the BBC and to stand by it as the broadcasters nervously waited for the real results to come in. In the first chapter of this section he explains in fascinating detail how he and his colleagues did it.

Given the complexity of what was happening in different parts of the country, to get a forecast that was no more than four seats out for any party was a phenomenal achievement. It was also the reward for developing over the last decade or so a much more reliable poll methodology than the sometimes hit or miss exit polls of the past. Now the contrast is with the traditional opinion polls and 'certainly an indication that the conventional (media?) wisdom about what the outcome of an election will be is often wrong'.

Mrs May claimed when she called the election that a big majority would give her a strengthened mandate for the imminent Brexit negotiations – she accused her opponents of trying to thwart the Brexit process and unspecified European politicians and officials of interfering in British politics. Tor Clark, associate professor at the University of Leicester, a former newspaper editor and political correspondent and a co-editor of this book, analyses the role Brexit played in the campaign.

He believes that Tory mistakes – particularly the U-turn over social care and Labour successes – producing a manifesto appealing to a public tiring of austerity – played their part in the result. In particular the young voters who had not bothered to vote in such numbers in the EU Referendum 'decided they had to turn out in the General Election to curb Mrs May's desire for a hard Brexit and maybe safeguard their own futures in post-Brexit Britain'.

Those young voters were a major factor in the pollsters' woes. David Cowling has worked for ITN and then the BBC, where he was head of political research, on every major UK election in the last thirty years. He has sympathy for the pollsters but nothing can hide the fact that their performance in the 2017 was another professional car crash. The problem partly lies, he thinks, in the polling companies' attempts to estimate how many young voters who say they'll vote will actually do it: they assumed that many of them would not. 'In 2017, with an increased overall turnout and more young people voting than before, it is easy to see how these otherwise sensible precautions blew up in the pollsters' faces'.

And Cowling is clear that this is not just an academic issue for psephologists and political geeks – when the polls are wrong it can skew the whole coverage of a campaign. In 2015 the media spent, in retrospect, ludicrous amounts of time on analysing a possible Labour/SNP government that was in reality never going to happen; this time round they encouraged the Tories to believe the election would be a walkover and the Conservatives' hubristic campaign, taking its core support for granted, was the consequence.

Ironically, the assumption among much of the media that the election was not a two horse race but a coronation may have helped Labour get its message across. Loughborough University's centre for research in communication and culture has a well-deserved international reputation for election studies. Professors David Deacon, John Downey, James Stanyer and Dominic Wring, together with university teacher David Smith have analysed how the media – print and broadcast – covered the election.

Their conclusion is that, although the media mis-read what was happening in the country and the newspapers were overwhelmingly hostile to Jeremy Corbyn in particular, their coverage played to Labour's strengths rather than the Conservatives'. While in most elections the process – the race – dominates the coverage, this time there was more focus on issues, partly because the race did not seem much of a story and partly because events – the Tories' mistakes over social care and the reaction to the horrific terrorist attacks in Manchester in London – meant there was more emphasis than usual on policies. 'Across the media, more coverage was devoted to health and health care rather than the economy and taxation; this distribution appeared to fit more closely with Labour's preferred agenda not the Conservatives'

Certainly for the pro-Conservative tabloids the election was a very different experience from the EU referendum a year before, where their whole-hearted endorsement of Brexit helped push Leave over the line, as Daily Express editor Hugh Whittow explains elsewhere in this book. Raymond Snoddy, the former Media Editor of The Times and one of the most respected analysts of the current media scene (and one of the co-editors of this book), reports how the tabloids hit Jeremy Corbyn with everything they had in terms of personal and political attacks.

Yet unlike the Referendum, many voters, particularly among the young, not only rejected their approach but in some cases reacted strongly against it on social media. For a generation more concerned with tuition fees, employment and housing, old stories of Jeremy's Corbyn's past encounters with supporters of the IRA and Hamas did not have the resonance the papers hoped they would have. Encouraged by social media, some young voters began to buy copies of the Sun and the Daily Mail not to read but to burn or recyle, unread: 'perhaps it was not ideal behaviour in a democracy but tellingly symbolic and embarrassing for the papers all the same'.

In such a polarised environment, the role of the broadcasters, under an obligation to report the election impartially, was more important than ever. Professor Justin Lewis and Stephen Cushion of Cardiff University have produced a series of definitive reports on broadcast impartiality. Their detailed analysis of the 2017 campaign makes uncomfortable reading for the broadcasters, particularly the BBC.

Although the coverage was balanced in terms of time, they found the framing of stories was skewed by the previous internal battles inside the Labour party and the hostility of many Labour MPs to Jeremy Corbyn's leadership. What turned out to be a hopelessly misconceived Tory focus on winning over traditional Labour seats was given too much credence. Far too much time was spent on meaningless vox-pops reflecting the conventional wisdom about the election (which turned out to be wrong). And, as in the EU Referendum, non-political experts found it hard to get a word in edgeways.

If Labour was the target for most of the press and had a tough time getting fair coverage on television, it was a different story on social media. Alex Connock, managing director of Endemol Shine North, describes an election where for the first time, social media had a decisive role in boosting Labour's appeal. 'Put simply, Labour were millennial, the Tories were so 20th century'.

The Conservatives found themselves outgunned in virtually every area of online campaigning. They failed to defend their own marginals, found that dubious attack ads rebounded and they never came to terms with the fact that Facebook was Labour territory. Jeremy Corbyn's Facebook had more than 4 million engagements from May 8 to June 8, while Theresa May had only just over 500,000: 'To attack Corbyn on Facebook was like attacking Lionel Messi in the Camp Nou'. The 2017 election looks like a turning point in the balance of power between social media and the mainstream.

Apart from the success of the exit poll, the only other piece of good news for the mainstream media was that Theresa May's decision not to take part in any election leaders' debates rebounded catastrophically – leaving her open to ridicule on air and reinforcing public doubts about her. Had she won, that decision would probably have been the death knell for leaders' debates in the UK, which since the success of the three big debates in 2010 have been under relentless pressure from the Conservatives to marginalise them and in 2017 to kill them off.

Sue Inglish as the BBC's head of political programmes, analysis and research, chaired the working group of broadcasters and politicians which finally broke the deadlock and achieved leaders' debates in 2010. The inside story of 2010 shows how fragile that achievement was – and from then on Lynton Crosby's hostility to that model resulted in David Cameron taking part in just one debate in 2015 and Theresa May refusing to do any debates in 2017. The public, particularly young voters, were not impressed. 'At the next general election, whenever it takes place and whoever the Conservative leader may be, one clear way to differentiate the campaign from the calamity of 2017 would be to announce immediately that he or she will debate with all comers'.

For thirty years Michael White has been one of the shrewdest as well as most entertaining political analysts, as political sketchwriter, political editor and assistant editor of The Guardian. For him, 2017 was the 'Selfie' election and a terrible miscalculation. The government did not have a coherent negotiating position on Brexit and would have been better focusing on the day job, but 'the Corbyn-led Labour party must have looked as temptingly vulnerable as the US Pacific Fleet in Pearl Harbour did that December day in 1941'.

Looking forward, he sees not much good coming out of the 2017 result. It was a protest election not a power election. Theresa May might hang on for a while for lack of an obvious successor. Jeremy Corbyn is scarcely a Clem Attlee of our times. 'A glimpse at his voting record and Attlee would have a fit'. Above all, the divisions on Brexit and the lack of any consensus over what the UK wants, let alone what the EU will offer in the negotiations have, if anything, been accentuated. Twelve months on from the events with which this book began, the election was 'only a respite, a lull in the encircling global storm'. Not for long.

How the exit poll got it All Right on the Night

The pollsters had a torrid time in the 2017 general election campaign, but the broadcasters' exit poll on election night accurately forecast a hung parliament. Professor John Curtice, the BBC's psephologist, explains how he and his colleagues did it

It is seemingly becoming part of the ritual of election night. At 10 pm Big Ben strikes, the broadcasters announce the results of their joint exit poll – and the country is shocked.

In 2005 the exit poll pronounced that Tony Blair would secure an overall majority of 66 contrary to the widespread expectation that it would be more like 100. In 2010 it said that, despite the dramatic rise in Liberal Democrat support in the polls, the party would end up with fewer seats than in 2005. Two years ago, the poll said that David Cameron was clearly set to continue as Prime Minister and that Labour and the Conservatives were not engaged in a dogfight to become the largest party.

Now most recently in 2017 the poll anticipated that, not only would the Prime Minister fail to deliver the landslide she was seeking, but that the Conservatives would lose their overall majority entirely. In detail, it forecast that the Conservatives would win 314 seats, Labour 266, the SNP 34, the Liberal Democrats 14, Plaid Cymru 3, and the Greens 1. In the event the Conservatives won 318 seats, Labour 262, the SNP 35, the Liberal Democrats 12, Plaid Cymru 4, and the Greens 1. In short, none of the estimates was more than four seats adrift of the eventual outcome.

So perhaps the country should not have been surprised that the exit poll was surprising – for surprises seem to be its forte. That it has consistently delivered the unexpected, and for the most part accurately, is certainly an indication that the conventional (media?) wisdom about what the outcome of an election will be is often wrong. That wisdom, of course, is heavily though not entirely driven by the opinion polls. However, an exit poll is a very different kind of exercise. Opinion polls attempt to interview, either by phone or via the internet, a representative sample of voters from across the whole country and ask them how they will vote.

John Curtice

An exit poll, in contrast, is conducted by approaching voters as they leave a limited number of polling stations and inviting them to indicate how they have just voted.

Choosing the polling stations

Central, then, to the conduct of an exit poll is the selection of the polling stations at which interviewers are positioned. This is not an easy task in Britain. In most countries, an election is counted separately within each polling station and the outcome of the vote at each polling station made publicly available. However, in Britain the practice is that the ballot boxes at each polling station are transferred to a central count and, once it has been ascertained that each ballot box contains the correct number of ballot papers, the ballot papers from different polling stations are mixed together before they are counted. As a result, nobody can know whether a particular sample of polling stations, however chosen, is representative of the whole country or not.

Meanwhile, both economics and resources dictate that any exit poll must cover a relatively small proportion of the many thousands of polling stations across Britain. At the same time, the level of support for the parties varies considerably from one locality to another. Consequently, there is a substantial risk that any selection of stations is not representative of the country at all. However, while the level of support for the parties varies considerably from place to place, the change in the parties' shares of the vote since the last election varies much less. There is thus much less risk that any selection of polling stations will prove atypical of the country if it is used to estimate change in party support rather than the level.

It is this insight which, following a suggestion first put forward by Prof. David Firth of Warwick University, has guided the methodology of the exit poll since 2005 (Curtice and Firth, 2008; Curtice et al., 2011; Firth, nd). Mind you, at first glance, it would seem it does not take us much further forward. For how can we estimate change in party support unless we know what the outcome was in a particular polling station last time, the very absence of which creates our difficulty in the first place? However, if we have previously conducted an exit poll we do have estimates of how the electorate voted locally at the polling stations that were covered by that previous poll. So, if we conduct an exit poll at the same locations this time we can derive an estimate of the change in party support at each polling station by comparing, station by station, the result of the new exit poll with that of the last one.

Not that this is always straightforward to achieve. Occasionally, the boundaries of the area served by a polling station are changed. Equally, a new housing development – or outward migration – may result in a considerable change in the composition of the electorate. But because the 2017 election took place just two years after its predecessor, for the most part these issues rarely arose this time around. We were able to return to all of the 141 polling districts that were covered by the 2015 survey; in the few instances where a boundary change had taken place, census data suggested it had not had a major impact on the kinds of people that voted at our station. Meanwhile, three new polling districts in three new constituencies were added to the sample; in these instances, a polling district was selected that appeared to be typical of the constituency in which it was located, and the outcome of the result in the relevant constituency as a whole in 2015 was used as the baseline for estimating the change in support at those polling stations.

Mock ballot papers

On polling day itself, the hard work was done by interviewers from gfk and Ipsos MORI who stood outside each of our 144 polling stations and invited a random sample of those leaving the station to indicate on a mock ballot paper (which was placed in a mock ballot box) how they have just voted. Interviewers were instructed to approach one in every n voters, where n was inversely related to the number of people registered to vote at the station; the aim was to approach roughly equal numbers of people at each station. In line with previous exit polls, nearly one in five refused to take part, and while we can undertake some checks on whether those who refuse are atypical in some way, for the most part we have to trust that they are not atypical. Meanwhile those who vote by post are not covered by the exercise at all; our assumption is that the change in party support amongst these voters will be the same as it is amongst those who do make it to the polling station.

This approach, then, gave us 144 estimates of the change in party support since 2015. But how were these turned into estimates of how many seats each party should win? First, they were analysed to identify significant and systematic differences in the estimated changes in party support. For example, in 2017 a number of indicators suggested the Labour party would perform better in places where the Remain vote in 2016 was relatively high, while the Conservatives would do better in places where Leave prospered twelve months ago. Equally, the poll suggested that the Liberal Democrat vote would often fall back heavily in seats that the party lost in 2015. Both patterns were in evidence when the results became known.

This analysis of the data gives us a sequence of equations that specify the estimated changes in party support and how those changes are expected to vary depending on one or more social, geographical or political characteristics of a constituency. These equations are solved for each constituency, thereby giving us a set of estimated changes in party support for each constituency. These estimated changes can then be applied to the actual result last time, and thus an estimated vote share for each party in each constituency obtained.

A balance of probabilities

There is then, one final wrinkle. Let us say, for example, that as a result of this exercise we estimate that the Conservatives will win 43% of the vote in a particular constituency, Labour 42%. Given all the uncertainties about the exercise, we cannot be sure that the Conservatives will win this constituency. In truth, they are no more than slight favourites to do so. In recognition of this, the estimated outcome in each constituency is then converted into an estimated probability for each party that they will win the seat. Thus, in our hypothetical example we might say that the Conservatives have a 52% probability of winning, Labour 48%. The total number of seats for each party broadcast at 10pm on election night are the sum of these probabilities across all seats.

The key feature how exit polls are conducted in Britain nowadays is then the focus on estimating change by comparing the results of two different exit polls. It is an approach which seems to serve well, though it certainly cannot be presumed that it will always be as accurate as it proved to be in 2017. As a result, editors, presenters, politicians and above all the audience have been given advance notice of what might emerge as the night unfolds – and, perhaps most importantly, a benchmark against which to measure and understand the implications of the early results as they unfold. It certainly provides some drama – and hopefully a little enlightenment too.

Acknowledgement

Many people contributed to the success of the 2017 exit poll, including Nick Moon, Roger Mortimore, Jouni Kuha, Stephen Fisher, Jonathan Mellon, Robert Ford, Patrick English, Colin Rallings and Michael Thrasher, as well as the editors and managers at the BBC, ITV and Sky who commissioned the exercise.

References

Curtice, J. and Firth, D. (2008), 'Exit polling in a cold climate: the BBC-ITV Experience in Britain in 2005', *Journal of the Royal Statistical Society Series A*, 171 (3): 509-39.

Curtice, J., Fisher, S. and Kuha, J. (2011), 'Confounding the Commentators: How the 2010 Exit Poll got it (more or less) right', *Journal of Elections, Public Opinion and Parties*, 21 (2): 211-35.

Firth, D. (nd), 'Exit Polling Explained'. Posted at http://www2.warwick.ac.uk/fac/sci/statistics/staff/academic-research/firth/exit-poll-explainer/, accessed on 16 June 2017

Note on contributor

John Curtice is Professor of Politics at the University of Strathclyde, senior research fellow at NatCen Social Research and President of the British Polling Council. He led the team of analysts of the BBC/ITV/Sky exit poll and presented its findings on the BBC Television election night programme.

Brexit and the 2017 General Election campaign

The 2017 election was framed by the Prime Minister, who called it 'the Brexit election', and though it didn't turn out the way Theresa May imagined, the decision to leave the EU overshadowed the campaign – before, during and after. Though in the end, thanks largely to Jeremy Corbyn, it turned out to be about an awful lot more than just Brexit, it was still Brexit that formed the backdrop to everything that happened, argues election-watcher Tor Clark

This was the election that should never have happened. Mrs May's predecessor as Tory leader and Prime Minister David Cameron had a working majority of 17 on being surprisingly re-elected in 2015. He didn't have to call a Referendum on EU membership for 2016, but he had promised it to his own Eurosceptic right wing – and he thought he'd win it.

As other chapters in this book point out, he didn't get much for Britain from his 'renegotiation' with the EU and entered the Referendum with a poor deal to sell. Not only that, but it was sold in a lacklustre way, not least by Labour leader Jeremy Corbyn and his party, many of whose traditional supporters backed Brexit in far greater numbers than expected.

David Cameron and Remain should not have lost the EU Referendum but they did, for all the reasons spelled out in the other sections of this book. Despite the relatively high turnout around 72 per cent, pro-Brexit older voters turned out more than pro-Remain younger voters and the poll was decided by just two per cent.

Cameron quit and was replaced as PM by Theresa May, who inherited his crown without a fight. But having got herself settled into 10 Downing Street, Mrs May revealed her priority would be to 'take back control' from the EU; so in response to perceived fears from the victorious 52 per cent about immigration, free movement of people around Europe would be ended.

The Europeans told her Britain could not be a member of the European Single Market, the UK's biggest export market, without free movement of people so her

Brexit became 'hard', i.e. outside the trading area. It seemed the Conservatives had made controlling immigration more important than protecting the UK's trade, and hence its economic prosperity.

Immediately Labour, the Liberal Democrats, the SNP and the Greens argued a 'hard Brexit' had not been on the EU Referendum ballot paper. They reminded voters it had been suggested the UK could still be in the Single Market even if it wasn't in the EU, as was Norway.

The Prime Minister gambles on a snap election

The Conservatives became an anti-immigration, hard Brexit party, persuading many Ukip voters to return to it. The opinion polls showed a strong Conservative lead.

Mrs May wanted a bigger majority to deliver departure from the EU and she wanted to be able to enact her own manifesto, rather than that bequeathed to her by Mr Cameron from his 2015 victory. She also, opportunistically, thought she could easily defeat a Labour Party sometimes calculated to be 20 per cent behind the Conservatives in the polls with a leader characterised as a liability.

So, in what looked at the time like a brilliant pre-emptive strike, on April 18 she called a snap election which she and her party sought to characterise around 'strong and stable leadership in the national interest'.

At the start of the electoral campaign, the Tories talked of little else than Brexit and Mrs May as being the only leader who could deliver it. She celebrated her colleague Ken Clarke's description of her as being 'a bloody difficult woman' in negotiations with the 27 other EU members and top Europeans brazenly leaked their disquiet at her strategy.

Then came the Tories' manifesto launch and the immediate U-turn on its social care policy, which she insisted in the campaign's greatest 'Emperor's New Clothes' moment, was not actually a U-turn. In fact the Conservatives were in a great deal of trouble with explaining this policy when the Manchester bomber struck and the campaign was suspended.

Security became an issue then, and again after the London Bridge attacks a week or so later. But towards the end of the campaign the Tories sought to return to what they thought was the safe ground of Mrs May as the country's only choice to get the UK a good Brexit deal – though many were by now asking how one difficult woman could secure any deal from 27 other people she had ridiculed and insulted.

Labour changes the message

The Labour Party's Brexit policy was much more woolly from the start, and it definitely wasn't hard. It wanted to secure workers' rights and economic prosperity. Labour was in a bind because Mr Corbyn, like his metropolitan middle class supporters did not object to immigration, but stressed its benefits. Meanwhile traditional working class Labour voters in its northern industrial strongholds appeared to have become strongly anti-immigration, voting Leave in 2016 and being tempted by Ukip on that policy alone.

Labour's shadow Brexit Secretary Sir Keir Starmer, a respected politician who had once held a proper job as Director of Public Prosecutions before becoming an MP, announced and discussed his party's strategy for leaving the EU in the first week of the campaign and then was virtually never heard of again, despite his being a capable performer.

Mr Corbyn unashamedly tried to move the whole campaign's focus onto other policies, perhaps recognising that day-to-day life for normal voters would go on despite Brexit hanging over them. Labour announced policies to tax high earners, end austerity and spend a lot of Government money on a range of policies from renationalising the railways to abolishing student fees.

As the campaign developed he grew more confident talking about real policies that affected real people, even when his party was branded 'tax and spend'.

It began to be said by the commentators that the Tories would win the election if they could keep the debate on Brexit, while they might suffer if it moved onto some of the many other issues bothering the electorate and being raised by Labour.

And though the Tories' traditional allies, the right-wing press, constantly demonised Mr Corbyn, television viewers got to see Mr Corbyn for themselves in as unbiased a way as possible and make up their own minds about him, as broadcast coverage over the course of the campaign was obliged by law to be balanced. If the Tory press had played a crucial part in securing Brexit in 2016, it was not to enjoy success in 2017.

The strange failure of the Lib Dems, and other parties

The Liberal Democrats, fresh from their spectacular by-election win in Richmond Park on the back of pushing their opposition to Brexit, seemed to be poised to make a strong bid for the votes of the 48 per cent of people who had voted Remain just a year before. However, strangely that aspect of their campaign just didn't seem to fly for them. It was the only major party unequivocally opposed to leaving the EU, but its strategy was confused by the problem that some of its traditional hunting grounds, especially in the South West, had voted Leave.

Leader Tim Farron never gave up trying to push the case against Brexit and had a nice clear policy on raising income tax by a penny to invest in health and social care, but bizarrely became constantly bogged down in his own personal religious beliefs on homosexuality. His pro-Remain message just didn't seem to cut through to the huge numbers of voters who might have been sympathetic.

Meanwhile on the right, with Nigel Farage gone and Brexit secured, Ukip voters deserted the party, either back to the Tories or to Labour. It lost its only seat and suffered catastrophic vote collapses in virtually every seat it fought. And, on the left, the Greens kept their one seat in Brighton, but again lost votes elsewhere in the UK.

The failed Scottish Independence referendum of 2014 had led to a remarkable Scottish National Party surge, leaving it with 56 out of 59 Scottish seats in the 2015 general election. Party leader Nicola Sturgeon used Scotland's vote to remain in the EU as an excuse to demand a second independence referendum for her country, but was slightly blindsided by Mrs May's snap election call, with the result that it all became very confused north of the border.

Scottish voters who wanted to remain in the UK seem to have decided to gather around whichever party was the SNP's main challenger in each seat, with the result that all three major UK parties regained seats in Scotland as the SNP lost 20 of its 2015 gains. The Tories, who had no seats at all north of the border only a dozen or so years beforehand, were surging back, sometimes with unprecedented swings of up to 20 per cent. If anything, in Scotland, independence trumped Brexit as an issue.

Young voters learn the lessons of Brexit

So Brexit was the reason for the election and let's not forget in the end pro-Brexit parties – the Conservatives and the Democratic Unionist Party in Northern Ireland – got the most votes and, at the time of writing immediately after the results, looked like they were about to work together to have a working majority to try to push through their policies in the House of Commons.

But to some extent it was Jeremy Corbyn's strategy of trying to move the election onto other policy areas which helped him unexpectedly increase Labour's share of the vote beyond a creditable and largely unexpected 40 per cent. And this gives us a clue to another perhaps crucial legacy of Brexit on the election.

Analysing the early results on election night, it seemed the Tories were increasing their vote, but that Labour were piling up their votes just a little bit more – we now know that increase was around two per cent. Comparing the 2017 results with the 2015 results it was clear the Ukip vote, some of the Liberal Democrat vote and a part of the Green vote was going to the two major parties, turning the British electoral landscape back into something resembling the 1970s (1974 to be precise).

But the shift of votes from minor to major parties didn't account for all the additional red and blue vote piles. Something else was happening; there were actually more votes in the system. Tory MPs were being re-elected with more votes than in 2015 but slimmer majorities over Labour, whose vote was often increasing even more.

As the night wore on it became apparent that turnout was increasing slightly, from about 67 per cent to about 69 per cent, but that pushed the general election turnout closer to the EU Referendum turnout figure than turnouts of previous elections. And it was the nature of these voters that proved crucial in the end.

Early analysis of the increased Labour vote suggests it was young voters who swelled their ranks. These young voters couldn't be scared by stories of Corbyn the leftie with the dodgy cap from the 80s. They didn't know much about such folk, as they weren't even born then. They liked the idea of getting rid of tuition fees, spending more public money and taxing the rich and weren't scared away by stories of Labour taking Britain back to the 1970s.

So in the end, though Theresa May wanted to capitalise on Brexit's 52 per cent majority and a widespread belief that even many of the Remainers had reluctantly accepted the inevitability of EU withdrawal, two factors directly created by Brexit might have thwarted her ambition.

Firstly, she had no evidence Britons wanted a hard Brexit. It hadn't been on the Referendum ballot paper and there was huge concern about both leaving the European Single Market trading area and getting a 'bad deal'. It seems likely both Remainers and soft Brexiteers turned to Labour.

But secondly and crucially, it may also have been the case that young voters, so tortured by the knowledge that if they had turned out in greater numbers in the EU Referendum there would have been no Brexit at all, decided they had to turn out in the General Election to curb Mrs May's desire for a hard Brexit and maybe safeguard their own futures in post-Brexit Britain.

If the legacy of the 2017 General Election is a better Brexit deal and a younger generation newly re-engaged with serious politics, it might prove to be a positive watershed moment. And though Brexit wasn't as central to the election as Mrs May and the Conservatives hoped, it did, in the end, dominate the whole campaign.

Note on contributor

Tor Clark is Associate Professor in Journalism at the University of Leicester. Previously he was Principal Lecturer in Journalism at De Montfort University in Leicester. Before that he edited two regional newspapers. He has been a political journalist since the 1980s and has covered every general election for newspapers or radio since 1992. He spent eight hours on election night 2017 in relative disbelief, covering the results as they came in for BBC Radio Leicester and has consequently given up predicting elections. He is co-editor of this book.

Déjà vu all over again

The pollsters - and the politicians - thought the only uncertainty the 2017 election was about the size of the predicted Conservative majority. But the whole campaign was based on a false premise. David Cowling analyses another car crash for the polling industry

The 2017 election result stunned everyone, including the leadership of both major parties. Understandably, the opinion poll companies found themselves in a very public firing line as soon as the election outcome became clear. For the pollsters themselves, this all had an ominous familiarity. Only two years earlier they had experienced a similar professional car crash and it is worth reminding ourselves of the scale of their 2015 under-achievement. During the six week election campaign in 2015, I monitored 92 voting intention polls. Among these, 17 suggested a dead heat between Conservative and Labour, leaving 75 which put one party ahead of another; and among these, 42 (56%) suggested Labour leads. In all, 81 polls registered a gap of between 0-3% between the two main parties when the final outcome was a Conservative lead of seven per cent.

For people of a certain age, the 2015 debacle carried echoes of a similar polling meltdown in the 1992 general election. The failure of the eve-of-election opinion polls to reflect the actual result of the 1992 general election *"was the most spectacular in the history of British election surveys"* according to the Market Research Society's investigative report published in July 1994 (*The Opinion Polls and the 1992 General Election*). During the 1992 election some 50 campaign polls had been published, 38 of which suggested small Labour leads when the outcome was a seven-point Conservative lead.

Emerging from the rubble in 2015, the polling companies looked to the 2016 EU Referendum for redemption. And whilst it is true that, overall, their results came closer to the final outcome in 2016, their performance fell short of restoring the industry's reputation.

Missing the Labour surge

Throughout the 2017 election campaign, some 79 voting intention polls were published. Nine polling companies published eve-of-poll forecasts and these final efforts produced a very accurate Conservative share of the vote; they averaged 44%, which was spot on. They were also reasonably accurate when forecasting vote shares for the Lib Dems, UKIP and Greens. Even before polling day, they had picked up the small decline in support for the Conservatives and the rise in support for Labour. However, Labour still proved to be the fly in their ointment. The average of the 2017 campaign eve-of-poll surveys suggested 36% support for Labour which was five-points adrift from the party's actual 41% share of the vote. For the majority of the pollsters, these low Labour ratings were beyond sampling error.

In five of the previous six general elections (2010 was the exception), the polling companies had overstated Labour's share of the vote. As a consequence, pollsters developed strategies for weighting samples that reduced this seemingly persistent Labour bias. They homed in on young voters who regularly over-stated their certainty to vote, as well as previous non-voters who said they would vote Labour next time but were thought to be likely serial offenders when it came to polling day. In 2017, with an increased overall turnout and more young people voting than before, it is easy to see how these otherwise sensible precautions blew up in the pollsters' faces. In addition, there is some suggestion of a late shift to Labour among older voters: a clear majority voted Conservative but not as many as suggested in the early campaign polls.

In Scotland, I recorded nine polls during the six-week election campaign and these captured the main story when it came to Labour and the Conservatives: a strong Labour recovery during the campaign and a doubling of Conservative support compared with the 2015 election. As for the SNP, all the polls showed them significantly below their 2015 share of almost 50% but only one recorded them below 40% support (they received 37% of the vote).

In Wales, the early YouGov polls ricocheted around until finally settling very close to the actual outcome.

A massive victory over expectations

In the immediate aftermath of the election, much was made of the calamitous Conservative performance. Yet the swing to Labour from the Conservatives in 2017 was 2% - a rather pedestrian performance in post-War general election history. Labour won 36 seats but lost six; and the Conservatives gained 20 seats but lost thirty-three. Given the post-election flights of fancy from Labour, we might be forgiven for thinking that ending up 64 seats short of a majority qualified as one of the greatest victories in the party's history. The 2017 election provided a massive victory over expectations for Labour in which they were able to overcome the gloomiest of predicted fates. But escaping the hangman's noose is not the same as coming out on top. Why did Labour not do better?

For all the fanfare about Jeremy Corbyn that followed Labour's better than expected defeat, before polling day he was always significantly behind Mrs May whenever the polls asked which party leader would make the best prime minister. Similarly, many more respondents preferred Mrs May and Philip Hammond to run the economy rather than Jeremy Corbyn and John McDonnell. Mr Corbyn scored poll leads as better representing the views of many voters compared to Mrs May, but the Prime Minister and the Conservative Government were perceived to be far better options for dealing with such issues as Brexit negotiations, national security and immigration.

What part, if any, did Brexit itself play in the election? It certainly featured high among the issues that respondents said were of most importance to them in deciding how they would vote. But, in the event, I think we are left with mixed messages. In this election, the Lib Dems tried to increase their dire 8% share of the vote in 2015 by carving as much support as they could out of the 48% Remain vote from 2016. It did not work: the party was left treading water in the shallows of British politics. If we consider 2017 election results in the constituencies with the largest Leave vote in 2016 and then compare these with seats with the largest vote for Remain, we find virtually no difference in Labour's performance (+8.7% in the strongest Brexit seats and +8.9% in the strongest Remain seats). However, in the strongest Brexit seats the Conservative vote increased by 9.9% (i.e. by more than Labour in those same seats) but by only 2.5% in the strongest Remain seats. This difference of outcomes for the Conservatives explains a number of their seat losses in Remain areas but also some of their gains and holds in Brexit areas.

How polls shape campaigns

Does any of this matter? Of course it does. Anyone who was half-awake during the 2015 election will know that the opinion polls shaped the politics of the entire campaign. A relentless series of polls, monotonously suggesting a hung parliament, in which Labour stood a good chance of becoming the largest single party, determined the media narrative. In the final days of that campaign you would have been forgiven for thinking you had woken up in the middle of a Holyrood election, with everyone discussing what concessions the SNP would demand from Labour in return for supporting their minority government. All complete rubbish as it turned out. What shape might the campaign have taken; what different questions might have been asked of politicians if the polls had pointed to the actual outcome of a majority Conservative Government?

In 2017, similarly, the polls shaped the early part of the campaign with their massive Conservative leads, suggesting majorities for Mrs May of 100-150 seats, or more. Would the Conservative campaign have been so hubristic if they had understood how much ill-feeling there was towards a number of their policies that could easily have coalesced around Labour but for the unpopularity of Jeremy Corbyn? The polls gave no indication that Mrs May's calamitous campaign performance could lead to a transformation in Jeremy Corbyn's standing; after all the polls had buried him long before.

It seems to me that we are left with imperfect polls but no alternative to them. Without them we are left drifting in a sea of self-serving spin and fraudulent speculation. The British Polling Council (comprising the companies that conduct political polling) has ruled out any public inquiry into the failure of the 2017 campaign opinion polls. The serious pollsters will undoubtedly return to their drawing boards; the less serious will either deny there was a problem, or if there was, it did not affect them.

The 2017 election delivered a complicated outcome: Labour won Canterbury for the first time in the seat's history, at the same time as they lost Stoke-on-Trent South for the first time since 1935. The Conservatives performed best among the white working class and Labour best among the middle class. The swings to Labour were greatest in London and the South of England and lowest in the North and the Midlands. In some areas, we seemed to be in a world turned upside down in 2017.

Should we really be surprised? In the 1900 general election, 99% of votes cast (in Britain were for the Conservative, Labour or Liberal parties. In the 2005 election, the comparable figure was 95%. However, in 2015 it crashed to 77%, in the most decisive rejection of the established political parties in our democratic history. The 2017 election saw the main party dominance in voting restored (back to 92% on the same measure) but I do not believe for one moment that the political volatility that exploded in 2015 has disappeared. It seems to me that the post-War settlement, whereby governments of whatever colour delivered rising standards of living has broken down for lots of people. And with it the default party loyalty that marked earlier decades. I believe the patience of many voters is wafer-thin and will remain so whichever individual or party is in the driving seat. The pollsters have a tough challenge to capture an accurate picture of this unstable political landscape but that is no less difficult than the journey the rest of us have to travel in order to find our way through it.

Note on the contributor

David Cowling is a visiting senior research fellow at the policy institute at King's College, London. He has been involved in the analysis of the polls in every UK general election since 1987, first as ITN's political analyst and then as the BBC's Editor of Political Research.

Two parts policy, one part process: News media coverage of the 2017 Election

Much of the media assumed the 2017 election would be a one-horse race, but analysis by Loughborough University's Centre for Communication and Culture shows Tory mistakes and a focus on policy issues helped turn it into almost a dead heat, say David Deacon, John Downey, David Smith, James Stanyer and Dominic Wring

One of the lessons we are supposed to take from the surprise outcome of the 2017 General Election is that the power and influence of traditional news media is in decline (e.g. Monbiot, 2017). While not denying the election raises important questions about the significance of digital platforms in campaigns (Chadwick, 2017), we argue it is too soon write off traditional outlets as politically irrelevant.

Several million voters still read the press and watch TV bulletins. There is wide agreement that the Conservatives' campaign was inept. Nevertheless, the Tories still secured the largest vote share and return of MPs. We will never know what would have happened had they not retained the fierce support of a significant number of newspapers. There are also dangers in overstating the distinctiveness of legacy and social media. In a hybridised information environment, many a filter bubble is fed by material from mainstream news organisations. Furthermore, the 2017 General Election was challenging in media terms for Theresa May and her party, even within the Tory press.

The Centre for Research in Communication and Culture conducted an audit of election news from May 5 to June 7. We analysed the main weekday outputs of five TV bulletins and ten national newspapers. Our research focused on the relative prominence of rival parties and politicians, the issue agenda, and the evaluative direction of press coverage. The findings show there were several portents of what was to come on polling day. The first sign was the Tories' failure to manage the issue agenda. Table 1 shows the top 10 campaign topics with discussion of the electoral process being the most prominent aspect of reporting. But the amount of this 'process coverage' – at roughly a third of the total – was far lower than in 2015. This meant a greater level of media engagement with policy content.

Table 1: Most prominent issues in news coverage

Rank	Issue	% (2017)	Difference from 2015
1	Electoral process	32.9%	-12.5%
2	Brexit/European Union	10.9%	+7.8%
3	Defence/Military/Security	7.2%	+4.7%
4	Health and health care provision	6.7%	=
5	Taxation	5.7%	-1.1%
6	Economy/Business/Trade	5.5%	-5.9%
7	Social Security	4.6%	+2.4%
8	Immigration	4.2%	+0.8%
9	Devolution & other constitutional issues	3.3%	-1.0%
10	Standards	3.0%	-0.3%

Notes: Percentages = (number of issues/total number of issues)*100, rounded.
Up to three issues could be coded per item.

There were several potential reasons for this. Process coverage is stimulated by electoral uncertainty but it was widely assumed the 2017 campaign was a 'one horse race' until some shock late polls suggested otherwise. This kind of coverage also thrives on conflict but at least one of the main protagonists was unwilling to indulge journalists in this way. Jeremy Corbyn has long expressed his distaste for spin and the 'theatrical abuse' that characterises so much political discourse. And, inadvertently, the major campaigning missteps – the leaking of the Labour manifesto and the Conservative's U-turn over social care – invited greater scrutiny of policy commitments. Whatever the reasons, the increased policy quotient did not seemingly fit well with the Conservatives' foregrounding of Theresa May's 'strong and stable' leadership qualities and apparent downgrading of their manifesto. Corbyn's team, on the other hand, were keen to promote policies over personalities.

In terms of substantive issues, things also worked to the Conservatives' disadvantage. The party's strategy was built around Brexit which was the most prominent substantive issue overall. But its presence varied considerably over the five weeks of formal campaigning, being dominant in only two weeks' coverage (see figure 1). Across the media, more coverage was devoted to health and health care rather than the economy and taxation; this distribution appeared to fit more closely with Labour's preferred agenda not the Conservatives'. Defence and security issues asserted themselves in the latter stages of the election, in part because of Labour's stance on Trident, but mainly due to the terrorist attacks in Manchester and London. In normal circumstances this might have helped the Conservatives, but Corbyn's attack on former Home Secretary May for cutting police numbers discomfited her Government.

Figure 1: Main issues by week

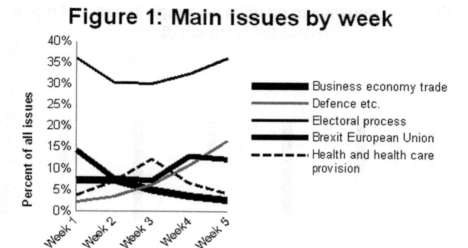

The Conservatives could of course count on the traditionally vociferous support of the 'Tory press' which sought to vilify Corbyn. Figure 2 compares the cumulative amount of positive to negative daily newspaper coverage each party received. Figure 3 weights these figures by circulation. These distributions demonstrate just how negative the treatment of Labour was, but they also show how this opprobrium was interrupted. Following the Conservatives' U-turn on their social care budget in week 3, aggregate coverage of the Tories became very negative. This hostility was pronounced when high circulation pro-Conservative titles such as the Daily Mail and The Sun were included.

Figure 2: negative to positive coverage in national press

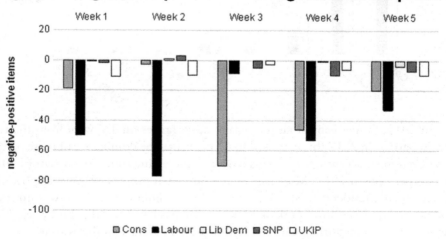

Figure 3: negative to positive coverage in national press (weighted by circulation)

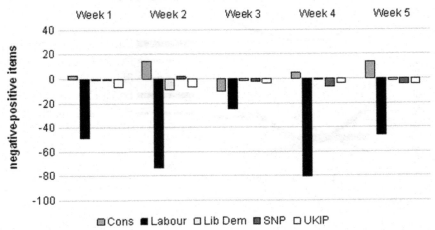

A major difference between the reporting of the 2017 General Election compared with the 2015 was the 'two party squeeze' in coverage (see figure 4).

Figure 4: prominence in the 2015 and 2017 General Elections

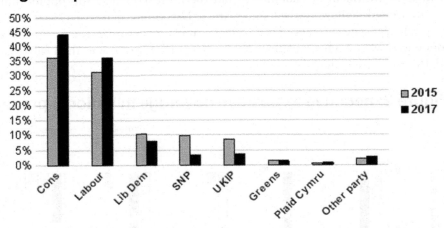

In 2015, 56 per cent of all politicians' appearances on TV were from the two main parties; in 2017 this increased to 67 per cent. The dominance of these parties was even more accentuated in press coverage, increasing from 70 per cent in 2015 to 84 per cent in 2017. Moreover, as the campaign progressed, coverage became increasingly presidentialised: May and Corbyn's combined presence was up from 30 per cent in week 1 to a peak of 39 per cent in week 4. Until the third week, May was more prominent than Corbyn, but in week 4 coverage of this was reversed. In the final week their media profiles were nearly equal. It was perhaps a portent of what was to come in a dramatic conclusion to a remarkable campaign which ended with a closer result than the overwhelming majority of experts had predicted.

References

Monbiot, G. (2017) 'The election's biggest losers? Not the Tories but the media, who missed the story', the Guardian, 14 June (https://www.theguardian.com/commentisfree/2017/jun/13/election-tories-media-broadcasters-press-jeremy-corbyn, accessed 14 June 2017)

Chadwick, A. (2017) 'Corbyn, Labour, Digital Media, and the 2017 UK Election', Medium, 9 June (https://medium.com/@andrew.chadwick/corbyn-labour-digital-media-and-the-2017-uk-election-ac0af06ea235, accessed 14 June)

Note on contributors

David Deacon is Professor of Communication and Media Analysis, Loughborough University. He has been involved in every Loughborough based Election news audit since 1992. He has written widely on political communication, election news reporting, media history and communication theory and research methods

John Downey is Professor of Comparative Media, Loughborough University. His research interests include political communication, digital media, international media and communication theory and research methods.

David Smith is University Teacher, Loughborough University. He has just completed his doctorate on national newspaper coverage of issues around immigration to Britain during general election campaigns over the 25 election campaigns between 1918 and 2010

James Stanyer is Professor of Communication and Media Analysis, Loughborough University. His research interests include news and democracy, new technologies and the exercise of political voice, and the personalisation of political communication.

Dominic Wring is Professor of Political Communication, Loughborough University. He has published widely on political marketing, the media, communication and politics. He co-founded and then convened the UK Political Studies Association's Media Politics Group.

A bad day for the Tory tabloids

The national press, so used to exercising its influence at election time, was forced to eat its words when the shock results of 2017 General Election became apparent. Young people and the social media they use for their news appear to have been far more influential than ever before, says Raymond Snoddy

For the right-wing tabloids it was election business as usual in 2017 – as raucous, committed and prejudiced against Labour as they have ever been.

The Sun had obviously saved up its bad headline pun – Don't Chuck Britain in the COR-BIN – with Jeremy Corbyn's head appearing out of a dustbin for the all-important election day, June 8.

Britain had to be saved from the 'catastrophe of a takeover by Labour's hard-left extremists' and apart from 'we've had enough of Jezza's rubbish … Vote Tory' the paper's busy front page managed to fit in ten charges aimed at the Labour leader.

They ranged from 'terrorists' friend,' and 'useless on Brexit' to 'open immigration' and 'Marxist extremist' with 'nuclear surrender' along the way.

In terms of crude propaganda the front-page under current Sun editor Tony Gallagher ranked up there with Kelvin MacKenzie's notorious attack on Neil Kinnock in 1992: "If Kinnock wins today will the last person to leave Britain please turn out the lights."

Then the Sun was able to claim, with at least some degree of plausibility, that it had contributed to John Major's unexpected victory, if not exactly being the one 'Wot Won It'.

The Daily Mail took a more positive note on its front-page election special by highlighting an eve-of poll appeal by Prime Minister Theresa May to 'reignite the British spirit'. Inside the paper there were 13 pages of darker, detailed warnings about how Corbyn 'will tax you while you work, he'll tax your garden and your home when you pass it to your loved ones'. Then it was on to accusing Labour of refusing to rip up rights to tackle terror and setting out a catalogue of all the things Labour's top team had said about Jeremy Corbyn in the past.

The Daily Express was predictable and rather uninspired – merely appealing to its readers to vote May 'or face disaster' combined with further demonising of 'EU boss Juncker', if that were possible. The paper quoted unnamed Brussels sources as saying European Commission President Jean-Claude Juncker wanted a Corbyn victory because then the Labour leader would be a prisoner of the Remainers.

The Sun, the Daily Mail and Daily Express supported the Conservatives as they always do, but they were not alone and backing for Theresa May also came from The Times, Daily Telegraph and Financial Times, with only two of the UK's national newspapers coming out against the Prime Minister.

Support for Jeremy Corbyn came from the Daily Mirror, traditionally Labour, and The Guardian, which sometimes hedges its bet by supporting the Liberal Democrats in general elections.

According to the opinion polls the Conservative-supporting national newspaper editors were going to get their way, despite the serious manifesto wobble in the middle of the campaign over social care funding and the so-called 'dementia tax'.

The efforts of the pollsters was best summed up by The Times on election day with its report that the Conservatives had taken a seven point lead over Labour in the final YouGov/Times poll of the campaign which, according to the paper, would have led to a 50-seat May majority. The poll said it had found a late dip in support for Labour.

An ICM/Guardian poll suggested a 12-point lead and 96-majority just ahead of the Comres/Independent which found a 10-point lead for May. The narrowing, but still substantial leads for the Conservatives, compared with the more than 20-per cent advantage which helped to encourage the Prime Minister to call the general election in the first place.

The only 'outlier', which is normal polling industry speak for a rogue poll that cannot be explained, came in the Mail on Sunday on June 4. The Survation poll for the paper found the Labour leader was continuing to narrow the Tory lead and put the Conservatives on 40 per cent with Labour on 39 per cent, barely enough for a wafer-thin May majority.

The poll was treated like a bit of a curiosity until the stroke of 10pm on election night when the polls closed and John Curtice of Strathclyde University (a contributor to this book) unveiled his BBC, ITV and Sky News exit poll which predicted, accurately, the political turmoil that was on the way. There would definitely be no landslides and although Mrs May would still be leading the largest party in the House of Commons there would be no Conservative majority. By morning it was clear she would have to depend on others – the ten MPs of the Democratic Unionist Party in Northern Ireland – to grimly try to hold unto power, at least for now.

What sort of campaign led to such an unexpected outcome and what does such a result say about the relative power and influence of the national press, broadcasters and the internet and social media? Has the world of electoral politics changed forever with an unstoppable move towards online?

While the anti-Corbyn attacks in the tabloids were sustained, there were few stories which were so new or dramatic that, of themselves, they would cause much of a shift in voting behaviour. The main thrust of the 'investigative' reporting concentrated on exposing the allegedly Marxist roots of both Corbyn and his Shadow Chancellor John McDonnell and chronicling every time across the years they appeared in public with supporters of the IRA, Hezbollah or Hamas. The historic nature of many of the encounters was eloquently illustrated by accompanying pictures which showed the grey-haired Corbyn with pristine brown hair and brown beard.

The allegations were given more current salience by the two interruptions of the election campaign by the tragic terrorist attacks in Manchester and on London Bridge and around nearby Borough Market. This enabled the Daily Mail to go on the attack again by labelling Corbyn, McDonnell and Shadow Home Secretary Diane Abbott as 'apologists for terror'. The Mail said it 'accuses this troika of befriending Britain's enemies and scorning the institutions that keep us safe'.

The Mail was prepared to accept that the Labour leader's expressions of horror over the atrocities, and sympathy for the families involved, were genuine. "But the ineluctable truth is that the Labour leader and his closest associates have spent their careers cosying up to those who hate our country, while pouring scorn on the police and security services and opposing anti-terror legislation over and over and over again," the paper said in a front page comment.

Mrs May was unable to take traditional Tory advantage of the terrorist threat as an issue because of the heavy media emphasis on the 22,000 police who had lost their jobs while she was Home Secretary.

There was none of the blatant bias of the tabloids from broadcasters – there can't be – because all are regulated and have a requirement to observe due impartiality. Historically this has enabled Labour and other opposition parties to make up ground in the battle to get their views over directly to the electorate, shaking off the tabloid attacks.

Perhaps stung by criticism of the way they covered the Referendum campaign (earlier in this book) there were signs of more robust questioning of politicians, almost everywhere apart from the BBC's One Show which sparked a debate about who puts out the bins.

Radio played a serious role in the campaign. Abbott was seriously undone when she revealed to Nick Ferrari on LBC Radio she did not have the faintest idea how much Labour's commitment to hire an additional 10,000 police officers would cost.

Corbyn himself stumbled when Emma Barrett on Radio 4's Woman's Hour pressed the Labour leader on how much Labour's promise to introduce free childcare for the under-twos would cost. He couldn't manage anything better than 'quite a lot of money'.

The BBC Election Debate became much more interesting following the last minute, inspired decision by Jeremy Corbyn to take part. This in turn exposed Theresa May to criticism and even on-air ridicule, when she refused to change her mind and debate the issues live on air with the leaders of the other British parties.

Naturally the Daily Mail praised Mrs May for her performance in the BBC's Question Time Show and demonised what it called 'Corbyn's Nuclear Meltdown' because the Labour leader refused 'to say whether he would defend Britain from nuclear attack'. Yet no analysis of conventional media coverage, or the performance of the opinion polls, even begins to explain how an apparently self-confident Prime Minister with a commanding lead in the polls could come so close to an immediate loss of office. In fact only Ruth Davidson and the 12 additional Tory MPs she delivered from Scotland saved Theresa May from that fate.

It is impossible to understand the political earthquake that hit the UK on June 8 without acknowledging the role of young voters and the social media they increasingly use enthusiastically. Further research will be needed to establish the precise numbers but there is little doubt that there was an enormous surge in young people both registering and voting. Encouraged by student unions and youth-facing web sites more than 1.2 million between the ages of 18 to 35 registered to vote following the calling of the general election, according to the Electoral Commission.

In 2015 Electoral Survey data found that among 18-24 year olds turnout was 58 per cent. Sky data suggested this time the percentage was 66.4 per cent, while there have even been suggestions, unconfirmed so far, it may have been as high as 72 per cent.

Such voters, particularly students, voted disproportionately in favour of Labour. A Guardian/ ICM poll found 57 per cent of 18-24-year-olds said they supported Labour with 22 per cent backing the Conservatives. Among students the lead was even greater – 65 per cent to 16 per cent.

The main issues driving unusual levels of political enthusiasm among younger voters included tuition fees and Labour's promise to abolish them, opposition to Brexit and to continuing austerity, plus a palpable taste for the avuncular style of Jeremy Corbyn. The Labour leader's message of 'hope' clearly resonated with them. There was no sign many of the pre-occupations of the right-wing tabloids – Corbyn's alleged meetings with the IRA or Middle East extremists before they were born, or the Labour leader's attitude to Trident – secured any traction among younger voters whatever.

At the very least the election results suggest the national newspaper industry's ability to influence the political climate in general elections is on the wane – the local and regional press have always been more balanced.

National newspaper sales continue to decline and buying newspapers is not a habit of the young. And while the online versions of the nationals have a reach that is unprecedented historically, increasingly they are being challenged by new online players. The Labour-supporting website The Canary, for example, claimed millions of hits during the election campaign. As research group Enders Analysis found: "In contrast to print coverage, most shared news and opinion content on social media was decidedly pro-Labour this election season."

The Canary and other left-leaning websites such as Evolve Politics and Skwawkbox not only attacked the Tories but also the mainstream media. Enders noted that Facebook's role in news distribution is growing steadily with half of the UK electorate active users. Facebook was also the main digital advertising platform for both main parties and although each adopted a negative tone towards their opponents to varying degrees there was, at least, no sign of fake news.

By general agreement among digital marketing specialists Labour won the online battle against the Conservatives for the first time and did it by spending far less money. Conservatives did not have the equivalent of Labour support group Momentum whose videos were watched by 13 million Facebook Users – 9.8 million of them in the UK. And on polling day to help rally the youth vote Labour spent sizeable sums promoting its Twitter hashtag - #forthemany.

As the technical term invented by former Sun editor MacKenzie has it – the Tory tabloids were forced to go for the 'reverse ferret' on June 9 – contradicting what they had argued so passionately only 24 hours before. For the Daily Mail it was the 'Gamble That Backfired', while the Daily Express went for 'May's Fight To Stay In Power'. The Sun – chose 'Mayhem' and still in its overnight edition asking plaintively on its front page: 'But is exit poll wrong?'

The Tory tabloids appeared terribly out of touch and more than a tad bewildered.

History may show 2017 marked the high water mark of the political influence of the right-wing national press and that the tide of social media will continue an inevitable rise.

As Will Hutton pointed out in The Observer young voters not only rejected the Tory tabloids but some took direct action against them – buying up copies of The Sun and immediately recycling them or burning copies of the Daily Mail. Perhaps it was not ideal behaviour in a democracy but tellingly symbolic and embarrassing for the papers all the same.

Note on contributor

Raymond Snoddy OBE, after studying at Queen's University in Belfast, worked on local and regional newspapers, before joining The Times in 1971. Five years later he moved to the Financial Times and reported on media issues before returning to The Times as media editor in 1995. At present, Snoddy is a freelance journalist writing for a range of publications. He presented NewsWatch on the BBC from its inception in 2004 until 2012. His other television work has included presenting Channel 4's award-winning series Hard News. Snoddy is the author of a biography of the media tycoon Michael Green, and of the acclaimed book on the British press, The Good, the Bad and the Ugly. He was awarded an OBE for his services to journalism in 2000. He is co-editor of this book.

Were the broadcasters impartial?

Equal time on television helped Labour defy predictions and was a factor in the dramatic shift in public opinion, but Stephen Cushion and Justin Lewis argue election television coverage could and should have been more balanced and impartial

At the beginning of the election campaign a Conservative landslide looked a foregone conclusion. Polls showed the Labour party lagging behind the Conservatives by between 16 and 22 points, a level of Tory supremacy that – even according to those pollsters who showed the narrowest margin – surpassed their landslide victory in 1983, when the Conservatives won by 15 points (42.4 per cent of the popular vote to Labour's 27.6 per cent).

After the second week of the campaign all the polling companies – ComRes, ICM, Kantar, Opinium, ORB, Survation and YouGov – reported numbers that added up to what the renowned psephologist David Butler has called the biggest poll shift in any election campaign since 1945. The Conservative lead was cut dramatically to between 5 and 14 points. Just a week before the campaign, this narrowed further to a lead of between one and 12 points.

There was an even more dramatic shift in how the public viewed party leaders. Before the campaign, polls showed strong approval ratings for Theresa May's party leadership and very negative ratings for Jeremy Corbyn. By May 25-26 YouGov reported a narrowing of the gap between them, but May still had a positive rating of +9 while Corbyn's was -28 (a 37 point gap in favour of May). But by June 1-2, Corbyn's rating had actually moved slightly ahead of May's (Corbyn -2 to May's -5). Similarly, when YouGov asked who would make the best Prime Minister just two months before the election, around half chose May while less than one fifth chose Corbyn. Immediately after the election, the two were neck and neck on 39 per cent.

Labour's final vote share after the election was just two per cent behind the Conservatives – within the margin of error of a number of polls (notably those that did *not* weight by 2015 turnout). But what all the polls agreed upon was a large and unprecedented swing to Labour during the campaign. How can this dramatic shift in public opinion be explained? There are, of course, moments when polls find immediate impact – we saw, for example, a boost in support for the Liberal Democrats following their leader Nick Clegg's performance in the 2010 TV debates – although in the past these shifts have been smaller and, in the case of the Liberal Democrats, often short-lived. Research more generally shows that changes in public perceptions generally take place over a much longer period (Lewis, 2001).

Why the public changed its mind

We would argue there were three main factors behind this shift. The first, and most widely discussed, is the general agreement that Corbyn ran a more open, energetic and spirited campaign than May. The Conservative leader tightly controlled her campaign appearances (Cushion, 2017a), dodged the TV debates and appeared a reluctant participant in one-on-one interviews. She became known as 'May-bot' to many journalists, sticking rigidly to her script about strong and stable leadership and evading difficult questioning. By contrast, Corbyn mixed openly with ordinary people, held well-attended rallies and campaigned passionately about the policies in Labour's manifesto.

Second, and perhaps more importantly, was the *contrast* between these campaigns and the lop-sided coverage of the two parties since Corbyn's election as Labour leader in 2015, which had created one of the widest gaps in support for the two main parties in post-World War II history. For the past two years, politics has often been dominated by the ability of the two main party leaders to control their parties. By this measure, May clearly beats Corbyn. While this is an important and legitimate issue, its primacy in political reporting meant insufficient attention has been paid to the very real policy choices which impact ordinary people, or to Corbyn's merits and May's deficiencies.

During the campaign veteran broadcaster David Dimbleby criticised media coverage of Labour under Jeremy Corbyn – both for its right-wing bias and its 'lazy pessimism' about Corbyn's viability as a potential Prime Minister (cited in Radio Times, 2017). The vitriol heaped upon Corbyn by a predominantly right-wing press has been well documented (Cammaerts et al, 2016), but it does raise questions about the impartiality of broadcast news over the preceding year. The Media Reform Coalition (2016), for example, found the BBC – unlike rival broadcasters – consistently focussed on the divisions within the Labour Party and Corbyn's poor leadership. There have also been moments where the BBC has been criticised about its treatment of Jeremy Corbyn. In January 2017, for example, the BBC Trust reprimanded the BBC's political editor Laura Kuenssberg for editing an interview with Corbyn on the BBC News at Six in ways that gave a false and negative impression of Labour's leader.

This is not a matter of wilful bias by the broadcasters, who are genuinely committed to impartiality – but it does show how news judgements are not always politically neutral. In focusing so much on Labour's divisions and what appeared to be fairly united Conservative Party (especially under May), both the press and broadcasters missed Corbyn's strengths (which saw him win two landslide leadership elections) and May's weaknesses. Just as important was the lack of interest in an emerging story about the underlying weakness of the Conservatives' focus on austerity and the economy it had created. While the Conservative record on employment won it plaudits, its poor record on GDP growth, productivity and earnings was given very little airtime.[1]

During the election campaign the rules about impartiality meant coverage focussed more centrally on comparing the policies of respective parties. As a consequence, it was arguably *the first time since Corbyn became leader* that Labour had received as much coverage as the Conservatives on substantive issues, in ways that allowed Corbyn to set out his stall.

The third reason involves the broadcast news coverage of the campaign itself, which we now explore in more detail.

Who won the airwar?

There has been much commentary about the importance of social media in the 2017 election campaign. Newspapers were overwhelmingly anti-Labour and, in the main, Conservative supporting (Deacon and Smith, 2017). But while the press remain an important source of news for older people, the overall influence of the Conservative press is declining. Few young people – who voted overwhelmingly for Labour in the election – regularly read newspapers. While they will have been exposed to right wing content on social media, in particular the Daily Mail or The Sun, they were perhaps more likely to come across left-wing and pro-Corbyn election stories on sites like Another Angry Voice, the Huffington Post, and The Canary. These types of sites, by and large, produced the most shared election stories on social media platforms like Facebook (Guardian 2017), while Jeremy Corbyn's following on both Facebook and Twitter was well ahead of Theresa May's.

Although broadcasters have long been aware of social media influence, it is not given the same agenda-setting power as the national press. Despite many newspapers losing readers, they continued to help set the agenda of broadcast news during the election campaign (Freedman and Schlosberg, 2017). Even within a fast changing media landscape, television news remains the dominant source of information for most voters. Even for under 45s nearly a third of people regularly tune into television news (Neilson and Sambrook 2016). Unlike partisan news circulating online, social media and many newspapers, UK broadcasters have a statutory obligation to remain 'duly impartial'. A team at Cardiff University monitored election news; Channel 5 at 5pm, Channel 4 at 7pm, BBC News at Ten,

ITV News at Ten and Sky News at 10pm and found Conservatives and Labour were given roughly equal time to air their views – see Table 1 – over the six week campaign. In focussing so heavily on Labour and the Conservatives, however, other parties may complain they were squeezed out of the election agenda. Broadcasters may argue they reflected the fact that over 80 per cent of the electorate voted for the two main parties, but that overlooks their role in helping to *construct* rather than just reflect public opinion.

Table 1: Share of party political airtime on UK television news evening bulletins

Conservative	39.4%
Labour	35.3%
Liberal Democrats	10.1%
UKIP	4%
Greens	1.5%
SNP	6.3%
Plaid	1.2%
Other	2.3%

The Conservatives' greater share of coverage can be explained by the airtime granted to the government immediately after the terrorist attacks in Manchester and London. Clearly, there is a fine line between governing and campaigning during an election campaign, with broadcasters having to respond quickly in highly challenging circumstances.

More importantly, perhaps, research by both Cardiff and Loughborough University (Cushion 2017b; Deacon and Smith, 2017) showed two related findings. First, broadcast coverage – especially around the period of the two manifesto launches – became more focused on policy issues. Second, while the Conservative Party (with the help of the press) successfully helped set the policy agenda in the 2015 election (Cushion et al. 2016; Cushion and Thomas 2017), the range of issues reported was more open in 2017.

Before the Manchester attack, Cardiff University's research showed that, after the launch of the manifestos a few weeks into the campaign, debates about the parties' policy was pushed to the top of the agenda (Cushion 2017b). In this week alone almost eight in ten television news items focussed on policy issues, compared to just under half the week before.

In many ways, this was the most critical week of the campaign, since it precipitated Labour's biggest surge in the polls. While some of this was negative – based on judgements about the leaking of Labour's manifesto – it also gave the party a platform to air their policy agenda. In the same week the Conservative

Party published its manifesto, including controversial social care reforms that many voters opposed, May quickly U-turned which was prominently reported on the evening news bulletins, including images of a tetchy press conference with journalists where she claimed: "Nothing has changed."

Once this occurred, we saw the emergence of a completely new news narrative – one that turned pre-election expectations upside down: Jeremy Corbyn, riding the crest of the poll surge, appeared the more confident and assured, while Theresa May appeared uncomfortable and less in control. Ironically, the lop-sided – and we would argue, somewhat short-sighted – nature of expectations before the election thereby worked to Labour's advantage. Neither of the two leaders underwent transformations in their leadership styles during the campaign, but, on television at least, they *appeared* to do so.

Equal time, but can conventional wisdom get in the way of equal treatment?

This, of course, raises questions about the nature of conventional wisdom amongst broadcast journalists, which under-estimated Corbyn's appeal and May's weaknesses, support for an anti-austerity agenda, and misunderstood the strength of feeling amongst younger people. The day after the election, Channel 4's anchor, Jon Snow, captured this sense about conventional wisdom – the belief that Corbyn was an electoral liability – by declaring: "I know nothing. We the media, the pundits and experts, know nothing."

On BBC radio, reporter Jonny Dymond acknowledged that because his interviews with members of the public seemed to reflect this conventional wisdom, he did not question them as perhaps (as the rapidly shifting polls indicated) he should have. Many columnists and commentators have since apologised for their misjudgement, acknowledging they had not registered Corbyn's appeal or the popularity of Labour policies.

Cardiff University's research found that, on broadcast news, despite the popularity of Labour's issues, the focus was often on Corbyn's leadership credentials and his (in)ability to appeal to voters (Cushion 2017c). This was evidenced in a number of ways, but here we focus on the use of live two-ways and vox pops (we use the phrase vox pops to refer to interviews with members of the public to convey a sense of public mood or sentiment).

Cardiff's research found that members of the public were, after politicians, the most quoted voice of broadcast TV, accounting for almost a quarter of airtime granted to sources – far more, for example, than independent experts (or indeed, from the more scientific evidence gathered by pollsters). While the instinct behind this may be democratic, it is not clear what viewers learn from them. According to the BBC guidelines, vox pops should be used as "a spread of opinions, reflecting, in a balanced way, the different strands of argument, OR, where appropriate, present an accurate and proportionate reflection of those whose opinions we have sought". Put more simply, vox pops are an *editorial construction of public opinion*.

However, while Labour and Conservative perspectives were represented in vox pops, their tone often *reflected conventional wisdom*. When the focus was on Labour, Corbyn's character and leadership was often questioned. So, for example, in BBC vox pops conducted in Liverpool early on the campaign (May 5), after one positive comment about Corbyn's integrity and authenticity, another member of the public had a longer exchange with the reporter about the Labour leader's credentials:

Vox pops: Dead. He's dead. He's got no personality. No presence. He's got no - he doesn't look strong, he looks weak, he looks like a wet cod all the time.

Reporter: Even though you are agreeing with all he says.

Vox pops: I love the guy, I do, I'm honest, I would like him to win but he's never going to win, never going to win, not in a million years.

One Channel 4 vox pops more simply put it, "I still believe in Labour [but not] plonker Corbyn". In other words, public opinion was often constructed as being sceptical of Corbyn despite polls showing many voters supported his policies (Cushion 2017c).

Corbyn's electoral appeal was questioned in more subtle ways by journalists during the campaign. In live two-ways, for example, *which made up close to a quarter of all TV news items* – political correspondents, at times, cast doubt on how far Corbyn's policies would appeal to voters. So, for example, after Labour's leaked manifesto a BBC correspondent focussed on Corbyn's leadership qualities and implied his policies may be too radical for many voters:

In the end, Huw, it comes down to faith, which Jeremy Corbyn has in abundance and in public trust, which as of now he presently lacks and needs to build up, if this whole plan is to become a radical plan for government and not simply end up as a sort of curiosity left over after a failed political experiment on June 8 (BBC, May 11).

By contrast, the Conservatives were often positioned in the centre-ground of British politics, with policies more likely to resonate with voters. As this BBC two-way illustrates after the launch of the Conservative's manifesto:

But I think more than anything, this idea of a mainstream politician for the mainstream tells us that she is determined to try to scoop up votes in every corner of the country, whether that's taking votes from Labour here in Yorkshire, from the SNP in Scotland, holding off the Lib Dem challenge in the south-west, or appealing to Ukip voters everywhere, she wants to take on all comers, and she wants to suggest that in 2017, the Tories can appeal, well, to just about everyone. (BBC, May 18)

And yet, far from Conservative policies being more popular than Labour's, the evidence suggested the contrary. During the campaign many of Labour's policy positions were widely supported, challenging the idea the party was too left wing for voters. ComRes polls, for instance, found a clear majority supported two Labour proposals to raise the minimum wage and increase the top rate of tax to 50p from 45p, while a majority also favoured renationalising the railways and the Royal Mail.

It is, of course, easy to be wise in hindsight, but there is a more general question raised by the heavy reliance of broadcasters on vox pops and two-ways, both of which are informed by journalistic and/or editorial judgement rather than a more scientific evidentiary base, and neither of which tend to explain or examine the stalls set out by the political parties. Broadcast coverage was at its best, we would argue, when it presented the policy options – both specific and broad brush – supported by well-informed context and scrutiny.

In rethinking election coverage, perhaps more time could be spent explaining the issues which most concern people, rather than – inaccurately – speculating about how the public think or the consequences of party strategy.

References

Cammaerts, B., DeCillia, B., Magalhães, J. and Jimenez-Martínez, C. (2106) *Journalistic Representations of Jeremy Corbyn in the British Press: From Watchdog to Attackdog*, London School of Economics and Political Science, http://www.lse.ac.uk/media@lse/research/pdf/JeremyCorbyn/Cobyn-Report.pdf accessed on 16 June 2017

Cushion, S. (2017a) 'It's time journalists exposed the spin behind politicians' campaign rallies', The Independent, http://www.independent.co.uk/voices/media-election-politics-news-journalism-expose-the-spin-a7718141.html accessed on 16 June 2017

Cushion, S. (2017b) 'Broadcasters are now talking policy – but the BBC are preoccupied with leadership', *New Statesman*, http://elections.newstatesman.com/the-650/broadcasters-are-now-talking-policy-but-the-bbc-are-preoccupied-with-leadership/ accessed on 16 June 2017

Cushion, S. (2017c) 'TV news coverage of the 2017 election isn't giving you the full picture – especially about Jeremy Corbyn', Conversation, http://theconversation.com/tv-news-coverage-of-the-2017-election-isnt-giving-you-the-full-picture-especially-about-jeremy-corbyn-77632 , accessed on 16 June 2016

Cushion, S. and Thomas, R. (2017) 'From quantitative precision to qualitative judgements: professional perspectives about the impartiality of television news during the 2015 UK General Election'. *Journalism*, Ifirst

Cushion, S. , Kilby, A., Thomas, R., Morani, M. and Sambrook, R. (2016) 'Newspapers, Impartiality and News Values in Television Journalism: Interpreting intermedia agenda-setting during the 2015 UK General Election campaign', *Journalism Studies*, Ifirst

Deacon, D. and Smith, D. (2017) 'How the Conservatives' media strategy collapsed during the election campaign' http://blog.lboro.ac.uk/crcc/general-election/conservatives-media-strategy-collapsed-election-campaign/, accessed on 16 June 2017

Freedman, D. and Schlosberg, J (2017) 'Right-wing newspaper headlines bring bias to the BBC', New Statesman, http://www.newstatesman.com/2017/05/right-wing-newspaper-headlines-bring-bias-bbc, accessed on 16 June 2017

Lewis, J. (2001) *Constructing Public Opinion*: How Political Elites Do What They Like and Why We Seem to Go Along with it. Chicago: Chicago University Press

Media Coalition Reform (2016) 'Should he stay or should he go? Television and online news coverage of the Labour Party in crisis', http://www.mediareform.org.uk/featured/stay-go-television-online-news-coverage-labour-party-crisis, accessed on 16 June 2017

Nielson, R. and Sambook, R. (2016) 'What is Happening to Television News?' http://reutersinstitute.politics.ox.ac.uk/publication/what-happening-television-news , acceesed on 16 June 2017

Radio Times (2017) 'David Dimbleby: Jeremy Corbyn has not had a fair deal at the hands of the press', http://www.radiotimes.com/news/2017-05-30/david-dimbleby-jeremy-corbyn-has-not-had-a-fair-deal-at-the-hands-of-the-press, accessed on 16 June 2017

The Guardian (2017) '25 most-shared articles about UK election are almost all pro-Labour', https://www.theguardian.com/politics/2017/jun/01/25-most-shared-articles-about-the-uk-election-labour-jeremy-corbyn, accessed on 16 June 2017

Note

[1] In a series of articles, economist Simon Wren-Lewis describes how Conservative claims about their 'strong and stable' management of the economy have been replicated rather than questioned. https://mainlymacro.blogspot.co.uk/

Note on contributors

Dr Stephen Cushion is a Reader at Cardiff University School of Journalism, Media and Cultural Studies. He is co-author of Reporting Elections: Rethinking the Logic of Campaign Coverage (Polity, 2018), and sole author of News and Politics: The Rise of Live and Interpretive Journalism (Routledge, 2015), The Democratic Value of News: Why Public Service Media Matter (Palgrave, 2012) and Television Journalism (Sage, 2012), and has published many academic journal articles and book chapters about journalism, news and politics, and co-authored several BBC Trust impartiality reviews.

Justin Lewis is Professor of Communication at Cardiff School of Journalism, Media and Cultural Studies. He has written widely about media, culture and politics. His books, since 2000, include Constructing Public Opinion (New York: Columbia University Press, 2001), Citizens or Consumers: What the media tell us about political participation (Open University Press, 2005), Shoot First and Ask Questions Later: Media Coverage of the War in Iraq (Peter Lang, 2006), Climate Change and the Media (Peter Lang, 2009) and The world of 24 hour news (Peter Lang, 2010). His most recent book is Beyond Consumer Capitalism: Media and the Limits to Imagination (Polity, 2013).

How to lose power on Facebook – social media in the 2017 UK General Election

Social media in the June 2017 UK General Election was the mirror image of the November US 2016 presidential vote. Almost everything was the same – just the other way round. says Alex Connock

Donald Trump triumphed in the 2016 US presidential election through upbeat alt-Right journalism plus echo-chamber social media activism. He bypassed the mainstream press with targeted, aggressive paid social advertising, which went viral and overwhelmed stodgy and technically clunky opposition. Commentators cried foul over fake news and supposed armies of mechanised bots, but the social media fight was really won organically. The right made more compelling content, and it made it faster.

In the UK election seven months later, it was same story but the other way around. This time, the newly-minted alt-Left swept the battlefield with an insurgent playbook, and it was the Right that looked static. Technical advertising and automation on either side was overwhelmed by the sheer passion and virality of an online movement on the Left.

There was really only one key thematic difference in this social media story. Despite all appearances before and since, Labour didn't actually win the election.

Viral charisma

"Some cause happiness wherever they go," observed Oscar Wilde. "Others *whenever* they go." Before even policies and technical tactics, the charismatic chasm between the two party leaders was the Ordnance Survey map of social media in the UK June 2017 election.

Corbyn had what SAS soldiers in the desert war called a 'battle nose'.[1]

Whether talking to someone's iPhone or a 10,000-person arena, he had the believable line for any given occasion to maximise social media engagement throughout the campaign. His would be the most popular election day post, with over 88,000 engagements and over 1.6m views. "This is our day. Our time. Our chance." Theresa May's characteristically miseryguts election morning message got just 12,000 engagements.[2]

Labour was massively outshared[3] on Facebook versus the Conservatives. Liam Corcoran of Newswhip wrote:[4] "The Labour Party and its politicians outperformed their Conservative rivals in the engagement stakes, on Facebook and elsewhere." Labour posted more: 229 stories to the Conservatives' 67, and 153 of them were videos, with higher engagement and shareability. On 25 May Corbyn's Facebook page outranked Theresa May's by ten times more views, and their growth was moving in opposite directions.[5][6] Corbyn's Facebook had 4,360,000 engagements from May 8 to June 8. Theresa May's just 554,000.

Put simply, Labour were millennial, the Tories were so 20th century.

Registration and turnout

Labour accumulated Millennials on Facebook and created registered voters. During the campaign, a record 1.05m 18 to 24-year-olds registered, including a quarter of a million – that's almost three per *second* – on deadline day alone. Two thirds of those voted for Corbyn.[7] Then crafty websites like My Nearest Marginal[8] pointed young people to their nearest marginal seat to go canvassing – for Labour.

Facebook was the consensus social media battleground. An Enders report estimated 56.4 per cent of UK population of voting age are Facebook users: all the young ones.[9] And over a six-week period, Facebook had 16m shares to Twitter's 2m.

Turnout in the election would hit 69 per cent, the highest since 1997. Labour would take student seats like Lincoln, Reading East and Nick Clegg's Sheffield Hallam. Momentum claimed Tory paid digital advertising was outflanked simply by the sharing by young people with friends and family, to the point that by election day one in four UK Facebook users had seen one – not bad for a media organisation with limited budget and no access to the TV stations.

Becoming ubiquitous (on Facebook) was the Tory Britain 2030 scaremongering video, which hit 7.8m views by mid June. A brilliantly simple conceit, typical of the best virals, it was a young girl talking to her Dad about the world lost.[10]

"And what's that ?"

"That's a free school meal."

"Why don't I get a free school meal ?"

Good question. Asking a question to which there is no positive answer is *the* sure-fire way to win a debate on social media – even assuming Tory voters were engaged in the social conversation. Theirs was a campaign in which the incumbent prime minister couldn't even be bothered to embrace the 20th century trope of a live political debate.

Tory strategy

At the start of the campaign, and fired up by the success of Brexit and Trump and the perceived weakness of the opposition, the Tory plan must have looked great in the PowerPoint. It would feature a relentless, aggressively-targeted social marketing exercise; smart media buying (mostly Facebook), some automation, and relentless demographically-focused attack ads. What could go wrong ?

What had already gone wrong were the assumptions lying behind social media targeting. Like a naïve medieval general, the Tories were advancing into enemy territory without securing their own. They didn't defend their own marginals, said Sam Jeffers, of Who Targets Me, which via user permissions was tracking more than 7,000 Facebook ads to nearly 12,000 voters. He showed that in Amber Rudd's close marginal of Hastings and Rye Labour advertised heavily, but not the Tories,[11] who were trying to geographically target their investment to marginal constituencies, which might explain their smaller reach and engagement levels.[12] According to the Telegraph[13], there were also no Tory adverts in Battersea in the final 48 hours of campaigning; it voted Labour, a 7,938 majority for the Conservative Jane Ellison overturned.

Not only that, but they weren't getting the 'earned' boost on their paid, from virality. Any social marketeer knows if you are paying for all your views and the thing isn't going viral, you are basically pushing a dead donkey up a glacier.

Attack ads

"Remember the golden rule of politics," Gerald Kaufman said: "Never kick a man until he's down." That underpinned the Tories' social media election strategy. Go after Corbyn everywhere, because he was weak. But the problem was that just wasn't so. To attack Corbyn on Facebook was like attacking Lionel Messi in the Camp Nou.

Tories made some questionable choices. Theresa May accused Corbyn of being opposed to using 'shoot to kill' to deal with terrorist incidents, based on a misleadingly headlined 18-month-old BBC video clip, and the party's social outlets backed it, even buying Google search term 'Jeremy Corbyn shoot to kill'. There was grey area open to social media feedback. The BBC Trust had said 'the report had not been duly accurate in how it framed the extract it used from Mr Corbyn's interview'.[14] That was grist to the mill for Opposition bloggers.

The Tory campaign was also targeted sub-optimally, sending to swing voters material that appealed largely to current supporters, according to data from We Are Social.[15] The material didn't pull in new and undecided voters, and 'strong and stable' didn't attract new support on social media.

Labour strategy

Meanwhile Labour was resolute in this election not to be beaten in Facebook advertising like it had been in 2015, according to an Enders report[16]. In the two intervening years advertising targeting on Facebook had seen interstellar evolution. Labour planned to spend £1m on targeted Facebook ads. That meant over a hundred million News Feed ad impressions.

That was the paid bit. What Labour really benefited from was a higher organic share rate. People wanted to send their friends more Labour stories than Tory ones. This worked for Labour-favouring press sites like The Independent, Guardian and Mirror. But where it really worked in the pro-Labour online publishers like The Canary and Evolve Politics, and even blogs like Another Angry Voice.

Labour also worked with social influencers – like grime artists. The hashtag #Grime4Corbyn went viral on Twitter[17] with Stormzy tweeting to his 710,000 followers: "Please please please vote. It's mad quick. Just go and do it, I used to think nah fuck it it's long what's my one lil vote gonna do."[18]

Emphasising the cultural divide, a comment on a Times piece about this complained: "Maybe voting should be limited to those who pay taxes?"

Another user replied: "They'd like to pay taxes but don't earn enough to in Tories zero-hours contract economy!"

Labour attacked too

Lest the impression were created that Labour stuck to purely positive messaging – in fact out of 2,314 Labour Party messages seen by Who Targets Me?, 60 per cent criticised other parties. Labour made an ad about 'dementia tax', in more than 200 constituencies.

Through Momentum, Labour had an insurgent force to deal the toughest attacks out – in the same way as Trump had been helped in the US by the numerous hard-core outlets of the Alt-Right, Breitbart included.

"Momentum were pushing out slick attack ads which allowed the Labour Party to stay above the fray," former press adviser to David Cameron, Giles Kenningham told The Guardian. "The Tories didn't have the equivalent third-party campaigning group in the rightwing space."[19]

A prescient Buzzfeed piece by political editor Jim Waterson[20] a month before the election christened the 'alt-Left'; sites like pay-as-you-feel blog Another Angry Voice[21] run by English tutor Thomas G Clark: "The most viral political journalist in the entire country." The site regularly gets 1.5k likes on its Facebook page, and [22] video views are in the hundreds of thousands. The featured video in June 2017, a rant about Theresa May's argument that she should be judged on her record, hit 1.1m.[23] The anger, presentation, social media-driven approach are all exactly reminiscent of the US alt-Right. Even the fonts are similar.

Waterson dubbed them: "Corbyn's outriders."

Buzzfeed analysis, just as it had done with pro-Trump social media in the US the year before[24], picked up that alt-media power: The Canary, Evolve Politics, Skwawkbox.[25] A Labour MP described them as 'the six nutters who sell the Socialist Workers Party newspaper in any town centre'.

As if the Alt-Right comparison were not clear enough, Skwawkbox described the media on its homepage in a way Trump would recognise: "We're proud that this blog has a track record of revealing news long before the 'MSM' either take an interest or care." MSM is Alt-Right speak for main stream media.

Did bots play a role ?

In the spring of 2017 there were claims that the Trump and Brexit campaigns had won in 2016 partly via the use of automated tools and fake users.[26] I make the case elsewhere in this book that whilst bots are real (social media channels know them by name, because they post comments improbably fast on new uploads) automation in Facebook advertising is not sinister but normal practice, and the case is far from proven than anything automated drove the massive organic social media enthusiasm behind Trump in 2016.

For the UK election, the Oxford Internet Institute research found posts using Labour-related hashtags dwarfed those featuring content about other parties, ultimately reaching 62 per cent of all tweets mentioning a party. Labour support spiked highest during the debate programmes: the Q&A with May and Corbyn on May 28, the election debate on May 31 that the Prime Minister opted out of.[27]

But was any of that impact from bots? 'High-frequency tweeting' increased in the same period, with more than 100,000 tweets sent from accounts that posted more than 50 times a day on just one hashtag. Such rapid rates of posting indicates automation, the Oxford authors say, although it may also just be a user with too much time on their hands.[28]

Meanwhile, and unlike in the US the year before, outright fake news sites flopped in the UK. An Oxford Internet Institute study found much lower levels of linking to 'junk news' stories than in the US election, at 11.4 per cent of the links shared vs 33.8 per cent in the US sample.

So there is a bit of evidence of automation. There is limited evidence of fake news linking. There is no evidence at all that it made much of a difference.

The final death of the tabloid press

"A newspaper should have no friends," said Joseph Pulitzer.

He wouldn't have said that about social media followers – since they are fast becoming the primary source of clout for newspapers, a quarter of whose web traffic derived in the election from Facebook (according to Comscore as reported by Enders). Building 'likes' is of existential commercial value, and not having enough likes can put the seal on your irrelevance.

Like Trump, Labour used alternative news channels. Enders pointed out that pro-Labour online publications with no direct print equivalents (The Canary and Evolve Politics) were reaching larger Facebook audiences for their content than most national news brands. Overall coverage weighted by distribution was much more left on social media than in print or on major news websites.[29]

Conclusion

In his otherwise brilliantly insightful May 6 piece about the rise of the Alt-Left, Buzzfeed journalist Jim Waterson said: "If polls are correct and Labour loses heavily, there will need to be a new narrative – and the early signs are that the mainstream media and Labour right will get much of the blame."[30]

Labour didn't lose heavily and it wasn't the Alt-Left that ended up needing a new narrative at all. It was the Tory party, it was the Government, and it was even the MSM – the mainstream media, left scratching their heads. After what hit them in June 2017, none will ever be the same again.

Notes

[1] Former SAS contributors in Ben Macintyre BBC TV series Rogue Warriors, February 2017

[2] https://www.newswhip.com/2017/06/labour-won-uks-social-media-election/

[3] https://www.newswhip.com/2017/05/heres-how-the-uk-election-is-playing-out-on-social-media/

[4] https://www.newswhip.com/2017/06/labour-won-uks-social-media-election/

[5] https://www.newswhip.com/2017/05/heres-how-the-uk-election-is-playing-out-on-social-media/

[6] https://www.newswhip.com/2017/06/labour-won-uks-social-media-election/

[7] Young voters go wild for old father grime Jeremy Corbyn and Labour, The Sunday Times, June 11, 2017, Gabriel Pogrund and Sanya Burgess

[8] https://myneareshttps://www.newswhip.com/2017/05/heres-how-the-uk-election-is-playing-out-on-social-media/tmarginal.com

[9] Enders Analysis report ' UK General Election online: news and advertising' published 7 June 2017

[10] https://www.facebook.com/PeoplesMomentum/videos/459077241104335/

[11] *Labour won social media election, digital strategists say*, Robert Booth and Alex Hern, The Guardian 9 June 2017

[12] https://www.newswhip.com/2017/06/labour-won-uks-social-media-election/

[13] http://www.telegraph.co.uk/technology/2017/06/09/conservatives-ran-ineffective-social-media-campaign-researchers/

[14] May attacks Corbyn's 'shoot to kill' stance as BBC clip is shared online, Martin Belam, Guardian, Monday 5 June 2017, https://www.theguardian.com/media/2017/jan/18/bbc-trust says-laura-kuenssberg-report-on-jeremy-corbyn-was-inaccurate-labour

[15] http://www.telegraph.co.uk/technology/2017/06/09/conservatives-ran-ineffective-social-media-campaign-researchers/

[16] Enders Analysis report ' UK General Election online: news and advertising' published 7 June 2017

[17] Young voters go wild for old father grime Jeremy Corbyn and Labour, The Sunday Times, June 11, 2017, Gabriel Pogrund and Sanya Burgess

[18] Stormzy twitter feed https://twitter.com/Stormzy1

[19] Quoted by Robert Booth and Alex Hern, The Guardian 9 June 2017

[20] The Rise Of The Alt-Left British Media, Jim Waterson, Buzzfeed May 6 2017

[21] http://anotherangryvoice.blogspot.co.uk

[22] https://www.facebook.com/Another-Angry-Voice-185180654855189/

[23] https://www.facebook.com/pg/Another-Angry-Voice-185180654855189/videos/?ref=page_internal

[24] Buzzfeed News – *is Analysis Shows How Viral Fake Election News Stories Outperformed Real News on Facebook* https://www.Buzzfeed.com/craigsilverman/viral-fake-election-news-outperformed-real-news-on-facebook

[25] https://www.buzzfeed.com/jimwaterson/the-rise-of-the-alt-Left

[26] Carole Cadwalladr, *Observer* (26 February 2017) *e Big Data Billionaire Waging War on Mainstream Media* https://www.theguardian.com/politics/2017/feb/26/robert-mercer-Breitbart-war-on-media-steve-bannon-donald-trump-nigel-farage

[27] Quoted by Alex Hern, Guardian 6 June 2017

[28] Quoted by Alex Hern, Guardian 6 June 2017

[29] Enders Analysis report ' UK General Election online: news and advertising' published 7 June 2017

[30] https://www.buzzfeed.com/jimwaterson/the-rise-of-the-alt-Left

Note on contributor

Alex Connock is Managing Director at TV production company Endemol Shine North, and has worked across viral advertising video production for many clients, including hit social platform LADbible, where for a period in 2016 he was head of video. He is also visiting professor at Salford, Sunderland and Manchester Metropolitan universities and Entrepreneur in Residence at Insead. He has recently completed a study with IpsosMori into the effectiveness of different styles of video in e-commerce.

The leaders' debates – will the historic achievement of 2010 ever be repeated?

The leaders' debates in 2010 were historic. They energised younger voters in particular but political self-interest in 2015 and 2017 put the debates in question. As the lessons of the 2017 campaign become clear, Sue Inglish asks: is the prospect for debates at the next election looking brighter?

"Tonight – who do you want to be your next Prime Minister?" These were David Dimbleby's opening words in the final Prime Ministerial election debate of the 2010 General Election. Despite several unsuccessful attempts at past elections, and after months of discussion, three historic election leaders' debates had finally made it on air. It was not the outcome we expected when we started the negotiations process eight months earlier. 1997 was the closest anyone had come to succeeding when John Major, tanking in the opinion polls, agreed to debate but Tony Blair was cooling on the idea. Richard Tait, who led the1997 ITV/ITN bid for debates, described it as: "A missed opportunity of epic proportions." (Tait 1998)

When Ric Bailey, the BBC's chief adviser politics, and I took up the challenge in 2009, we were not optimistic. In his comprehensive study of the debates, Ric Bailey concludes that the parties' decisions on whether to take part are based: "… squarely on political self-interest. Either incumbency or a substantial opinion poll lead – or both – always meant agreeing to debates presented too high a risk for one or other of the parties." (Bailey 2012).

Why 2010 was different

David Cameron first called for debates in May 2007, even offering to drive Gordon Brown to the studio to take part. Brown was initially reluctant using the dubious excuse that he and Cameron debated every week at Prime Minister's Questions – an argument resurrected by Theresa May seven years later. But by the summer of 2009, Labour had privately decided that Gordon Brown, languishing in the polls, had nothing to lose and the party, short of cash to fight the campaign, could see the attraction of debates paid for by the broadcasters.

In early September Sky surprised everyone by unilaterally announcing a campaign for debates and threatened to empty chair anyone who didn't turn up. The BBC and ITV declined to take part in a campaign feeling it was not compatible with their duty of impartiality. It wasn't the most auspicious start to the broadcasters' united front but undoubtedly the process was given a kick-start. The broadcasters' negotiating team[1] agreed to work closely together, essential if we were to avoid the political parties playing us off against each other. The election could be as soon as April and one of the lessons learned from the 97 failure was that time was of the essence.

The participation of the Liberal Democrats was a major stumbling block in 1997 but since excluding them in 2010 would almost certainly have led to a successful legal challenge, we decided to include them on equal terms. To keep it simple, all three broadcasters adopted the same format: 90 minutes in prime-time with questions from a live audience, one debate a week for three weeks of the campaign.

Three leaders, three debates and three broadcasters – clear and simple. This was the proposal on the table in December 2009 when two representatives each from the Conservatives and Labour, and three from the Liberal Democrats* met the broadcasters. It was the first time in the history of debates negotiations that the process had reached that point. It subsequently became clear the Conservatives and Labour had already met separately to discuss the proposal.

We expected some push-back from the Conservatives or Labour on the inclusion of Liberal Democrats on an equal basis but to our surprise it didn't happen. The Conservatives came to regret this. There were intense discussions about the live audience: what was its role, how would it be selected, was applause allowed? We agreed that half of each debate would be themed and the broadcasters would draw lots to decide the allocation of themes and the order of the debates. ITV drew home affairs in the first debate, the second debate on foreign affairs went to Sky and the BBC drew the final debate on the economy. This was later to prove a significant complication.

Labour's last-minute wobble

Just before Christmas 2009 the parties and broadcasters announced they had reached agreement on the key principles. Now it would be hard but not impossible, for any party to pull out. Finally, the broadcasters began to believe debates would happen. Over the following weeks we worked through the details, agreeing where we could and putting to one side anything problematic for later resolution. This process built up trust, which was to prove vital when with a final agreement tantalisingly close, a problem arose which looked as though it could sink the entire project. The Labour Party negotiators had not realised the significance of the BBC's economy debate taking place in the last full week of the campaign. Gordon Brown was insistent the first debate should be on the economy where he felt he had the advantage. For two nerve-wracking weeks in February the process stalled. There was increasing concern that David Cameron, encouraged by favourable opinion polls, might decide debates were too risky after all and use Labour's last-minute wobble as an excuse to abandon the whole process. At last on March 1, 2010, Labour accepted that the economy would be in the last debate and agreement was finally reached.

The debates were the highlight of the campaign. The leaders of the three biggest parties debated the key election issues with each other for four-and-a-half hours live, on prime-time television. 22m people saw the debates. Two thirds of people surveyed said they learned something new and up to 70 per cent said they knew more about the parties' policies. One of the most striking features was the response of young people, turned off by conventional politics and traditionally hard to reach with political programmes. 18-24 year olds seemed to have been particularly energised by the debates with more than half saying they had become 'more interested' in the campaign and 75 per cent said they had learnt something about the parties' policies (Coleman 2011).

The verdict from both supporters and critics was that the debates were here to stay but the broadcasters' team had their doubts. In Ric Bailey's opinion the debates happened in 2010 'because – for once – both the largest UK political parties concluded there was electoral advantage in debates and – also for the first time – the main broadcasters worked closely together to overcome the significant practical obstacles'. He added presciently: "Just because debates have happened once, it is far from certain they will be here next time round." (Bailey 2012).

What went wrong in 2015?
Leading Conservatives had come to the view that the 2010 debates were a mistake. Allowing the Liberal Democrats to take part had in their opinion cost them votes and denied David Cameron a majority. Lynton Crosby, who took over responsibility for the Conservatives' election strategy in 2012, made it clear privately that negotiating with the broadcasters over debates was not the way they did it in Australia and he was not in favour of a 'cartel' of broadcasters dictating the terms.

In addition the political landscape was more complex. With UKIP increasing its vote in local elections and coming first in the 2014 European Parliament elections, a debate with only the three parties who took part in 2010 was increasingly untenable. In October 2014 the broadcasters, now joined by Channel 4, proposed three debates, one including UKIP, to be scheduled every two weeks during the campaign.

The Greens launched a vocal campaign to be included, backed in a piece of flagrant political self-interest by David Cameron. Nicola Sturgeon, riding high in the polls, demanded a place on the stage too. Mindful of the closely fought legal challenge from the SNP to the BBC debate in the 2010, the broadcasters produced a new proposal to reflect the increasingly multi-party state of the UK.

Just weeks before the campaign, David Cameron made a final offer to take part in a single seven party debate of 90 minutes before the beginning of the campaign. The broadcasters responded: "We have given your proposal serious consideration but we don't think it achieves the goal of providing our viewers with election debates that can properly explore a reasonably full range of issues… all we can do … is to provide a fair forum for debates to take place. It will always remain the decision of individual leaders whether or not to take part. The debates will go ahead open to all the invited leaders right up to the broadcast."

The deadlock was eventually broken with agreement on a range of different programmes.

Sky and Channel 4 produced a programme just before the start of campaign with David Cameron and Ed Miliband, appearing separately facing questions from a live studio audience and interviewed by Jeremy Paxman. David Cameron appeared in a single, seven party debate on ITV during the campaign. The BBC held a five party opposition leaders' debate and a special Question Time with Cameron, Miliband and Clegg separately taking questions from a live audience. 21m people saw some of the four programmes, slightly fewer than the 2010 debates, and the principle of election leaders' debates survived, but only just. The unified approach of the broadcasters had taken a battering and at the EU Referendum in 2016 the individual broadcasters arranged debates with the rival campaigns separately.

The 2017 General Election

When the snap election was called in April 2017, Mrs May, sitting on what looked like an impregnable lead in the polls, immediately ruled out taking part in debates preferring, she said, to meet people on the doorstep. ITV went ahead with a leaders' debate though Jeremy Corbyn too declined to appear. Critics dismissed the programme as an irrelevance as the leaders who appeared represented just 16 per cent of the electorate. The viewing figures were disappointing but ITV deserves great credit for sticking to the principle that election debates are a vital part of the democratic process.

With the Conservative campaign running into trouble over the so-called 'dementia tax' and buoyed by his increasingly successful campaign, Jeremy Corbyn decided at the last minute to take part in the BBC debate. Theresa May's refusal to participate – Amber Rudd stood in for her – was the focus of stinging criticism. As Caroline Lucas pithily put it: "The first rule of leadership is to show up." For a campaign focused on the leadership of Theresa May, her refusal to debate, combined with her 'Maybot' repetition of slogans like 'strong and stable government' turned out to be a fatal mistake. As Matthew Paris said in The Spectator: "Not taking part in TV debates was supposed to appear commanding: above the silly shouting match. It has ended up making her look frit."

Will leaders' debates happen next time?

When the final verdicts are written on the 2017 debacle, the Prime Minister's refusal to debate will be one glaring example of her failure to communicate with the electorate, particularly young voters who were particularly enthusiastic about debates and played a key role in the election result. At the next general election, whenever it takes place and whoever the Conservative leader may be, one clear way to differentiate the campaign from the calamity of 2017 would be to announce immediately that he or she will debate with all comers. And as Andrew Hawkins executive chairman of the research consultancy ComRes says, 'at national level, there is now an expectation that party leaders are accessible, open and willing to debate. It was clear back in 2010 that the TV debate genie was out of the bottle. After this election, only a fool would make the mistake of refusing to take part' (Hawkins 2017).

The broadcasters must be ready to seize the opportunity to establish once again the principle that leaders' debates are a unique chance for voters to engage with the democratic process. At a time of political turmoil and public distrust of politics, it is a principle worth fighting for.

Notes

[1] The negotiating teams were:

(1) Sky - Jonathan Levy, Chris Birkett; ITV - Michael Jermey; ITN - Jonathan Munro; BBC – Ric Bailey, Sue Inglish

(2) Conservatives – Andy Coulson, Michael Salter; Labour – David Muir, Justin Forsyth; Liberal Democrats – Lord Oates, Lena Pietsch, Lord Sharkey

References

Bailey, Ric (2012) Squeezing out the Oxygen – or Reviving Democracy? The History and Future of TV Election Debates in the UK. Oxford: Reuters Institute for the Study of Journalism

Coleman, Stephen (2011) Leaders in the Living Room. Oxford: Reuters Institute for the Study of Journalism

Hawkins, Andrew (2017), Election Unpredictability, available online at http://comresupdates.eu.com/DCJ-4ZXXA-6A1LMCQO13/cr.aspx, accessed 19 June 2017

Tait, Richard (1998) 'The Debate that Never Happened', in Crewe, Ivor, Gosschalk, Brian, Bartle, John, Why Labour Won the General Election of 1997. London: Cass, pp.205-214

Note on contributor

Sue Inglish is chair of the International News Safety Institute (INSI) and an independent governor of the Westminster Foundation for Democracy. She was in charge of the BBC's political output from 2005 to 2015 as head of political programmes, analysis and research. She had joined the BBC from ITN where she had been foreign editor and deputy editor of Channel 4 News and editor of itn.co.uk and LBC. She chaired the working party which delivered the 2010 leaders debates.

The 'selfie' election

With a huge lead in the polls, a much-derided opponent and the overwhelming support of most of Fleet Street, what could possibly go wrong for the Tories? Michael White analyses the mistakes that all but wrecked Theresa May's premiership

With hindsight the real surprise about Theresa May's "selfie" election on June 8th was that Britain's political leadership and London-heavy mainstream media, most voters too, should – yet again - have approached a major decision at the ballot box confident that they already knew the outcome. Had not most opinion-formers predicted that the Remain camp would win the EU referendum in 2016? Had they not dismissed any prospect of a Conservative majority emerging from the 2015 general election? Until the last minute they had shown similar insouciance about the result of the Scottish independence referendum the previous autumn and got a nasty scare.

Slow learners should have taken the heaviest hint imaginable on a wildly improbable November day when the huckster property tycoon, reality TV star and pathological liar, Donald Trump, was elected 45th President of the United States, despite being 3 million votes short of his opponent. But no. On April 18th Mrs May reversed her previous assurances that there would be no snap election before her two-year Brexit Odyssey. The chief focus of speculation immediately became which side of 100 seats her overall Commons majority would be. Labour's Jeremy Corbyn was derided and abused as a hapless punchbag. Instead what unfolded over the next seven weeks was a popular revolt which saw the bearded left-wing pacifist, a lifelong vegetarian and teetotaller of genially herbivorous temperament, coming within 2% of outpolling her – and all but wrecking May's rookie premiership.

Handbrake U-turns

As Fleet St's hard-boiled pundits did one of their collective handbrake U-turns, much attention was focussed on the sheer complacent ineptitude of the Tory campaign, the stilted and defensive rigidity of May's own performance. Far from

398

being "strong and stable," as her Australian campaign chief, Lynton Crosby, insisted she should proclaim herself at every TV opportunity (May reportedly hated the phrase, but did as she was told), her brittle, presidential focus on herself served chiefly to highlight inadequacies which voters had previously been happy to regard as the self-contained determination of a Home Counties vicar's only child. The contrast with Corbyn, pragmatically rebooting his placard-waving persona – no more Mr Angry from genial Uncle Jeremy – could hardly have been more stark. Controlled photo-ops or big and enthusiastic crowds? What was there not to like?

Instant analysis sought to place May's humiliation safely inside the evolving narrative across mature and economically developed democracies throughout the western world. In an increasingly globalised, tech-driven setting many voters, those who had lost jobs, job security or pay increases over recent decades, felt "forgotten," "overlooked" or "left behind" in the race towards robotics and McJobs. Their economic fears were reinforced by cultural ones, social liberalism (the gay marriage movement often a touchstone) and multiculturalism (jihadis are not social liberals). The two streams merged in recurring alarm at historic wave of south-to-north migration, itself a mixture of economic aspiration and the flight from poverty, corruption or war.

Populism Right and Left

From Austria and Hungary on the EU's eastern flank through the Netherlands and France, to Britain and the US, a surge of spiky, nationalistic populism was the most visible response, often with an authoritarian tinge. Economic populism emerged in both traditional right-wing forms; lower taxes or anti-government rhetoric, and in left-wing ones; more social protection and nationalisation, an end to austerity budget-balancing by piling higher taxes on the tax-shy rich or corporations. With characteristic indifference to consistency or philosophy, Donald Trump managed to face both ways, enraging Republican purists even as he captured their party by appealing to the Rust Belt's heartfelt, justified sense of neglect.

Despite her forays into law and order rhetoric – accentuated by the two terrorist attacks, in Manchester and London, during the campaign - and her opponents' efforts to paint her as a near-fascist Theresa May was hard to fit into the populist mould: an unpopulist perhaps. As for talk of voters rejecting "the political elite" or the "establishment" such labels were more easily pinned on the ousted Etonian, David Cameron, and his sacked chancellor, George Osborne.

If revenge is a dish best served cold Mr Osborne, by now editor of the London Evening Standard, would soon get his as a fast-food take-away, piping hot. Yet fellow-Bullingdon Club hearty, Boris Johnson, and his posse of well-fed public school allies, including (well below the salt) Nigel Farage, had managed to pass themselves off as grassroots anti-Establishment insurgents during the Brexit campaign. After all, the Manhattan billionaire, Trump, who claimed Brexit as his precursor, would also don the mantle of poor man's friend. Ancient Romans knew that dodge, performed by Senate populists.

The oft-repeated charge that politicians were "out of touch" with the concerns of ordinary people was also on voters' disaffection indictment. That too was more readily pinned on Hillary Clinton, the Democrats' self-imposed heir to Bill, than on mild Mrs May. Clinton's condemnation of Trump's troops as "deplorables" was itself deplorable. Nearly beaten for her party's nomination by Bernie Sanders, a less lovable but more substantial radical than Corbyn, she was so bad that even Trump beat her. Armed with a 20% poll lead May was so bad on the campaign that even Corbyn nearly beat her. She would never have risked a snap election against a more formidable foe.

A sense of *entitlement*

May was less remote from voters than Clinton who pandered to identity politics rather than hammer the blatant fantasies of Trump business career and election promises. Encouraged by her joint chief-of-staff, the bearded Nick Timothy, an admirer of the interventionist instincts of his Brummie hero Joseph Chamberlain (1836-1914) the prime minister made a clumsy attempt at centre-left pandering with policies Team May felt would resonate with ex-UKIP and wavering Labour voters in the Midlands and North, the "just about managing" voters she had talked about. But all this was undercut by the nature of her decision to stage an election three years early and the manner in which she did it. It smacked of a sense of *entitlement*, the charge against Cameron, Clinton and that host of ageing French politicians who thought it was their turn to be president – and keep family members on the state's payroll.

But every such disaster is custom-made with its own local peculiarities. Ostensibly May called the election to "strengthen her negotiating hand" for the Brexit ordeal ahead. Allies interpreted that as meaning that an enhanced majority would provide a mandate to face down so-called "Remoaners" lurking on both backbenches, those in cabinet seeking a less economically-damaging "soft Brexit" and the unruly House of Lords, awash with experienced veterans of European realities, less prone to romanticism or zeal. It would also dispel persistent notions in Brussels that the Brits would eventually repent their referendum folly and ask to stop the ticking clock of Article 50 withdrawal which May had imperiously triggered *before* calling her "selfie" election. Second referendum thoughts at the point of a financial gun is the EU way with recalcitrants, at least with smaller ones.

'Crush the Saboteurs'

Still relishing its "Enemies of the People" attack on the Supreme Court, demagogic and deranged though it was, the Daily Mail loyally summed up May's declared strategy as being to "Crush the Saboteurs." Some suspected that what No 10 was really hoping to achieve was buy two more years head room beyond the previously scheduled 2020 election. It would provide time in which she and David Davis, her Brexit chief, could reach sensible compromises with EU negotiator, Michel Barnier and those 27 veto-holding member states, not to mention with a pragmatic majority of MPs and peers. The "saboteurs" whom ex-Remain's May might need to crush might well turn out to be Europhobic Tory zealots, including the Mail itself.

Obviously it would be impolitic to say so at this stage. Besides, the Corbyn-led Labour party must have looked as temptingly vulnerable as the US Pacific Fleet in Pearl Harbour did that December day in 1941. Is it wise to crush an enfeebled opposition? Effective democracies need an effective opposition to keep the executive on its toes. Wouldn't a government which had just triggered Article 50 without a coherent negotiating strategy that voters – or Europe – could understand have better spend its time and energy doing the day job?

There was an echo of May's apparent wish to put her own and her party's tactical interests before those of the country in Scotland. Here Nicola Sturgeon had been using the SNP's hegemonic victory 2015 – 56 Westmister seats out of 59 – to renew persistent demands for a second "once in a generation" referendum on Scottish independence, staged before the final Brexit deal would be known. The Scottish First Minister had a legitimate grievance in that Scotland had voted Remain on June 23. But so had Northern Ireland, the economic powerhouse of London and other big cities too, a fact the "winner take all" Brexiteers had chosen to ignore.

'52% minus 48% equals 100%'

It was May who had compounded their "52% minus 48% equals 100%" formula and opted to make control of Britain's borders and judicial "sovereignty" her Brexit priority. Her reading of the Brexit runes had alarmed senior economic ministers like chancellor, Philip Hammond. Sturgeon's demand that, at very least, Scotland should stay inside the EU's single market, preferably the customs union too, found some contradictory echo in Belfast where the pro-Brexit Democratic Unionists (DUP) were noisily keen to keep an open EU land border to the south. Everyone was interpreting a binary referendum result to suit their own purposes. The June 8 election would resolve nothing.

But, as with Gerry Adams's manoeuvres on Sinn Finn's behalf, the SNP's real prize was – as usual – the independence which Scots voters had rejected (this time by 55% to 45%) in 2014. Polling data showed that most Scots voters – some more pro-Brexit than pro-independence - felt the government in Holyrood should also be concentrating on the day job. Scotland's economic performance, standards in public services like schools and the police, were slipping after 10 years of SNP rule. Flat-lining world oil prices offered no North Sea panacea solutions to Scotland's fiscal deficit.

At least Sturgeon, a more experienced and adept politician than May, was braced for losses on June 8, though not the 21 net loss that has restored a better balance to Scotland's politics. May's complacency led her to reject any TV debates with her opponents, Corbyn included. Her control freak's insecurity, reminiscent of Gordon Brown's, let Timothy dominate the manifesto-writing that excluded both Crosby and cannier elected ministers. The result was the well-meant but half-baked plan to include the legacy equity in elderly voters' homes in future care bills. It was far more progressive than many of Corbyn's Christmas Tree proposals – made by a leadership which still expected a Tory majority around 50 on polling day – notably his £11 billion student loans bribe to middle class undergraduates. Such policies need more preparatory work than it got.

'Corbyn Chaos'
A U-turn on the misnamed "dementia tax" (actually a dementia lottery) followed compounded by May's insistence: "Nothing has changed." But everything had changed, the policy and the election's trajectory. In the closing days the Praetorian tabloids dusted off their favourite "Project Fear" headlines and threw everything they could at Corbyn and his agit-prop shadow chancellor John McDonnell, their fiscal irresponsibility, their decades old infatuation with the friends of terrorists and the enemies of NATO. Shadow Home Secretary, Diane Abbott, would have been in their sightlines too, but she had already recused herself from the campaign after a series of interview mishaps.

"Corbyn Chaos," screamed more excitable newspapers for whom the campaign had become an old-fashioned Labour vs Tories struggle. UKIP was fast fading and the Lib Dems struggling to get traction for a re-run of Brexit. Both minor party leaders would resign after polling day: Nick Clegg was out, Vince Cable back and busy scheming. Yet something even more significant than May's muddle was going on beneath the mainstream media radar. The Tories were fighting the kind of targeted social media war – strength and personal leadership – which had previously worked in Australia, the US and Britain. But in a fast-moving media market for young people it had also failed.

In contrast Corbyn's shock troops, the young and tech savvy people working with old lefties and entryists in Momentum, were devising crude but cleverly pitched films for the YouTube millions like "Daddy, Why Do You Hate Me" ("Because, I voted for Theresa May in 2017"). Were they any worse than the billboard posters and party political broadcasts of yesteryear? No, but they went viral and got out usually apathetic or lazy young voters and infected groups in their 30s and 40s too. Corbyn's 40% vote share was up 10% on Ed Miliband's, higher than Tony Blair's third win in 2005.

A protest election
Voters everywhere like to kick incumbents these days. But this was surely a protest election, not a power election: May remains prime minister until her party can find a better one. In a small talent pool that will take longer than some suppose. Even

more strongly entrenched Corbyn, the moral victor, has understandably enjoyed his unexpected success and new-found popularity as what sentimental middle class converts, the Guardian and Observer reading sceptics, are now calling the Clem Attlee of our times. A glimpse at his voting record and Attlee would have a fit.

But reality will kick back in soon enough and John McDonnell – no Uncle John - was quick to speed up the process with calls for street protest to get May and her new DUP allies out. She may have been hopeless again in her response to the Grenfell Tower fire catastrophe, itself a sobering event. But her clumsiness is at least as authentic as Corbyn's Uncle Jeremy performance or John McDonnell's Pollyanna-ish budget maths. Next time, whenever it comes, the markets will be forced to take a Labour manifesto seriously, so the manifesto should be more serious than the backward-looking exercise cobbled together in 2017.

So much in Britain cries out for radical reform, but such reform is always hard, courageous work. The unfolding tech revolution and Brexit accentuate the challenges – and the opportunities. On June 8 voters saved themselves from May-ite triumphalism, from Scottish independence (at least for now) and from a temperamentally ill-suited and unprepared Corbyn premiership. But it was only a respite, a lull in the encircling global storm.

Note on contributor

Michael White is a former assistant editor of the Guardian and wrote for the paper for more than 45 years, as a reporter, foreign correspondent and columnist. He was political editor from 1990-2006, having previously been the paper's Washington correspondent (1984-88) and parliamentary sketchwriter (1977-84). He joined the Guardian as the late arts sub editor from the Evening Standard's reporters' room in 1971

Postscript:

We can do better, but the job remains the same

Nick Robinson concludes that there is a new fight to be fought: convincing a new generation that sharing facts and debate across the divide is no bad thing

We didn't get it right. We didn't see it coming. We must try harder. That is where any assessment of the media's reporting of Brexit and Trump and the rise of Jeremy Corbyn should begin. With humility.

Although it is fair to point out that the politicians themselves – whether Johnson and Gove, or Trump, or Corbyn and May – were as surprised by the results as most pollsters and pundits. Next come the questions – many of which have been examined in this book.

Do we spend too long in the campaign bubble? Undoubtedly – although the BBC and other broadcasters made great efforts in the 2017 election to hear more directly from voters. Did we downplay the significance of groups of voters, opinions and areas that are 'not where elections are won and lost?' Certainly – we did not see or find a way to highlight the dramatic shifts of opinion in the US rust belt or the UK's northern industrial towns or amongst the under 45s.

Did we fail to see the propaganda, which did not rely on television or the press or an old-fashioned leaflet through the door? Again yes. Finally, are we still better at reporting the campaign horserace than equipping voters to assess the truth of the claims and counter claims? Once again yes – although the BBC's Reality Check team did provide regular robust analysis of the claims and counter claims.

Finally, there must be a determination to keep learning the lessons rather than allow ourselves to get distracted by the next campaign – and the lesson of recent times is that, like those proverbial buses, you can wait a long time for a national vote only to find three or four come along at the same time. The political and media world we operate in has changed dramatically but we have yet to change adequately in response.

A decade and a half ago the BBC commissioned market research that found – surprise surprise – that viewers and listeners and readers struggled to follow let alone make sense of the stories on the news. They were baffled by the jargon – 'whips' and 'backbenchers' and the like – and confused by stories that appeared to have emerged from nowhere and which they lacked the background knowledge to make sense of. What they wanted, the researchers concluded, was a 'trusted guide'. It was a phrase adopted by the then Director General Greg Dyke.

Long before that phrase was ever used the early giants of broadcasting, men like Richard Dimbleby, were just that. Imagine, though, if he had reported on that 'Italian spaghetti harvest' this year rather than 60 years ago. Twitter would light up with smart arses pointing out that it was April 1. Facebook would carry posts accusing the BBC of peddling fake news or of filling the news with trivia whilst willfully ignoring news that didn't suit its agenda. Finally, Twitter would fill with conspiracy theories that Dimbleby owned shares in a spaghetti farm and was, therefore, guilty of corruption.

In the old media world many of us grew up everyone knew their place – it was the media equivalent of Downtown Abbey. Today's media world is more like Breaking Bad.

We broadcasters can no longer expect to be trusted simply because we are, well, broadcasters. Just as MPs, the police, the church and even doctors no longer enjoy the automatic trust they once did. We have to earn trust each and every day and that means being more willing than we have been to question our approach, to be open about the limits of what we do and do not know and to admit our mistakes swiftly and honestly.

This is not going to be easy in an atmosphere in which politicians and their cheerleaders are targeting broadcasters with the clear intention of discrediting us, undermining our credibility and, ultimately, persuading people to switch off and stop watching, listening and reading.

There have, of course, always been furious complaints of broadcast bias from politicians. And I do mean always. Long before Blair's clash with the BBC over the Iraq war or Thatcher's over the Falklands or coverage of the IRA, a young Winston Churchill launched an assault on the BBC for its coverage of the General Strike in 1926. You cannot, he argued, be impartial between 'the fireman and the fire'.

What is different now is that today's political leaders are not trying to influence the coverage of this or that story or to damage the reputation of programmes, presenters or correspondents they don't like. They see attacks on those they deride as the MSM – the mainstream media – as a key part of their political strategy. In order to succeed they need to convince people not to believe 'the news'. There is method behind what some regard as the madness of The Donald's attacking the 'failing' press as purveyors of fake news. What's more, campaigners on the left as well as the right have been watching and learning.

In Europe, politicians of the left as well as the right have launched assaults on the media. Italy's Beppe Grillo has described the Italian media as "the opium of the people, they hide the truth to reassure you, while you slowly die." In Germany the right-wing Alternative for Germany party (AfD) have revived the Nazi insult 'lugenpresse' meaning 'lying press'.

In this country, the same approach has been pursued by followers (although, happily, not always by their leaders) of each new anti-establishment force – backers of Scottish independence, Ukip, the Greens, the Leave campaign and, most recently, Jeremy Corbyn.

This is no longer a lazy clap line delivered to a party conference or to the raise the morale of a crowd of the party faithful. It is guerilla war being fought on social media, day after day and hour after hour.

Trump's election ensured that people are now familiar with the influence of the 'Alt-right' media and Breitbart in particular. In the 2017 general election the 'Alt-left' came of age with sites like The Canary, Another Angry Voice, The Skwawkbox, Novara Media and Evolve Politics. Their posts are shared and, therefore, read more than mainstream political journalism. So far, so unsurprising. What is worth reflecting on is the fact – uncovered by the excellent Political Editor of Buzzfeed, Jim Waterson – that what generates the most shares and likes is allegations of media bias or prejudice and sloppiness.

(By the way you'll read these stories on Facebook, the place where 'real people' get most of their news and not on Twitter to which so many journalists and political activists and, dare I say, readers of this book are addicted.)

The founders of Alt-right and Alt-left sites sometimes claim they are just as impartial as the MSM. Occasionally they are open about the fact that they are first and foremost political activists trying to 'build a new media for a different politics' as Novara Media puts it, declaring that [our journalism is always politically committed; rather than seeking to moderate between two sides of a debate, our output actively intends to feed back into political action'.

Much has been written about the growth of so-called 'identity politics' – politics based not on broad based parties but on national, regional or class identity. A growing number of people are being drawn to what you might call 'identity journalism'. They seek out, read and share stories that re-affirm their sense of who they are and, just as importantly, their prejudice about their opponents or anyone who criticizes their cause or leader.

The risk here is that we will follow the trend in the United States where right wing activists get their news from one outlet, Fox News, whilst liberals get their from watching MSNBC or CNN. The consequence is that there are no shared facts around which public debates can revolve. So it was that the debate about health care reform in the US – which politicians on all sides agree is long overdue – descended into an argument about whether President Obama was planning to create 'death panels' to decide who lived or died, or whether his critics wanted to condemn the poor to a premature death.

In the face of this risk we need to re-make the case for impartiality from first principles remembering that there is nothing God given about the idea. Those of us who grew up with the lofty ideals of the BBC, ITN and, indeed, Sky News, take the standards they set for granted. It is, though, an artificial, legal constraint on the freedom to broadcast, which could as easily be scrapped as it was introduced in the 1920s.

We need to explain that no-one is born impartial. We are all, inevitably, influenced by our background and upbringing, knowledge and experience, beliefs and prejudices but we broadcasters do endeavor to get as close to the truth as we can each.

I have now grown used to repeated allegations that I am not impartial but one claim that has kept resurfacing has taught me a great deal about the new world we now live in. Is it true, I have been asked repeatedly, that you said 'I hate all poor people'?

Resisting the temptation to respond sarcastically that I'd been rumbled, I looked for the source. It appeared as one of a series of 'Facts about the BBC' listed on a meme along with the 'fact'– which could be disproved by a quick Wikipedia search – that I 'went to Eton with David Cameron'.

I mentioned this recurring falsehood to someone at a party who blushed before confessing that she'd invented these 'facts' for a satirical online piece exposing the paranoia of the BBC's critics. She'd also written an alternative alleging that 'the Biased Broadcasting Corporation' was leftwing in which I was alleged to have said that, 'I love taxes. Hang the rich'. Her joke has been widely circulated, read and believed by partisans who are hungry for anything that feeds their anger.

The lesson of Trump, Brexit and the 2017 General Election is that we can and must fight to convince a new generation that all that you read and watch and listen to is not the same. Yes, we get things wrong. Yes, we can do better. Yes, we have lots to learn but we do not come to work to make the case for a party, a leader or a cause. Our job is to report and investigate, question, analyse and explain.

Notes on the contributor
Nick Robinson is one of the presenters of BBC Radio 4's Today programme. He is a former Political Editor of the BBC.